ROBERT G

COMPLETE POEMS

Volume III

Robert Graves Programme
General Editor: Patrick J.M. Quinn

Centenary Selected Poems
edited by Patrick J.M. Quinn

Collected Writings on Poetry
edited by Paul O'Prey

Complete Short Stories
edited by Lucia Graves

Complete Poems I
edited by Beryl Graves and Dunstan Ward

Complete Poems II
edited by Beryl Graves and Dunstan Ward

Complete Poems III
edited by Beryl Graves and Dunstan Ward

The White Goddess:
A Historical Grammar of Poetic Myth
edited by Grevel Lindop

I, Claudius and *Claudius the God*
edited by Richard Francis

Sergeant Lamb of the Ninth and *Proceed, Sergeant Lamb*
edited by Caroline Zilboorg

Robert Graves

COLLECTED POEMS
Volume 3

Edited by Beryl Graves and
Dunstan Ward

CARCANET

First published in Great Britain in 1999 by
Carcanet Press Limited
4th Floor, Conavon Court
12–16 Blackfriars Street
Manchester M3 5BQ

A CIP catalogue record for this book
is available from the British Library.
ISBN 1 85754 280 0

The publisher acknowledges financial
assistance from the Arts Council of England

Funded by THE ARTS COUNCIL OF ENGLAND

Set in Meridien by XL Publishing Services, Tiverton
Printed and bound in England by SRP Ltd, Exeter

CONTENTS

ACKNOWLEDGEMENTS

The editors wish to thank the following individuals and institutions for enabling us to examine materials, and for permission to quote from them: the Henry W. and Albert A. Berg Collection, New York Public Library, Astor, Lennox and Tilden Foundations; the Poetry/Rare Books Collection, University Libraries, State University of New York at Buffalo; the National Library of Scotland, Edinburgh; the St John's College Robert Graves Trust, Oxford; Ms Shelley Cox, Rare Books Librarian, and the Morris Library, Southern Illinois University at Carbondale; Ms Lorna Knight, Curator of Manuscripts, and the Carl A. Kroch Library, Cornell University; Mr George Newkey-Burden, and the staff of the *Daily Telegraph* Library; Mr Michael Meredith, Curator, and the College Library, Eton College; Mr William S. Reese, and Mr Terry Halliday, Literary Manager, William Reese Company, New Haven, Connecticut; Mr D.M. Bownes, Assistant Curator, Royal Welch Fusiliers Regimental Museum, Caernarvon; the Harry Ransom Humanities Research Center, University of Texas at Austin; Ms Lori N. Curtis, Associate Curator of Special Collections, and the McFarlin Library, University of Tulsa, Oklahoma; Mr Christopher G. Petter, Special Collections Librarian, and the University Library, University of Victoria, British Columbia, Canada. Once again, special thanks are due to the Curator of the Poetry/Rare Books Collection, SUNY at Buffalo, Professor Robert J. Bertholf, for his help and encouragement, and to Dr Michael Basinski, Assistant Curator.

We are grateful to the Board of Literary Management of the late Laura (Riding) Jackson for permission to reprint 'Midsummer Duet', from Laura Riding's *Collected Poems* (London: Cassell, 1938; and Manchester: Carcanet, and New York: Persea Books, 1980), copyright © 1938, 1980; and 'Majorcan Letter, 1935', from *Focus*, 4 (Dec. 1935). The Board, 'in conformity with her wish', asks us 'to record that, in 1941, Laura (Riding) Jackson renounced, on grounds of linguistic principle, the writing of poetry: she had come to hold that "poetry obstructs general attainment to something better in our linguistic way-of-life than we have".'

As with the two previous volumes, Ms Lucia Graves's advice and her assistance with research have been invaluable.

Among the many others who have helped us in various ways, we should like particularly to thank Señora Elena Lambea and Mr William Graves; Mr Tomás Graves; Mr Simon Gough; Mr Carl R.

Hahn; Mrs Stella Irwin; Dr Christopher Simon; Mr Reg Ward; and Ms Juli Simon, who shared her manuscripts and her knowledge of the late poems with us.

This edition is indebted to Robert Graves's bibliographers, Fred. H. Higginson and William Proctor Williams; the editor of his selected letters, Paul O'Prey; and his biographer, Richard Perceval Graves.

Dunstan Ward gratefully acknowledges a grant from the British Academy to visit libraries and collections in the United States, and the support of the University of London's British Institute in Paris.

Finally, we wish again to thank Dr Robyn Marsack, our meticulous and understanding editor.

INTRODUCTION

Fierce poems of our past –
How can they ever die,
Condemned by love to last
Word for word and exactly
Under a wide and changeful sky?

('If No Cuckoo Sings')

With its 666 poems, this third and final volume of Robert Graves's *Complete Poems* is considerably larger than either Volume I (1910-1926) or Volume II (1927-1959). Graves's last period was his most prolific: nearly half the total number of poems in his books were written in the fifteen years from 1960 to 1975. Volume III also contains 112 'Uncollected Poems' (published only in periodicals and the press, between 1910 and 1974), and 69 poems selected from his unpublished and posthumously published work.

'Love is the main theme and origin of true poems', Graves affirmed in 1965.[1] Most of the poems of the last period are, indeed, love poems; their focus is 'the personal Muse', an incarnation (as he had come to believe) of the Goddess.[2] The period can thus be divided into three: 1960-63, 1963-66 and 1966-75, corresponding to Graves's relationships with his so-called 'muses', though the continuities are perhaps more significant than the contrasts.[3] During the first, Graves sought to 'dramatize, truthfully and factually, the vicissitudes of a poet's dealings with the White Goddess, the Muse, the perpetual Other Woman'.[4] His quest then turned to the White Goddess's 'mysterious sister', the Black Goddess of Wisdom, who 'represents a miraculous certitude in love'.[5]

Graves's 'muses' were the source not only of his inspiration but also of frequent disquiet. In the later work there are still, however, a number of witty, light-hearted or ironic poems. It was this ability to distance himself – clearly seen in his foreword to *Colophon to 'Love Respelt'* – that to a large extent helped him through some

[1] 'Lecture One, 1965', *PCP*, p.116, republished as 'The Duende', *CWP*, p.473. For the bibliographical notes and abbreviations, see pp.421-4.

[2] See 'The Personal Muse', *OAP*, pp.57-81, and *CWP*, pp.336-53.

[3] For the detailed personal background to the poems concerned with Graves's 'muses', see *SL 2* and *RPG 3*, *passim*.

[4] 'Intimations of the Black Goddess', *MBG*, p.151; see the note on *MP61*.

[5] 'Intimations of the Black Goddess', *MBG*, p.162, and *CWP*, p.397; see the note on 'The Hearth' (*MDWI*).

painful emotional situations. (For example, he wrote 'Ann at Highwood Hall' in a few days at a particularly distressing time in his personal life.)[6]

The twenty-three books of verse that Graves published during this period include three *Collected Poems*. In the 1965 volume he suppressed almost a quarter of the contents of *Collected Poems 1959*, mainly on the grounds of suspected 'lovelessness';[7] but he reprinted the mass of recent love poetry, as he did again in his last volume, published in 1975 when he was eighty: the final version of his 'spiritual autobiography'[8] was designed to tell 'one story only' . . .

Graves's fame as a poet reached its height in the 1960s. Each new book of poems received virtually unanimous praise from the reviewers (until the predictable reaction).[9] The 1961 paperback edition of *The White Goddess* made him even 'something of a cult-figure'.[10] His lectures as Professor of Poetry at Oxford in 1961-65 drew exceptional audiences, and their publication, among half a dozen books of essays, ensured a wider circulation for his views. He gave numerous talks and readings; besides his frequent visits to the United States, he travelled to Greece, Hungary, Poland, Russia, Mexico and Australia. He was awarded a gold medal at the 1968 Mexican 'Cultural Olympics', and, later that year, the Queen's Gold Medal for Poetry. But he was never part of the literary establishment, remaining obstinately removed.

In his last years Graves suffered increasingly from ill health and loss of memory, yet to the end he worked as he had always done, producing draft upon draft in his life-long 'obsession about getting poems *right*'.[11] Among the latest poems are some of his most poignant: 'The Moon's Last Quarter', 'The Unpenned Poem', 'The Green Woods of Unrest'; he left over fifty completed poems in manuscript. Until he could no longer write, he continued to 'treat poetry with a single-minded devotion which may be called religious'.[12]

---

[6] Diary, 25-27 Feb., 1963.

[7] 'Foreword', *CP65*; see note.

[8] 'Foreword', *PS51*; see *Complete Poems*, Volume II, pp.345-6.

[9] See the note on *P65-68*.

[10] *WG61*, revised edition, edited by Grevel Lindop (Manchester: Carcanet, 1997, and London: Faber, 1999), Introduction, p.xvii.

[11] Graves to James Reeves, 3 June 1954; *SL 2*, p.136.

[12] 'The Poet and his Public', *CrP*, p.185.

All the known uncollected poems have been included in this volume, several of them not previously recorded; any further poems traced will be added to the edition in the future.

In making what is inevitably a personal selection from over two hundred unpublished and posthumously published poems, the editors have given priority to poems whose publication Graves approved, but which was prevented by some external factor (as was the case, for example, with 'Diotima Dead'). Apart from these, they have chosen poems that were treated by Graves as 'finished'[13] (or that reached a comparably 'finished' state), and which are, in their judgement, of literary, historical or biographical interest, and representative of Graves's poetry at the time.

The arrangement of the poems from Graves's books of verse corresponds to the first editions, and follows the order within them. 'From' before the title of a book (e.g. 'From *Food for Centaurs*') indicates the omission of a poem or poems already included in an earlier book (or incorporated into a later poem); the complete contents are given in the notes.

The uncollected poems are in order of first publication. The unpublished and posthumously published poems are in order of composition, to the extent that it has been possible to determine this.

In accordance with Graves's practice, this edition prints the latest texts of the poems. It compares these, in the notes, with the versions in the first editions or, for uncollected poems, the versions first published. (His extensive revisions during composition, between periodical and book publication, and in the course of reprintings would require a full-scale variorum edition.)

The poems from books and the uncollected poems appear in the last version that Graves published, with further revisions incorporated, and the unpublished and posthumously published poems in the version of the latest manuscript/typescript. Anomalies and misprints have been corrected in the light of manuscripts and previous printings, as reported in the notes (under 'Emendations'). When an earlier printed variant in wording or punctuation has been adopted, it has been checked wherever possible against manuscripts and proofs, as have the texts of the uncollected poems.

Where Graves republished a poem with substantive revisions, the principal differences between the version in the first edition of the book of verse concerned (or, for uncollected poems, the version

[13] See, for example, the note on 'Historical Particulars'.

first published) and the last version are recorded in the notes. All changes in wording are given, with omitted lines or stanzas; punctuation changes are given when they involve a change in sense; the main modifications in layout and typography are also indicated. Although studied in the course of preparing this edition, revisions intervening between first and last book publication are noted only exceptionally, as are manuscript and (save for uncollected poems) periodical variants.

The notes also give background information on the poems, with quotations from and/or references to other poems, letters, diaries and prose works.

The poems have been printed flush left, as in *Collected Poems 1975*. Titles provided editorially are in square brackets. Some details of punctuation – ellipses, the use of single quotation marks (double for quotations within them), punctuation relative to quotation marks and italics – have been normalized in line with Graves's later practice; and some inconsistent spelling has been altered (though the earlier use of the hyphenated form of certain words – 'to-day', 'to-morrow' – has been respected, as in the successive *Collected Poems*). American spelling in uncollected poems has been Anglicized. Where Graves used an ampersand (&) in the manuscript of an unpublished poem it has been spelt out ('and'), except in the notes. Inconsistencies in the capitalization of titles in upper-and-lower-case in the contents lists have been removed.

Where required, line numbers have been inserted in poems of over thirty lines which are not in stanzas, to make reference easier.

An asterisk after the title of a poem from one of Graves's books of verse indicates a note at the back of the volume. There are notes on all the 'Uncollected Poems' and the 'Unpublished and Posthumously Published Poems'; in the last section, a dagger (†) after the title of a poem indicates that it was posthumously published.

From FOOD FOR CENTAURS

(1960)

TWICE OF THE SAME FEVER

No one can die twice of the same fever?
    Tell them it is untrue:
Have we not died three deaths, and three again,
    You of me, I of you?

The chill, the frantic pulse, brows burning,
    Lips broken by thirst –
Until, in darkness, a ghost grieves:
    'It was I died the first.'

Worse than such death, even, is resurrection.
    Do we dare laugh away
Disaster, and with a callous madrigal
    Salute the new day?

ESTABLISHED LOVERS*

The established lovers of an elder generation
Dead from the waist down, every man of them,
Have now expired for sure
And, after nine days' public threnody,
Lapse to oblivion, or literature . . .
Clerks of Establishment must therefore search
For faces fit to people the blank spaces.

Faces enough are found, to pretend modesty
And mask their yearning for the public call:
Pluperfect candidates
Having long ceased to live as lovers do . . .
Clerks of Establishment, checking the dates,
Can feel no qualm in recommending Orders,
Titles and honorary love-doctorates.

Observe him well, the scarlet-robed academician
Stalled with his peers, an Order on his breast,
And (who could doubt it?) free
Of such despairs and voices as attended
His visits to the grotto below sea
Where once he served a glare-eyed Demoness
And swore her his unswerving verity.

THE QUIET GLADES OF EDEN*

All such proclivities are tabulated –
By trained pathologists, in detail too –
The obscener parts of speech compulsively
Shrouded in Classic Latin.

But though my pleasure in your feet and hair
Is ungainsayable, let me protest
(Dear love) I am no trichomaniac
And no foot-fetichist.

If it should please you, for your own best reasons,
To take and flog me with a rawhide whip,
I might (who knows?) surprisedly accept
This earnest of affection.

Nothing, agreed, is alien to love
When pure desire has overflowed its baulks;
But why must private sportiveness be viewed
Through public spectacles?

Enough, I will not claim a heart unfluttered
By these case-histories of aberrancy;
Nevertheless a long cool draught of water,
Or a long swim in the bay,

Serves to restore my wholesome appetite
For you and what we do at night together:
Which is no more than Adam did with Eve
In the quiet glades of Eden.

HEROES IN THEIR PRIME*

Theseus: was he an old, bald King of Athens
By folly forced into self-banishment,
Who cursed his own twelve tribes from Mount Gargettus
And sailed for Scyros, glowering discontent?

No, but that tall youth who laid low Procrustes,
Sinis and Scyron, bandits of repute,
And in a labyrinthine lair at Cnossus
The Minotaur by night did execute.

Bellerophon: was he a tattered outcast
Seldom descried on the rough Xanthian plain,
Whom Pegasus had pitched into a thorn-bush,
Thus rudely closing his presumptuous reign?

No, but that hero, smiled on by Athene,
Scourge both of Amazons and Solymi,
Who quenched Chimaera's fiery exhalations
With arrows shot at her from a clear sky.

Jason: was Jason a chap-fallen beggar
Whom the prophetic prow of Argo slew
When back he crawled to die in shame at Corinth
Loathed by the gods, and by his shipmates too?

No, but that single-sandalled young Magnesian,
Fearless and fond, the cynosure of Greece,
Who by your kindly aid, Queen Aphrodite,
Seduced Medea and fetched home the Fleece.

And Nestor: was he Agamemnon's Nestor,
Whose grey beard wagged beside the walls of Troy
And wagged still more, long after Troy had fallen,
Anent his exploits as a beardless boy?

Yes, that was he: revered by Prince Achilles,
Odysseus, Diomede and many more –
Not the young braggart quaking at the tree-top
In terror of a Calydonian boar.

CATKIND

Through the window,
Listening carefully,
I overheard a low
Moonlight murmur from an olive-tree –
Three cats rehearsed the virtues of catkind:
Catkind's silky tread and devious mind,
Catkind's quiet economy
(Cleansing itself with wash of its own body),
Catkind's nonchalance,
Catkind's persistence,
Catkind's circumambulance,
Its fealty to the Queen of Cats above –
'But when we love,' they wailed, 'alas, we LOVE!'

TWO CHILDREN*

You were as venturesome as I was shy:
Eager and inquisitive your eye.
    You set a nap on the plum, a haze on the rose,
And shooting stars across the wintry sky
    Flashed by in volleys for me when you chose.

None spoke with you, I alone worshipped you,
Child of the wave, child of the morning dew,
And in my dreams went chasing here and there
A fugitive beacon – your moon-yellow hair.

HERE LIVE YOUR LIFE OUT!*

Window-gazing, at one time or another
In the course of travel, you must have startled at
Some coign of true felicity. 'Stay!' it beckoned,
'Here live your life out!' If you were simple-hearted
The village rose, perhaps, from a broad stream
Lined with alders and gold-flowering flags –
Hills, hay-fields, orchards, mills – and, plain to see,
The very house behind its mulberry-tree
Stood, by a miracle, untenanted!

Alas, you could not alight, found yourself jolted
Viciously on; public conveyances
Are not amenable to casual halts,
Except in sternly drawn emergencies –
Bandits, floods, landslides, earthquakes or the like –
Nor could you muster resolution enough
To shout: 'This is emergency, let me out!'
Rushing to grasp their brakes; so the whole scene
Withdrew forever. Once at the terminus
(As your internal mentor will have told you),
It would have been pure folly to engage
A private car, drive back, sue for possession.
Too far, too late:
Already bolder tenants were at the gate.

JOAN AND DARBY*

My friends are those who find agreement with me
In large measure, but not absolutely.
Little children, parasites and God
May flatter me with absolute agreement –
For no one lives more cynical than God.

As for my love, I gifted my heart to her
Twenty years ago, without proviso,
And in return she gifted hers to me;
Yet still they beat as two, unyielding in
Their honest, first reluctance to agree.

Other seasons, other thoughts and reasons,
Other fears or phases of the moon:
In loving-kindness we grow grey together –
Like Joan and Darby in their weather-lodge
Who never venture out in the same weather.

SUPERMAN ON THE RIVIERA

Looked tough, was tall and permanently bronzed
(I should guess Berkeley, do not quote me, though)
Not an ounce above the statutory weight,
Two hundred pounds, most of it bone and muscle;
Blue-eyed, with jutting chin and jutting brows.
The nose, however, did not command the chin.
Myself, I would rather have no chin at all
Than one that dared be wiser than its boss.
As for his mouth, a man-sized Cupid bow,
Curved for kissing a diminutive mother
And flashing teen-age smiles of high intent:
Was that the cause, or was it one more symptom,
Of his twin habits – equally repulsive
To us inveterate Western Europeans –
Downing a midday pint of raw cow's milk
And treating France's noblest vintages
Like bath-tub gin whenever he got high?

THE PICTURE NAIL

I brought a Death of Nelson home, where I
Hung it, by inadvertence, on a fly.
  Down crashed the heavy frame, off the fly flew,
And how my curses rang! Frankly, I own
To a sad lack of humour when alone –
  Like you, by God, and you, and even you!

OLD WORLD DIALOGUE*

'Is this,' she asked, 'what the lower orders call . . . ?'
'Yes, yes,' replied her lover, Lord Whitehall,
'But, hush!, the expression is a trifle crude – '
'*Much* too good for them,' cried Lady Ermintrude.

'Nevertheless,' resumed the tactless peer,
'Those who excel at it – pray, do not sneer –
Are, by and large, of obscure parentage.
One girl I knew – '
'Take that!' she shouted, red with rage.

THE WERE-MAN

Alone, alone and well alone at last,
Sentries by stealth outwitted, frontiers passed!
Yet walking alien thoroughfares you brood
Fearfully on the man by this feat rescued.

Never before, though trusted friends were few,
Though your own love of loves her oath outgrew,
Though off to the loud wars your children ran,
Never before closeted with a were-man.

Loathing his sylvan company, unable
To bed with him or set his place at table,
A savage life you lead, condemned to share
Your hearth with one whose habitat is nowhere.

THE PERSON FROM PORLOCK*

. . . At that moment the Author was unfortunately called out by a person on business from Porlock and on his return found to his mortification that though he retained some vague recollection of his vision, yet with the exception of eight or ten scattered lines and images, all the rest had passed away.

Coleridge's preface to *Kubla Khan: A Fragment*

Unkind fate sent the Porlock person
To collect fivepence from a poet's house;
Pocketing which old debt he drove away,
Heedless and gay, homeward bound for Porlock.

O Porlock person, habitual scapegoat,
Should any masterpiece be marred or scotched,
I wish your burly fist on the front door
Had banged yet oftener in literature!

From THE PENNY FIDDLE

(1960)

THE PENNY FIDDLE*

Yesterday I bought a penny fiddle
      And put it to my chin to play,
But I found that the strings were painted,
      So I threw my fiddle away.

A gipsy girl found my penny fiddle
      As it lay abandoned there;
When she asked me if she might keep it,
      I told her I did not care.

Then she drew such music from the fiddle
      With help of a farthing bow,
That I offered five shillings for the secret.
      But, alas, she would not let it go.

ROBINSON CRUSOE*

Robinson Crusoe cut his coats
      Not too narrow, not too big,
From the hides of nanny-goats;
      Yet he longed to keep a pig.

Robinson Crusoe sat in grief,
      All day long he sometimes sat,
Gazing at the coral reef,
      Grumbling to his favourite cat.

'Queen of Pussies,' he would say,
      'Two things I am sure about:
Bacon should begin the day,
      "Pork!" should put the candle out.'

THE SIX BADGERS*

As I was a-hoeing, a-hoeing my lands,
Six badgers walked up, with white wands in their hands.
They formed a ring round me and, bowing, they said:
'Hurry home, Farmer George, for the table is spread!
There's pie in the oven, there's beef on the plate:
Hurry home, Farmer George, if you would not be late!'

So homeward went I, but could not understand
Why six fine dog-badgers with white wands in hand
Should seek me out hoeing, and bow in a ring,
And all to inform me so common a thing!

JOCK O' BINNORIE*

King Duncan had a fool called Leery
    And gave him very high pay
To tell him stories after dinner,
    A new one every day;
But if the stories failed him
    (As Leery did agree)
The King would call his merry men all
    And hang him from a tree.

Leery began with Jim o' Binnorie
    Who danced on Stirling Rock
And emptied a peck of pickled eels
    All over his brother Jock;
Yet Jock refrained from unkind words
    That many a lad might use,
And while Jim slept on a load of hay
    Put five live eels in his shoes.

Leery had told nine hundred tales
    And found no others to tell,
He started from the first once more –
    King Duncan knew it well.
'Old friends are best, dear Fool,' he cried,
    'And old yarns heard again.
You may tell me the story of Jock o' Binnorie
    Every night of my reign!'

From MORE POEMS 1961

(1961)

LYCEIA*

All the wolves of the forest
Howl for Lyceia,
Crowding together
In a close circle,
Tongues a-loll.

A silver serpent
Coiled at her waist
And a quiver at knee,
She combs fine tresses
With a fine comb:

Wolf-like, woman-like,
Gazing about her,
Greeting the wolves;
Partial to many,
Yet masked in pride.

The young wolves snarl,
They snap at one another
Under the moon.
'Beasts, be reasonable,
My beauty is my own!'

Lyceia has a light foot
For a weaving walk.
Her archer muscles
Warn them how tightly
She can stretch the string.

I question Lyceia,
Whom I find posted
Under the pine trees
One early morning:
'What do the wolves learn?'

'They learn only envy,'
Lyceia answers,
'Envy and hope,
Hope and chagrin.
Would you howl too
In that wolfish circle?'
She laughs as she speaks.

SYMPTOMS OF LOVE*

Love is a universal migraine,
A bright stain on the vision
Blotting out reason.

Symptoms of true love
Are leanness, jealousy,
Laggard dawns;

Are omens and nightmares –
Listening for a knock,
Waiting for a sign:

For a touch of her fingers
In a darkened room,
For a searching look.

Take courage, lover!
Could you endure such grief
At any hand but hers?

THE SHARP RIDGE

Since now I dare not ask
Any gift from you, or gentle task,
Or lover's promise – nor yet refuse
Whatever I can give and you dare choose –
Have pity on us both: choose well
On this sharp ridge dividing death from hell.

UNDER THE OLIVES*

We never would have loved had love not struck
Swifter than reason, and despite reason:
Under the olives, our hands interlocked,
We both fell silent:
Each listened for the other's answering
Sigh of unreasonableness –
Innocent, gentle, bold, enduring, proud.

THE VISITATION*

Drowsing in my chair of disbelief
I watch the door as it slowly opens –
A trick of the night wind?

Your slender body seems a shaft of moonlight
Against the door as it gently closes.
Do you cast no shadow?

Your whisper is too soft for credence,
Your tread like blossom drifting from a bough,
Your touch even softer.

You wear that sorrowful and tender mask
Which on high mountain tops in heather-flow
Entrances lonely shepherds;

And though a single word scatters all doubts
I quake for wonder at your choice of me:
Why, why and why?

FRAGMENT*

Are you shaken, are you stirred
By a whisper of love?
Spell-bound to a word
Does Time cease to move,
Till her calm grey eye
Expands to a sky
And the clouds of her hair
Like storms go by?

APPLE ISLAND*

Though cruel seas like mountains fill the bay,
Wrecking the quayside huts,
Salting our vineyards with tall showers of spray;

And though the moon shines dangerously clear,
Fixed in another cycle
Than the sun's progress round the felloe'd year;

And though I may not hope to dwell apart
With you on Apple Island
Unless my breast be docile to the dart –

Why should I fear your element, the sea,
Or the full moon, your mirror,
Or the halved apple from your holy tree?

THE FALCON WOMAN

It is hard to be a man
Whose word is his bond
In love with such a woman,

When he builds on a promise
She lightly let fall
In carelessness of spirit.

The more sternly he asks her
To stand by that promise
The faster she flies.

But is it less hard
To be born such a woman
With wings like a falcon
And in carelessness of spirit
To love such a man?

TROUGHS OF SEA*

'Do you delude yourself?' a neighbour asks,
Dismayed by my abstraction.
But though love cannot question love
Nor need deny its need,

Pity the man who finds a rebel heart
Under his breastbone drumming
Which reason warns him he should drown
In midnight wastes of sea.

Now as he stalks between tormented pines
(The moon in her last quarter)
A lissom spectre glides ahead
And utters not a word.

Waves tasselled with dark weed come rearing up
Like castle walls, disclosing
Deep in their troughs a ribbed sea-floor
To break his bones upon.

– Clasp both your hands under my naked foot
And press hard, as I taught you:
A trick to mitigate the pangs
Either of birth or love.

THE LAUGH*

Your sudden laugh restored felicity –
Everything grew clear that before would not:
The impossible genies, the extravagants,
Swung in to establish themselves fairly
As at last manageable elements
In a most daylight-simple plot.
It was the identity of opposites
Had so confused my all too sober wits.

THE DEATH GRAPPLE*

Lying between your sheets, I challenge
A watersnake in a swoln cataract
Or a starved lioness among drifts of snow.

Yet dare it out, for after each death grapple,
Each gorgon stare borrowed from very hate,
A childish innocent smile touches your lips,
Your eyelids droop, fearless and careless,
And sleep remoulds the lineaments of love.

THE STARRED COVERLET*

A difficult achievement for true lovers
Is to lie mute, without embrace or kiss,
Without a rustle or a smothered sigh,
Basking each in the other's glory.

Let us not undervalue lips or arms
As reassurances of constancy,
Or speech as necessary communication
When troubled hearts go groping through the dusk;

Yet lovers who have learned this last refinement –
To lie apart, yet sleep and dream together
Motionless under their starred coverlet –
Crown love with wreaths of myrtle.

THE INTRUSION*

Going confidently into the garden
Where she made much of you four hours ago
You find another person in her seat.

If your scalp crawls and your eyes prick at sight
Of her white motionless face and folded hands
Framed in such thunderclouds of sorrow,

Give her no word of consolation, man,
Dissemble your own anguish,
Withdraw in silence, gaze averted –
This is the dark edge of her double-axe:
Divine mourning for what cannot be.

PATIENCE

Almost I could prefer
A flare of anger
To your dumb signal of displeasure.

Must it be my task
To assume the mask
Of not desiring what I may not ask?

On a wide bed,
Both arms outspread,
I watch the spites do battle in my head,

Yet know this sickness
For stubborn weakness
Unconsonant with your tenderness.

O, to be patient
As you would have me patient:
Patient for a thousand nights, patient!

THE CURE

No lover ever found a cure for love
Except so cruel a thrust under the heart
(By her own hand delivered)
His wound was nine long years in healing,
Purulent with dead hope,
And ached yet longer at the moon's changes . . .
More tolerable the infection than its cure.

HAG-RIDDEN*

I awoke in profuse sweat, arms aching,
Knees bruised and soles cut to the raw –
Preserved no memory of that night
But whipcracks and my own voice screaming.
Through what wild, flinty wastes of fury,
Hag of the Mill,
Did you ride your madman?

TURN OF THE MOON*

Never forget who brings the rain
In swarthy goatskin bags from a far sea:
It is the Moon as she turns, repairing
Damages of long drought and sunstroke.

Never count upon rain, never foretell it,
For no power can bring rain
Except the Moon as she turns; and who can rule her?

She is prone to delay the necessary floods,
Lest such a gift might become obligation,
A month, or two, or three; then suddenly
Not relenting but by way of whim
Will perhaps conjure from the cloudless west
A single rain-drop to surprise with hope
Each haggard, upturned face.

Were the Moon a Sun, we would count upon her
To bring rain seasonably as she turned;
Yet no one thinks to thank the regular Sun
For shining fierce in summer, mild in winter –
Why should the Moon so drudge?

But if one night she brings us, as she turns,
Soft, steady, even, copious rain
That harms no leaf nor flower, but gently falls
Hour after hour, sinking to the tap roots,
And the sodden earth exhales at dawn
A long sigh scented with pure gratitude,
Such rain – the first rain of our lives, it seems,
Neither foretold, cajoled, nor counted on –
Is woman giving as she loves.

THE SECRET LAND*

Every woman of true royalty owns
A secret land more real to her
Than this pale outer world:

At midnight when the house falls quiet
She lays aside needle or book
And visits it unseen.

Shutting her eyes, she improvises
A five-barred gate among tall birches,
Vaults over, takes possession.

Then runs, or flies, or mounts a horse
(A horse will canter up to greet her)
And travels where she will;

Can make grass grow, coax lilies up
From bud to blossom as she watches,
Lets fish eat from her palm;

Has founded villages, planted groves
And hollowed valleys for brooks running
Cool to a land-locked bay.

I never dared question my love
About the government of her queendom
Or its geography,

Nor followed her between those birches,
Setting one leg astride the gate,
Spying into the mist.

Yet she has pledged me, when I die,
A lodge beneath her private palace
In a level clearing of the wood
Where gentians grow and gillyflowers
And sometimes we may meet.

SELDOM YET NOW*

Seldom yet now: the quality
Of this fierce love between us –
Seldom the encounter,
The presence always,
Free of oath or promise.

And if we were not so
But birds of similar plumage caged
In the peace of every day,
Would we still conjure wildfire up
From common earth, as now?

TO MYRTO OF MYRTLES*

Goddess of Midsummer, how late
  You let me understand
My lines of head, life, fate
  And heart: a broad M brand
  Inerasable from either hand.

ANCHISES TO APHRODITE*

Your sceptre awes me, Aphrodite,
   The knot-of-wisdom in your grasp.
Though you have deigned my couch to warm
   And my firm neck in love to clasp,

How am I more than a man-lion
   To you a goddess, the world's queen?
Ten thousand champions of your choice
   Are gone as if they had not been.

Yet while you grant me power to stem
   The tide's unalterable flow,
Enroyalled I await your pleasure
   And starve if you would have it so.

A LOST WORLD*

'Dear love, why should you weep
      For time's remorseless way?
Though today die in sleep
      And be called yesterday,
      We love, we stay.'

'I weep for days that died
      With former love that shone
On a world true and wide
      Before this newer one
      Which yours shines on.'

'Is this world not as true
      As that one ever was
Which now has fled from you
      Like shadows from the grass
      When the clouds pass?'

'Yet for that would I weep
      Kindly, before we kiss:
Love has a faith to keep
      With past felicities
      That weep for this.'

THE DANGEROUS GIFT*

Were I to cut my hand
    On that sharp knife you gave me
    (That dangerous knife, your beauty),
I should know what to do:
    Bandage the wound myself
And hide the blood from you.

A murderous knife it is,
    As often you have warned me:
    For if I looked for pity
Or tried a wheedling note
    Either I must restore it
Or turn it on my throat.

SURGICAL WARD: MEN*

Something occurred after the operation
To scare the surgeons (though no fault of theirs),
Whose reassurance did not fool me long.
Beyond the shy, concerned faces of nurses
A single white-hot eye, focusing on me,
Forced sweat in rivers down from scalp to belly.
I whistled, gasped or sang, with blanching knuckles
Clutched at my bed-grip almost till it cracked:
Too proud, still, to let loose Bedlamite screeches
And bring the charge-nurse scuttling down the aisle
With morphia-needle levelled. . . .
                                        Lady Morphia –
Her scorpion kiss and dark gyrating dreams –
She in mistrust of whom I dared out-dare,
Two minutes longer than seemed possible,
Pain, that unpurposed, matchless elemental
Stronger than fear or grief, stranger than love.

NIGHTFALL AT TWENTY THOUSAND FEET

A black wall from the east, toppling, arches the tall sky over
To drown what innocent pale western lights yet cover
Cloud banks of expired sunset; so goodbye, sweet day!
From earliest green you sprang, in green tenderly glide away . . .
Had I never noticed, on watch before at a humbler height,
That crowding through dawn's gate come night and dead of night?

THE SIMPLETON

To be defrauded often of large sums,
A whole year's income, even,
By friends trusted so long and perfectly
He never thought to ask receipts from them:
Such had been his misfortune.

He did not undervalue money, sighed for
Those banknotes, warm in the breast pocket,
For want of which his plans were baulked;
But could not claim that any man had left him
In complete poverty.

Easier to choke back resentment,
Never to sue them, never pit in court
His unsupported oath against theirs;
Easier not to change a forsworn friend
For a sworn enemy.

Easier, too, to scoff at legal safeguards,
Promissories on pale-blue foolscap
Sealed, signed, delivered before witnesses.
What legal safeguard had a full wallet
Carried among a crowd?

But though he preened himself on calmly
Cancelling irrecoverable debts,
It vexed him not to know
Why all his oldest, dearest friends conspired
To pluck him like a fowl.

TWO RHYMES ABOUT FATE AND MONEY*

'Neighbour, neighbour, don't forget:
    Thirty shillings due tomorrow!'
Fate and mammon rule us yet,
In the midst of life we are in debt,
    Here to pay and gone to borrow.

*

How and why
Poets die,
    That's a dismal tale:
Some take a spill
On Guinea Hill,
    Some drown in ale,

Some get lost
At sea, or crossed
    In love with cruel witches,
But some attain
Long life and reign
    Like Popes among their riches.

THE TWO WITCHES*

O sixteen hundred and ninety-one,
Never was year so well begun,
Backsy-forsy and inside out,
The best of years to ballad about.

On the first fine day of January
I ran to my sweetheart Margery
And tossed her over the roof so far
That down she fell like a shooting star.

But when we two had frolicked and kissed
She clapped her fingers about my wrist
And tossed me over the chimney stack,
And danced on me till my bones did crack.

Then, when she had laboured to ease my pain,
We sat by the stile of Robin's Lane,
She in a hare and I in a toad
And puffed at the clouds till merry they glowed.

We spelled our loves until close of day.
I wished her good-night and walked away,
But she put out a tongue that was long and red
And swallowed me down like a crumb of bread.

BURN IT!*

Fetch your book here.
That you have fought with it for half a year
(Christmas till May)
Not intermittently but night and day
Need but enhance your satisfaction
In swift and wholesome action.

Write off the expense
Of stationery against experience,
And salvage no small beauties or half-lines.
You took the wrong turn, disregarded signs
Winking along your track,
Until too close-committed to turn back.

Fetch the book here
And burn it without fear,
Grateful at least that, having gone so far,
You still know what truth is and where you are,
With better things to say
In your own bold, unmarketable way.

SONG: COME, ENJOY YOUR SUNDAY!*

Into your outstretched hands come pouring
Gifts by the cornucopiaful –
        What else is lacking?
Come, enjoy your Sunday
While yet you may!

Cease from unnecessary labours,
Saunter into the green world stretching far,
        Light a long cigar,
Come, enjoy your Sunday
While yet you may!

What more, what more? You fended off disaster
In a long war, never acknowledging
        Any man as master;
Come, enjoy your Sunday
While yet you may!

Are you afraid of death? But death is nothing:
The leaden seal set on a filled flask.
        If it be life you ask,
Come, enjoy your Sunday
While yet you may!

On a warm sand dune now, sprawling at ease
With little in mind, learn to despise the sea's
        Unhuman restlessness:
Come, enjoy your Sunday
While yet you may!

From COLLECTED POEMS 1961

(1961)

RUBY AND AMETHYST*

Two women: one as good as bread,
    Bound to a sturdy husband.
Two women: one as rare as myrrh,
    Bound only to herself.

Two women: one as good as bread,
    Faithful to every promise.
Two women: one as rare as myrrh,
    Who never pledges faith.

The one a flawless ruby wears
    But with such innocent pleasure
A stranger's eye might think it glass
    And take no closer look.

Two women: one as good as bread,
    The noblest of the city.
Two women: one as rare as myrrh,
    Who needs no public praise.

The pale rose-amethyst on her breast
    Has such a garden in it
Your eye could trespass there for hours,
    And wonder, and be lost.

About her head a swallow wheels
    Nor ever breaks the circuit:
Glory and awe of womanhood
    Still undeclared to man.

Two women: one as good as bread,
    Resistant to all weathers.
Two women: one as rare as myrrh,
    Her weather still her own.

From THE MORE DESERVING CASES

(1962)

THE MILLER'S MAN*

The imperturbable miller's man
Whose help the boy implored, drowning,
Drifting slowly past the mill,
Was a stout swimmer, yet would not come between
The river-god and his assured victim.

Soon he, too, swimming in the sun,
Is caught with cramp; and the boy's ghost
Jeers from the reeds and rushes.
But he drowns valiantly in silence,
This being no one's business but his own.

Let us not reckon the miller's man
With Judas or with Jesus,
But with the cattle, who endure all weathers,
Or with the mill-wheel foolishly creaking,
Incurious of the grain in the bins.

JULY 24TH*

July the twenty-fourth, a day
Heavy with clouds that would not spill
On the disconsolate earth.

Across the road in docile chorus
School-children raised their morning hymn to God
Who still forgot their names and their petitions.

'What an age to be born in!' cried old Jamboree.
'Two world wars in one generation!'
'However,' said I, 'the plum crop should be heavy!'

What was the glass doing? The glass was low.
The Germans claimed to have stormed the town of Rostov.
Sweden dismissed the claim as premature.

Not a single painter left in the neighbourhood –
All were repainting ruined Exeter.
We had no earthly right to grumble . . . No?

I was reading a book about bone artifacts
In the age of the elk or woolly rhinoceros.
Already, it seems, man had a high culture.

A clerk wrote from the Ministry of Labour
To ask what reasons (if any) would prevent me
From serving in the Devonshire Home Guard.

Soon the Americans would be here: the patter
Of their rubber heels sounding like summer rain.
So pleasantly passed my forty-seventh birthday.

SAFE RECEIPT OF A CENSORED LETTER*

As the war lengthened, the mail shrank:
And now the Military Censor's clerk
Caught up with correspondence twelve months old –
But letters in a foreign language waited
Five months more.

'Time,' he said, 'is the best Censor:
Secret movements of troops and guns, even,
Become historical, cease to concern.
These uninterpretable items may be
Passed at last.'

Your letter was among the favoured –
Dateless familiar gossip of the village.
Thus you (who died a year ago) succeed,
Old rogue, in circumventing a more rigid
Censorship.

From NEW POEMS 1962

(1962)

RECOGNITION

When on the cliffs we met, by chance,
I startled at your quiet voice
And watched the swallows round you dance
Like children that had made a choice.

Simple it was, as I stood there,
To penetrate the mask you wore,
Your secret lineage to declare
And your lost dignities restore.

Yet thus I earned a poet's fee
So far out-distancing desire
That swallows yell in rage at me
As who would set their world on fire.

THE WATCH*

Since the night in which you stole
Like a phantom to my bed,
Seized my throat and from it wrung
Vows that could not be unsaid,

Here beneath my arching ribs
Red-hot embers, primed to be
Blown upon by winds of love,
Scorch away mortality.

Like sledgehammers my two fists,
My broad forehead grim with pride,
Muscles corded on my calves
And my frame gigantified.

Yet your watching for an hour
That our mutual stars will bless
Proves you more entranced than I
Who go parched in hope of less.

NAME DAY

Tears of delight that on my name-day
She gave me nothing, and in return
Accepted every gift I heaped upon her –
Call me the richest poet alive!

UNCALENDARED LOVE*

The first name cut on a rock, a King's,
Marked the beginning of time's annals;
And each new year would recapitulate
The unkind sloughings and renewals
Of the death-serpent's chequered coat.

But you with me together, together, together,
Survive ordeals never before endured:
We snatch the quill out of Enoch's hand
To obliterate our names from his black scroll –
Twin absentees of time.

Ours is uncalendared love, whole life,
As long or brief as befalls. Alone, together,
Recalling little, prophesying less,
We watch the serpent, crushed by your bare heel,
Rainbow his scales in a deathward agony.

THE MEETING

We, two elementals, woman and man,
Approached each other from far away:
I on the lower wind, she on the upper.

And the faith with which we came invested
By the blind thousands of our twin worlds
Formed thunder clouds about us.

Never such uproar as when we met,
Nor such forked lightning; rain in a cataract
Tumbled on deserts dry these thousand years.

What of the meteorologists?
They said nothing, turned their faces away,
Let the event pass unrecorded.

And what of us? We also said nothing.
Is it not the height of silent humour
To cause an unknown change in the earth's climate?

LACK*

Born from ignoble stock on a day of dearth
He tramps the roads, trailing his withered branch,
And grudges every beauty of the wide earth.

Lack is his name, and although in gentleness
You set him honourably at the high table
And load his plate with luxury of excess,

Crying: 'Eat well, brother, and drink your fill',
Yet with hunger whetted only, he boasts aloud:
'I have never begged a favour, nor ever will!'

His clothes are sad, but a burly wretch is he,
Of lustreless look, slack mouth, a borrowed wit,
And a sigh that would charm the song-bird from her tree.

Now he casts his eye in greed upon your demesne
With open mockery of a heart so open
It dares this gallows-climber to entertain.

NOT AT HOME

Her house loomed at the end of a Berkshire lane,
Tall but retired. She was expecting me;
And I approached with light heart and quick tread,
Having already seen from the garden gate
How bright her knocker shone – in readiness
For my confident rap? – and the steps holystoned.
I ran the last few paces, rapped and listened
Intently for the rustle of her approach. . . .

No reply, no movement. I waited three long minutes,
Then, in surprise, went down the path again
To observe the chimney stacks. No smoke from either.
And the curtains: were they drawn against the sun?
Or against what, then? I glanced over a wall
At her well-tended orchard, heavy with bloom
(Easter fell late that year, Spring had come early),
And found the gardener, bent over cold frames.

'Her ladyship is not at home?'
'No, sir.'
'She was expecting me. My name is Lion.
Did she leave a note?'
'No, sir, she left no note.'
'I trust nothing has happened. . . ?'
'No, sir, nothing. . . .
And yet she seemed preoccupied: we guess
Some family reason.'
'*Has* she a family?'
'That, sir, I could not say. . . . She seemed distressed –
Not quite herself, if I may venture so.'
'But she left no note?'
'Only a verbal message:
Her ladyship will be away some weeks
Or months, hopes to return before midsummer,
And, please, you are not to communicate.
There was something else: about the need for patience.'

The sun went in, a bleak wind shook the blossom,
Dust flew, the windows glared in a blank row. . . .
And yet I felt, when I turned slowly away,
Her eyes boring my back, as it might be posted
Behind a curtain slit, and still in love.

HORIZON*

On a clear day how thin the horizon
Drawn between sea and sky,
Between sea-love and sky-love;
And after sunset how debatable
Even for an honest eye.

'Do as you will tonight,'
Said she, and so he did
By moonlight, candlelight,
Candlelight and moonlight,
While pillowed clouds the horizon hid.

Knowing-not-knowing that such deeds must end
In a curse which lovers long past weeping for
Had heaped upon him: she would be gone one night
With his familiar friend,
Granting him leave her beauty to explore
By moonlight, candlelight,
Candlelight and moonlight.

GOLDEN ANCHOR

Gone: and to an undisclosed region,
Free as the wind, if less predictable.
Why should I grieve, who have no claim on her?
My ring circles her finger, from her neck
Dangles my powerful jade. All is not lost
While still she wears those evident tokens
And no debts lie between us except love.

Or does the golden anchor plague her
As a drag on woman's liberty? Longing
To cut the cable, run grandly adrift,
Is she warned by a voice what wide misfortune
Ripples from ill faith? – therefore temporizes
And fears to use the axe, although consorting
With lovelessness and evil?

What should I say or do? It was she chose me,
Not contrariwise. Moreover, if I lavished
Extravagant praise on her, she deserved all.
I have been honest in love, as is my nature;
She secret, as is hers. I cannot grieve
Unless for having vexed her by unmasking
A jewelled virtue she was loth to use.

LION LOVER*

You chose a lion to be your lover –
Me, who in joy such doom greeting
Dared jealously undertake
Cruel ordeals long foreseen and known,
Springing a trap baited with flesh: my own.

Nor would I now exchange this lion heart
For a less furious other,
Though by the Moon possessed
I gnaw at dry bones in a lost lair
And, when clouds cover her, roar my despair.

Gratitude and affection I disdain
As cheap in any market:
Your naked feet upon my scarred shoulders,
Your eyes naked with love,
Are all the gifts my beasthood can approve.

IBYCUS IN SAMOS*

The women of Samos are lost in love for me:
Nag at their men, neglect their looms,
And send me secret missives, to my sorrow.

I am the poet Ibycus, known by the cranes,
Each slender Samian offers herself moon-blanched
As my only bride, my heart's belovèd;

And when I return a calm salute, no more,
Or a brotherly kiss, will heap curses upon me:
Do I despise her warm myrrh-scented bosom?

She whom I honour has turned her face away
A whole year now, and in pride more than royal
Lacerates my heart and hers as one.

Wherever I wander in this day-long fever,
Sprigs of the olive-trees are touched with fire
And stones twinkle along my devious path.

Who here can blame me if I alone am poet,
If none other has dared to accept the fate
Of death and again death in the Muse's house?

Or who can blame me if my hair crackles
Like thorns under a pot, if my eyes flash
As it were sheets of summer lightning?

POSSESSED

To be possessed by her is to possess –
Though rooted in this thought
Build nothing on it.

Unreasonable faith becomes you
And mute endurance
Even of betrayal.

Never expect to be brought wholly
Into her confidence.
Being natural woman

She knows what she must do, not why;
Balks your anticipation
Of pleasure vowed;

Yet, no less vulnerable than you,
Suffers the dire pangs
Of your self-defeat.

THE WINGED HEART*

Trying to read the news, after your visit,
When the words made little sense, I let them go;
And found my heart suddenly sprouting feathers.

Alone in the house, and the full honest rain
After a devil's own four-day sirocco
Still driving down in sheets across the valley –

How it hissed, how the leaves of the olives shook!
We had suffered drought since earliest April;
Here we were already in October.

I have nothing more to tell you. What has been said
Can never possibly be retracted now
Without denial of the large universe.

Some curse has fallen between us, a dead hand,
An inhalation of evil sucking up virtue:
Which left us no recourse, unless we turned

Improvident as at our first encounter,
Deriding practical care of how or where:
Your certitude must be my certitude.

And the tranquil blaze of sky etherializing
The circle of rocks and our own rain-wet faces,
Was that not worth a lifetime of pure grief?

IN TRANCE AT A DISTANCE*

It is easy, often, and natural even,
To commune with her in trance at a distance;
To attest those deep confessionary sighs
Otherwise so seldom heard from her;
To be assured by a single shudder
Wracking both hearts, and underneath the press
Of clothes by a common nakedness.

Hold fast to the memory, lest a cold fear
Of never again here, of nothing good coming,
Should lure you into self-delusive trade
With demonesses who dare masquerade
As herself in your dreams, and who after a while
Skilfully imitate her dancing gait,
Borrow her voice and vocables and smile.

It is no longer – was it ever? – in your power
To catch her close to you at any hour:
She has raised a wall of nothingness in between
(Were it something known and seen, to be torn apart,
You could grind its heartless fragments into the ground);
Yet, taken in trance, would she still deny
That you are hers, she yours, till both shall die?

THE WREATH*

A bitter year it was. What woman ever
Cared for me so, yet so ill-used me,
Came in so close and drew so far away,
So much promised and performed so little,
So murderously her own love dared betray?
Since I can never be clear out of your debt,
Queen of ingratitude, to my dying day,
You shall be punished with a deathless crown
For your dark head, resist it how you may.

IN HER PRAISE*

This they know well: the Goddess yet abides.
Though each new lovely woman whom she rides,
Straddling her neck a year or two or three,
Should sink beneath such weight of majesty
And, groping back to humankind, gainsay
The headlong power that whitened all her way
With a broad track of trefoil – leaving you,
Her chosen lover, ever again thrust through
With daggers, your purse rifled, your rings gone –
Nevertheless they call you to live on
To parley with the pure, oracular dead,
To hear the wild pack whimpering overhead,
To watch the moon tugging at her cold tides.
Woman is mortal woman. She abides.

THE ALABASTER THRONE*

This tall lithe Amazon armed herself
With all the cunning of a peasant father
Who, fled to Corinth from starved Taenarum,
Had cherished her, the child of his new wealth,
Almost as though a son.

From Corinth she embarked for Paphos
Where white doves, circling, settled on her palms
And a sudden inspiration drew us
To heap that lap with pearls, almost as though
Ignorant of her antecedents.

Which was the Goddess, which the woman?
Let the philosophers break their teeth on it!
She had seized an empty alabaster throne
And for two summers, almost, could deny
Both Taenarum and Corinth.

A RESTLESS GHOST

Alas for obstinate doubt: the dread
Of error in supposing my heart freed,
All care for her stone dead!
Ineffably will shine the hills and radiant coast
Of early morning when she is gone indeed,
Her divine elements disbanded, disembodied
And through the misty orchards in love spread –
When she is gone indeed –
But still among them moves her restless ghost.

BETWEEN MOON AND MOON*

In the last sad watches of night
Hardly a sliver of light will remain
To edge the guilty shadow of a waned moon
That dawn must soon devour.
                                        Thereafter, another
Crescent queen shall arise with power –
So wise a beauty never yet seen, say I:
A true creature of moon, though not the same
In nature, name or feature –
Her innocent eye rebuking inconstancy
As if Time itself should die and disappear.

So was it ever. She is here again, I sigh.

BEWARE, MADAM!*

Beware, madam, of the witty devil,
The arch intriguer who walks disguised
In a poet's cloak, his gay tongue oozing evil.

Would you be a Muse? He will so declare you,
Pledging his blind allegiance,
Yet remain secret and uncommitted.

Poets are men: are single-hearted lovers
Who adore and trust beyond all reason,
Who die honourably at the gates of hell.

The Muse alone is licensed to do murder
And to betray: weeping with honest tears
She thrones each victim in her paradise.

But from this Muse the devil borrows an art
That ill becomes a man. Beware, madam:
He plots to strip you bare of woman-pride.

He is capable of seducing your twin-sister
On the same pillow, and neither she nor you
Will suspect the act, so close a glamour he sheds.

Alas, being honourably single-hearted,
You adore and trust beyond all reason,
Being no more a Muse than he a poet.

THE CLIFF EDGE

Violence threatens you no longer:
It was your innocent temerity
Caused us to tremble: veterans discharged
From the dirty wars of life.

Forgive us this presumption: we are abashed –
As when a child, straying on the cliff's edge,
Turns about to ask her white-faced brothers:
'Do you take me for a child?'

ACROBATS

Poised impossibly on the high tight-rope
        Of love, in spite of all,
They still preserve their dizzying balance
And smile this way or that,
        As though uncertain on which side to fall.

OUZO UNCLOUDED*

Here is ouzo (she said) to try you:
Better not drowned in water,
Better not chilled with ice,
Not sipped at thoughtfully,
Nor toped in secret.
Drink it down (she said) unclouded
At a blow, this tall glass full,
But keep your eyes on mine
Like a true Arcadian acorn-eater.

THE BROKEN GIRTH

Bravely from Fairyland he rode, on furlough,
Astride a tall bay given him by the Queen
From whose couch he had leaped not a half-hour since,
Whose lilies-of-the-valley shone from his helm.

But alas, as he paused to assist five Ulstermen
Sweating to raise a recumbent Ogham pillar,
Breach of a saddle-girth tumbled Oisín
To common Irish earth. And at once, it is said,
Old age came on him with grief and frailty.

St Patrick asked: would he not confess the Christ? –
Which for that Lady's sake he loathed to do,
But northward loyally turned his eyes in death.
It was Fenians bore the unshriven corpse away
For burial, keening.
                    Curse me all squint-eyed monks
Who misconstrue the passing of Finn's son:
Old age, not Fairyland, was his delusion.

INKIDOO AND THE QUEEN OF BABEL*

When I was a callant, born far hence,
You first laid hand on my innocence,
But sent your champion into a boar
That my fair young body a-pieces tore.

When I was a lapwing, crowned with gold,
Your lust and liking for me you told,
But plucked my feathers and broke my wing –
Wherefore all summer for grief I sing.

When I was a lion of tawny fell,
You stroked my mane and you combed it well,
But pitfalls seven you dug for me
That from one or other I might not flee.

When I was a courser, proud and strong,
That like the wind would wallop along,
You bated my pride with spur and bit
And many a rod on my shoulder split.

When I was a shepherd that for your sake
The bread of love at my hearth would bake,
A ravening wolf did you make of me
To be thrust from home by my brothers three.

When I tended your father's orchard close
I brought you plum, pear, apple, and rose,
But my lusty manhood away you stole
And changed me into a grovelling mole.

When I was simple, when I was fond,
Thrice and thrice did you wave your wand,
But now you vow to be leal and true
And softly ask, will I wed with you?

THREE SONGS FOR THE LUTE

I

TRUTH IS POOR PHYSIC

A wild beast falling sick
Will find his own best physic –
        Herb, berry, root of tree
Or wholesome salt to lick –
        And so run free.

But this I know at least
Better than a wild beast:
        That should I fall love-sick
And the wind veer to East,
        Truth is poor physic.

II

IN HER ONLY WAY

When her need for you dies
        And she wanders apart,
Never rhetoricize
        On the faithless heart,

But with manlier virtue
        Be content to say
She both loved you and hurt you
        In her only way.

III

HEDGES FREAKED WITH SNOW

No argument, no anger, no remorse,
        No dividing of blame.
There was poison in the cup – why should we ask
        From whose hand it came?

No grief for our dead love, no howling gales
        That through darkness blow,
But the smile of sorrow, a wan winter landscape,
        Hedges freaked with snow.

THE AMBROSIA OF DIONYSUS AND SEMELE*

Little slender lad, toad-headed,
For whom ages and leagues are dice to throw with,
Smile back to where entranced I wander
Gorged with your bitter flesh,
Drunk with your Virgin Mother's lullaby.

Little slender lad, lightning engendered,
Grand master of magicians:
When pirates stole you at Icaria
Wild ivy gripped their rigging, every oar
Changed to a serpent, panthers held the poop,
A giant vine sprouted from the mast crotch
And overboard they plunged, the whey-faced crew!

Lead us with your song, tall Queen of earth!
Twinned to the god, I follow comradely
Through a first rainbow-limbo, webbed in white,
Through chill Tyrrhenian grottoes, under water,
Where dolphins wallow between marble rocks,
Through sword-bright jungles, tangles of unease,
Through halls of fear ceilinged with incubi,
Through blazing treasure-chambers walled with garnet,
Through domes pillared with naked Caryatids –
Then mount at last on wings into pure air,
Peering down with regal eye upon
Five-fruited orchards of Elysium,
In perfect knowledge of all knowledges.

And still she drowsily chants
From her invisible bower of stars.
Gentle her voice, her notes come linked together
In intricate golden chains paid out
Slowly across brocaded cramoisy,
Or unfold like leaves from the jade-green shoot
Of a rising bush whose blossoms are her tears. . . .
O, whenever she pauses, my heart quails
Until the sound renews.

Little slender lad, little secret god,
Pledge her your faith in me,
Who have ambrosia eaten and yet live.

THE UNNAMED SPELL*

Let us never name that royal certitude,
That simultaneous recognition
When first we stood together,

When I saw you as a child astonished,
Years before, under tall trees
By a marching sound of wind:

Your heart sown with a headlong wisdom
Which every grief or joy thereafter
Rooted still more strongly.

Naming is treacherous, names divide
Truth into lesser truths, enclosing them
In a coffin of counters –

Give the spell no name, liken it only
To the more than tree luxuriating
Seven ells above earth:

All heal, golden surprise of a kiss,
Wakeful glory while the grove winters,
A branch Hell-harrowing,

Of no discoverable parentage,
Strangeling scion of varied stocks
Yet true to its own leaf,

Secret of secrets disclosed only
To who already share it,
Who themselves sometimes raised an arch –
Pillared with honour; its lintel, love –
And passed silently through.

From MAN DOES, WOMAN IS

(1964)

A TIME OF WAITING*

The moment comes when my sound senses
Warn me to keep the pot at a quiet simmer,
Conclude no rash decisions, enter into
No random friendships, check the runaway tongue
And fix my mind in a close caul of doubt –
Which is more difficult, maybe, than to face
Night-long assaults of lurking furies.

The pool lies almost empty; I watch it nursed
By a thin stream. Such idle intervals
Are from waning moon to the new – a moon always
Holds the cords of my heart. Then patience, hands;
Dabble your nerveless fingers in the shallows;
A time shall come when she has need of them.

EXPECT NOTHING

Give, ask for nothing, hope for nothing,
Subsist on crumbs, though scattered casually
Not for you (she smiles) but for the birds.
Though only a thief's diet, it staves off
Dire starvation, nor does she grow fat
On the bread she crumbles, while the lonely truth
Of love is honoured, and her word pledged.

NO LETTER

Be angry yourself, as well you may,
But why with her? She is no party to
Those avaricious dreams that pester you.
Why knot your fists as though plotting to slay
Even our postman George (whose only due
Is a small Christmas box on Christmas Day)
If his delivery does not raise the curse
Of doubt from your impoverished universe?

THE WHY OF THE WEATHER*

Since no one knows the why of the weather
Or can authoritatively forecast
More than twelve hours of day or night, at most,
Every poor fool is licensed to explain it
As Heaven's considered judgement on mankind,
And I to account for its vagaries, Myrto,
By inklings of your unaccountable mind.

IN TIME

In time all undertakings are made good,
All cruelties remedied,
Each bond resealed more firmly than before –
Befriend us, Time, Love's gaunt executor!

FIRE WALKER

To be near her is to be near the furnace.
Fortunate boy who could slip idly through,
Basket in hand, culling the red-gold blossom,
Then wander on, untaught that flowers were flame,
With no least smell of scorching on his clothes!
I, at a greater distance, charred to coal,
Earn her reproach for my temerity.

DEED OF GIFT

After close, unembittered meditation
        She gave herself to herself, this time for good;
        Body and heart re-echoed gratitude
For such a merciful repudiation
        Of debts claimed from them by the neighbourhood –

Not only friends, and friends of friends, but lovers
        Whom in the circumstances few could blame
        (Her beauty having singed them like a flame)
If they had hoarded under legal covers
        Old promissory notes signed with her name.

And though to stand once more on the firm road
        From which by misadventure she had strayed,
        So that her journey was that much delayed,
Justified the default of duties owed,
        What debt of true love did she leave unpaid?

AT BEST, POETS*

Woman with her forests, moons, flowers, waters,
And watchful fingers:
We claim no magic comparable to hers –
At best, poets; at worst, sorcerers.

SHE IS NO LIAR*

She is no liar, yet she will wash away
Honey from her lips, blood from her shadowy hand,
And, dressed at dawn in clean white robes will say,
Trusting the ignorant world to understand:
'Such things no longer are; this is today.'

A LAST POEM*

A last poem, and a very last, and yet another –
O, when can I give over?
Must I drive the pen until blood bursts from my nails
And my breath fails and I shake with fever,
Or sit well wrapped in a many-coloured cloak
Where the moon shines new through Castle Crystal?
Shall I never hear her whisper softly:
'But this is truth written by you only,
And for me only; therefore, love, have done'?

THE PEARL*

When, wounded by her anger at some trifle,
I imitate the oyster, rounding out
A ball of nacre about the intrusive grit,
Why should she charge me with perversity
As one rejoicing in his own torn guts
Or in the lucent pearl resultant
Which she disdainfully strings for her neck?
Such anger I admire; but could she swear
That I am otherwise incorrigible?

THE LEAP

Forget the rest: my heart is true
And in its waking thought of you
Gives the same wild and sudden leap
That jerks it from the brink of sleep.

BANK ACCOUNT

Never again remind me of it:
There are no debts between us.
Though silences, half-promises, evasions
Curb my impatient spirit
And freeze the regular currency of love,
They do not weaken credit. Must I demand
Sworn attestations of collateral,
Forgetting how you looked when first you opened
Our joint account at the Bank of Fate?

JUDGEMENT OF PARIS*

What if Prince Paris, after taking thought,
Had not adjudged the apple to Aphrodite
But, instead, had favoured buxom Hera,
Divine defendress of the marriage couch?
What if Queen Helen had been left to squander
Her beauty upon the thralls of Menelaus,
Hector to die unhonoured in his bed,
Penthesileia to hunt a poorer quarry,
The bards to celebrate a meaner siege?
Could we still have found the courage, you and I,
To embark together for Cranaë
And consummate our no less fateful love?

MAN DOES, WOMAN IS*

Studiously by lamp-light I appraised
The palm of your hand, its heart-line
Identical with its head-line;
And you appraised the approving frown.

I spread my cards face-upwards on the table,
Not challenging you for yours.
Man does; but woman is –
Can a gamester argue with his luck?

THE AMPLE GARDEN*

However artfully you transformed yourself
Into bitch, vixen, tigress,
I knew the woman behind.

Light as a bird now, you descend at dawn
From the poplar bough or ivy bunch
To peck my strawberries,

And have need indeed of an ample garden:
All my fruits, fountains, arbours, lawns
In fief to your glory.

You, most unmetaphorically you:
Call me a Catholic, so devout in faith
I joke of love, as Catholics do of God,
And scorn all exegesis.

TO MYRTO ABOUT HERSELF

Fierce though your love of her may be,
    What man alive can doubt
I love her more? Come now, agree
Not to turn rivalrous of me,
    Lest you and I fall out!

And should her law make little sense
    Even at times to you,
Love has its own sure recompense:
To love beyond all reason – hence
    Her fondness for us two.

What she pursues we neither know
    Nor can we well inquire;
But if you carelessly bestow
A look on me she did not owe
    It comes at her desire.

THE THREE-FACED

Who calls her two-faced? Faces, she has three:
The first inscrutable, for the outer world;
The second shrouded in self-contemplation;
The third, her face of love,
Once for an endless moment turned on me.

DAZZLE OF DARKNESS

The flame guttered, flared impossibly high,
Went out for good; yet in the dazzle of darkness
I saw her face ashine like an angel's:
Beauty too memorable for lamentation,
Though doomed to rat and maggot.

MYRRHINA*

O, why judge Myrrhina
As though she were a man?
She obeys a dark wisdom
(As Eve did before her)
Which never can fail,
Being bound by no pride
Of armorial bearings
Bequeathed in tail male.

And though your blood brother
Who dared to do you wrong
In his greed of Myrrhina
Might plead a like wisdom
The fault to excuse,
Myrrhina is just:
She has hanged the poor rogue
By the neck from her noose.

FOOD OF THE DEAD*

Blush as you stroke the curves – chin, lips and brow –
Of your scarred face, Prince Orpheus: for she has called it
Beautiful, nor would she stoop to flattery.
Yet are you patient still, when again she has eaten
Food of the dead, seven red pomegranate seeds,
And once more warmed the serpent at her thighs
For a new progress through new wards of hell?

EURYDICE*

'I am oppressed, I am oppressed, I am oppressed' –
Once I utter the curse, how can she rest:
No longer able, weeping, to placate me
With renewed auguries of celestial beauty?

Speak, fly in her amber ring; speak, horse of gold!
What gift did I ever grudge her, or help withhold?
In a mirror I watch blood trickling down the wall –
Is it mine? Yet still I stand here, proud and tall.

Look where she shines, with a borrowed blaze of light
Among the cowardly, faceless, lost, unright,
Clasping a naked imp to either breast –
Am I not oppressed, oppressed, three times oppressed?

She has gnawn at corpse-flesh till her breath stank,
Paired with a jackal, grown distraught and lank,
Crept home, accepted solace, but then again
Flown off to chain truth back with an iron chain.

My own dear heart, dare you so war on me
As to strangle love in a mad perversity?
Is ours a fate can ever be forsworn
Though my lopped head sing to the yet unborn?

TO BEGUILE AND BETRAY*

To beguile and betray, though pardonable in women,
Slowly quenches the divine need-fire
By true love kindled in them. Have you not watched
The immanent Goddess fade from their brows
When they make private to her mysteries
Some whip-scarred rogue from the hulks, some painted clown
From the pantomime – and afterwards accuse you
Of jealous hankering for the mandalot
Rather than horror and sick foreboding
That she will never return to the same house?

I WILL WRITE

He had done for her all that a man could,
And, some might say, more than a man should.
Then was ever a flame so recklessly blown out
Or a last goodbye so negligent as this?
'I will write to you,' she muttered briefly,
Tilting her cheek for a polite kiss;
Then walked away, nor ever turned about. . . .

Long letters written and mailed in her own head –
There are no mails in a city of the dead.

BIRD OF PARADISE*

At sunset, only to his true love,
The bird of paradise opened wide his wings
Displaying emerald plumage shot with gold
Unguessed even by him.
                                        True, that wide crest
Had blazoned royal estate, and the tropic flowers
Through which he flew had shown example
Of what brave colours gallantry might flaunt,
But these were other. She asked herself, trembling:
'What did I do to awake such glory?'

THE METAPHOR

The act of love seemed a dead metaphor
For love itself, until the timeless moment
When fingers trembled, heads clouded,
And love rode everywhere, too numinous
To be expressed or greeted calmly:
O, then it was, deep in our own forest,
We dared revivify the metaphor,
Shedding the garments of this epoch
In scorn of time's wilful irrelevancy;
So at last understood true nakedness
And the long debt to silence owed.

SONG: A PHOENIX FLAME*

In my heart a phoenix flame
   Darts and scorches me all day –
Should a fierce sun do the same,
   I die away.

O for pools with sunken rocks,
   Minnow-haunted mountain brooks,
Blustering gales of Equinox,
   Cold, green nooks.

Who could boast a careless wit,
   Doubly roasted, heart and hide,
Turning on the Sun's red spit,
   Consumed inside?

SECRECY*

Lovers are happy
When favoured by chance,
But here is blessedness
Beyond all happiness,

Not to be gainsaid
By any gust of chance,
Harvest of one vine,
Gold from the same mine:

To keep which sacred
Demands a secrecy
That the world might blame
As deceit and shame;

Yet to publish which
Would make a him and her
Out of me and you
That were both untrue.

Let pigeons couple
Brazenly on the bough,
But royal stag and hind
Are of our own mind.

JOSEPH AND MARY

They turned together with a shocked surprise –
He, old and fabulous; she, young and wise –
Both having heard a newborn hero weep
In convalescence from the stroke of sleep.

AN EAST WIND

Beware the giddy spell, ground fallen away
Under your feet, wings not yet beating steady:
An ignorant East Wind tempts you to deny
Faith in the twofold glory of your being –
You with a thousand leagues or more to fly.

'Poised in air between earth and paradise,
Paradise and earth, confess which pull
Do you find the stronger? Is it of homesickness
Or of passion? Would you be rather loyal or wise?
How are these choices reconcilable?'

Turn from him without anger. East Wind knows
Only one wall of every foursquare house,
Has never viewed your northern paradise
Nor watched its queen tending her jewelled boughs,
But always from the same sick quarter blows.

DANCE OF WORDS*

To make them move, you should start from lightning
And not forecast the rhythm: rely on chance,
Or so-called chance for its bright emergence
Once lightning interpenetrates the dance.

Grant them their own traditional steps and postures
But see they dance it out again and again
Until only lightning is left to puzzle over –
The choreography plain, and the theme plain.

A BLIND ARROW

Though your blind arrow, shot in time of need
Among the shadowy birches, did indeed
Strike, as you knew it must, the assassin's heart,
Never disparage a trained bowman's art.

THE OLEASTER*

Each night for seven nights beyond the gulf
A storm raged, out of hearing, and crooked flashes
Of lightning animated us. Before day-break
Rain fell munificently for the earth's need. . . .

No, here they never plant the sweet olive
As some do (bedding slips in a prepared trench),
But graft it on the club of Hercules
The savage, inexpugnable oleaster
Whose roots and bole bunching from limestone crannies
Sprout impudent shoots born only to be lopped
Spring after Spring. Theirs is a loveless berry. . . .

By mid-day we walk out, with naked feet,
Through pools on the road, gazing at waterfalls
Or a line of surf, but mostly at the trees
Whose elegant branches rain has duly blackened
And pressed their crowns to a sparkling silver.

Innumerable, plump with promise of oil,
The olives hang grass-green, in thankfulness
For a bitter sap and bitter New Year snows
That cleansed their bark. . . .
                                        Forgive me, dearest love,
If nothing I can say be strange or new.
I am no child of the hot South like you,
Though in rock rooted like an oleaster.

THE SEPTUAGENARIAN

Youth is the ruggedest burden that can score
Your septuagenarian shoulder:
If you should threaten, as before, to powder
Rocks with bare heels, or rend the oak asunder
With naked fingers, you can now no more
Plead youthful benefit of metaphor.
Such unsubstantiated boasts will be
Substantial evidence of senility.

NON COGUNT ASTRA

Come, live in Now and occupy it well.
Prediction's no alternative to forethought
Despite at least four hundred arts of scrying
The dubious future, such as to study birds,
Or bull's guts, or sheep droppings, or wine lees
In an alabaster cup. True, the most ancient,
Most exact discipline, astrology,
Comes hallowed by a college of gowned mantics
Who still cast horoscopes only by stars
Apparent to the still unaided eye –

And of whom a few, the best, focus their powers
On exact horary configurations, then
At an agreed moment brusquely sweep away
Zodiacal signs, conjunctions, trines,
And reinduce a pure, archaic vision;
Yet disregard all false astrologers
Who dare lay greedy or compulsive hands
On the stars you sped at your nativity
Along their courses and forbad to canker
The rose of love or blunt the blade of honour:
No public hangmen these, but servants chosen
To wear bright livery at your house gate;
And favour you the more, the less you fear them.

SONG: SWORD AND ROSE

The King of Hearts a broadsword bears,
   The Queen of Hearts, a rose –
Though why, not every gambler cares
   Or cartomancer knows.

Be beauty yours, be honour mine,
   Yet sword and rose are one:
Great emblems that in love combine
   Until the dealing's done;

For no card, whether small or face,
   Shall overtrump our two
Except that Heart of Hearts, the Ace,
   To which their title's due.

ENDLESS PAVEMENT

In passage along an endless, eventless pavement,
None but the man in love, as he turns to stare
At the glazed eyes flickering past, will remain aware
Of his own, assured, meticulous, rustic tread –
As if pavement were pebbles, or rocks overgrown by grasses;
And houses, trees with birds flying overhead.

IN DISGUISE*

Almost I welcome the dirty subterfuges
Of this unreal world closing us in,
That present you as a lady of high fashion
And me as a veteran on the pensioned list.

Our conversation is infinitely proper,
With a peck on either cheek as we meet or part –
Yet the seven archons of the heavenly stair
Tremble at the disclosure of our seals.

A MEASURE OF CASUALNESS

Too fierce the candlelight; your gentle voice
Roars as in dream: my shoulder-nooks flower;
A scent of honeysuckle invades the house,
And my fingertips are so love-enhanced
That sailcloth feels like satin to them.
Teach me a measure of casualness
Though you stalk into my room like Venus naked.

IN TIME OF ABSENCE

Lovers in time of absence need not signal
With call and answering call:
By sleight of providence each sends the other
A clear, more than coincidental answer
To every still unformulated puzzle,
Or a smile at a joke harboured, not yet made,
Or power to be already wise and unafraid.

THE GREEN CASTLE

The first heaven is a flowery plain;
The second, a glass mountain;
The third, likewise terrestrial,
Is an orchard-close unclouded
By prescience of death or change
Or the blood-sports of desire:
Our childhood paradise.

The next three heavens, known as celestial,
Are awkward of approach.
Mind is the prudent rider; body, the ass
Disciplined always by a harsh bit,
Accepts his daily diet of thorns
And frugal, brackish water;
Holds converse with archangels.

The seventh heaven, most unlike those others,
We once contrived to enter
By a trance of love; it is a green castle
Girdled with ramparts of blue sea
And silent but for the waves' leisured wash.
There Adam rediscovered Eve:
She wrapped him in her arms.

An afterglow of truth, still evident
When we had fallen earthward,
Astonished all except the born blind.
Strangers would halt us in the roadway:
'Confess where you have been.'
And, at a loss, we replied stumblingly:
'It was here, it was nowhere –
Last night we lodged at a green castle,
Its courtyard paved with gold.'

NOT TO SLEEP*

Not to sleep all the night long, for pure joy,
Counting no sheep and careless of chimes,
Welcoming the dawn confabulation
Of birds, her children, who discuss idly
Fanciful details of the promised coming –
Will she be wearing red, or russet, or blue,
Or pure white? – whatever she wears, glorious:
Not to sleep all the night long, for pure joy,
This is given to few but at last to me,
So that when I laugh and stretch and leap from bed
I shall glide downstairs, my feet brushing the carpet
In courtesy to civilized progression,
Though, did I wish, I could soar through the open window
And perch on a branch above, acceptable ally
Of the birds still alert, grumbling gently together.

THE HEARTH*

Here it begins: the worm of love breeding
Among red embers of a hearth-fire
Turns to a chick, is slowly fledged,
And will hop from lap to lap in a ring
Of eager children basking at the blaze.

But the luckless man who never sat there,
Nor borrowed live coals from the sacred source
To warm a hearth of his own making,
Nor bedded lay under pearl-grey wings
In dutiful content,

How shall he watch at the stroke of midnight
Dove become phoenix, plumed with green and gold?
Or be caught up by jewelled talons
And haled away to a fastness of the hills
Where an unveiled woman, black as Mother Night,
Teaches him a new degree of love
And the tongues and songs of birds?

THAT OTHER WORLD*

Fatedly alone with you once more
As before Time first creaked:
Sole woman and sole man.

Others admire us as we walk this world:
We show them kindliness and mercy,
So be it none grow jealous
Of the truth that echoes between us two,
Or of that other world, in the world's cradle,
Child of your love for me.

THE BEDS OF GRAINNE AND DIARMUID*

How many secret nooks in copse or glen
We sained for ever with our pure embraces,
No man shall know; though indeed master poets
Reckon one such for every eve of the year,
To sain their calendar.
                                        But this much is true:
That children stumbling on our lairs by chance
In quest of hazel-nuts or whortleberries
Will recognize the impress of twin bodies
On the blue-green turf, starred with diversity
Of alien flowers, and shout astonishment.
Yet should some amorous country pair, presuming
To bask in joy on any bed of ours,
Offend against the love by us exampled,
Long ivy roots will writhe up from beneath
And bitterly fetter ankle, wrist and throat.

RAIN OF BRIMSTONE

Yet if they trust by lures or spells
   To exorcize the tall angel,
Love, from this ancient keep by us
   Now long frequented,

And if frustration turns their wits,
   So that they bawl in hell's fury
Battering at our gate all night
   With oaken cudgels,

Are we to blame for sparing them
   The voice of truth which they deny us?
Should we not darkly leave the town
   To its rain of brimstone?

CONSORTIUM OF STONES*

The stones you have gathered, of diverse shapes,
Chosen from sea strand, lake strand, mountain gully:
Lay them all out on a basalt slab together
But allow intervals for light and air,
These being human souls; and reject any
With crumpled calceous edges and no feature
That awakes loving correspondence.

Start at this pair: blue flint, grey ironstone,
Which you ring around with close affinities
In every changeless colour, hatched, patched, plain –
Curve always answering curve; and angle, angle.

Gaps there may be, which next year or the next
Will fill to a marvel: never jog Time's arm,
Only narrow your eyes when you walk about
Lest they miss what is missing. The agreed intent
Of each consortium, whether of seven stones,
Or of nineteen, or thirty-three, or more,
Must be a circle, with firm edges outward,
Each various element aware of the sum.

THE BLACK GODDESS*

Silence, words into foolishness fading,
Silence prolonged, of thought so secret
We hush the sheep-bells and the loud cicada.

And your black agate eyes, wide open, mirror
The released firebird beating his way
Down a whirled avenue of blues and yellows.

Should I not weep? Profuse the berries of love,
The speckled fish, the filberts and white ivy
Which you, with a half-smile, bestow
On your delectable broad land of promise
For me, who never before went gay in plumes.

BROKEN NECK

'Some forty years ago or maybe more,'
Pronounced the radiologist, 'you broke
Your neck: that is to say, contrived to fracture
Your sixth cervical vertebra – see here,
The picture's clear – and between sixth and seventh
Flattened this cartilage to uselessness:
Hence rheumatism. Surely you recall
Some incident? We all do foolish things
While young, and obstinately laugh them off –
Till they catch up with us in God's good time.
Let me prescribe you a Swiss analgesic
Which should at least. . . .'
                                        Love, I still laugh it off
And all Swiss mercenary alleviations,
For though I broke my neck in God's good time
It is in yours alone I choose to live.

O

'O per se O, O per se O!',
The moribund grammarian cried
To certain scholars grouped at his bedside,
Spying the round, dark pit a-gape below:
'O per se O!'

WOMAN OF GREECE

By your knees they rightly clasp you,
  Strong sons of your bed,
Whom you get, kneeling; and bear, kneeling;
  Kneeling, mourn for dead.

THE COLOURS OF NIGHT

The Moon never makes use of the Sun's palette.
Admire her silvery landscapes, but abstain
From record of them: lest you be later tempted
To counterfeit the dangerous colours of Night
Which are man's blood spurted on moving cloud.

BETWEEN TRAINS

Arguing over coffee at the station,
Neither of us noticed her dark beauty,
Though she sat close by, until suddenly
Three casual words – does it matter what they were? –
Spoken without remarkable intonation
Or accent, so bewildered him and me,
As it were catching the breath of our conversation,
That each set down his coffee-cup, to stare.
'You have come for us?' my lips cautiously framed –
Her eyes were almost brighter than I could bear –
But she rose and left, unready to be named.

TO THE TEUMESSIAN VIXEN*

Do not mistake me: I was never a rival
   Of that poor fox who pledged himself to win
Your heart by gnawing away his brush. Who ever
   Proved love was love except by a whole skin?

THE HUNG WU VASE*

With women like Marie no holds are barred.
Where do they get the gall? How can they do it?

She stormed out, slamming the hall door so hard
That a vase on the gilt shelf above – you knew it,
Loot from the Summer Palace at Pekin
And worth the entire contents of my flat –
Toppled and fell. . . .
                                        I poured myself straight gin,
Downing it at a gulp. 'So that was that!'

The bell once more. . . . Marie walked calmly in,
Observed broken red porcelain on the mat,
Looked up, looked down again with condescension,
Then, gliding past me to retrieve a glove
(Her poor excuse for this improper call),
Muttered: 'And one thing I forgot to mention:
Your Hung Wu vase was phoney, like your love!'

How can they do it? Where do they get the gall?

LA MEJICANA

Perfect beneath an eight-rayed sun you lie,
   Rejoiced at his caresses. Yours is a land
For pumas, chillis, and men dark of eye;
   Yet summon me with no derisive hand
From these remote moon-pastures drenched in dew –
And watch who burns the blacker: I or you.

LAMIA IN LOVE*

Need of this man was her ignoble secret:
Desperate for love, yet loathing to deserve it,
She wept pure tears of sorrow when his eyes
Betrayed mistrust in her impeccable lies.

AFTER THE FLOOD*

Noah retrieves the dove again,
   Which bears him in its bill
A twig of olive to explain
That, if God sends them no more rain,
   The world may prosper still.

Shem, Ham and Japheth raise a shout,
   But weeks on end must wait
Till Father Noah, venturing out,
Can view the landscape all about
   And prophesy their fate.

'Where have the waters of God's Flood
   Dispersed?' God only knew.
What Noah saw was miles of mud,
Drowned rogues, and almond trees in bud
   With blossom peeping through.

'Bold lads, in patience here abide!
   This mire around the ark
By wind or sun must well be dried
Before we set against her side
   The planks to disembark.'

Obedient sons, a virtuous wife,
   Flocks, cattle, jars of seeds,
Crook, coulter, halter, pruning-knife –
Noah forecasts a brave new life
   Agreeable to his needs.

Exult with him at the clear sky,
   Proud Noahs of today,
For though we here and there descry
Morasses that no sun can dry
   (Regret them how we may),

God's rainbow is a glorious toy,
   His wine a cheerful drink,
And since He chooses to destroy
Folk better dead, we wish Him joy,
   While choking at the stink.

A LATE ARRIVAL

A Libyan pilgrim-ship tied up at Joppa
Twenty-four hours late, on a Wednesday morning.
The poor Jew from Cyrene hired no ass
But trudged, by way of Gimzo and Beth Horon,
Three hundred stadia to Jerusalem.

That Friday morning, close to the Western Gate
Where his son Alexander welcomed him,
He was tapped on the wrist by a Roman sergeant
And, though with little on his conscience, jumped
In excusable fright. The grinning sergeant said:
'A work of charity awaits you, sir!'

Foot-sore Simon, thus impressed to shoulder
The eight-foot oaken cross-piece of a cross
Towards Jeremiah's grotto – now already
Late for a family gathering and, far worse,
Contaminated by this unclean baulk –
Vented his rage on the condemned bandit:

'Poor fool! Betrayed to those Boethan traitors
By one of your own men, my son reports!
How long had you known Judah of Cherioth?
Seven years, or more? Alas, what innocence!
So long, and never peered into his heart?
I heard him once, far too loud in your praise
(Three Passovers ago, it must have been),
And all but naming you the Appointed King . . .
I am told that Judah, jealous for your honour
Yet jealous of you, boasting he knew best,
Pleaded for your protective custody;
Loved you, he said, but loved our nation more.'

Since the poor stumbling felon made no answer,
Though his lips moved, as it might be in prayer,
Simon thought pityingly of Alexander:
What a disgrace for his own son to see him
Hauled off to attend a Roman crucifixion!
Why had God's hand delayed that Lybian ship?

Later the man spoke in a small, dry voice:
'May God forgive me and my servant too –
We both thought we knew better than our lord.'

SONG: WITH NO RETURN

If you keep your heart so true
   That her oaks take fire and burn,
And her foxes dance for you
All together in full view,
   Paradise is here to earn,
   Peace to learn:
She will pledge you, as she must,
To a trust beyond all trust
   With no manner of return.

ALL I TELL YOU FROM MY HEART

I begged my love to wait a bit
Although the sky was clear:
'I smell a shower of rain,' said I,
'And you'll be caught, I fear.'
'You want to keep me trapped,' she said,
'And hold my hand again. . . .'
But not ten minutes had she gone
When how the rain did rain!

'Alas, dear love, so wet you are –
You should have trusted me!
For all I tell you from my heart
Is sure as prophecy.'

I begged my love to wait a bit
And watch the faggots blaze.
'There's music on the march,' said I,
'To cheer whoever stays.'
'You want to keep me trapped,' she said,
'O, every night's the same. . . .'
But not ten minutes had she gone
When in the fiddlers came!

'Alas, dear love, what tunes they played –
You should have trusted me!
For all I tell you from my heart
Is sure as prophecy.'

I begged my love to take good heed
When walking through the wood,
And warned her of a random rogue
Who brought the world no good.
'You want to keep me trapped,' she said,
'And roll me in your bed. . . .'
But scarce a hundred yards from home
She lost her maidenhead.

'Alas, dear love, it is too late –
You should have trusted me!
For all I told you from my heart
Was sure as prophecy.'

THE UNDEAD

To be the only woman alive in a vast hive of death
Is a strange predicament, granted! Innumerable zombies
With glazed eyes shuffle around at their diurnal tasks,
Keep the machines whirring, drudge idly in stores and bars,
Bear still-born zombie children, pack them off to school
For education in science and the dead languages,
Divert themselves with moribund travesties of living,
Lay mountainous bets on horses never seen to run,
Speed along highways in conveyor-belt automobiles
But, significantly enough, often dare overshoot
The traffic signals and *boing!* destroy themselves again,
Earning expensive funerals. (These, if at last they emerge
From the select green cemetery plots awarded them
On their twenty-first death-days by sombre uncles and aunts,
Will become zombies of the second degree, reverenced
Nationwide in church or synagogue.)
Nevertheless,
Let none of this daunt you, child! Accept it as your fate
To live, to love, knowingly to cause true miracles,
Nor ever to find your body possessed by a cold corpse.
For one day, as you choose an unfamiliar side-street
Keeping both eyes open, alert, not apprehensive,
You shall suddenly (this is a promise) come to a brief halt:
For striding towards you on the same sidewalk will appear
A young man with the halo of life around his head,
Will catch you reassuringly by both hands, asseverating
In phrases utterly unintelligible to a zombie
That all is well: you are neither diseased, deranged, nor
mistaken,
But merely undead. He will name others like you, no less alive:
Two girls and a man, all moneyless immigrants arrived
Lately at a new necropolitan conurbation.
'Come with me, girl, and join them! The dead, you will observe,
Can exercise no direct sanctions against the living
And therefore doggedly try to omit them from all the records.
Still, they cannot avoid a certain morbid fascination
With what they call our genius. They will venture questions
But never wait for an answer – being doubtless afraid
That it will make their ears burn, or their eyes prick with tears –
Nor can they countermand what orders we may issue.'

Nod your assent, go with him, do not even return to pack!
When five live people room together, each rates as a million –
But encourage the zombies to serve you, the honest creatures,
For though one cannot ameliorate their way of death
By telling them true stories or singing them real songs,
They will feel obscurely honoured by your warm presence.

From ANN AT HIGHWOOD HALL

(1964)

ANN AT HIGHWOOD HALL

Ann ran away from home, where she had been
The third-but-youngest child of seventeen;
Since her poor mother's death that drunken man,
Ann's father, had thrown cups and plates at Ann
And once – he saw her polishing the stairs –
Asked, who was *she* to give herself such airs?

Ann, dressed in rags and an old tattered shawl,
Marched resolutely off to Highwood Hall,
Making herself invisible (for she
Had learned this trick from harsh necessity),
Then stole past valets, footmen, pages, grooms,
White marble statues, chambermaids with brooms,
And up the curving staircase carpeted
In green, down corridors all hung in red,
To the Duke's private room where twin fire-dogs
Crouched under a huge pile of crackling logs.

Ann entered calmly, chose a book, sat down
And began reading with a thoughtful frown.
In flounced the Duchess. Ann gave her a smile
But still continued reading a long while
Until the Duchess, watched by the Duke's cat,
Rang for the butler: 'Browne, remove this brat,
His Grace the Duke's latest discovery,
And bring her back attired more decently.'

The butler, Browne, led Ann to a large tub
Full of hot water. She enjoyed her scrub
And having her fair tresses tied in braids
Most elegantly by two lady's maids,
And being dressed in muslin. Thereupon
She sauntered back, but found the Duchess gone.

Now, Ann had learned at home: SILENCE IS BEST,
And since the Duke was seldom told what guest
His Duchess had invited – this gay pair
Let half the English peerage picnic there –
Ann took for granted she was welcome too,
And later felt it neither strange nor new
That now she dined in state at the Duke's board
As though the heiress of some powerful lord.

She sang to her own lute, lay long a-bed,
Swooned fashionably, embroidered with gold thread,
Danced, rode to hounds, was held in high regard,
Refused two Earls . . .
But here her story (starred
With royal visits, royal compliments,
Odes to her beauty, duels, tournaments,
Portraits by rival painters) dims at last
With the Duke's execution and a vast
Ruin engulfing all his relatives . . .

Thieves plundered Highwood Hall. Yet Ann still lives:
A lovely lady in her attic room
Working, folk say, by starlight at a loom,
Invisible to most eyes, but not all,
And well content with rags and tattered shawl.

ST VALENTINE'S DAY

Tell me truly, Valentine,
What you most require.
Off I'll hurry, back I'll fetch
All your heart's desire:

Stockings for your jaunty legs,
Staddles for your ricks,
String to tie the pickle-jar,
Straw to make bricks,

Silver salvers for your board,
Satin for your bed,
And scented suds to blow you bubbles,
Green, blue, yellow and red.

I HAVE A LITTLE COUGH, SIR*

'I have a little cough, sir,
    In my little chest, sir,
All night long I cough, sir,
    I can never rest, sir,
And every time I cough, sir,
    It leaves a little pain, sir –
Cough, cough, cough, sir:
    There it is again, sir!'

'O Doctor Millikan,
    I shall surely die!'
'Yes, pretty Susan –
    So one day shall I.'

JOSEPH AND JESUS*

(from the Spanish)

Said Joseph unto Mary,
    'Be counselled by me:
Fetch your love child from the manger,
    For to Egypt we must flee.'

As Mary went a-riding
    Up the hill out of view,
The ass was much astonishèd
    How like a dove he flew.

Said Jesus unto Joseph,
    Who his soft cheek did kiss:
'There are thorns in your beard, good sir.
    I askèd not for this.'

Then Joseph brought to Jesus
    Hot paps of white bread
Which, when it burned that pretty mouth,
    Joseph swallowed in his stead.

LOVE RESPELT

(1965)

THE RED SHOWER

Live sparks rain from the central anvil
    In a red shower. Let all beware
Who read the event as history, frowning at
    What they may find of madness there:
    Felicity endangering despair.

ABOVE THE EDGE OF DOOM

Bats at play taunt us with 'guess how many',
And music sounds far off, tempered by sea.
Above the edge of doom sits woman
Communing with herself. 'Dear love,' says she,
As it were apostrophizing cat or dog,
'Sometimes by a delicate glance and gesture
You almost seem to understand me,
Poor honest creature of the blue eyes,
Having crept closer to my sealed bosom
With your more desperate faith in womankind
Than any other since I first flowered.

It may be best you cannot read my mind.'

WILD CYCLAMEN*

'What can I do for you?' she asked gently.
I reached for pen and paper: 'Draw me flowers!'

She pursed her lips – O the smooth brown forehead,
The smooth lids drooped, intent on their task –
And drew me wild Majorcan cyclamen
(Not yet in season) extravagantly petalled,
Then laughed and tossed me back the picture.

'It is nothing,' she said; yet that cyclamen odour
Hung heavy in the room for a long while;
And when she was gone, I caught myself smiling
In her own crooked way, trying to make my eyes
Sparkle like hers, though ineffectually,
Till I fell asleep; for this was my sick-bed
And her visits brief, by order.

GIFT OF SIGHT*

I had long known the diverse tastes of the wood,
Each leaf, each bark, rank earth from every hollow;
Knew the smells of bird's breath and of bat's wing;
Yet sight I lacked: until you stole upon me,
Touching my eyelids with light finger-tips.
The trees blazed out, their colours whirled together,
Nor ever before had I been aware of sky.

*BATXÓCA**

Firm-lipped, high-bosomed, slender Queen of Beanstalk Land,
Who are more to me than any woman upon this earth
Though you live from hand to mouth, keeping no certain hours,
Disguising your wisdom with unpracticality
And your elusiveness with hugs for all and sundry,
Flaunting green, yellow and scarlet, suddenly disappearing
In a whirlwind rage and flurry of skirts, always alone
Until found, days later, asleep on a couch of broom
And incommunicable until you have breakfasted –
By what outrageous freak of dissimilarity
Were you forced, noble Batxóca, to fall so deep in love
With me as to demand marriage, despite your warning
That you and I must on no account be seen together –
A Beanstalk Queen, no less, paired with a regular man!

Did you wistfully, perhaps, expect me to say 'no'?

THE SNAP-COMB WILDERNESS

Magic is tangled in a woman's hair
For the enlightenment of male pride.
To slide a comb uxoriously
Through an even swell of tresses undisturbed
By their cascade from an exact parting
Could never hearten or enlighten me –
Not though her eyes were bluer than blue sea.
Magic rules an irreducible jungle
Dark as eclipse and scented with despair,
A stubborn snap-comb wilderness of hair,
Each strand a singular, wild, curling tree.

CHANGE*

'This year she has changed greatly' – meaning you –
My sanguine friends agree,
And hope thereby to reassure me.

No, child, you never change; neither do I.
Indeed all our lives long
We are still fated to do wrong,

Too fast caught by care of humankind,
Easily vexed and grieved,
Foolishly flattered and deceived;

And yet each knows that the changeless other
Must love and pardon still,
Be the new error what it will:

Assured by that same glint of deathlessness
Which neither can surprise
In any other pair of eyes.

A COURT OF LOVE

Were you to break the vow we swore together,
The vow, I said, would break you utterly:
Despite your pleas of duty elsewhere owed,
You could no longer laugh, work, heal, do magic,
Nor in the mirror face your own eyes.

They have summoned me before their Court of Love
And warned me I must sign for your release
Pledging my word never again to draft
A similar pact, as one who has presumed
Lasting felicity still unknown in time.
What should I do? Forswear myself for you?
No man in love, plagued by his own scruples
Will ever, voluntarily, concede
That women have a spirit above vows.

BLACK

Black drinks the sun and draws all colours to it.
I am bleached white, my truant love. Come back,
And stain me with intensity of black.

BETWEEN HYSSOP AND AXE

To know our destiny is to know the horror
Of separation, dawn oppressed by night:
Is, between hyssop and axe, boldly to prove
That gifted, each, with singular need for freedom
And haunted, both, by spectres of reproach,
We may yet house together without succumbing
To the low fever of domesticity
Or to the lunatic spin of aimless flight.

GOLD AND MALACHITE*

After the hour of illumination, when the tottering mind
Has been by force delivered from its incubus of despair,
When all the painted, papier mâché, Mexican faces
Of demons grinning at you from hell's vaulted roof
Fade and become angelic monitors of wisdom –
Slowly the brisk intelligence wakes, to mutter questions
Of when, where, how; and which should be the first step forward. . . .

Now is the crucial moment you were forewarned against.
Stop your ears with your fingers, guard unequivocal silence
Lest you discuss wisdom in the language of unwisdom;
Roam instead through the heaped treasury of your heart:
You will find her, from whom you have been so long estranged,
Chin to knees, brooding apart on gold and malachite.
But beware again: even a shy embrace would be too explicit –
Let her learn by your gait alone that you are free at last.

AMBIENCE

The nymph of the forest, only in whose honour
These birds perform, provides an ambience
But never leads the chorus: even at dawn
When we awake to whistle, flute and pipe,
Astonished they can so extemporize
Their own parts, as it were haphazard
Each in his own time, yet avoid discordance
Or domineering, however virtuose
Or long sustained each voluntary of love.
The rare silences, too, appear like sound
Rather than pause for breath or meditation. . . .
Nor is the same piece ever given twice.

THE VOW*

No vow once sworn may ever be annulled
Except by a higher law of love or mercy –
Search your heart well: is there a lie hidden
Deep in its convolutions of resolve?

For whom do you live? Can it be yourself?
For whom then? Not for this unlovely world,
Not for the rotting waters of mischance,
Nor for the tall, eventual catafalque.

You live for her who alone loves you,
Whose royal prerogative can be denied
By none observant of the awakening gasps
That greet her progress down whatever hall.

Your vow is to truth, not practicality;
To honour, not to the dead world's esteem;
To a bed of rock, not to a swan's-down pillow;
To the tears you kiss away from her black eyes.

They lament an uninstructible world of men
Who dare not listen or watch, but challenge proof
That a leap of a thousand miles is nothing
And to walk invisibly needs no artifice.

THE FROG AND THE GOLDEN BALL

She let her golden ball fall down the well
   And begged a cold frog to retrieve it;
For which she kissed his ugly, gaping mouth –
   Indeed, he could scarce believe it.

And seeing him transformed to his princely shape,
   Who had been by hags enchanted,
She knew she could never love another man
   Nor by any fate be daunted.

But what would her royal father and mother say?
  They had promised her in marriage
To a cousin whose wide kingdom marched with theirs,
  Who rode in a jewelled carriage.

'Our plight, dear heart, would appear past human hope
  To all except you and me: to all
Who have never swum as a frog in a dark well
  Or have lost a golden ball.'

'What then shall we do now?' she asked her lover.
  He kissed her again, and said:
'Is magic of love less powerful at your Court
  Than at this green well-head?'

THOSE WHO CAME SHORT

Those who came short of love for me or you,
Where are they now? Ill-starred and bitter-mouthed,
Cursing us for their own contrariness,
Each having fallen in turn, head over heels,
From that illusive heaven at which they flew.

Are we then poison of love-perfection
To all but our own kind? Should we beware
Of handling such intemperate shaggy creatures
As leap on us like dogs to be cosseted
And, after, claim full rights of jealousy?

At once too simple and too various
Except for ourselves, should we awhile conceal
Our studies from the world, in cool forbearance
Watching each night for another dawn to break
And the last guest to straggle home?

WHOLE LOVE

Every choice is always the wrong choice,
Every vote cast is always cast away –
How can truth hover between alternatives?

Then love me more than dearly, love me wholly,
Love me with no weighing of circumstance,
As I am pledged in honour to love you:

With no weakness, with no speculation
On what might happen should you and I prove less
Than bringers-to-be of our own certainty.
Neither was born by hazard: each foreknew
The extreme possession we are grown into.

THIS HOLY MONTH*

The demon who throughout our late estrangement
Followed with malice in my footsteps, often
Making as if to stumble, so that I stumbled
And gashed my head against a live rock;
Who tore my palms on butcher's broom and thorn,
Flung me at midnight into filthy ditches
And multiplied the horrors of this house
When back I limped again to a hard bed;
Who simultaneously plagued you too
With sleeplessness, dismay and darkness,
Paralysed your hands, denied you air –
We both know well he was the same demon,
Arch-enemy of rule and calculation,
Who lives for our love, being created from it,
Astonishes us with blossom, silvers the hills
With more than moonlight, summons bees in swarms
From the Lion's mouth to fill our hives with honey,
Turns flesh into fire, and eyes into deep lakes;
And so may do once more, this holy month.

THE BLOW*

You struck me on the face and I, who strike
Only to kill, stood in confusion like
Death's fool: your ugly blow
Had fallen soft as snow.

Love me for what I am, with liberty
To curb my rage; I love you for what will be –
Your urgent sun – therefore
Acquitting you of error.

Laughter becomes us: gift of the third eye
That passes nothing by.

THE IMPOSSIBLE

Dear love, since the impossible proves
  Our sole recourse from this distress,
Claim it: the ebony ritual-mask of no
  Cannot outstare a living yes.

Claim it without despond or hate
  Or greed; but in your gentler tone
Say: 'This is ours, the impossible,' and silence
  Will give consent it is ours alone.

The impossible has wild-cat claws
  Which you would rather meet and die
Than commit love to time's curative venom
  And break our oath; for so would I.

THE FETTER*

Concerned, against our wish, with a sick world,
Self-neglectful, tuned to knock or summons,
We make amends for follies not our own.

We have taken love through a thousand deaths;
Should either try to slip our iron fetter,
It bites yet deeper into neck and arm.

As for that act of supererogation,
The kiss in which we secretly concur,
Let laughter mitigate its quiet excess.

Could we only be a simple, bickering pair
In the tied cottage of a small estate,
With no tasks laid on us except to dig,
Hoe, fatten geese and scrape the quarter's rent,
How admirable our close interdependence;
Our insecurity how fortunate!

IRON PALACE*

We stood together, side by side, rooted
At the iron heart of circumambient hills,
Parents to a new age, weeping in awe
That the lot had fallen, of all mankind, on us
Now sealed as love's exemplars.

We could not prevaricate or argue,
Citing involvement in some alien scene,
Nor plead unworthiness: none else would venture
To live detached from force of circumstance
As history neared its ending.

We told no one. These were not strange dreams
Recalled at breakfast with a yawning smile,
Nor tales for children, on the verge of sleep,
Who ask no questions. Our predicament
Remained a silent burden.

We had no token or proof, and needed none
Of what we learned that day; but laughed softly
Watching our hands engage, in co-awareness
That these red hills warned us, on pain of death,
Never to disengage them.

Woman, wild and hard as the truth may be,
Nothing can circumvent it. We stand coupled
With chains, who otherwise might live apart
Conveniently paired, each with another,
And slide securely graveward.

TRUE JOY*

Whoever has drowned and awhile entered
The adamantine gates of afterwards,
Stands privileged to reject heavenly joy
(Though without disrespect for God's archangels)
With 'never again' – no moon, no herbs, no sea,
No singular love of women.

True joy, believe us, is to groan and wake
From the hallelujah choir on Fiddler's Green,
With lungs now emptied of salt water,
With gradual heat returning to clammed veins
In the first flicker of reanimation,
Repossession of now, awareness
Of her live hands and lips, her playful voice,
Her smooth and wingless shoulders.

TOMORROW'S ENVY OF TODAY*

Historians may scorn the close engagement
Of Moon with Lion that we have witnessed
Here in this lair, here in this numinous grove,
May write me down as imbecile, or presume
A clot of madness festering in your heart –
Such is tomorrow's envy of today.

Today we are how we are, and how we see:
Alive, elate, untrimmed, without hazard
Of supersession: flowers that never fade,
Leaves that never shrivel, truth persistent
Not as a prophecy of bliss to fall
A thousand generations hence on lovers
More fortunately circumstanced than we,
But as a golden interlock of power
Looped about every bush and branching tree.

THE HIDDEN GARDEN

Nor can ambition make this garden theirs,
Any more than birds can fly through a window pane.
When they hint at passwords, keys and private stairs,
We are tempted often to open the front gate,
Which has no lock, and haul them bodily in,
Abashed that there they wait, disconsolate.

And yet such pity would be worse than pride:
Should we admit as love their vain self-pity,
The gate must vanish and we be left outside.

THE WEDDING

When down I went to the rust-red quarry
I was informed, by birds, of your resolve
To live with me for ever and a day –
The day being always new and antecedent.
What could we ask of Nature? Nothing more
Than to outdo herself in our behalf.

Blossoms of caper, though they smell sweet,
Have never sailed the air like butterflies
Circling in innocent dance around each other
Over the cliff and out across the bay;
Nor has broom-blossom scorched a man's finger
With golden fire, kindled by sun.

Come, maids of honour and pages chosen
To attend this wedding, charged to perform
Incomparable feats – dance, caper-blossom!
Scorch, blossom of broom, our married fingers –
Though crowds of almost-men and almost-women
Howl for their lost immediacy.

WHAT WILL BE, IS*

Manifest reason glared at you and me
Thus ringed with love. Entire togetherness
Became for us the sole redress.

Together in heart, but our over-eager bodies
Distrained upon for debt, we shifted ground;
Which brought mistiming. Each cried out in turn,
And with a complementary delusion:
'I am free; but you? Are you still bound?'

In blood the debts were paid. Hereafter
We make no truce for manifest reason
From this side of the broad and fateful stream
Where wisdom rules from her dark cave of dream
And time is corrigible by laughter.

Moon and Sun are one. Granted, they ride
Paths unconformable to the calendar,
And seldom does a New Moon coincide
With a New Year; yet we agree:
'What will be, is' – rejoicing at a day
Of dolphins jostling in the blue bay,
Eagles in air, and flame on every tree.

*SON ALTESSE**

Alone, you are no more than many another
Gay-hearted, greedy, passionate noblewoman;
And I, alone, no more than a slow-witted
Passionate, credulous knight, though skilled in fight.

Then if I hail you as my Blessed Virgin
This is no flattery, nor does it endow you
With private magics which, when I am gone,
May flatter rogues or drunken renegades.

Name me your single, proud, whole-hearted champion
Whose feats no man alive will overpass;
But they must reverence you as I do; only
Conjoined in fame can we grow legendary.

Should I ride home, vainglorious after battle,
With droves of prisoners and huge heaps of spoil,
Make me dismount a half-mile from your door;
To walk barefoot in dust, as a knight must.

Yet never greet me carelessly or idly,
Nor use the teasing manners learned at Court,
Lest I be ambushed in a treacherous pass –
And you pent up in shame's black nunnery.

EVERYWHERE IS HERE*

By this exchange of eyes, this encirclement
You of me, I of you, together we baffle
Logic no doubt, but never understanding;
And laugh instead of choking back the tears
When we say goodbye.
                                        Fog gathers thick about us
Yet a single careless pair of leaves, one green, one gold,
Whirl round and round each other skippingly
As though blown by a wind; pause and subside
In a double star, the gold above the green.

Everywhere is here, once we have shattered
The iron-bound laws of contiguity,
Blazoning love as an eagle with four wings
(Their complementary tinctures counterchanged)
That scorns to roost in any terrene crag.

SONG: THE FAR SIDE OF YOUR MOON*

The far side of your moon is black,
    And glorious grows the vine;
Ask anything of me you lack,
    But only what is mine.

Yours is the great wheel of the sun,
    And yours the unclouded sky;
Then take my stars, take every one,
    But wear them openly,

Walking in splendour through the plain
    For all the world to see,
Since none alive shall view again
    The match of you and me.

DELIVERANCE*

Lying disembodied under the trees
(Their slender trunks converged above us
Like rays of a five-fold star) we heard
A sudden whinnying from the dark hill.

Our implacable demon, foaled by love,
Never knew rein or saddle; though he drank
From a stream winding by, his blue pastures
Ranged far out beyond the stellar mill.

He had seared us two so close together
That death itself might not disjoin us;
It was impossible you could love me less,
It was impossible I could love you more.

We were no calculating lovers
But gasped in awe at our deliverance
From a too familiar prison,
And vainly puzzled how it was that now
We should never need to build another,
As each, time after time, had done before.

CONJUNCTION*

What happens afterwards, none need enquire:
They are poised there in conjunction, beyond time,
At an oak-tree top level with Paradise:
Its leafy tester unshaken where they stand
Palm to palm, mouth to mouth, beyond desire,
Perpetuating lark song, perfume, colour,
And the tremulous gasp of watchful winds,

Past all unbelief, we know them held
By peace and light and irrefragable love –
Twin paragons, our final selves, resistant
To the dull pull of earth dappled with shade:
Myself the forester, never known to abandon
His vigilant coursing of the greenwood's floor,
And you, dryad of dryads, never before
Yielding her whole heart to the enemy, man.

NOTHING NOW ASTONISHES*

A month of vigilance draws to its close
With silence of snow and the Northern Lights
In longed-for wordlessness.

This rainbow spanning our two worlds
Becomes more than a bridge between them:
They fade into geography.

Variegated with the seven colours
We twist them into skeins for hide and seek
In a lovers' labyrinth.

Can I be astonished at male trembling
Of sea-horizons as you lean towards them?
Nothing now astonishes.

You change, from a running drop of pure gold
On a silver salver, to the white doe
In nut-groves harbouring.

Let me be changed now to an eight-petalled
Scarlet anemone that will never strain
For the circling butterfly.

Rest, my loud heart. Your too exultant flight
Had raised the wing-beat to a roar
Drowning seraphic whispers.

I'D DIE FOR YOU*

I'd die for you, or you for me,
So furious is our jealousy –
And if you doubt this to be true
Kill me outright, lest I kill you.

From COLLECTED POEMS 1965

(1965)

GRACE NOTES*

It was not the words, nor the melody,
   Not the beat, nor the pace;
It was that slow suspension of our breathing
   As we watched your face,
And the grace-notes, unrecordable on the clef,
   Sung only by a spirit in grace.

GOOD NIGHT TO THE OLD GODS

Good night, old gods, all this long year so faint
You propped your heavy eyelids up with shells!
Though once we honoured you who ruled this land
One hundred generations and ten more,
Our mood has changed: you dribble at the mouth,
Your dark-blue fern-tattoos are faded green,
Your thunderous anger wanes to petulance,
And love to groanings of indifference.
What most you crave is rest in a rock-cave,
Seasonally aroused by raucous gulls
Or swallows, nodding off once more to sleep.

We lay you in a row with cool palm wine
Close at your elbows, should you suffer thirst,
And breadfruit piled on rushes by your feet;
But will not furnish you a standing guard –
We have fish to net and spear, taro to hoe,
Pigs to fatten, coco-trees to climb;
Nor are our poets so bedulled in spirit
They would mount a platform, praising in worn verse
Those fusillades of lightning hurled by you
At giants in a first day-break of time:
Whom you disarmed and stretched in a rock-cave
Not unlike this – you have forgotten where.

THE SWEET-SHOP ROUND THE CORNER*

The child dreaming along a crowded street
Lost hold of his mother, who had turned to greet
Some neighbour, and mistakenly matched his tread
With a strange woman's. 'Buy me sweets,' he said,
Waving his hand, which he found warmly pressed;
So dragged her on, boisterous and self-possessed:
'The sweet-shop's round the corner!' Both went in,
And not for a long while did the child begin
To feel a dread that something had gone wrong:
Were Mother's legs so lean, or her shoes so long,
Or her skirt so patched, or her hair tousled and grey?
Why did she twitter in such a ghostly way?
'*O Mother, are you dead?*'
What else could a child say?

DOUBLE BASS

He coils so close about his double-bass,
Serpentine and entranced,
That they form a single creature:
Which man-instrument writhes and complains,
Mouth of disaster, skeleton limbs a-twitch,
Cavernous belly booming,
Insistent fingers torturing us to love,
Its deep-gulped fumes of marihuana
Blinding our eyes with scarlet streamers. . . .

Again I turn, for your laugh-nod to lend me
Measured reassurance of sanity.

DESCENT INTO HELL

Christ harrowed Hell in pity for all damned souls
Who had perverted innocence and honour –
It was a Sabbath, the day given to rest –
But none rose with him, and his journey grieved
The hearts even of such as loved him best.

THE PARDON

Should not the white lie and the unkept promise,
   Though distant from black lie and broken vow,
Demand a kiss of pardon afterwards
   From the sworn lover? So I kiss you now,
Counting on my own pardon: who but I
   Provoked both unkept promise and white lie?

POINT OF NO RETURN

When the alcoholic passed the crucial point
Of no return, he sold his soul to priests
Who, mercifully, would not deny him drink
But remitted a thousand years of purgatory
On this condition: that he must now engage
A woman's pity, beseeching her to cure him,
Wearing her down with betterment and relapse,
Till he had won a second soul for glory,
At the point of no return.

A SHIFT OF SCENE

To lie far off, in bed with a foul cough,
And a view of elms and roofs and six panes' worth
Of clear sky; here to watch, all the day long,
For a dove, or a black cat, or a puff of smoke
To cause a shift of scene – how could it do so? –
Or to take a pen and write – what else is there
To write but: 'I am not dead, not quite, as yet
Though I lie far off, in bed with a foul cough
And a view of elms and roofs and six panes' worth
Of clear sky'? Tell me, love, are you sick too
And plagued like me with a great hole in the mind
Where all those towers we built, and not on sand,
Have been sucked in and lost; so that it seems
No dove, and no black cat, nor puff of smoke
Can cause a shift of scene and fetch us back
To where we lie as one, in the same bed?

From SEVENTEEN POEMS MISSING FROM 'LOVE RESPELT'

(1966)

COCK IN PULLET'S FEATHERS*

Though ready enough with beak and spurs,
You go disguised, a cock in pullet's feathers,
Among those crowing, preening chanticleers.
But, dear self, learn to love your own body
In its full naked glory,
Despite all blemishes of moles and scars –
As she, for whom it shines, wholly loves hers.

DEAD HAND

Grieve for the loveless, spiritless, faceless men
Without alternative but to protract
Reason's mortmain on what their hearts deny –
Themselves – and owed small courtesy beyond
The uncovered head, as when a hearse goes by.

ARREARS OF MOONLIGHT*

My heart lies wrapped in red under your pillow,
My body wanders banished among the stars;
On one terrestrial pretext or another
You still withhold the extravagant arrears
Of moonlight that you owe us,
Though the owl whoops from a far olive branch
His brief, monotonous, night-long reminder.

WHAT DID YOU SAY?

She listened to his voice urgently pleading,
So captivated by his eloquence
She saw each word in its own grace and beauty
Drift like a flower down that clear-flowing brook,
And draw a wake of multicoloured bubbles.
But when he paused, intent on her reply,
She could stammer only: 'Love, what did you say?' –
As loath as ever to hold him in her arms
Naked, under the trees, until high day.

LURE OF MURDER*

A round moon suffocates the neighbouring stars
With greener light than sun through vine-leaves.
Awed by her ecstasy of solitude
I crouch among rocks, scanning the gulf, agape,
Whetting a knife on my horny sole.

Alas for the lure of murder, dear my love!
Could its employment purge two moon-vexed hearts
Of jealousy more formidable than death,
Then each would stab, stab, stab at secret parts
Of the other's beloved body where unknown
Zones of desire imperil full possession.

But never can mortal dagger serve to geld
This glory of ours, this loving beyond reason –
Death holds no remedy or alternative:
We are singled out to endure his lasting grudge
On the tall battlements of nightfall.

THE GORGE*

Yonder beyond all hopes of access
Begins your queendom; here is my frontier.
Between us howl phantoms of the long dead,
But the bridge that I cross, concealed from view
Even in sunlight, and the gorge bottomless,
Swings and echoes under my strong tread
Because I have need of you.

ECSTASY OF CHAOS*

When the immense drugged universe explodes
In a cascade of unendurable colour
And leaves us gasping naked,
This is no more than ecstasy of chaos:
Hold fast, with both hands, to that royal love
Which alone, as we know certainly, restores
Fragmentation into true being.

STOLEN JEWEL*

You weep whole-heartedly – your shining tears
Roll down for sorrow, not like mine for joy.
Dear love, should we not scorn to treat each other
With palliatives and with placebos?

Under a blinding moon you took from me
This jewel of wonder, but unaware
That it was yielded only on condition
Of whole possession; that it still denies you
Strength or desire for its restitution.

What do you fear? My hand around your throat?
What do I fear? Your dagger through my heart?
Must we not rage alone together
In lofts of singular high starriness?

THE EAGRE*

Suddenly the Eagre mounts upstream
And a tall youth on dolphin back
Outdares my blue eyes and your black.

THE SNAPPED THREAD*

Desire, first, by a natural miracle
United bodies, united hearts, blazed beauty;
Transcended bodies, transcended hearts.

Two souls, now unalterably one
In whole love always and for ever,
Soar out of twilight, through upper air,
Let fall their sensuous burden.

Is it kind, though, is it honest even,
To consort with none but spirits –
Leaving true-wedded hearts like ours
In enforced night-long separation,
Each to its random bodily inclination,
The thread of miracle snapped?

FORTUNATE CHILD

For fear strangers might intrude upon us
You and I played at being strangers,
But lent our act such verisimilitude
That when at last, by hazard, we met alone
In a secret glen where the badger earths
We had drawn away from love: did not prepare
For melting of eyes into hearts of flowers,
For a sun-aureoled enhancement of hair,
For over-riding of death on an eagle's back –
Yet so it was: sky shuddered apart before us
Until, from a cleft of more than light, we both
Overheard the laugh of a fortunate child
Swung from those eagle talons in a gold cloth.

LOVING TRUE, FLYING BLIND*

How often have I said before
That no soft 'if', no 'either-or',
Can keep my obdurate male mind
From loving true and flying blind? –

Which, though deranged beyond all cure
Of temporal reason, knows for sure
That timeless magic first began
When woman bared her soul to man.

Be bird, be blossom, comet, star,
Be paradisal gates ajar,
But still, as woman, bear you must
With who alone endures your trust.

THE NEAR ECLIPSE*

Out shines again the glorious round sun –
After his near-eclipse when pools of light
Thrown on the turf between leaf shadows
Grew crescent-shaped like moons – dizzying us
With paraboles of colour: regal amends
To our own sun mauled barbarously
By the same wide-mouthed dragon.

DANCING FLAME*

Pass now in metaphor beyond birds,
Their seasonal nesting and migration,
Their airy gambols, their repetitive song;
Beyond the puma and the ocelot
That spring in air and follow us with their eyes;
Beyond all creatures but our own selves,
Eternal genii of dancing flame
Armed with the irreproachable secret
Of love, which is: never to turn back.

BIRTH OF ANGELS

Never was so profound a shadow thrown
On earth as by your sun: a black roundel
Harbouring an unheard-of generation
Fledged by the sun ablaze above your own –
Wild beyond words, yet each of them an angel.

ON GIVING

Those who dare give nothing
Are left with less than nothing;
Dear heart, you give me everything,
Which leaves you more than everything –
Though those who dare give nothing
Might judge it left you nothing.

Giving you everything,
I too, who once had nothing,
Am left with more than everything
As gifts for those with nothing
Who need, if not our everything,
At least a loving something.

From COLOPHON TO 'LOVE RESPELT'

(1967)

THE P'ENG THAT WAS A K'UN*

(*Adapted from the Chinese of Lao Tse*)

In Northern seas there roams a fish called K'un,
Of how many thousand leagues in length I know not,
Which changes to a bird called P'eng – its wing-span
Of how many thousand leagues in width I know not.
Every half-year this P'eng, that was a K'un,
Fans out its glorious feathers to the whirlwind
And soars to the most Southerly pool of Heaven.

The Finch and Sparrow, thus informed, debated:
'We by our utmost efforts may fly only
To yonder elm. How can the P'eng outdo us?'
Though, indeed, neither started as a fish.

LIKE OWLS*

The blind are their own brothers; we
Form an obscure fraternity
Who, though not destitute of sight
Know ourselves doomed from birth to see,
Like owls, most clearly in half light.

IN PERSPECTIVE

What, keep love in *perspective*? – that old lie
Forced on the Imagination by the Eye
Which, mechanistically controlled, will tell
How rarely table-sides run parallel;
How distance shortens us; how wheels are found
Oval in shape far oftener than round;
How every ceiling-corner's out of joint;
How the broad highway tapers to a point –
Can all this fool us lovers? Not for long:
Even the blind will sense that something's wrong.

THE UTTER RIM*

But if that Cerberus, my mind, should be
Flung to earth by the very opiate
That frees my senses for undared adventure,
Waving them wide-eyed past me to explore
Limitless hells of disintegrity,
Endless, undifferentiatable fate
Scrolled out beyond the utter rim of nowhere,
Scrolled out . . . . . .
                                        who on return fail to surrender
Their memory trophies, random wisps of horror
Trailed from my shins or tangled in my hair?

BOWER-BIRD

The Bower-bird improvised a cool retreat
For the hen he honoured, doing his poor best
With parrot-plumage, orchids, bones and corals,
To engage her fancy.
                                        But this was no nest . . .
So, though the Penguin dropped at his hen's feet
An oval stone to signal: 'be my bride',
And though the Jackdaw's nest was glorified
With diamond rings and brooches massed inside,
It was the Bower-bird who contented me
By not equating love with matrimony.

MIST*

Fire and Deluge, rival pretenders
To ruling the world's end; these cannot daunt us
Whom flames will never singe, nor floods drown,
While we stand guard against their murderous child
Mist, that slily catches at love's throat,
Shrouding the clear sun and clean waters
Of all green gardens everywhere –
The twitching mouths likewise and furtive eyes
Of those who speak us fair.

THE WORD*

The Word is unspoken
Between honest lovers:
They substitute a silence
Or wave at a wild flower,
Sighing inaudibly.

That it exists indeed
Will scarcely be disputed:
The wildest of conceptions
Can be reduced to speech –
Or so the Schoolmen teach.

You and I, thronged by angels,
Learned it in the same dream
Which startled us by moon-light,
And that we still revere it
Keeps our souls aflame.

'God' is a standing question
That still negates an answer.
The Word is not a question
But simple affirmation,
The antonym of 'God'.

Who would believe this Word
Could have so long been hidden
Behind a candid smile,
A sweet but hasty kiss
And always dancing feet?

PERFECTIONISTS*

Interalienation of their hearts
It was not, though both played resentful parts
In proud unwillingness to share
One house, one pillow, the same fare.
It was perfectionism, they confess,
To know the truth and ask for nothing less.

Their fire-eyed guardians watched from overhead:
'These two alone have learned to love,' they said,
'But neither can forget
They are not worthy of each other yet.'

PRISON WALLS*

Love, this is not the way
To treat a glorious day:
To cloud it over with conjectured fears,
Wiping my eyes before they brim with tears
And, long before we part,
Mourning the torments of my jealous heart.

That you have tried me more
Than who else did before,
Is no good reason to prognosticate
My last ordeal: when I must greet with hate
Your phantom fairy prince
Conjured in childhood, lost so often since.

Nor can a true heart rest
Resigned to second best –
Why did you need to temper me so true
That I became your sword of swords, if you
Must nail me on your wall
And choose a painted lath when the blows fall?

Because I stay heart-whole,
Because you bound your soul
To mine, with curses should it wander free,
I charge you now to keep full faith with me
Nor can I ask for less
Than your unswerving honest-heartedness.

Then grieve no more, but while
Your flowers are scented, smile
And never sacrifice, as others may,
So clear a dawn to dread of Judgement Day –
Lest prison walls should see
Fresh tears of longing you let fall for me.

A DREAM OF HELL

You reject the rainbow
Of our Sun castle
As hyperbolic;

You enjoin the Moon
Of our pure trysts
To condone deceit;

Lured to violence
By a lying spirit,
You break our troth.

Seven wide, enchanted
Wards of horror
Lie stretched before you,

To brand your naked breast
With impious colours,
To band your thighs.

How can I discharge
Your confused spirit
From its chosen hell?

You who once dragged me
From the bubbling slime
Of a tidal reach,

Who washed me, fed me,
Laid me in white sheets,
Warmed me in brown arms,

Would you have me cede
Our single sovereignty
To your tall demon?

OUR SELF

When first we came together
It was no chance foreshadowing
Of a chance happy ending.
The case grows always clearer
By its own worse disorder:
However reasonably we oppose
That unquiet integer, our self, we lose.

BITES AND KISSES*

Heather and holly,
Bites and kisses,
A courtship-royal
On the hill's red cusp.
Look up, look down,
Gaze all about you –
A livelier world
By ourselves contrived:

Swan in full course
Up the Milky Way,
Moon in her wildness,
Sun ascendant
In Crab or Lion,
Beyond the bay
A pride of dolphins
Curving and tumbling
With bites and kisses . . .

Or dog-rose petals
Well-starred by dew,
Or jewelled pebbles,
Or waterlilies open
For the dragon-flies
In their silver and blue.

SUN-FACE AND MOON-FACE

We twin cherubs above the Mercy Seat,
Sun-face and Moon-face,
Locked in the irrevocable embrace
That guards our children from defeat,
Are fire not flesh; as none will dare deny
Lest his own soul should die.

FREEHOLD*

Though love expels the ugly past
Restoring you this house at last –
This generous-hearted mind and soul
Reserved from alien control –
How can you count on living free
From sudden jolts of history,
From interceptive sigh or stare
That heaves you back to how-things-were
And makes you answerable for
The casualties of bygone war?
Yet smile your vaguest: make it clear
That then was then, but now is here.

THE NECKLACE*

Variegated flowers, nuts, cockle-shells
And pebbles, chosen lovingly and strung
On golden spider-webs with a gold clasp
For your neck, naturally: and each bead touched
By a child's lips as he stoops over them:
Wear these for the new miracle they announce –
All four cross-quarter-days beseech you –
Your safe return from shipwreck, drought and war,
Beautiful as before, to what you are.

A BRACELET

A bracelet invisible
For your busy wrist,
Twisted from silver
Spilt afar,
From silver of the clear Moon,
From her sheer halo,
From the male beauty
Of a shooting star.

BLACKENING SKY*

Lightning enclosed by a vast ring of mirrors,
Instant thunder extravagantly bandied
Between red cliffs no hawk may nest upon,
Triumphant jetting, passion of deluge: ours –
With spray that stuns, dams that lurch and are gone. . . .

But against this insensate hubbub of subsidence
Our voices, always true to a fireside tone,
Meditate on the secret marriage of flowers
Or the bees' paradise, with much else more;
And while the sky blackens anew for rain,
On why we love as none ever loved before.

BLESSED SUN

Honest morning blesses the Sun's beauty;
Noon, his endurance; dusk, his majesty;
Sweetheart, our own twin worlds bask in the glory
And searching wisdom of that single eye –
Why must the Queen of Night on her moon throne
Tear up their contract and still reign alone?

LION-GENTLE

Love, never disavow our vow
Nor wound your lion-gentle:
Take what you will, dote on it, keep it,
But pay your debts with a grave, wilful smile
Like a woman of the sword.

SONG: THE PALM TREE*

Palm-tree, single and apart
        In your serpent-haunted land,
Like the fountain of a heart
        Soaring into air from sand –
None can count it as a fault
That your roots are fed with salt.

Panniers-full of dates you yield,
        Thorny branches laced with light,
Wistful for no pasture-field
        Fed by torrents from a height,
Short of politics to share
With the damson or the pear.

Never-failing phoenix tree
        In your serpent-haunted land,
Fount of magic soaring free
        From a desert of salt sand;
Tears of joy are salty too –
Mine shall flow in praise of you.

SPITE OF MIRRORS*

O what astonishment if you
Could see yourself as others do,
Foiling the mirror's wilful spite
That shows your left cheek as the right
And shifts your lovely crooked smile
To the wrong corner! But meanwhile
Lakes, pools and puddles all agree
(Bound in a vast conspiracy)
To reflect only your stern look
Designed for peering in a book –
No easy laugh, no glint of rage,
No thoughts in cheerful pilgrimage,
No start of guilt, no rising fear,
No premonition of a tear.

How, with a mirror, can you keep
Watch on your eyelids closed in sleep?
How judge which profile to bestow
On a new coin or cameo?
How, from two steps behind you, stare
At your firm nape discovered bare
Of ringlets as you bend and reach
Transparent pebbles from the beach?
Love, if you long for a surprise
Of self-discernment, hold my eyes
And plunge deep down in them to see
Sights never long withheld from me.

PRIDE OF LOVE*

I face impossible feats at your command,
Resentful at the tears of love you shed
For the faint-hearted sick who flock to you;
But since all love lies wholly in the giving,
Weep on: your tears are true,
Nor can despair provoke me to self-pity
Where pride alone is due.

HOODED FLAME

Love, though I sorrow, I shall never grieve:
Grief is to mourn a flame extinguished;
Sorrow, to find it hooded for the hour
When planetary influences deceive
And hope, like wine, turns sour.

INJURIES*

Injure yourself, you injure me:
Is that not true as true can be?
Nor can you give me cause to doubt
It works the other way about;
So what precautions must I take
Not to be injured for love's sake?

HER BRIEF WITHDRAWAL*

'Forgive me, love, if I withdraw awhile:
It is only that you ask such bitter questions,
Always another beyond the extreme last.
And the answers astound: you have entangled me
In my own mystery. Grant me a respite:
I was happier far, not asking, nor much caring,
Choosing by appetite only: self-deposed,
Self-reinstated, no one observing.
When I belittled this vibrancy of touch
And the active vengeance of these folded arms
No one could certify my powers for me
Or my saining virtue, or know that I compressed
Knots of destiny in a careless fist,
I who had passed for a foundling from the hills
Of innocent and flower-like phantasies,
Though minting silver by my mere tread . . . .
Did I not dote on you, I well might strike you
For implicating me in your true dream.'

THE CRANE

The Crane lounes loudly in his need,
        And so for love I loune:
Son to the sovereign Sun indeed,
        Courier of the Moon.

STRANGENESS*

You love me strangely, and in strangeness
I love you wholly, with no parallel
To this long miracle; for each example
Of love coincidence levels a finger
At strangeness undesigned as unforeseen.

And this long miracle is to discover
The inmost you and never leave her;
To show no curiosity for another;
To forge the soul and its desire together
Gently, openly and for ever.

Seated in silence, clothed in silence
And face to face – the room is small
But thronged with visitants –
We ask for nothing: we have all.

From THE POOR BOY WHO FOLLOWED HIS STAR

(1968)

HIDE AND SEEK

The trees are tall, but the moon small,
My legs feel rather weak,
For Avis, Mavis and Tom Clarke
Are hiding somewhere in the dark
And it's my turn to seek.

Suppose they lay a trap and play
A trick to frighten me?
Suppose they plan to disappear
And leave me here, half-dead with fear,
Groping from tree to tree?

Alone, alone, all on my own
And then perhaps to find
Not Avis, Mavis and young Tom
But monsters to run shrieking from,
Mad monsters of no kind?

THE HERO*

Slowly with bleeding nose and aching wrists
After tremendous use of feet and fists
He rises from the dusty schoolroom floor
And limps for solace to the girl next door,
Boasting of kicks and punches, cheers and noise,
And far worse damage done to bigger boys.

AT SEVENTY-TWO

At seventy-two,
Being older than you,
I can rise when I please
Without slippers or shoes
And go down to the kitchen
To eat what I choose –
Jam, tomatoes and cheese –
Then I visit the garden
And wander at ease
Past the bed where what grows is
A huge clump of roses
And I swing in the swing
Set up under the trees
My mouth full of biscuits,
My hat on my knees.

From POEMS 1965–1968

(1968)

SONG: HOW CAN I CARE?*

How can I care whether you sigh for me
While still I sleep alone swallowing back
The spittle of desire, unmanned, a tree
Pollarded of its crown, a dusty sack
Tossed on the stable rack?

How can I care what coloured frocks you wear,
What humming-birds you watch on jungle hills,
What phosphorescence wavers in your hair,
Or with what water-music the night fills –
Dear love, how can I care?

SONG: THOUGH ONCE TRUE LOVERS

Though once true lovers,
We are less than friends.
What woman ever
So ill-used her man?
That I played false
Not even she pretends:
May God forgive her,
For, alas, I can.

SONG: CHERRIES OR LILIES

Death can have no alternative but Love,
Or Love but Death.
Acquaintance dallying on the path of Love,
Sickness on that of Death,
Pause at a bed-side, doing what they can
With fruit and flowers bought from the barrow man.

Death can have no alternative but Love,
Or Love but Death.
Then shower me cherries from your orchard, Love,
Or strew me lilies, Death:
For she and I were never of that breed
Who vacillate or trifle with true need.

SONG: CROWN OF STARS*

Lion-heart, you prowl alone
True to Virgin, Bride and Crone;
None so black of brow as they
Now, tomorrow, yesterday.
Yet the night you shall not see
Must illuminate all three
As the tears of love you shed
Blaze about their single head
And a sword shall pierce the side
Of true Virgin, Crone and Bride
Among mansions of the dead.

SONG: FIG TREE IN LEAF*

One day in early Spring
Upon bare branches perching
        Great companies of birds are seen
        Clad all at once in pilgrim green
Their news of love to bring:

Their fig tree parable,
For which the world is watchful,
        Retold with shining wings displayed:
        Her secret flower, her milk, her shade,
Her scarlet, blue and purple.

SONG: DEW-DROP AND DIAMOND*

The difference between you and her
(Whom I to you did once prefer)
Is clear enough to settle:
She like a diamond shone, but you
Shine like an early drop of dew
Poised on a red rose-petal.

The dew-drop carries in its eye
Mountain and forest, sea and sky,
With every change of weather;
Contrariwise, a diamond splits
The prospect into idle bits
That none can piece together.

SONG: JUST FRIENDS

Just friend, you are my only friend –
You think the same of me
And swear our love must never end
Though lapped in secrecy,
As all true love should be.
They ask us: 'What about you two?'
I answer 'Only friends' and you:
'Just friends' gently agree.

SONG: OF COURSE

No, of course we were never
Off course in our love,
Being nourished by manna
That dripped from above,

And our secret of loving
Was taught us, it seems,
By ravens and owlets
And fast-flowing streams.

We had sealed it with kisses,
It blazed from our eyes,
Yet all was unspoken
And proof against lies.

For to publish a secret
Once learned in the rain
Would have meant to lose course
And not find it again.

So this parting, of course,
Is illusion, not fate,
And the love in your letters
Comes charged overweight.

SONG: THREE RINGS FOR HER

Flowers remind of jewels;
Jewels, of flowers;
Flowers, of innocent morning;
Jewels, of honest evening –
Emerald, moonstone, opal –
For so I mean, and meant.
Jewels are longer lasting –
Emerald, moonstone, opal;
Opal, emerald, moonstone:
Moonstone, opal, emerald –
And wear a livelier scent.

SINCÈREMENT

J'étais confus à cet instant.
Quelle honte d'avoir écrit
L'adverbe aveugle 'sincèrement' –
'Je t'aime' m'aurait suffi
Sans point et sans souci.

DANS UN SEUL LIT

Entre deux belles femmes dans un seul lit
Cet homme, se sentant interdit,
Des convenances n'ose pas faire foin
Mais opte pour elle qu'il aime le moins.

Entre deux beaux hommes en pareil cas,
Une dame sans mœurs si délicats
Mais sans s'exprimer en termes crus,
Se penche vers lui qu'elle aime le plus.

IS NOW THE TIME?

If he asks, 'Is now the time?', it is not the time.
She turns her head from his concern with time
As a signal not to haste it;
And every time he asks:'Is now the time?'
A hundred nights are wasted.

TWINS

Siamese twins: one, maddened by
The other's moral bigotry,
Resolved at length to misbehave
And drink them both into the grave.

SAIL AND OAR

Woman sails, man must row:
Each, disdainful of a tow,
Cuts across the other's bows
Shame or fury to arouse –
And evermore it shall be so,
Lest man sail, or woman row.

GOOSEFLESH ABBEY*

Nuns are allowed full liberty of conscience.
Yet might this young witch, when she took the veil,
Count on an aged Abbess's connivance
At keeping toad-familiars in her cell?
Some called it liberty; but others, licence –
And how was she to tell?

THE HOME-COMING

At the tangled heart of a wood I fell asleep,
Bewildered by her silence and her absence –
As though such potent lulls in love were not
Ordained by the demands of pure music.

A bird sang: 'Close your eyes, it is not for long –
Dream of what gold and crimson she will wear
In honour of your oak-brown.'

It was her hoopoe. Yet, when the spread heavens
Of my feast night glistened with shooting stars
And she walked unheralded up through the dim light
Of the home lane, I did not recognize her –
So lost a man can be
Who feeds on hopes and fears and memory.

WITH THE GIFT OF A LION'S CLAW

Queen of the Crabs, accept this claw
Plucked from a Lion's patient paw;
It shall propel her forward who
Ran sideways always hitherto.

WIGS AND BEARDS

In the bad old days a bewigged country Squire
Would never pay his debts, unless at cards,
Shot, angled, urged his pack through standing grain,
Horsewhipped his tenantry, snorted at the arts,
Toped himself under the table every night,
Blasphemed God with a cropful of God-damns,
Aired whorehouse French or lame Italian,
Set fashions of pluperfect slovenliness
And claimed seigneurial rights over all women
Who slept, imprudently, under the same roof.

Taxes and wars long ago ploughed them under –
'And serve the bastards right' the Beards agree,
Hurling their empties through the café window
And belching loud as they proceed downstairs.
Latter-day bastards of that famous stock,
They never rode a nag, nor gaffed a trout,
Nor winged a pheasant, nor went soldiering,
But remain true to the same hell-fire code
In all available particulars
And scorn to pay their debts even at cards.
Moreunder (which is to subtract, not add),
Their ancestors called themselves gentlemen
As they, in the same sense, call themselves artists.

PERSONAL PACKAGING, INC.

Folks, we have zero'd in to a big break-thru:
Our boys are learning how to package *people*
By a new impermeable-grading process
In cartons of mixed twenties – all three sexes!

Process involves molecular adjustment
To micro-regulated temperatures,
Making them unexpendable time-wise
Thru a whole century . . . Some clients opt for
Five thousand years, or six, in real deep freeze –
A chance what sensible guy would kick against
To pile up dollars at compound interest?
Nor do we even propose that they quit smoking
Or, necessarily, be parted from their wives.

WORK ROOM

Camp-stool for chair once more and packing case for table;
All histories of doubt extruded from this room
With its menacing, promising, delusive, toppling bookshelves;
Nothing now astir but you in my fresh imagination,
And no letters but yours ever demanding answers.
To start all over again; indeed, why should I not? –
With a new pen, clean paper, full inkpot.

THE ARK

Beasts of the field, fowls likewise of the air,
Came trooping, seven by seven or pair by pair;
And though from Hell the arch-fiend Samael
Bawled out 'Escapist!' Noah did not care.

ALL EXCEPT HANNIBAL

Trapped in a dismal marsh, he told his troops:
'No lying down, lads! Form your own mess-groups
And sit in circles, each man on the knees
Of the man behind; then nobody will freeze.'

They obeyed his orders, as the cold sun set,
Drowsing all night in one another's debt,
All except Hannibal himself, who chose
His private tree-stump – he was one of those!

THE BEGGAR MAID AND KING COPHETUA

To be adored by a proud Paladin
Whom the wide world adored,
To queen it over countless noblewomen:
What fame was hers at last,
What lure and envy!

Yet, being still a daughter of the mandrake
She sighed for more than fame;
Not all the gold with which Cophetua crowned her
Could check this beggar-maid's
Concupiscence.

Sworn to become proverbially known
As martyred by true love,
She took revenge on his victorious name
That blotted her own fame
For woman's magic.

True to her kind, she slipped away one dawn
With a poor stable lad,
Gaunt, spotted, drunken, scrawny, desperate,
Mean of intelligence
As bare of honour.

So pitiable indeed that when the guards
Who caught them saw the green
Stain on her finger from his plain brass ring
They gaped at it, too moved
Not to applaud her.

FOR EVER

Sweetheart, I beg you to renew and seal
With a not supererogatory kiss
Our contract of 'For Ever'.
                                        Learned judges
Deplore the household sense 'interminable':
True love, they rule, never acknowledges
Future or past, only a perfect now. . . .
But let it read 'For Ever', anyhow!

*JUGUM IMPROBUM**

Pyrrha, jugo tandem vitulum junges-ne leoni?
Sit tibi dilectus, num stricto verbere debet
Compelli pavitans medium moriturus in ignem?

DE ARTE POETICA

De minimis curat non Lex, utcumque poeta.

SIT MIHI TERRA LEVIS

Ante mortem qui defletus
        Solis lucem repperit
Ante Mortem perquietus,
        Erato, domum redit.

ASTYMELUSA†*

'Astymelusa!'
                    Knees at your approach
Suddenly give, more than in sleep or death –
As well they may; such love compels them.
'Astymelusa!'
                    But no answer comes.
Crowned with a leafy crown, the girl passes
Like a star afloat through glittering sky,
Or a golden flower, or drifted thistledown.

† A fragment by the Dorian Greek poet Alcman, seventh century B.C., found among the Oxyrhynchus papyri.

TOUSLED PILLOW

She appeared in Triad – Youth, Truth, Beauty –
Full face and profiles whispering together
All night at my bed-foot.
                              And when dawn came
At last, from a tousled pillow resolutely
I made my full surrender:
'So be it, Goddess, claim me without shame
And tent me in your hair.'
                              Since when she holds me
As close as candlewick to candleflame
And from all hazards free,
My soul drawn back to its virginity.

TO BE IN LOVE*

To spring impetuously in air and remain
Treading on air for three heart-beats or four,
Then to descend at leisure; or else to scale
The forward-tilted crag with no hand-holds;
Or, disembodied, to carry roses home
From a Queen's garden – this is being in love,
Graced with *agilitas* and *subtilitas*
At which few famous lovers ever guessed
Though children may foreknow it, deep in dream,
And ghosts may mourn it, haunting their own tombs,
And peacocks cry it, in default of speech.

FACT OF THE ACT

On the other side of the world's narrow lane
You lie in bed, your young breasts tingling
With imagined kisses, your lips puckered,
Your fists tight.

Dreaming yourself naked in my arms,
Free from discovery, under some holm oak;
The high sun peering through thick branches,
All winds mute.

Endlessly you prolong the moment
Of your delirium: a first engagement,
Silent, inevitable, fearful,
Honey-sweet.

Will it be so in fact? Will fact mirror
Your virginal ecstasies:
True love, uncircumstantial,
No blame, no shame?

It is for you, now, to say 'come';
It is for you, now, to prepare the bed;
It is for you as the sole hostess
Of your white dreams –

It is for you to open the locked gate,
It is for you to shake red apples down,
It is for you to halve them with your hands
That both may eat.

Yet expectation lies as far from fact
As fact's own after-glow in memory;
Fact is a dark return to man's beginnings,
Test of our hardihood, test of a wilful
And blind acceptance of each other
As also flesh.

TO OGMIAN HERCULES*

Your Labours are performed, your Bye-works too,
Your ashes gently drift from Oeta's peak.
Here is escape then, Hercules, from empire.

Lithe Hebë, youngest of all Goddesses,
Who circles on the Moon's broad threshing-floor
Harboured no jealousy for Megara,
Augë, Hippolytë, Deianeira,
But grieved for each in turn. You broke all hearts,
Burning too Sun-like for a Grecian bride.

Rest your immortal head on Hebë's lap;
What wars you started let your sons conclude.
Meditate a new Alphabet, heal wounds,
Draw poets to you with long golden chains
But still go armed with club and lion's pelt.

ARROW SHOTS

Only a madman could mistake,
    When shot at from behind a tree,
The whizz and thud that arrows make –
    Yours, for example, fired at me.

Some bows are drawn to blind or maim,
    I have known others drawn to kill,
But truth in love is your sole aim
    And proves your vulnerary skill.

Though often, drowsing at mid-day,
    I wince to find myself your mark,
Let me concede the hit, but say:
    'Your hand is steadiest after dark.'

SHE TO HIM

To have it, sweetheart, is to know you have it
Rather than think you have it;
To think you have it is a wish to take it,
Though afterwards you would not have it –
And thus a fear to take it.
Yet if you know you have it, you may take it
And know that still you have it.

WITHIN REASON

You have wandered widely through your own mind
And your own perfect body;
Thus learning, within reason, gentle one,
Everything that can prove worth the knowing.

A concise wisdom never attained by those
Bodiless nobodies
Who travel pen in hand through others' minds,
But without reason,
Feeding on manifold contradiction.

To stand perplexed by love's inconsequences
Like fire-flies in your hair
Or distant flashes of a summer storm:
Such are the stabs of joy you deal me
Who also wander widely through my mind
And still imperfect body.

THE YET UNSAYABLE

It was always fiercer, brighter, gentler than could be told
Even in words quickened by Truth's dark eye:
Its absence, whirlpool; its presence, deluge;
Its time, astonishment; its magnitude,
A murderous dagger-point.
                                        So we surrender
Our voices to the dried and scurrying leaves
And choose our own long-predetermined path
From the unsaid to the yet unsayable
In silence of love and love's temerity.

NONE THE WISER

They would be none the wiser, even could they overhear
My slurred ecstatic mumbling or grow somehow aware
Of eyes ablaze behind shut lids in the attic gloom.

Even if they adjured me on pain of death to disclose
All that I see and am when I so absent myself,
What would they make of steady, somnolent light-rings
Converging, violet-blue or green hypnotic gold,
Upon a warded peep-hole, as it were a rift in Space,
Through which I peer, as it might be into your eyes,
And pass disembodied, a spiral wisp or whorl
Tall, slanted, russet-red, crowned with a lunar nimbus? –
To you the central flow, the glow, the ease, the hush
Of music drawn through irrecoverable modes.
And then such after-glory, meteors across the heart
When I awake, astonished, in the bed where once you dreamed.

'Metaphysical', they would comment lamely, 'metaphysical';
But you would smile at me for leaving so much out.

THE NARROW SEA

With you for mast and sail and flag,
And anchor never known to drag,
Death's narrow but oppressive sea
Looks not unnavigable to me.

THE OLIVE-YARD*

Now by a sudden shift of eye
The hitherto exemplary world
Takes on immediate wildness
And birds, trees, winds, the very letters
Of our childhood's alphabet, alter
Into rainbowed mysteries.

Flesh is no longer flesh, but power;
Numbers, no longer arithmetical,
Dance like lambs, fly like doves;
And silence falls at last, though silken branches
Gently heave in the near olive-yard
And vague cloud labours on.

Whose was the stroke of summer genius
Flung from a mountain fastness
Where the griffon-vulture soars
That let us read our shrouded future
As easily as a book of prayer
Spread open on the knee?

BEYOND GIVING

(1969)

PART I

SONG: TO A ROSE

Queen of Sharon in the valley,
Clasp my head your breasts between:
Darkly blind me to your beauty –
Rose renowned for blood-red berries
Ages earlier than for fragrant
Blossom and sweet hidden honey,
Save by studious bees.

SONG: DREAM WARNING*

A lion in the path, a lion;
A jewelled serpent by the sun
Hatched in a desert silence
And stumbled on by chance;
A peacock crested with green fire,
His legs befouled in mire;
Not less, an enlacement of seven dreams
On a rainbow scale returning
To the drum that throbs against their melodies
Its dark insistent warning.

SONG: BEYOND GIVING

There is a giving beyond giving:
        Yours to me
Who awoke last night, hours before the dawn,
        Set free
By one intolerable lightning stroke
        That ripped the sky
To understand what love withholds in love,
        And why.

TRIAL OF INNOCENCE*

Urged by your needs and my desire,
I first made you a woman; nor was either
Troubled by fear of hidden evil
Or of temporal circumstance;
For circumstances never alter cases
When lovers, hand in hand, face trial
Pleading uncircumstantial innocence.

POISONED DAY

The clouds dripped poisonous dew to spite
A day for weeks looked forward to. True love
Sickened that evening without remedy:
We neither quarrelled, kissed, nor said good-night
But fell asleep, our arms around each other,
And awoke to the gentle hiss of rain on grass
And thrushes calling that the worst was over.

SUPERSTITION*

Forget the foolishness with which I vexed you:
Mine was a gun-shy superstition
Surviving from defeat in former loves
And banished when you stood staring aghast
At the replacement of your sturdy lover
By a disconsolate waif.

Blame the foul weather for my aching wounds,
Blame ugly history for my wild fears,
Nor ever turn from your own path; for still
Despite your fancies, your white silences,
Your disappearances, you remain bound
By this unshakeable trust I rest in you.

Go, because inner strength ordains your journey,
Making a necessary occasion seem
No more than incidental. Love go with you
In distillation of all past and future –
You, a clear torrent flooding the mill-race,
Forcing its mill to grind
A coarse grain into flour for angels' bread.

IN THE NAME OF VIRTUE*

In the name of Virtue, girl,
Why must you try so hard
In the hard name of Virtue?
Is not such trying, questioning?
Such questioning, doubting?
Such doubting, guessing?
Such guessing, not-knowing?
Such not-knowing, not-being?
Such not-being, death?
Can death be Virtue?

Virtue is from listening
To a private angel,
An angel overheard
When the little-finger twitches –
The bold little-finger
That refused education:
When the rest went to college
And philosophized on Virtue,
It neither went, nor tried.

Knowing becomes doing
When all we need to know
Is how to check our pendulum
And move the hands around
For a needed golden instant
Of the future or past –
Then start time up again
With a bold little-finger
In Virtue's easy name.

WHAT WE DID NEXT*

What we did next, neither of us remembers. . . .
Still, the key turned, the wide bronze gate creaked open
And there before us in profuse detail
Spread Paradise: its lawns dappled with petals,
Pomegranate trees in quincunx, corn in stooks;
Plantations loud with birds, pools live with fish,
And unborn children blue as bonfire-smoke
Crouching entranced to see the grand serpent
Writhe in and out of long rock-corridors,
Rattling his coils of gold –
Or the jewelled toad from whose immense mouth
Burst out the four great rivers. . . . To be there
Was always to be there, without grief, always,
Superior to all chance, or change, or death. . . .

What we did next, neither of us remembers.

COMPACT*

My love for you, though true, wears the extravagance of centuries;
Your love for me is fragrant, simple and millennial.
Smiling without a word, you watch my extravagances pass;
To check them would be presumptuous and unmaidenly –
As it were using me like an ill-bred schoolboy.

Dear Live-apart, when I sit confused by the active spites
Tormenting me with too close sympathy for fools,
Too dark a rage against hidden plotters of evil,
Too sour a mind, or soused with sodden wool-bales –
I turn my eyes to the light smoke drifting from your fire.

Our settled plan has been: never to make plans –
The future, present and past being already settled
Beyond review or interpretative conjecture
By the first decision of truth that we clasped hands upon:
To conserve a purity of soul each for the other.

SONG: NEW YEAR KISSES

Every morning, every evening,
Kisses for my starving darling:
On her brow for close reflection,
On her eyes for patient watching,
On her ears for watchful listening,
On her palms for careful action,
On her toes for fiery dancing –
Kisses that outgo perfection –
On her nape for secrecy,
On her lips for poetry,
On her bosom bared for me
Kisses more than three times three.

SONG: THE CLOCKS OF TIME*

The clocks of time divide us:
You sleep while I wake –
No need to think it monstrous
Though I remain uneasy,
Watchful, albeit drowsy,
Communing over wastes of sea
With you, my other me.

Too strict a concentration,
Each on an absent self,
Distracts our prosecution
Of what this love implies:
Genius, with its complexities
Of working backwards from the answer
To bring a problem near.

But when your image shortens
(My eyes thrown out of focus)
And fades in the far distance –
Your features indistinguishable,
Your gait and form unstable –
Time's heart revives our closeness
Hand in hand, lip to lip.

GOLD CLOUD*

Your gold cloud, towering far above me,
Through which I climb from darkness into sleep
Has the warmth of sun, rain's morning freshness
And a scent either of wood-smoke or of jasmine;
Nor is the ascent steep.

Our creature, Time, bends readily as willow:
We plan our own births, that at least we know,
Whether in the lovely moment of death
Or when we first meet, here in Paradise,
As now, so years ago.

SONG: BASKET OF BLOSSOM*

Jewels here lie heaped for you
Under jasmine, under lilac –
Leave them undisclosed awhile;
If the blossoms be short-lasting
Smile, but with your secret smile.

I have always from the first
Made my vow in honour's name
Only thus to fetch you jewels,
Never vaunting of the same.

SONG: WHEREVER WE MAY BE*

Wherever we may be
There is mindlessness and mind,
There is lovelessness and love,
There is self, there is unself,
Within and without;
There is plus, there is minus;
There is empty, there is full;
There is God, the busy question
In denial of doubt.

There is mindlessness and mind,
There is deathlessness and death,
There is waking, there is sleeping,
There is false, there is true,
There is going, there is coming,
But upon the stroke of midnight
Wherever we may be,
There am I, there are you.

WHAT IS LOVE?*

But what is love? Tell me, dear heart, I beg you.
Is it a reattainment of our centre,
A core of trustful innocence come home to?

Is it, perhaps, a first wild bout of being,
The taking of our own extreme measure
And for a few hours knowing everything?

Or what is love? Is it primeval vision
That stars our course with oracles of danger
And looks to death for timely intervention?

SONG: THE PROMISE*

While you were promised to me
But still were not yet given,
There was this to be said:
Though wishes might be wishes,
A promise was a promise –
Like the shadow of a cedar,
Or the moon overhead,
Or the firmness of your fingers,
Or the print of your kisses,
Or your lightness of tread,
With not a doubt between us
Once bats began their circling
Among the palms and cedars
And it was time for bed.

SONG: YESTERDAY ONLY

Not today, not tomorrow,
Yesterday only:
A long-lasting yesterday
Devised by us to swallow
Today with tomorrow.

When was your poem hidden
Underneath my pillow,
When was your rose-bush planted
Underneath my window –
Yesterday only?

Green leaves, red roses,
Blazoned upon snow,
A long-lasting yesterday,
Today with tomorrow,
Always and only.

PART II

SEMI-DETACHED*

Her inevitable complaint or accusation
Whatever the Major does or leaves undone,
Though, being a good wife, never before strangers,
Nor, being a good mother, ever before their child . . .
With no endearments except for cats and kittens
Or an occasional bird rescued from cats . . .
Well, as semi-detached neighbours, with party-walls
Not altogether sound-proof, we overhear
The rare explosion when he retaliates
In a sudden burst of anger, although perhaps
(We are pretty sure) apologizing later
And getting no forgiveness or reply.

He has his own resources – bees and gardening –
And, we conclude, is on the whole happy.
They never sleep together, as they once did
Five or six years ago, when they first arrived,
Or so we judge from washing on their line –
Those double sheets are now for guests only –
But welcome streams of visitors. How many
Suspect that the show put on by both of them,
Of perfect marital love, is apology
In sincere make-believe, for what still lacks?

If ever she falls ill, which seldom happens,
We know he nurses her indefatigably,
But this she greets, we know, with sour resentment,
Hating to catch herself at a disadvantage,
And crawls groaning downstairs to sink and oven.
If he falls ill she treats it as affront –
Except at the time of that car-accident
When he nearly died, and unmistakable grief
Shone from her eyes for almost a whole fortnight,
But then faded . . .
He receives regular airmail
In the same handwriting, with Austrian stamps.
Whoever sends it, obviously a woman,
Never appears. Those are his brightest moments.
Somehow they take no holidays whatsoever
But are good neighbours, always ready to lend
And seldom borrowing. Our child plays with theirs;
Yet we exchange no visits or confidences.
Only once I penetrated past their hall –
Which was when I fetched him in from the wrecked car
And alone knew who had caused the accident.

IAGO

Iago learned from that old witch, his mother,
How to do double murder
On man and woman fallen deep in love;
Lie first to her, then lie again to him,
Make each mistrustful of the honest other.
Guilt and suspicion wear the same sick face –
Two deaths will follow in a short space.

AGAINST WITCHCRAFT*

No smile so innocent or angelic
As when she nestled to his wounded heart,
Where the slow poison worked within
And eggs of insane fever incubated . . .

Out, witch, out! Here are nine cloves of garlic
That grew repellent to the Moon's pull;
Here too is every gift you ever gave him,
Wrapped in a silken cloth.
Your four-snake chariot awaits your parting
And here I plant my besom upside down.

TROUBLESOME FAME

To be born famous, as your father's son,
   Is a fate troublesome enough, unless
Like Philip's Alexander of Macedon
   You can out-do him by superb excess
Of greed and profligacy and wantonness.

To become famous as a wonder-child
   Brings no less trouble, with whatever art
You toyed precociously, for Fame had smiled
   Malevolence at your birth . . . Only Mozart
Played on, still smiling from his placid heart.

To become famous while a raw young man
  And lead Fame by the nose, to a bitter end,
As Caesar's nephew did, Octavian
  Styling himself Augustus, is to pretend
Peace in the torments that such laurels lend.

To become famous in your middle years
  For merit not unblessed by accident –
Encountering cat-calls, missiles, jeers and sneers
  From half your uncontrollable parliament –
Is no bad fate, to a good sportsman sent. . . .

But Fame attendant on extreme old age
  Falls best. What envious youth cares to compete
With a lean sage hauled painfully upstage,
  Bowing, gasping, shuffling his frozen feet –
A ribboned hearse parked plainly down the street?

TOLLING BELL*

'But why so solemn when the bell tolled?'
'Did you expect me to stand up and caper?'
'Confess, what are you trying to hide from me?
Horror of death?'
                    'That seventeenth-century
Skeletal effigy in the Church crypt?'
'Or is it fear, perhaps, of a second childhood?
Of incurable sickness? Or of a strange someone
Seated in your own chair at your own table?
Or worse, of that chair gone?'
                              'Why saddle me
With your own nightmares?'
                              'Fear of the other world?'
'Be your own age! What world exists but ours?'
'Distaste for funerals?'
                    'Isn't it easier
To play the unweeping corpse than the pall-bearer?'
'Why so mysterious?'
                    'Why so persistent?'
'I only asked why you had looked solemn

When the bell tolled.'
'Angered, not solemn, angered
By all parochially enforced grief.
Death is a private, ungainsayable act.'
'Privately, then, what does Death mean to you?'
'Only love's gentle sigh of consummation,
Which I have little fear of drawing too soon.'

BLANKET CHARGE*

This fever doubtless comes in punishment
For crimes discovered by your own conscience:
You lie detained here on a blanket charge
And between blankets lodged.

So many tedious hours of light and dark
To weigh the incriminatory evidence –
With your head somewhat clearer by midday
Than at its midnight worst.

Ignorance of the Law is no defence
In any Court; but can you plead 'not guilty
Of criminal intent' without a lawyer
To rise on your behalf?

However long the sentence passed on you,
The term served here will, you assume, be taken
Into consideration; you have proved,
Surely, a model prisoner?

The worst is finding where your fault lay
In all its pettiness; do you regret
It was not some cardinal, outrageous sin
That drew crowds to the gibbet?

THE STRAYED MESSAGE

Characteristic, nevertheless strange:
Something went badly wrong at the Exchange,
And my private message to you, in full detail,
Got broadcast over eleven frequencies
With the usual, though disquieting, consequences
Of a torrential amatory fan-mail.

SONG: THE SUNDIAL'S LAMENT*

(*Air: The Groves of Blarney*)

Since much at home on
My face and gnomon,
The sun refuses
Daylight to increase;
Yet certain powers dare
Miscount my hours there
Though sun and shadow
Still collogue in peace.

These rogues aspire
To act Hezekiah
For whom Isaiah
In a day of trial,
All for delaying
His end by praying
Turned back the shadow
On my honest dial.

Nay, Sirs, though willing
To abase the shilling
From noble twelvepence
To the half of ten,
Pray go no further
On this path of murther:
If hours be Dismalized,
Sure, I'm finished then.

POEM: A REMINDER*

Capital letters prompting every line,
Lines printed down the centre of each page,
Clear spaces between groups of these, combine
In a convention of respectable age
To mean: 'Read carefully. Each word we chose
Has rhythm and sound and sense. This is not prose.'

poem: a reminder

capitallett
-ers prompting ev
-eryline lines printed down the
cen
-tre of each page clear

spaces between

groups of these combine in a con
v
e
n
t
i
o
n
of respectable age to mean read
care
-fully each word we chose has

rhythm and
sound and
sense this is
notprose

*ANTORCHA Y CORONA, 1968**

Píndaro no soy, sino caballero
De San Patricio; y nuestro santo
Siglos atrás se hizo mejicano.

Todos aquí alaban las mujeres
Y con razón, como divinos seres –
Por eso entrará en mis deberes

A vuestra Olimpiada mejicana
El origen explicar de la corona:
En su principio fué femenina. . . .

Antes que Hercules con paso largo
Metros midiera para el estadio
Miles de esfuerzos así alentado –

Ya antes, digo, allí existia
Otra carrera mas apasionada
La cual presidia la Diosa Hera.

La virgen que, a su fraternidad
Supero con maxima velocidad
Ganaba el premio de la santidad:

La corona de olivo. . . . Me perdonará
El respetable, si de Atalanta
Sueño, la corredora engañada

Con tres manzanas, pero de oro fino. . . .
Y si los mitos griegos hoy resumo
Es que parecen de acuerdo pleno,

A la inventora primeval del juego,
A la Santa Madre, más honores dando
Que no a su portero deportivo.

En tres cientas trece Olimpiadas
Este nego la entrada a las damas
Amenazandolas, ai, con espadas!

Aquí, por fin, brindemos por la linda
Enriqueta de Basilio: la primera
Que nos honra con antorcha y corona.†

† This poem, with its English translation, was read at the Mexican Cultural Olympiads and awarded the Gold Medal for Poetry.

TORCH AND CROWN, 1968*

(*English translation of the foregoing*)

No Pindar, I, but a poor gentleman
Of Irish race. Patrick, our learned saint,
Centuries past made himself Mexican.

All true-bred Mexicans idolize women
And with sound reason, as divine beings,
I therefore owe it you as my clear duty

At your Olympics, here in Mexico,
To explain the origin of the olive crown:
In the Golden Age women alone could wear it.

Long before Hercules with his huge stride
Paced out the circuit of a stadium,
Provoking men to incalculable efforts,

Long, long before, in Argos, had been run
Even more passionately, a girls' foot race
Under the watchful eye of Mother Hera.

The inspired runner who outstripped all rivals
Of her sorority and finished first
Bore off that coveted and holy prize –

The olive crown. Ladies and gentlemen,
Forgive me if I brood on Atalanta,
A champion quarter-miler tricked one day

By three gold apples tumbled on her track;
And if I plague you with these ancient myths
That is because none of them disagrees

In paying higher honours to the foundress
Of all competitive sport – the Holy Mother –
Than to her sportive janitor, Hercules.

Three hundred and thirteen Olympic Games
Hercules held, though warning off all ladies,
Even as audience, with the naked sword!

So homage to Enriqueta de Basilio
Of Mexico, the first girl who has ever
Honoured these Games with torch and olive crown!

ARMISTICE DAY, 1918*

What's all this hubbub and yelling,
   Commotion and scamper of feet,
With ear-splitting clatter of kettles and cans,
   Wild laughter down Mafeking Street?

O, those are the kids whom we fought for
   (You might think they'd been scoffing our rum)
With flags that they waved when we marched off to war
   In the rapture of bugle and drum.

Now they'll hang Kaiser Bill from a lamp-post,
   Von Tirpitz they'll hang from a tree. . . .
We've been promised a 'Land Fit for Heroes' –
   What heroes we heroes must be!

And the guns that we took from the Fritzes,
   That we paid for with rivers of blood,
Look, they're hauling them down to Old Battersea Bridge
   Where they'll topple them, souse, in the mud!

But there's old men and women in corners
   With tears falling fast on their cheeks,
There's the armless and legless and sightless –
   It's seldom that one of them speaks.

And there's flappers gone drunk and indecent
   Their skirts kilted up to the thigh,
The constables lifting no hand in reproof
   And the chaplain averting his eye. . . .

When the days of rejoicing are over,
   When the flags are stowed safely away,
They will dream of another wild 'War to End Wars'
   And another wild Armistice day.

But the boys who were killed in the trenches,
   Who fought with no rage and no rant,
We left them stretched out on their pallets of mud
   Low down with the worm and the ant.

THE MOTES

You like to joke about young love
   Because (let me be just)
In your dead courts and corridors
Motes dance upon no sunbeams
   But settle down as dust.

From POEMS ABOUT LOVE

(1969)

IF AND WHEN

She hates an *if*, know that for sure:
Whether in cunning or self-torture,
Your *ifs* anticipate the *when*
That womankind conceals from men.

From POEMS 1968–1970

(1970)

SONG: THE SIGIL

Stumbling up an unfamiliar stairway
    Between my past and future
And overtaken by the shadowy mind
    Of a girl dancing for love,
    I glanced over my shoulder.

She had read my secret name, that was no doubt,
    For which how could I blame her?
Her future paired so gently with my own,
    Her past so innocently,
    It flung me in a fever.

Thereupon, as on every strange occasion,
    The past relived its future
With what outdid all hopes and fantasies –
    How could I not concede
    My sigil in its favour?

SONG: TWINNED HEART

Challenged once more to reunite,
        Perfect in every limb
But screened against the intrusive light
        By ghosts and cherubim,

I call your beauty to my bed,
        My pride you call to yours
Though clouds run maniac overhead
        And cruel rain down pours,

With both of us prepared to wake
        Each in a bed apart,
True to a spell no power can break:
        The beat of a twinned heart.

SONG: OLIVE TREE

Call down a blessing
On that green sapling,
A sudden blessing
For true love's sake
On that green sapling
Framed by our window
With her leaves twinkling
As we lie awake.
Two birds flew from her
In the eye of morning
Their folded feathers
In the sun to shake.

Augury recorded,
Vision rewarded
With an arrow flying
With a sudden sting,
With a sure blessing,
With a double dart,
With a starry ring,
With music from the mountains
In the air, in the heart
This bright May morning
Re-echoing.

SONG: ONCE MORE

These quiet months of watching for
An endless moment of once more
May not be shortened,

But while we share them at a distance,
In irreproachable persistence,
Are strangely brightened.

And these long hours of perfect sleep
When company in love we keep,
By time unstraitened,

Yield us a third of the whole year
In which to embrace each other here,
Sleeping together, watching for
An endless moment of once more
By dreams enlightened.

SONG: VICTIMS OF CALUMNY

Equally innocent,
Confused by evil,
Pondering the event,
Aloof and penitent,
With hearts left sore
By a cruel calumny,
With eyes half-open now
To its warped history,
But undeceivably
Both in love once more.

LOVE GIFTS

Though love be gained only by truth in love
Never by gifts, yet there are gifts of love
That match or enhance beauty, that indeed
Fetch beauty with them. Always the man gives,
Never the woman – unless flowers or berries
Or pebbles from the shore.
                                        She welcomes jewels
To ponder and pore over tremblingly
By candlelight. 'Why does he love me so,
Divining my concealed necessities?'
And afterwards (there is no afterwards
In perfect love, nor further call for gifts)
Writes: 'How you spoil me!', meaning: 'You are mine',
But sends him cornflowers, pinks and columbine.

MANKIND AND OCEAN

You celebrate with kisses the good fortune
Of a new and cloudless moon
(Also the tide's good fortune),
Content with July fancies
To brown your naked bodies
On the slopes of a sea-dune.

Mankind and Ocean, Ocean and mankind:
Those fatal tricks of temper,
Those crooked acts of murder
Provoked by the wind –
I am no Ocean lover,
Nor can I love mankind.

To love the Ocean is to taste salt,
To drink the blood of sailors,
To watch the waves assault
Mast-high a cliff that shudders
Under their heartless hammers. . . .
Is wind alone at fault?

VIRGIN MIRROR

Souls in virginity joined together
  Rest unassailable:
Ours is no undulant fierce rutting fever
  But clear unbroken lunar magic able
  To mirror loves illimitable.

When first we chose this power of being
  I never paused to warn you
What ruinous charms the world was weaving;
  I knew you for a child fostered in virtue
  And swore no hand could hurt you.

Then should I suffer nightmares now
  Lest you, grown somewhat older,
Be lured to accept a worldly where and how,
  Carelessly breathing on the virgin mirror,
  Clouding love's face for ever?

SECRET THEATRE

When from your sleepy mind the day's burden
Falls like a bushel sack on a barn floor,
Be prepared for music, for natural mirages
And for night's incomparable parade of colour.

Neither of us daring to assume direction
Of an unforeseen and fiery entertainment,
We clutch hands in the seventh row of the stalls
And watch together, quivering, astonished, silent.

It is hours past midnight now; a flute signals
Far off; we mount the stage as though at random,
Boldly ring down the curtain, then dance out our love:
Lost to the outraged, humming auditorium.

HOW IT STARTED

It started, unexpectedly of course,
At a wild midnight dance, in my own garden,
To which indeed I was not invited:
I read: 'Teen-agers only.'

In the circumstances I stayed away
Until you fetched me out on the tiled floor
Where, acting as an honorary teen-ager,
I kicked off both my shoes.

Since girls like you must set the stage always,
With lonely men for choreographers,
I chose the step, I even called the tune;
And we both danced entranced.

Here the narrator pauses circumspectly,
Knowing me not unpassionate by nature
And the situation far from normal:
Two apple-seeds had sprouted. . . .

Recordable history began again
With you no longer in your late teens
And me socially (once more) my age –
Yet that was where it started.

BRIEF REUNION

Our one foreboding was: we might forget
How strangely close absence had drawn us,
How close once more we must be drawn by parting –
Absence, dark twin of presence!

Nor could such closeness be attained by practice
Of even the most heroic self-deceit:
Only by inbred faculties far wiser
Than any carnal sense –

Progress in which had disciplined us both
To the same doting pride: a stoicism
Which might confuse, at every brief reunion,
Presence with pangs of absence.

And if this pride should overshoot its mark,
Forcing on us a raw indifference
To what might happen when our hearts were fired
By renewed hours of presence?

Could we forget what carnal pangs had seized us
Three summers past in a burst of moonlight,
Making us more possessive of each other
Than either dared concede? – a prescience
Of the vast grief that each sublunary pair
Transmits at last to its chance children
With tears of violence.

THE JUDGES

Crouched on wet shingle at the cove
In day-long search for treasure-trove –
Meaning the loveliest-patterned pebble,
Of any colour imaginable,
Ground and smoothed by a gentle sea –
How seldom, Julia, we agree
On our day's find: the perfect one
To fetch back home when day is done,
Splendid enough to stupefy
The fiercest, most fastidious eye –
Tossing which back we tell the sea:
'Work on it one more century!'

LOVE AND NIGHT*

Though your professions, ages and conditions
Might seem to any sober person
Irreconcilable,

Yet still you claim the inalienable right
To kiss in corners and exchange long letters
Patterned with well-pierced hearts.

When judges, dazzled by your blazing eyes,
Mistake you both for Seventh Day Adventists
(Heaven rest their innocent souls!)

You smile impassively and say no word –
The why and how of magic being tabu
Even in courts of Law.

Who could have guessed that your unearthly glow
Conceals a power no judgement can subdue,
Nor act of God, nor death?

Your love is not desire but certainty,
Perfect simultaneity,
Inheritance not conquest;

Long silences divide its delicate phases
With simple absence, almost with unbeing,
Before each new resurgence.

Such love has clues to a riddling of the maze:
Should you let fall the thread, grope for it,
Unawed by the thick gloom.

Such love illuminates the far house
Where difficult questions meet their answers
And lies get scoured away.

Your powers to love were forged by Mother Night –
Her perfect discipline of thought and breath –
Sleep is their sustenance.

You prophesy without accessories:
Her words run splashed in light across your walls
For reading as you wake.

But Night, no doubt, has deathless other secrets
Guarded by her unblinking owls against
All clumsy stumbling on them.

CHILD WITH VETERAN

You were a child and I your veteran;
An age of violence lay between us,
Yet both claimed citizenship of the same land
Conversing in our own soft, hidden language,
Often by signs alone.

Our eyelids closed, little by little,
And we fell chained in an enchantment
Heavier than any known or dreamed before,
Groping in darkness for each other's fingers
Lifting them to our lips.

Here brooded power beyond comparison,
Tremendous as a thousand bee-stings
Or a great volley of steel-tipped arrows
With which to take possession of a province
That no one could deny us,
For the swift regeneration of dead souls
And the pride of those undead.

PURIFICATION*

'He numbed my heart, he stole away my truth,
He laid hands on my body.
Never had I known ecstasy like that:
I could have flown with him to the world's end
And thought of you no more.'

'Wake, dearest love, here in my own warm arms,
That was a nightmare only.
You kept the wall-side, leaving me the outer,
No demon slid between us to molest you.
This is a narrow bed.'

I would have brought her breakfast on a tray
But she seemed haunted still
By terror that in nine short months, maybe,
A demon's litter, twitching scaly tails
Would hang from either breast.

And still she shuddered inconsolably
All day; our true love-magic
Dwindled and failed. 'He swore to take me
The round of Paris, on his midnight tours,
Fiddling for me to dance.'

Thus to have murdered love even in dream
Called for purification;
And (as the Great Queen yearly did at Paphos)
Down to the sea she trod and in salt water
Renewed virginity.

POWERS UNCONFESSED*

Diffidently, when asked who might I be,
I agreed that, yes, I ruled a small kingdom
Though, like yourself, free to wander abroad
Hatless, barefooted and incognito.

Abruptly we embraced – a strange event,
The casual passers-by taking less notice
Than had this been a chance meeting of cousins –
Nor did we argue over protocol.

You, from your queendom, answerable only
To royal virtue, not to a male code,
Knew me for supernatural, like yourself,
And fell at once head over heels in love;
As I also with you – but lamentably
Never confessed what wrathful powers attest
The Roman jealousy of my male genius.

PANDORA*

But our escape: to what god did we owe it,
Pandora, my one love?
White-faced we lay, apart and all but dead.

In place of magic had you offered fancy
(Being still a girl and over-credulous)
To honour my poor genius? –
And with your careless innocence of death
Concealed the mischief and those unseen Spites
For long months haunting you and me, your Titan,
Chasing away the honey-bees of love?

Though my acute dream-senses, apprehending,
Warned me with fevers, chills and violences
That the postern gate was forced
And the keep in instant peril,
Why did my eyes stay blind and my ears deaf?

And this escape: to what god did we owe it,
Or to what unborn child?

SOLOMON'S SEAL*

Peace is at last confirmed for us:
A double blessing, heavily priced,
Won back as we renew our maiden hearts
In a magic known to ourselves only,
Proof against furious tides of error
And bitter ironies of the self-damned:

Perfect in love now, though not sharing
The customary pillow – and our reasons
Appear shrouded in dark Egyptian dreams
That recreate us as a single being
Wholly in love with love.

Under each pyramid lies inverted
Its twin, the sister-bride to Pharaoh,
And so Solomon's seal bears witness.

Therefore we neither plead nor threaten
As lovers do who have lost faith –
Lovers not riven together by an oath
Sworn on the very brink of birth,
Nor by the penetrative ray of need
Piercing our doubled pyramid to its bed.

All time lies knotted here in Time's caress,
And so Solomon's seal bears witness.

TO PUT IT SIMPLY

Perfect reliance on the impossible
   By strict avoidance of all such conjecture
As underlies the so-called possible:
   That is true love's adventure.

Put it more simply: all the truth we need
   Is ours by curious preknowledge of it –
On love's impossibility agreed,
   Constrained neither by horoscope nor prophet.

Or put it still more simply: all we know
Is that love is and always must be so.

TO TELL AND BE TOLD

What is it I most want in all the world?
To be with you at last, alone in the world,
And as I kiss with you to tell and be told.

A child you no more are, yet as a child
You foresaw miracles when no more a child –
So spread a bed for us, to tell and be told.

You wear my promises on rings of gold,
I wear your promise on a chain of gold:
For ever and once more to tell and be told.

THE THEME OF DEATH

Since love is an astonished always
Challenging the long lies of history,
Yesterday when I chose the theme of death
You shook a passionate finger at me:
'Wake from your nightmare! Would you murder love?
Wake from your nightmare!'

No, sweetheart! Death is nightmare when conceived
As God's Last Judgement, or the curse of Time –
Its intransgressible bounds of destiny;
But love is an astonished always
With death as affidavit for its birth
And timeless progress.

What if these tombs and catafalques conspire,
Menacing us with gross ancestral fears,
To dissipate my living truth, and yours,
To induct us into ritual weeping?
Our love remains a still astonished always,
Pure death its witness.

AT THE WELL

To work it out even a thought better
Than ever before – yet a thought rare enough
To raise a sigh of wonder –
That is your art (he said) but mine also
Since first I fell upon the secret
And sighed for wonder that our dry mouths
After a world of travel
Were drawn together by the same spell
To drink at the same well.

Coincidence (she said) continues with us,
Secret by secret,
Love's magic being no more than obstinacy
In love's perfection –
Like the red apple, highest on the tree
Reserved for you by me.

LOGIC*

Clear knowledge having come
Of an algebraic queendom,
Compulsive touch and tread
By a public voice dictated
Proclaims renewed loyalty
To a defunct geometry:
Blue-prints of logic –

Logic, tricking the tongue
With its fool's learning,
Prescribed excess,
Devoted emptiness,
With dull heart-burning
For a forgotten peace,
For work beyond employment,
For trust beyond allegiance,
For love beyond enjoyment,
For life beyond existence,
For death beyond decease.

ROBBERS' DEN

They have taken Sun from Woman
And consoled her with Moon;
They have taken Moon from Woman
And consoled her with Seas;
They have taken Seas from Woman
And consoled her with Stars;
They have taken Stars from Woman
And consoled her with Trees;
They have taken Trees from Woman
And consoled her with Tilth;
They have taken Tilth from Woman
And consoled her with Hearth;
They have taken Hearth from Woman
And consoled her with Praise –
Goddess, the robbers' den that men inherit
They soon must quit, going their ways,
Restoring you your Sun, your Moon, your Seas,
Your Stars, your Trees, your Tilth, your Hearth –
But sparing you the indignity of Praise.

THE ACCOMPLICE

Mercury, god of larceny
And banking and diplomacy,
Marks you as his accomplice.

No coins hang from his watch-chain
Where once he used to wear them:
He has done with toys like these.

Would you prove your independence
By entering some Order
Or taking your own life?

He will, be sure, divinely
Revenge the moral fervour
Of your disloyalties.

For his fistful of signed contracts
And million-dollar bank-notes
Bear witness to his credit
With your colleagues, friends, assistants
And your own faithful wife.

FIRST LOVE

Darling, if ever on some night of fever
But with your own full knowledge . . .
Darling, confess how it will be if ever
You violate your true-love pledge
Once offered me unprompted,
Which I reciprocated
Freely, fully and without restraint
Nor ever have abjured since first we kissed?
Will that prove you a liar and me a saint,
Or me a fool and you a realist?

THROUGH A DARK WOOD

Together, trustfully, through a dark wood –
But headed where, unless to the ancient, cruel,
Inescapable, marital pitfall
With its thorny couch for the procreation
Of love's usurpers or interlopers?
Or worse by far, should each be trapped singly
But for true-love's sake gulp down a jealousy
And grief at not having suffered jointly. . . .

Together, through a dark wood, trustfully.

IN THE VESTRY

It is over now, with no more need
For whispers, for brief messages posted
In the chestnut-tree, for blank avoidance
Of each other's eyes at festivals,
For hoarded letters, for blossom-tokens,
For go-betweens or confidants.

Well, are you glad that all is over now?
Be as truthful as you dare.
Posted at last as would-be man and wife
Behaving as the Lord Himself enjoined,
Repudiating your lascivious past,
Each alike swearing never to retrieve it,
Particularly (God knows) with someone else –
Marriage being for procreation only –
Are you both glad and sure that all is over?

WHEN LOVE IS NOT

'Where is love when love is not?'
   Asked the logician.
'We term it Omega Minus,'
   Said the mathematician.

'Does that mean marriage or plain Hell?'
   Asked the logician.
'I was never at the altar,'
   Said the mathematician.

'Is it love makes the world go round?'
   Asked the logician.
'Or you might reverse the question,'
   Said the mathematician.

THE REITERATION

The death of love comes from reiteration:
A single line sung over and over again –
No prelude and no end.

The word is not, perhaps, 'reiteration' –
Nature herself repunctuates her seasons
With the same stars, flowers, fruits –
Though love's foolish reluctance to survive
Springs always from the same mechanical fault:
The needle jumps its groove.

MAN OF EVIL*

But should I not pity that poor devil,
Such a load of guilt he carries?
He debauched the daughter of his benefactor –
A girl of seventeen – her brother too,
At the same drunken picnic.

Pushes hard drugs, abstains from them himself;
His first wife ended in a mad-house,
The second was found drowned in a forest pool –
The Coroner, observing his distress,
Called for an open verdict.

And so on, oh and so on – why continue?
He complains always of his luckless childhood
And fills commiserating eyes with tears.
The truth is: he was evil from the womb
And both his parents knew it.

He cowers and sponges when his guilt is plain
And his bank-account runs dry.
O, that unalterable black self-pity,
Void of repentance or amendment,
Clouding his Universe!

But who can cast out evil? We can only
Learn to diagnose that natal sickness,
The one known cure for which, so far, is death.
Evil is here to stay unendingly;
But so also is Love.

THE RAFT

Asleep on the raft and forced far out to sea
By an irresistible current:
No good, no good!

O for a sister island! Ships were scarce
In that unhomely latitude,
And he lacked food.

No canoes would row out to his rescue;
No native ever called him brother –
What was brotherhood?

He asked another question: which to choose?
A drowning vision of damnation
Or slow starvation?

Even savages, hungry for his flesh,
Would offer him a happier exit;
And he need not fight.

Yet, having always drifted on the raft
Each night, always without provision,
Loathing each night,

So now again he quaked with sudden terror
Lest the same current, irresistibly
Reversed, should toss him back
Once more on the same shore –
As it did every night.

THE UNCUT DIAMOND

This is ours by natural, not by civil, right:
An uncut diamond, found while picnicking
Beside blue clay here on the open veldt!
It should carve up to a walnut-sized brilliant
And a score of lesser gems.

What shall we do? To be caught smuggling stones
Assures us each a dozen years in gaol;
And who can trust a cutting-agency?
So, do you love me?
                    Or must I toss it back?

MY GHOST*

I held a poor opinion of myself
When young, but never bettered my opinion
(Even by comparison)
Of all my fellow-fools at school or college.

Passage of years induced a tolerance,
Even a near-affection, for myself –
Which, when you fell in love with me, amounted
(Though with my tongue kept resolutely tied)
To little short of pride.

Pride brought its punishment: thus to be haunted
By my own ghost whom, much to my disquiet,
All would-be friends and open enemies
Boldly identified and certified
As me, including him in anecdotal
Autobiographies.

Love, should you meet him in the newspapers,
In planes, on trains, or at large get-togethers,
I charge you, disregard his foolish capers;
Silence him with a cold unwinking stare
Where he sits opposite you at table
And let all present watch amazed, remarking
On how little you care.

THE RISK

Though there are always doctors who advise
Fools on the care of their own foolish bodies,
And surgeons ready to rush up and set
Well-fractured arms or thighs, never forget
That you are your own body and alone
Can give it a true medical opinion
Drawn not from catalogued analogies
But from a sense of where your danger lies,
And how it obstinately defies the danger.

Your body, though yourself, can play the stranger
As when it falls in love, presuming on
Another's truth and perfect comprehension,
And fails to ask you: dare it run the risk
Of a mild cardiac lesion or slipped disk?

SOMETHING TO SAY

(*Dialogue between Thomas Carlyle and Lewis Carroll*)

T.C. 'Would you care to explain
Why they fight for your books
With already too many
Tight-packed on their shelves
(Many hundreds of thousands
Or hundreds of millions)
As though you had written
Those few for themselves?'

L.C. 'In reply to your query:
I wrote for one reason
And only one reason
(That being my way):
Not for fame, not for glory,
Nor yet for distraction,
But oddly enough
I had something to say.'

T.C. 'So you wrote for one reason?
Be damned to that reason!
It may sound pretty fine
But relinquish it, pray!
There are preachers in pulpits
And urchins in playgrounds
And fools in asylums
And beggars in corners
And drunkards in gutters
And bandits in prisons
With all the right reasons
For something to say.'

OCCASIONALIA

RESEARCH AND DEVELOPMENT: CLASSIFIED

We reckon Cooke our best chemist alive
And therefore the least certain to survive
Even by crediting his way-out findings
To our Department boss, Sir Bonehead Clive.

Those Goblins, guessing which of us is what
(And, but for Cooke, we're far from a bright lot),
Must either pinch his know-how or else wipe him.
He boasts himself quite safe. By God, he's not!

In fact, we all conclude that Cooke's one hope
Is neither loud heroics nor soft soap:
Cooke must defect, we warn him, to the Goblins,
Though even they may grudge him enough rope.

THE IMMINENT SEVENTIES

Man's life is threescore years and ten,†
  Which God will surely bless;
Still, we are warned what follows then –
  Labour and heaviness –

And understand old David's grouch
  Though he (or so we're told)
Bespoke a virgin for his couch
  To shield him from the cold. . . .‡

Are not all centuries, like men,
  Born hopeful too and gay,
And good for seventy years, but then
  Hope slowly seeps away?

True, a new geriatric art
  Prolongs our last adventures
When eyes grow dim, when teeth depart:
  For glasses come, and dentures –

Helps which these last three decades need
  If true to Freedom's cause:
Glasses (detecting crimes of greed)
  Teeth (implementing laws).

† Psalms 40. 10.
‡ I Kings 1. 1-15.

CAROL OF PATIENCE*

Shepherds armed with staff and sling,
  Ranged along a steep hillside,
Watch for their anointed King
  By all prophets prophesied –
Sing patience, patience,
Only still have patience!

Hour by hour they scrutinize
   Comet, planet, planet, star,
Till the oldest shepherd sighs:
   'I am frail and he is far.'
Sing patience etc.

'Born, they say, a happy child;
   Grown, a man of grief to be,
From all careless joys exiled,
   Rooted in eternity.'
Sing patience etc.

Then another shepherd said:
   'Yonder lights are Bethlehem;
There young David raised his head
   Destined for the diadem.'
Sing patience etc.

Cried the youngest shepherd: 'There
   Our Redeemer comes tonight,
Comes with starlight on his hair,
   With his brow exceeding bright.'
Sing patience etc.

'Sacrifice no lamb nor kid,
   Let such foolish fashions pass;
In a manger find him hid,
   Breathed upon by ox and ass.'
Sing patience etc.

Dance for him and laugh and sing,
   Watch him mercifully smile,
Dance although tomorrow bring
   Every plague that plagued the Nile!
Sing patience, patience,
Only still have patience!

H

H may be N for those who speak
Russian, although long E in Greek;
And cockneys, like the French, agree
That H is neither N nor E
Nor Hate's harsh aspirate, but meek
And mute as in *Humanity*.

INVITATION TO BRISTOL

'Come as my doctor,
Come as my lawyer,
Or come as my agent
(First practise your lies)
For Bristol is a small town
Full of silly gossip
And a girl gets abashed by
Ten thousand staring eyes.'

'Yes, I'll come as your lawyer
Or as your god-father,
Or even as Father Christmas? –
Not half a bad disguise –
With a jingle of sleigh bells,
A sack full of crackers
And a big bunch of mistletoe
For you to recognize.'

THE PRIMROSE BED*

The eunuch and the unicorn
    Walked by the primrose bed;
The month was May, the time was morn,
    Their hearts were dull as lead.

'Ah, unicorn,' the eunuch cried,
  'How tragic is our Spring,
With stir of love on every side,
  And loud the sweet birds sing.'

Then, arm and foreleg intertwined,
  Both mourned their cruel fate –
The one was single of his kind,
  The other could not mate.

THE STRANGLING IN MERRION SQUARE

None ever loved as Molly loved me then,
    With her whole soul, and yet
How might the patientest of Irishmen
    Forgive, far less forget
Her long unpaid and now unpayable debt?
There's scarce a liveried footman in the Square
But can detail you how and when and where.

THE AWAKENING

Just why should it invariably happen
That when the Christian wakes at last in Heaven
He finds two harassed surgeons watching by
In white angelic smocks and gloves, and why
Looking so cross and (as three junior nurses
Trundle the trolley off with stifled curses)
Why joking that the X-ray photograph
Must have been someone else's – what a laugh! – ?

Now they may smoke. . . . A message from downstairs
Says: 'Matron says, God's due soon after Prayers.'

From THE GREEN-SAILED VESSEL

(1971)

THE HOOPOE TELLS US HOW*

Recklessly you offered me your all,
Recklessly I accepted,
Laying my large world at your childish feet
Beyond all bounds of honourable recall:
Wild, wilful, incomplete.

Absence reintegrates our pact of pacts –
The hoopoe tells us how:
With bold love-magic, Moon in *Leo*,
Sun in *Pisces*, blossom upon bough.

PART I

THE WAND*

These tears flooding my eyes, are they of pain
Or of relief: to have done with other loves,
To abstain from childish folly?

It has fallen on us to become exemplars
Of a love so far removed from gallantry
That we now meet seldom in a room apart
Or kiss goodnight, or even dine together
Unless in casual company.

For while we walk the same green paradise
And confidently ply the same green wand
That still restores the wilting hopes of others
Far more distressed than we,
How can we dread the broad and bottomless mere
Of utter infamy sunk below us
Where the eggs of hatred hatch?

FIVE*

Five beringed fingers of Creation,
Five candles blazing at a shrine,
Five points of her continuous pentagram,
Five letters in her name – as five in mine.
I love, therefore I am.

*QUINQUE**

Quinque tibi luces vibrant in nomine: quinque
  Isidis in stella cornua sacra deae.
Nonne etiam digitos anuli quinque Isidis ornant?
  Ornant te totidem, Julia. . . . Sum, quod amo.

ARROW ON THE VANE

Suddenly, at last, the bitter wind veers round
From North-East to South-West. It is at your orders;
And the arrow on our vane swings and stays true
To your direction. Nothing parts us now.
What can I say? Nothing I have not said,
However the wind blew. I more than love,
As when you drew me bodily from the dead.

GORGON MASK

When the great ship ran madly towards the rocks
An unseen current slewed her into safety,
A dying man ashore took heart and lived,
And the moon soared overhead, ringed with three rainbows,
To announce the birth of a miraculous child.
Yet you preserved your silence, secretly
Nodding at me across the crowded hall.

The ship carried no cargo destined for us,
Nor were her crew or master known to us,
Nor was that sick man under our surveillance,
Nor would the child ever be born to you,
Or by me fathered on another woman –
Nevertheless our magic power ordained
These three concurrent prodigies.

Stranger things bear upon us. We are poets
Age-old in love: a full reach of desire
Would burn us both to an invisible ash. . . .
Then hide from me, if hide from me you must,
In bleak refuge among nonentities,
But wear your Gorgon mask of divine warning
That, as we first began, so must we stay.

TO BE POETS*

We are two lovers of no careless breed,
Nor is our love a curiosity
(Like honey-suckle shoots from an oak tree
Or a child with two left hands) but a proud need
For royal thought and irreproachable deed;
What others write about us makes poor sense,
Theirs being a no-man's land of negligence.

To be poets confers Death on us:
Death, paradisal fiery conspectus
For those who bear themselves always as poets,
Who cannot fall beneath the ignoble curse
(Whether by love of self, whether by scorn
Of truth) never to die, never to have been born.

WITH A GIFT OF RINGS

It was no costume jewellery I sent:
True stones cool to the tongue, their settings ancient,
Their magic evident.
Conceal your pride, accept them negligently
But, naked on your couch, wear them for me.

CASSE-NOISETTE

As a scurrying snow-flake
Or a wild-rose petal
Carried by the breeze,
Dance your nightly ballet
On the set stage.

And although each scurrying
Snow-flake or rose-petal
Resembles any other –
Her established smile,
Her well-schooled carriage –

Dance to Rule, ballet-child;
Yet never laugh to Rule,
Never love to Rule!
Keep your genius hidden
By a slow rage.

So let it be your triumph
In this nightly ballet
Of snow-flakes and petals,
To present love-magic
In your single image –
With a low, final curtsey
From the set stage.

THE GARDEN

Enhanced in a tower, asleep, dreaming about him,
The twin buds of her breasts opening like flowers,
Her fingers leafed and wandering . . .
                                                            Past the well
Blossoms an apple-tree, and a horde of birds
Nested in the close thickets of her hair
Grumble in dreamy dissonance,
Calling him to the garden, if he dare.

THE GREEN-SAILED VESSEL

We are like doves, well-paired,
Veering across a meadow –
Children's voices below,
Their song and echo;

Like raven, wren or crow
That cry and prophesy,
What do we not foreknow,
Whether deep or shallow?

Like the tiller and prow
Of a green-sailed vessel
Voyaging, none knows how,
Between moon and shadow;

Like the restless, endless
Blossoming of a bough,
Like tansy, violet, mallow,
Like the sun's afterglow.

Of sharp resemblances
What further must I show
Until your black eyes narrow,
Furrowing your clear brow?

DREAMING CHILDREN

They have space enough, however cramped their quarters,
   And time enough, however short their day,
In sleep to chase each other through dream orchards
   Or bounce from rafters into buoyant hay.

But midnight thunder rolls, with frequent flashes,
   Wild hail peppers the farm-house roof and walls,
Wild wind sweeps from the North, flattening the bushes
   As with a crash of doom chain-lightning falls.

Split to its tap-roots, their own favourite oak-tree
   Glows like a torch across the narrow heath.
She shudders: 'Take me home again! It scares me!
   Put your arms round me, we have seen death!'

THE PROHIBITION*

You were by my side, though I could not see you,
Your beauty being sucked up by the moon
In whose broad light, streaming across the valley,
We could match colours or read the finest print,
While swart tree shadows rose from living roots
Like a stockade planted against intrusion.

But since dawn spread, birds everywhere wakeful
And the sun risen masterly from the East,
Where are you now? Not standing at my side
But gone with the moon, sucked away into daylight,
All magic vanished, save for the rare instant
When a sudden arrow-shot transfixes me.

Marry into your tribe, bear noble sons
Never to call me father – which is forbidden
To poets by the laws of moon magic,
The Goddess being forever a fierce virgin
And chastening all love with prohibition
Of what her untranslatable truth transcends.

SERPENT'S TAIL

When you are old as I now am
I shall be young as you, my lamb;
For lest love's timely force should fail
The Serpent swallows his own tail.

UNTIL WE BOTH . . .*

Until we both . . .
Strolling across Great Park
With a child and a dog, greeting the guardian lions
At the royal entrance, slowly rounding the mere
Where boats are sailed all day, this perfect Sunday,
Counting our blessings peacefully enough . . .

Until we both, at the same horrid signal,
The twelfth stroke of a clock booming behind us,
Sink through these nonchalant, broad, close-cut lawns
To a swirling no-man's land shrouded in smoke
That feeds our kisses with bright furnace embers,
And we beg anguished mercy of each other,
Exchanging vow for vow, our lips blistered . . .

Until we both . . .
Until we both at once . . .
Have you more courage, love, even than I
Under this final torment?
Shall we ever again greet our guardian lions
And the boats on the Great Mere?

THE MIRACLE*

No one can understand our habit of love
Unless, trudging perhaps across the moor
Or resting on a tree-stump, deep in thought,
He has been scorched, like me, by summer lightning
And every blade of grass etherialized.

Which must have happened at some sudden turn
Of love, neither invited nor foreseen,
Nor are such miracles ever repetitious
Unless in their long deep-drawn gasp of wonder
And fierce awareness of its origin.

Do they astonish always as renewal
Of truth after impossible variance,
With tongues of flame spurting from bush and tree?

THE ROSE*

When was it that we swore to love for ever?
When did this Universe come at last to be?
The two questions are one.

Fetch me a rose from your rose-arbour
To bless this night and grant me honest sleep:
Sleep, not oblivion.

TESTAMENT*

Pure melody, love without alteration,
Flame without smoke, cresses from a clean brook,
The sun and moon as it were casting dice
With ample falls of rain,
Then comes the peaceful moment of appraisal,
The first and last lines of our testament,
With you ensconced high in the castle turret,
Combing your dark hair at a silver mirror,
And me below, sharpening my quill again.

This body is now yours; therefore I own it.
Your body is now mine; therefore you own it.
As for our single heart, let it stay ours
Since neither may disown it
While still it flowers in the same dream of flowers.

THE CRAB-TREE*

Because of love's infallibility,
Because of love's insistence –
And none can call us liars –
Spring heaps your lap with summer buds and flowers
And lights my mountain peaks with Beltane fires.

The sea spreads far below; its blue whale's-back
Forcing no limit on us;
We watch the boats go by
Beyond rain-laden ranks of olive trees
And, rising, sail in convoy through clear sky.

Never, yet always. Having at last perfected
Utter togetherness
We meet nightly in dream
Where no voice interrupts our confidences
Under the crab-tree by the pebbled stream.

THREE LOCKED HOOPS*

Yourself, myself and our togetherness
Lock like three hoops, exempt from time and space.
Let preachers preach of sovereign trinities,
Yet can such ancient parallels concern us
Unless they too spelt He and She and Oneness?

CLIFF AND WAVE*

Since first you drew my irresistible wave
To break in foam on your immovable cliff,
We occupy the same station of being –
Not as in wedlock harboured close together,
But beyond reason, co-identical.
Now when our bodies hazard an encounter,
They dread to engage the fury of their senses,
And only in the brief dismay of parting
Will your cliff shiver or my wave falter.

PART II

THOSE BLIND FROM BIRTH*

Those blind from birth ignore the false perspective
Of those who see. Their inward-gazing eyes
Broaden or narrow no right-angle;
Nor does a far-off mansion fade for them
To match-box size.

Those blind from birth live by their four sound senses.
Only a fool disguises voice and face
When visiting the blind. Smell, tread and hand-clasp
Announce just why, and in what mood, he visits
That all-observant place.

FOOLS*

There is no fool like an old fool,
   Yet fools of middling age
Can seldom teach themselves to reach
   True folly's final stage.

Their course of love mounts not above
   Some five-and-forty years,
Though God gave men threescore and ten
   To scald with foolish tears.

THE GATEWAY

After three years of constant courtship
Each owes the other more than can be paid
Short of a single bankruptcy.
                                        Both falter
At the gateway of the garden; each advances
One foot across it, hating to forgo
The pangs of womanhood and manhood;
Both turn about, breathing love's honest name,
Too strictly tied by bonds of miracle
And lasting magic to be easily lured
Into acceptance of concubinage:
Its deep defraudment of their regal selves.

ADVICE FROM A MOTHER

Be advised by me, darling:
If you hope to keep my love,
Do not marry that man!

I cannot be mistaken:
There is murder on his conscience
And fear in his heart.

I knew his grandparents:
The stock is good enough,
Clear of criminal taint.

And I find no vice in him,
Only a broken spirit
Which the years cannot heal;

And gather that, when younger,
He volunteered for service
With a secret police;

That one day he had orders
From a number and a letter
Which had to be obeyed,

And still cannot confess,
In fear for his own life,
Nor make reparation.

The dead in their bunkers
Call to him every night:
'Come breakfast with us!'

No gentleness, no love,
Can cure a broken spirit;
I forbid you to try.

A REDUCED SENTENCE

They were confused at first, being well warned
That the Governor forbade, by a strict rule,
All conversation between long-term prisoners –
Except cell-mates (who were his own choice);
Also, in that mixed prison, the two sexes
Might catch no glimpse whatever of each other
Even at fire-drill, even at Church Service.

Yet soon – a most unusual case – this pair
Defied the spirit, although not the letter,
Of his harsh rules, using the fourth dimension
For passage through stone walls and cast-iron doors
As coolly as one strolls across Hyde Park:
Bringing each other presents, kisses, news.

By good behaviour they reduced their sentence
From life to a few years, then out they went
Through three-dimensional gates, gently embraced . . .
And walked away together, arm in arm. . . .
But, home at last, halted abashed and shaking
Where the stairs mounted to a double bed.

THE GENTLEMAN*

That he knows more of love than you, by far,
And suffers more, has long been his illusion.
His faults, he hopes, are few – maybe they are
With a life barred against common confusion;
But that he knows far less and suffers less,
Protected by his age, his reputation,
His gentlemanly sanctimoniousness,
Has blinded him to the dumb grief that lies
Warring with love of love in your young eyes.

COMPLAINT AND REPLY*

I

After our death, when scholars try
To arrange our letters in due sequence,
No one will envy them their task,
You sign your name so lovingly
So sweetly and so neatly
That all must be confounded by
Your curious reluctance,
Throughout this correspondence,
To answer anything I ask
Though phrased with perfect prudence . . .
Why do you wear so blank a mask,
Why always baulk at a reply
Both in and out of sequence,
Yet sign your name so lovingly,
So sweetly and so neatly?

II

Oh, the dark future! I confess
Compassion for your scholars – yes.
Not being myself incorrigible,
Trying most gallantly, indeed,
To answer what I cannot read,
With half your words illegible
Or, at least, any scholar's guess.

SONG: RECONCILIATION

The storm is done, the sun shines out,
  The blackbird calls again
With bushes, trees and long hedgerows
  Still twinkling bright with rain.

Sweet, since you now can trust your heart
  As surely as I can,
Be still the sole woman I love
  With me for your sole man.

For though we hurt each other once
  In youthful blindness, yet
A man must learn how to forgive
  What women soon forget.

KNOBS AND LEVERS

Before God died, shot while running away,
He left mankind His massive hoards of gold:
Which the Devil presently appropriated
With the approval of all major trusts
As credit for inhumanizable
Master-machines and adequate spare-parts.

Men, born no longer in God's holy image,
Were graded as ancillary knobs or levers
With no Law to revere nor faith to cherish.
'You are free, Citizens,' old Satan crowed;
And all felicitated one another
As quit of patriarchal interference.

This page turns slowly: its last paragraph
Hints at a full-scale break-down implemented
By famine and disease. Nevertheless
The book itself runs on for five more chapters.
God died; clearly the Devil must have followed.
But was there not a Goddess too, God's mother?

THE VIRUS*

We can do little for these living dead
Unless to help them bury one another
By an escalation of intense noise
And the logic of computers.
They are, we recognize, past praying for –
Only among the moribund or dying
Is treatment practical.

Faithfully we experiment, assuming
That death is a still undetected virus
And most contagious where
Men eat, smoke, drink and sleep money:
Its monstrous and unconscionable source.

DRUID LOVE*

No Druid can control a woman's longing
Even while dismally foreboding
Death for her lover, anguish for herself
Because of bribes accepted, pledges broken,
Breaches hidden.
                                        More than this, the Druid
May use no comminatory incantations
Against either the woman or her lover,
Nor ask what punishment she herself elects.

But if the woman be herself a Druid?
The case worsens: he must flee the land.
Hers is a violence unassessable
Save by herself – ultimate proof and fury
Of magic power, dispelling all restraint
That princely laws impose on those who love.

PROBLEMS OF GENDER*

Circling the Sun, at a respectful distance,
Earth remains warmed, not roasted; but the Moon
Circling the Earth, at a disdainful distance,
Will drive men lunatic (should they defy her)
With seeds of wintry love, not sown for spite.

Mankind, so far, continues undecided
On the Sun's gender – grammars disagree –
As on the Moon's. Should Moon be god, or goddess:
Drawing the tide, shepherding flocks of stars
That never show themselves by broad daylight?

Thus curious problems of propriety
Challenge all ardent lovers of each sex:
Which circles which at a respectful distance,
Or which, instead, at a disdainful distance?
And who controls the regal powers of night?

CONFESS, MARPESSA*

Confess, Marpessa, who is your new lover?
Could he be, perhaps, that skilful rough-sea diver
Plunging deep in the waves, curving far under
Yet surfacing at last with controlled breath?

Confess, Marpessa, who is your new lover?
Is he some ghoul, with naked greed of plunder
Urging his steed across the gulf of death,
A brood of dragons tangled close beneath?

Or could he be the fabulous Salamander,
Courting you with soft flame and gentle ember?
Confess, Marpessa, who is your new lover?

*JUS PRIMAE NOCTIS**

Love is a game for only two to play at,
Nor could she banish him from her soft bed
Even on her bridal night, *jus primae noctis*
Being irreversibly his. He took the wall-side
Long ago granted him. Her first-born son
Would claim his name, likeness and character.
Nor did we ask her why. The case was clear:
Even though that lover had been nine years dead
She could not banish him from her soft bed.

WORK DRAFTS*

I am working at a poem, pray excuse me,
Which may take twenty drafts or more to write
Before tomorrow night,
But since no poem should be classed with prose,
I must not call it 'work', God knows –
Again, excuse me!

My poem (or non-poem) will come out
In the *New Statesman* first, no doubt,
And in hard covers gradually become
A handsome source of supplementary income,
Selected for *Great Poems* – watch the lists –
And by all subsequent anthologists.

Poems are not, we know, composed for money
And yet my work (or play)-drafts carefully
Hatched and cross-hatched by puzzling layers of ink
Are not the detritus that you might think:
They fetch from ten to fifty bucks apiece
In sale to Old Gold College Library
Where swans, however black, are never geese –
Excuse me and excuse me, pray excuse me!

From POEMS 1970–1972

(1972)

HER BEAUTY

Let me put on record for posterity
The uniqueness of her beauty:
Her black eyes fixed unblinking on my own,
Cascading hair, high breasts, firm nose,
Soft mouth and dancer's toes.

Which is, I grant, cautious concealment
Of a new Muse by the Immortals sent
For me to honour worthily –
Her eyes brimming with tears of more than love,
Her lips gentle, moving secretly –

And she is also the dark hidden bride
Whose beauty I invoke for lost sleep:
To last the whole night through without dreaming –
Even when waking is to wake in pain
And summon her to grant me sleep again.

ALWAYS

Slowly stroking your fingers where they lie,
Slowly parting your hair to kiss your brow –
For this will last for always (as you sigh),
Whatever follows now.

Always and always – who dares disagree
That certainty hangs upon certainty?
Yet who ever encountered anywhere
So unendurably circumstanced a pair
Clasped heart to heart under a blossoming tree
With such untamable magic of despair,
Such childlike certainty?

DESERT FRINGE

When a live flower, a single name of names,
Thrusts with firm roots into your secret heart
Let it continue ineradicably
To scent the breeze not only on her name-day
But on your own: a hedge of roses fringing
Absolute desert strewn with ancient flints
And broken shards and shells of ostrich eggs –
Where no water is found, but only sand,
And yet one day, we swear, recoverable.

THE TITLE OF POET

Poets are guardians
Of a shadowy island
With granges and forests
Warmed by the Moon.

Come back, child, come back!
You have been far away,
Housed among phantoms,
Reserving silence.

Whoever loves a poet
Continues whole-hearted,
Her other loves or loyalties
Distinct and clear.

She is young, he is old
And endures for her sake
Such fears of unease
As distance provokes.

Yet how can he warn her
What natural disasters
Will plague one who dares
To neglect her poet? . . .
For the title of poet
Comes only with death.

DEPTH OF LOVE

Since depth of love is never gauged
By proof of appetites assuaged,
Nor dare you set your body free
To take its passionate toll of me –
And with good reason –
What now remains for me to do
In proof of perfect love for you
But as I am continue,
The ecstatic bonds of monk or nun
Made odious by comparison?

BREAKFAST TABLE

Breakfast peremptorily closes
The reign of Night, her dream extravagances
Recalled for laughter only.

Yet here we sit at our own table,
Brooding apart on spells of midnight love
Long irreversible:

Spells that have locked our hearts together,
Never to falter, never again to stray
Into the fierce dichotomy of Day;
Night has a gentler laughter.

THE HALF-FINISHED LETTER

One day when I am written off as dead –
My works widely collected, rarely read
Unless as Literature (examiners
Asking each student which one he prefers
And how to classify it), my grey head
Slumped on the work-desk – they will find your name
On a half-finished letter, still the same
And in my characteristic characters:
That's one thing will have obdurately lasted.

THE HAZEL GROVE*

To be well loved,
Is it not to dare all,
Is it not to do all,
Is it not to know all?
To be deep in love?

A tall red sally
Had stood for seventy
Years by the pool
(And that was plenty)
Before I could shape
My harp from her poll.

Now seven hundred
Years will be numbered
In our hazel grove
Before this vibrant
Harp falls silent –
For lack of strings,
Not for lack of love.

PITY

Sickness may seem a falling out of love,
With pleas for pity – love's lean deputy.
If so, refuse me pity, wait, love on:
Never outlaw me while I yet live.
The day may come when you too, falling sick,
Implore my pity. Let me, too, refuse it
Offering you, instead, my pitiless love.

SILENT VISIT*

I was walking my garden
Judiciously, calmly,
Curved mattock in hand
Heavy basket on shoulder,
When all of a sudden

You kissed me most kindly
From forehead to chin,
Though arriving unseen
As a pledge of love-magic
And wordlessly even.

Had you come, long-announced,
Wearing velvets and silk
After travels of grandeur
From Greece to the Yemen,
Socotra and Aden

With no rapture of silence
Nor rapture of absence –
No poem to greet you,
No burst of green glory
From trees in my garden. . . .

But you came, a grown woman,
No longer the child
Whom I loved well enough
When your age was just seven –
Who would enter alone
The close thickets of Eden
And there would run wild.

CORONET OF MOONLIGHT

Such was the circumstance of our first love:
Sea, silence, a full moon.
Nevertheless, even the same silence
Amended by a distant nightingale
From the same past, and gently heaving surf,
Brings me no sure revival of our dream –
For to be surely with you is to sleep,
Having well earned my coronet of moonlight
By no mere counting of processional sheep.

SONG: TO BECOME EACH OTHER*

To love you truly
   I must become you,
And so to love you
   I must leave behind
All that was not you:
   All jewelled phantoms,
All fabrications
   Of a jealous mind.

For man and woman
   To become each other
Is far less hard
   Than would seem to be:
An eternal serpent
   With eyes of emerald
Stands curled around
   This blossoming tree.

Though I seem old
   As a castle turret
And you as young
   As the grass beneath
It is no great task
   To become each other
Where nothing honest
   Goes in fear of death.

HEAVEN*

Laugh still, write always lovingly, for still
You neither will nor can deny your heart,
Which always was a poet's,
Even while our ways are cruelly swept apart.
But though the rose I gave you in your childhood
Has never crumbled yellowing into dust
Neither as yet have needles pricked your conscience,
Which also is a poet's,
To attempt the miracles which one day you must.

Meanwhile reject their Heaven, but guard our own
Here on this needle-point, immediately
Accessible, not sprawled like theirs across
Limitless outer space. If to those angels
We seem a million light-years yet unborn,
And cannot more concern them than they us,
Let our own Heaven, with neither choir nor throne
Nor janitor, rest inexpugnable
And private for our gentler love alone.

GROWING PAINS

My earliest love, that stabbed and lacerated,
Must I accept it as it seemed then –
Although still closely documented, dated
And even irreversibly annotated
By your own honest pen?

Love never lies, even when it most enlarges
Dimensions, griefs, or charges,
But, come what must, remains
Irrevocably true to its worst growing pains.

FRIDAY NIGHT*

On the brink of sleep, stretched in a wide bed,
   Rain pattering at the windows
And proud waves booming against granite rocks:
   Such was our night of glory.

Thursday had brought us dreams only of evil,
   As the muezzin warned us:
'Forget all nightmare once the dawn breaks,
   Prepare for holy Friday!'

Friday brings dreams only of inward love
   So overpassing passion
That no lips reach to kiss, nor hands to clasp,
   Nor does foot press on foot.

We wait until the lamp has flickered out
   Leaving us in full darkness,
Each still observant of the other's lively
   Sighs of pure content.

Truth is prolonged until the grey dawn:
   Her face floating above me,
Her black hair falling cloudlike to her breasts,
   Her lovely eyes half-open.

THE PACT

The identity of opposites had linked us
In our impossible pact of only love
Which, being a man, I honoured to excess
But you, being woman, quietly disregarded –
Though loving me no less –
And, when I would have left you, envied me
My unassuageable positivity.

POOR OTHERS*

Hope, not Love, twangles her single string
Monotonously and in broken rhythms.
Can Hope deserve praise?

I fell in love with you, as you with me.
Hope envies us for being otherwise
Than honest Hope should be.

No charm avails against the evil eye
Of envy but to spit into our bosoms
And so dissemble

That we are we and not such luckless others
As hope and tremble,
Shifting the blame to fathers or to mothers
For being themselves, not others:
Alas, poor others!

A TOAST TO DEATH*

This is, indeed, neither the time nor the place
For victory celebrations. Victory over what?
Over Death, his grinning image and manifesto
Of which, as children, we have been forewarned
And offered a corpse's frigid hand to kiss.

Contrariwise, let me raise this unsteady glass
In a toast to Death, the sole deviser of life,
Our antenatal witness when each determined
Sex, colour, humour, religion, limit of years,
Parents, place, date of birth –
A full conspectus, with ourselves recognized
As viable capsules lodged in the fifth dimension,
Never to perish, time being irrelevant,
And the reason for which, and sole excuse, is love –
Tripled togetherness of you with me.

THE YOUNG SIBYL

The swing has its bold rhythm,
Yet a breeze in the trees
Varies the music for her
As down the apples drop
In a row on her lap.

Though still only a child
She must become our Sibyl,
A holder of the apple
Prophesying wild
Histories for her people.

Five apples in a row,
Each with ruddy cheeks,
So too her own cheeks glow
As the long swing creaks,
Pulsing to and fro.

RECORDS

Accept these records of pure love
With no end or beginning, written for
Yourself alone, not the abashed world,
Timeless therefore –

Whose exaltations clearly tell
Of a past pilgrimage through hell,
Which in the name of love I spare you.
Hell is my loneliness, not ours,
Else we should harrow it together.

Love, have you walked worse hells even than I,
Through echoing silence where no midge or fly
Buzzes – hells boundless, without change of weather?

THE FLOWERING ALOE*

The century-plant has flowered, its golden blossom
Showering honey from seven times our height:
Now the stock withers fast and wonder ends.
Yet from its roots eventually will soar
Another stock to enchant your great-grandchildren
But vex my jealous, uninvited ghost,
These being no blood of mine.

CIRCUS RING

How may a lover draw two bows at once
Or ride two steeds at once,
Firm in the saddle?
Yet these are master-feats you ask of me
Who loves you crazily
When in the circus ring you rock astraddle
Your well-matched bay and grey –
Firing sharp kisses at me.

AGELESS REASON*

We laugh, we frown, our fingers twitch
Nor can we yet prognosticate
How we shall learn our fate –
The occasion when, the country which –
Determined only that this season
Of royal tremulous possession
Shall find its deathless reason.

AS WHEN THE MYSTIC

To be lost for good to the gay self-esteem
That carried him through difficult years of childhood,
To be well stripped of all tattered ambitions
By his own judgement, now scorning himself
As past redemption –
                this is anticipation
Of true felicity, as when the mystic
Starved, frightened, purged, assaulted and ignobled
Drinks Eleusinian ambrosia
From a gold cup and walks in Paradise.

UNPOSTED LETTER*

(1963)

Do you still love, once having shared love's secret
With a man born to it?
Then sleep no more in graceless beds, untrue
To love, where jealousy of the secret
May scorch away your childlike sheen of virtue –
Did he not confer crown, orb and sceptre
On a single-hearted, single-fated you?

BIRTH OF A GODDESS*

It was John the Baptist, son to Zechariah,
Who assumed the cloak of God's honest Archangel
And mouthpiece born on Monday, Gabriel,
And coming where his cousin Mary span
Her purple thread or stitched a golden tassel
For the curtain of the Temple Sanctuary,
Hailed her as imminent mother, not as bride –
Leaving the honest virgin mystified.

Nor would it be a man-child she must bear:
Foreseen by John as a Messiah sentenced
To ransom all mankind from endless shame –
But a Virgin Goddess cast in her own image
And bearing the same name.

BEATRICE AND DANTE

He, a grave poet, fell in love with her.
She, a mere child, fell deep in love with love
And, being a child, illumined his whole heart.

From her clear conspect rose a whispering
With no hard words in innocency held back –
Until the day that she became woman,

Frowning to find her love imposed upon:
A new world beaten out in her own image –
For his own deathless glory.

THE DILEMMA*

Tom Noddy's body speaks, not so his mind;
   Or his mind speaks, not so Tom Noddy's body.
Undualistic truth is hard to find
   For the distressed Tom Noddy.

Mind wanders blindly, body misbehaves;
   Body sickens, mind at last repents,
Each calling on the heart, the heart that saves,
   Disposes, glows, relents.

Which of these two must poor Tom's heart obey:
   The mind seduced by logical excess
To misbehaviour, or its lonely prey –
   The unthinking body sunk in lovelessness?

THE WALL

A towering wall divides your house from mine.
You alone hold the key to the hidden door
That gives you secret passage, north to south,
Changing unrecognizably as you go.
The south side borders on my cherry orchard
Which, when you see, you smile upon and bless.
The north side I am never allowed to visit;
Your northern self I must not even greet,
Nor would you welcome me if I stole through.

I have a single self, which never alters
And which you love more than the whole world
Though you fetch nothing for me from the north
And can bring nothing back. To be a poet
Is to have no wall parting his domain,
Never to change. Whenever you stand by me
You are the Queen of poets, and my judge.
Yet you return to play the Mameluke
Speaking a language alien to our own.

WOMEN AND MASKS*

Translated from Gábor Devecseri's Hungarian

Women and masks: an old familiar story.
Life slowly drains away and we are left
As masks of what we were. The living past
Rightly respects all countenances offered
As visible sacrifices to the gods
And clamps them fast even upon live faces.
Let face be mask then, or let mask be face –
Mankind can take its ease, may assume godhead.
Thus God from time to time descends in power
Graciously, not to a theologian's hell
But to our human hell enlaced with heaven.

Let us wear masks once worn in the swift circlings
And constant clamour of a holy dance
Performed always in prayer, in the ecstasy
Of love-hate murder – today's children always
Feeling, recording, never understanding.

Yet this old woman understands, it seems,
At least the unimportance of half-knowledge,
Her face already become mask, her teeth
Wide-gapped as though to scare us, her calm face
Patterned with wrinkles in unchanging grooves
That outlive years, decades and centuries.
Hers is a mask remains exemplary
For countless generations. Who may wear it?
She only, having fashioned it herself.
So long as memory lasts us, it was hers.
Behind it she assembles her rapt goodness,
Her gentle worth already overflooding
The mask, her prison, shaming its fierce, holy
Terror: for through its gaping sockets always
Peer out a pair of young and lovely eyes.

TILTH

('Robert Graves, the British veteran, is no longer in the poetic swim. He still resorts to traditional metres and rhyme, and to such out-dated words as *tilth*; withholding his 100% approbation also from contemporary poems that favour sexual freedom.'
From a New York critical weekly)

Gone are the drab monosyllabic days
When 'agricultural labour' still was *tilth*;
And '100% approbation', *praise*;
And 'pornographic modernism', *filth* –
Yet still I stand by *tilth* and *filth* and *praise*.

THE LAST FISTFUL

He won her Classic races, at the start,
With a sound wind, strong legs and gallant heart;
Yet she reduced his fodder day by day
Till she had sneaked the last fistful away –
When, not unnaturally, the old nag died
Leaving her four worn horseshoes and his hide.

THE TRADITIONALIST

Respect his obstinacy of undefeat,
His hoarding of tradition,
Those hands hung loosely at his side
Always prepared for hardening into fists
Should any fool waylay him,
His feet prepared for the conquest of crags
Or a week's march to the sea.

If miracles are recorded in his presence
As in your own, remember
These are no more than time's obliquities
Gifted to men who still fall deep in love
With real women like you.

THE PREPARED STATEMENT

The Prepared Statement is a sure stand-by
For business men and Ministers. A lie
Blurted by thieves caught in the very act
Shows less regard, no doubt, for the act's fact
But more for truth; and all good thieves know why.

ST ANTONY OF PADUA

Love, when you lost your keepsake,
The green-eyed silver serpent,
And called upon St Antony
  To fetch it back again,
The fact was that such keepsakes
Must never become idols
And meddle with the magic
  That chains us with its chain:
Indeed the tears it cost you
By sliding from your finger
Was Antony's admonishment
  That magic must remain
Dependent on no silver ring
Nor serpent's emerald eyes
But equally unalterable,
  Acceptable and plain . . .
Yet none the less St Antony
(A blessing on his honesty!)
Proved merciful to you and me
  And found that ring again.

BROKEN COMPACT

It was not he who broke their compact;
But neither had he dared to warn her
How dangerous was the act.
It might have seemed cruel blackmail,
Not mere foreknowledge, to confess
What powers protected and supported him
In his mute call for singleheartedness.

It was she indeed who planted the first kiss,
Pleading with him for true togetherness –
Therefore her faults might well be charged against him.
She dared to act as he had never dared.
Nor could he change: his heart remaining full,
Commanded by her, yet unconquerable,
Blinding her with its truth.
                                        So, worse than blind,
He suffered more than she in body and mind.

A DREAM OF FRANCES SPEEDWELL

I fell in love at my first evening party.
You were tall and fair, just seventeen perhaps,
Talking to my two sisters. I kept silent
And never since have loved a tall fair girl,
Until last night in the small windy hours
When, floating up an unfamiliar staircase
And into someone's bedroom, there I found her
Posted beside the window in half-light
Wearing that same white dress with lacy sleeves.
She beckoned. I came closer. We embraced
Inseparably until the dream faded.
Her eyes shone clear and blue. . . .

Who was it, though, impersonated you?

THE ENCOUNTER*

Von Masoch met the Count de Sade
  In Hell as he strode by.
'Pray thrash me soundly, Count!' he begged.
  His lordship made reply:

'What? Strike a lacquey who *enjoys*
  Great blows that bruise and scar?'
'I love you, Count,' von Masoch sighed,
  'So cruel to me you are.'

AGE GAP

My grandfather, who blessed me as a child
Shortly before the Diamond Jubilee,
Was born close to the date of Badajoz
And I have grandchildren well past your age –
One married, with a child, expecting more.

How prudently you chose to be a girl
And I to be a boy! Contrary options
Would have denied us this idyllic friendship –
Boys never fall in love with great-grandmothers.

NIGHTMARE OF SENILITY

Then must I punish you with trustfulness
Since you can trust yourself no more and dread
Fresh promptings to deceive me? Or instead
Must I reward you by deceiving you,
By heaping coals of fire on my own head?
Are truth and friendship dead?

And why must I, turning in nightmare on you,
Bawl out my lies as though to make them true?
O if this Now were once, when pitifully
You dressed my wounds, kissed and made much of me,
Though warned how things must be!

* * * * * *

Very well, then: my head across the block,
A smile on your pursed lips, and the axe poised
For a merciful descent. Ministering to you
Even in my torment, praising your firm wrists,
Your resolute stance. . . . How else can I protect you
From the curse my death must carry, except only
By begging you not to prolong my pain
Beyond these trivial years?
                                        I am young again.
I watch you shrinking to a wrinkled hag.
Your kisses grow repulsive, your feet shuffle
And drag. Now I forget your name and forget mine . . .

No matter, they were always equally 'darling'.
Nor were my poems lies; you made them so
To mystify our friends and our friends' friends.
We were the loveliest pair: all-powerful too,
Until you came to loathe me for the hush
That our archaic legend forced on you.

ABSENT CRUSADER

An ancient rule prescribed for true knights
Was: 'Never share your couch with a true lady
Whom you would not care in honour to acknowledge
As closest to your heart, on whose pure body
You most would glory to beget children
And acknowledge them your own.'

The converse to which rule, for fine ladies,
No knight could preach with firm authority;
Nor could he venture to condemn any
Who broke the rule even while still sharing
Oaths of love-magic with her absent knight,
Telling herself: 'This is not love, but medicine
For my starved animal body; and my right.
Such peccadilloes all crusades afford –
As when I yield to my own wedded Lord.'

DREAM RECALLED ON WAKING

The monstrous and three-headed cur
Rose hugely when she stroked his fur,
Using his metapontine tail
To lift her high across the pale.

Ranging those ridges far and near
Brought blushes to her cheek, I fear,
Yet who but she, the last and first
Could dare what lions never durst?

Proud Queen, continue as you are,
More steadfast than the Polar Star,
Yet still pretend a child to be
Gathering sea-wrack by the sea.

COLOPHON

Dutifully I close this book. . . .
Its final pages, with the proud look
Of timelessness that your love lends it,
Call only for a simple Colophon
(Rose, key or shepherd's crook)
To announce it as your own
Whose coming made it and whose kiss ends it.

From TIMELESS MEETING

(1973)

THE PROMISED BALLAD

This augurs well; both in their soft beds
Asleep, unwakably far removed,
Nevertheless as near as makes no odds –
Proud fingers twitching, all but touching.

What most engages him are his own eyes
Beautified by dreaming how one day
He will cast this long love-story as a ballad
For her to sing likewise –
How endless lovers will accept its marvels
As true, which they must be indeed:
Freed of dark witches and tall singing devils.

THE IMPOSSIBLE DAY

A day which never could be yesterday
Nor ever can become tomorrow,
Which framed eternity in a great lawn
Beside the appletrees, there in your garden –
We never shall dismiss it.

Threats of poverty, or of long absence,
Foreknowledge of ten thousand strokes
Threatened against our love by a blank world –
How suddenly they vanished and were gone;
We had fallen in love for ever.

Our proof of which, impossibility,
Was a test of such true magic
As no one but ourselves could answer for.
Both of us might be dead, but we were not,
Our light being still most needed.

And if some unannounced oppression breaks
To chase the governing stars from a clear sky,
Thunder rolling at once from west and east
What should we lovers fear from such a scene
Being incontestably a single heart?

Then say no more about eternity
That might compel us into fantasy:
One day remains our sure centre of being,
Substance of curious impossibility
At which we stand amazed.

THE POET'S CURSE

Restore my truth, love, or have done for good –
Ours being a simple compact of the heart
Guiding each obstinate body
And slow mind regularly –
Each always with a proud faith in the other's
Proud faith in love, though often wrenched apart
By the irresistible Nightmare that half-smothers –
But bound for ever by the poet's curse
Intolerably guarding ill from worse.

SEVEN YEARS*

Where is the truth to indulge my heart,
These long years promised –
Truth set apart,
Not wholly vanished.
I still have eyes for watching,
Hands for holding fast,
Legs for far-striding,
Mouth for truth-telling –
Can the time yet have passed,
For loving and for listening?

LOVE AS LOVELESSNESS

What she refused him – in the name of love
And the hidden tears he shed –
She granted only to such soulless blades
As might accept her casual invitation
To a loveless bed.

Each year of the long seven gnawed at her heart,
Yet never would she lay
Tokens of his pure love under her pillow
Nor let him meet, by chance, her new bedfellow;
Thus suffering more than he.

Seven years had ended, the fierce truth was known.
Which of these two had suffered most?
Neither enquired and neither cared to boast:
'Not you, but I. It was myself alone.'
In loneliness true love burns to excess.

THE SCARED CHILD

It is seven years now that we first loved –
Since you were still a scared and difficult child
Confessing less than love prompted,
Yet one night coaxed me into bed
With a gentle kiss
And there blew out the candle.
Had you then given what your tongue promised,
Making no fresh excuses
And never again punished your true self
With the acceptance of my heart only,
Not of my body, nor offered your caresses
To brisk and casual strangers –
How would you stand now? Not in love's full glory
That jewels your fingers immemorially
And brines your eyes with bright prophetic tears.

AS ALL MUST END

All ends as all must end,
And yet cannot end
The way that all pretend,
Nor will it have been I
Who forged the obtrusive lie
But found sufficient wit
To contradict it.

Never was there a man
Not since this world began
Who could outlie a woman:
Nor can it have been you
Who tore our pact in two
And shaking your wild head
Laid a curse on my bed.

I hid in the deep wood,
Weeping where I stood,
Berries my sole food,
But could have no least doubt
That you would search me out,
Forcing from me a kiss
In its dark recesses.

TOUCH MY SHUT LIPS

Touch my shut lips with your soft forefinger,
Not for silence, but speech –
Though we guard secret words of close exchange,
Whispering each with each,
Yet when these cloudy autumn nights grow longer
There falls a silence stronger yet, we know,
Than speech: a silence from which tears flow.

THE MOON'S LAST QUARTER*

So daylight dies.
The moon's in full decline,
Nor can those misted early stars outshine her.
But what of love, counted on to discount
Recurrent terror of the moon's last quarter?

Child, take my hand, kiss it finger by finger!
Can true love fade? I do not fear death
But only pity, with forgetfulness
Of love's timeless vocabulary

And an end to poetry
With death's mad aircraft rocketing from the sky.
Child, take my hand!

TRUE EVIL

All bodies have their yearnings for true evil,
A pall of darkness blotting out the heart,
Nor can remorse cancel luckless events
That rotted our engagements with Heaven's truth;
These are now history. Therefore once more
We swear perpetual love at love's own altar
And reassign our bodies, in good faith,
To faith in their reanimated souls.

But on our death beds shall our flaming passions
Revert in memory to their infantile
Delight of mocking the stark laws of love?
Rather let death concede a warning record
Of hells anticipated but foregone.

WHEN AND WHY

When and why we two need never ask –
It is not, we know, our task
Though both stand bound still to accept
The close faith we have always kept
With contradictions and the impossible:
To work indeed as one for ever
In rapt acknowledgment of love's low fever.

THE WINDOW PANE

To bed, to bed: a storm is brewing.
Three natural wonders – thunder, lightning, rain –
Test our togetherness. The window pane,
Regaling us with vistas of forked lightning,
Grants our mortality fair warning;
And every stroke reminds us once again
How soon true love curves round to its beginning.

PRIDE OF PROGENY

While deep in love with one another,
Those seven long earlier years, we two
Would often kiss, lying entranced together
Yet never do what simpler lovers do
In generous pride of generous progeny;
Counting ourselves as poets only,
We judged it false to number more than two.

THAT WAS THE NIGHT*

That was the night you came to say goodnight,
Where from the roof hung gargoyles of protection
And our eyes ached, but not intolerably,
The scene for once being well:
We had no now that did not spell forever
Though traffic growled and wild cascades of rain
Rattled against each streaming window pane.

They had gone at last, we reassured each other,
Even those morbid untranslatable visions
Whose ancient terrors we were pledged to accept,
Whose broken past lay resolutely elsewhere.
Hell, the true worldly Hell, proved otherwise:
Dry demons having drunk our marshes dry.

SONG: THE QUEEN OF TIME

Two generations bridge or part us.
The case, we grant, is rare –
Yet while you dare, I dare:
Our curious love being age-long pledged to last,
Posterity, even while it ridicules,
Cannot disprove the past.

Neither of us would think to hedge or lie –
Too well we know the cost:
Should the least canon of love's law be crossed,
Both would be wholly lost –
You, queen of time, and I.

SHOULD I CARE?

'Should I care,' she asked, 'his heart being mine,
If his body be another's? –
Should I long for children and a full clothes-line?
Children, indeed, need mothers,
But do they still need fathers?
And now that money governs everything
Should a country need a king?'

TIMELESS MEETING

To have attained an endless, timeless meeting
By faith in the stroke which first engaged us,
Driving two hearts improbably together
Against all faults of history
And bodily disposition –

What does this mean? Prescience of new birth?
But one suffices, having paired us off
For the powers of creation –
Lest more remain unsaid.

Nor need we make demands or deal awards
Even for a thousand years:
Who we still are we know.

Exchange of love-looks came to us unsought
And inexpressible:

To which we stand resigned.

ENVOI

There is no now for us but always,
Nor any I but we –
Who have loved only and love only
From the hilltops to the sea
In our long turbulence of nights and days:
A calendar from which no lover strays
In proud perversity.

AT THE GATE

(1974)

OURS IS NO WEDLOCK*

Ours is no wedlock, nor could ever be:
We are more, dear heart, than free.
Evil surrounds us – love be our eye-witness –
Yet while a first childish togetherness
Still links this magic, all terror of lies
Fades from our still indomitable eyes:
We love, and none dares gibe at our excess.

THE DISCARDED LOVE POEM

Should I treat it as my own
Though loth to recall
The occasion, the reason,
The scorn of a woman
Who let no tears fall?

It seems no mere exercise
But grief from a wound
For lovers to recognize:
A scar below the shoulder,
White, of royal size.

How did she treat the occasion?
In disdainful mood?
Or as death to her womanhood?
As the Devil's long tooth?
As the end of all truth?

EARLIER LOVERS*

First came fine words softening our souls for magic,
Next came fine magic, sweetening hope with sex;
Lastly came love, training both hearts for grief –
Magical grief that no honour could vex.

Was it ever granted earlier true lovers –
Whether equally bruised need not concern us –
To anticipate such hand-in-hand conformity?
If so, how were they named? And was their glory
Fixed by an oath you never dared deny me?

FAST BOUND TOGETHER

Fast bound together by the impossible,
The everlasting, the contempt for change,
We meet seldom, we kiss seldom, seldom converse,
Sharing no pillow in no dark bed,
Knowing ourselves twin poets, man with woman,
A millennial coincidence past all argument,
All laughter and all wonder.

£. s. d.

When *Libra, Solidus, Denarius*
Ruled our metallic currency,
They satisfied and steadied us: –
Pounds, shillings, pence, all honest British money.

True, the gold *libra* weighed twelve ounces once.
The *solidus*, gold equally,
Worth twenty-five *denarii* –
Money that did not burn,
Money which in its turn . . .

'What happened to the *solidus*?' you ask me.
Reduced at last to an unsilvered shilling
Of twelve *denarii* – 'pence', or bronze money –
It faded pitifully into the blue . . .
As for the *libra*, having done with gold,
It languished among paper promises
Based on hopes, lies and shrewd financial guesses.
But mourn for the French *sou*, as is most proper:
Three hundred ounces, once, all of pure copper.

THREE WORDS ONLY*

Tears from our eyes
Start out suddenly
Until wiped away
By the gentle whisper
Of three words only.

And how should we stifle
Grief and jealousy
That would jerk us apart
Were it not for an oracle
Of three words only?

Three words only,
Full seven years waiting
With prolonged cruelty
Night by night endured
For three words only.

Sweetheart, I love you
Here in the world's eye
And always shall do
With a perfect faith
In three words only.

Let us boast ourselves
Still to be poets
Whose power and whose faith
Hang at this tall altar
Of three words only.

TRUE MAGIC*

Love, there have necessarily been others
When we are forced apart
Into far-off continents and islands
Either to sleep alone with an aching heart
Or admit casual lovers . . .

Is the choice murderous? Seven years have passed
Yet each remains the other's perfect love
And must continue suffering to the last . . .
Can continence claim virtue in preserving
An oath hurtful and gruelling?

Patience! No firm alternative can be found
To absolute love; we therefore plead for none
And are poets, thriving all hours upon true magic
Distilled from poetry – such love being sacred
And its breach wholly beyond absolution.

THE TOWER OF LOVE

What demon lurked among those olive-trees,
Blackening your name, questioning my faith,
Raising sudden great flaws of desperate wind,
Making a liar of me?
Confess: was it the demon Jealousy?

Has there been any gift in these eight years
That ever you refused when gently asked?
Or that I ever chose to refuse you –
For fear of loving you too dearly –
However much I had failed to demand?

Forgive, and teach me to forgive myself.
This much we know: lifting our faith above
All argument and idle contradiction,
We have won eternity of togetherness
Here in this tall tower blessed for us alone.

THE LOVE LETTER

It came at last, a letter of true love,
Not asking for an answer,
Being itself the answer
To such perversities of absence
As day by day distress us –
Spring, summer, autumn, winter –
With due unhappiness and unease.

What may I say? What must I not say?
Ours is an evil age, afflicting us
With acts of unexampled cruelty
Even in this fast circle of friends,
Offering no choice between disease and death –
With love balanced above profound deeps . . .
Yet here is your love letter.

Why must we never sleep in the same bed
Nor view each other naked
Though our hearts and minds require it
In proof of honest love?
Can it be because poetic magic
Must mount beyond all sensual choosing
To a hidden future and forgotten past?

SONG: SEVEN FRESH YEARS

Two full generations
Had parted our births
Yet still I could love you
Beyond all concealment,
All fear, all reproach,
Until seven fresh years
Ruling distance and time
Had established our truth.

Love brooded undimmed
For a threatening new age,
So we travelled together
Through torment and error
Beyond jealousy's eras
Of midnight and dawn,
Until seven fresh years
Ruling distance and time
Had established our truth.

AS A LESS THAN ROBBER

You can scarcely grant me now
What was already granted
In bland self-deprivation
Only to other debtors
To whom you owed nothing.

And had I cause for complaint
After my honest absence
That for seven long years
I never dared insist
That you should keep faith?

Now in reward for waiting,
Being still a mere nobody,
Let me plead without reproach
As a less than robber
That I am owed nothing.

SINGLENESS IN LOVE

And the magic law long governing our lives
As poets, how should it be rightly phrased?
Not as injunction, not as interdiction,
But as true power of singleness in love
(The self-same power guarding the fifth dimension
In which we live and move
Perfect in time gone by and time foreknown)
Our endless glory to be bound in love,
Nor ever lost by cheating circumstance.

LOVE CHARMS

How closely these long years have bound us
Stands proved by constant imminence of death –
On land, on water, and in the sky –
As by our love-charms worn on the same finger
Against a broken neck or sudden drowning –
Should we debate them?

To have done with quarrels and misunderstandings
Seems of small import even though emphasizing
The impossibility of a fatal breach.
And yet how strange such charms may seem, how wanton,
And forced on us by what? Not by the present
Nor the past either, nor the random future:
Here we lie caught in love's close net of truth.

AT THE GATE*

Where are poems? Why do I now write none?
This can mean no lack of pens, nor lack of love,
But need perhaps of an increased magic –
Where have my ancient powers suddenly gone?

Tonight I caught a glimpse of her at the gate
Grappling a monster never found before,
And jerking back its head. Had I come too late?
Her eyes blazed fire and I could look no more.

What could she hold against me? Never yet
Had I lied to her or thwarted her desire,
Rejecting prayers that I could never forget,
Stealing green leaves to light an alien fire.

THE MOON'S TEAR*

Each time it happened recklessly:
No poet's magic could release her
From those feckless unfathomable demands
Of anger and imprudence,
Those pleas of cruelly injured innocence.

Why should he keep so strange a woman
Close at his elbow fitfully observing
The end of a world that was?
Must he fetch a moon's black tear to tame her
For ever and a day?

SONG: FROM OTHERWHERE OR NOWHERE*

Should unknown messengers appear
From otherwhere or nowhere,
Treat them with courtesy,
Listen most carefully,
Never presume to argue.
Though the sense be unintelligible,
Accept it as true.

Otherwhere is a lonely past,
Nowhere a far future
To which love must have access
In time of loneliness.
Listen most carefully:
Though the sense be unintelligible,
Accept it as true.

A distant flower-garden,
A forgotten forest,
Islands on a lake
Teeming with salmon,
Its waters dark blue –
Though the sense be unintelligible,
Accept it as true.

NAME

Caught by the lure of marriage,
Casting yourself in prospect
As perfect wife and mother
Through endless years of joy,
Be warned by one who loves you
Never to name your first-born
Until you know the father
And: is it girl or boy?

Nine months in mortal darkness
Let it debate the future,
Reviewing its inheritance
Through three-score generations,
From both sides of the family,
A most exacting game;
Then, just before delivery,
Prepare for a soft whisper
As it reveals its name.

TWO DISCIPLINES*

Fierce bodily control, constant routine,
Precision and a closely smothered rage
Alike at ballet-school and the manège:
These harden muscles, these bolster the heart
For glorious records of achievement
To glow in public memory apart.
Which disciplines (ballet and horsemanship)
Have proved no less reciprocally exclusive –
Note their strange differences in gait and carriage –
Than permissivity and Christian marriage.

THE UGLY SECRET*

Grow angry, sweetheart, if you must, with me
Rather than with yourself. This honest shoulder
Will surely shrug your heaviest blow away,
So you can sleep the sounder.

As for the ugly secret gnawing at you
Which you still hide for fear of hurting me,
Here is my blank pledge of forgiveness –
Nor need you ever name the enemy,
Nor need I ever guess.

THREE YEARS WAITING*

Have we now not spent three years waiting
For these preposterous longings to make sense –
Mine and what I divine to be your secret
Since gently you tighten your lips on its conclusion
Though never registering a copyright?

Since these are poems in their first making,
Let us refrain from secret consideration
Of their bewildered presence.
What is a poem
Unless a shot in the night with a blind arrow
From a well-magicked bowstring?

From COLLECTED POEMS 1975

(1975)

THE CRYSTAL

Incalculably old,
True gift from true king –
Crystal with streaks of gold
For mounting in a ring –
Be sure this gem bespeaks
A sunrise love-making:
To kiss, to have, to hold.

A CHARM FOR SOUND SLEEPING*

A charm for sound sleeping,
A charm against nightmares,
A charm against death –
Without rhyme, without music,
Yet short of deceit?

How to master such magic,
How acquire such deep knowledge,
How secure such full power?
Would you shrink from her answer?
Would you dare face defeat?

For to work out of time,
To endure out of space,
To live within her truth –
That alone is full triumph
And honour complete.

THE NEW ETERNITY

We still remain we;
The how and where now being stationary
Need not henceforth concern us;
Nor this new eternity
Of love prove dangerous
Even though it still may seem
Posted and hidden past all dream.

HISTORY OF THE FALL

But did not Adam, Eve's appointed playmate,
Honour her as his goddess and his guide,
Finding her ten times hardier than himself:
Resistant to more sickness and worse weather?
Did he not try his muscles in Eve's service –
Fell trees, shoulder vast boulders, run long errands?

Hers was a pure age, until humankind
Ate flesh like the wild beasts. Fruits, roots, and herbs
Had been their diet before world-wide drought
Forced famine on them: before witless Adam
Disobeyed orders, tossing sacred apples
From Eve's green tree, driving and butchering deer,
Teaching his sons to eat as now he ate.

Eve forced the family from their chosen Eden . . .
And Cain killed Abel, battening on the corpse.

ELSEWHERE

Either we lodge diurnally here together
Both in heart and in mind,
Or awhile you lodge elsewhere –
And where, dear heart, is *Elsewhere*?

Elsewhere may be your casual breach of promise –
Unpunishable since unbound by oath –
Yet still awhile *Elsewhere.*

As a veteran I must never break my step,
As a poet I must never break my word,
Lest one day I should suddenly cease to love you
And remain unloved elsewhere.
Come, call on me tonight –
Not marching, love, but walking.

WHAT CAN WE NOT ASK?*

What can we not ask you?
Being a woman
You still alert the world and, still being men,
We never dare gainsay you, nor yet venture
To descend the mountain when your bells chime
The midday feast and nature gives assent.

Whatever hours they strike, you are found true
To your lovely self and to yourself only:
Silent yet still uncontradictable.
Did we ever see you stumble, taking thought?

What rights have men in such divinity,
Widely though they may move within its shade,
Abstaining still from prayers?

TWO CRUCIAL GENERATIONS*

Two crucial generations parted them,
Though neither chargeable as an offence –
Nor could she dare dismiss an honest lover
For no worse crime than mere senility,
Nor could he dare to blame her, being himself
Capable of a passionate end to love
Should she show signs of mocking at old age?
Then why debate the near impossible
Even in fitful bouts of honest rage?

TO COME OF AGE*

At last we could keep quiet, each on his own,
Signalling silently though memorably
His news or latest unnews.

When younger we had spent those wintry evenings
In shoutings and wild laughter –
We dared not come of age.

Unless obsessed by love none of us changed.
How could we change? Has true love ever changed?
Not in our day, but only in another's.

Tell me, my heart of hearts, I still beseech you:
When dare we reasonably come of age?

SEPTEMBER LANDSCAPE

Olive-green, sky-blue, gravel-brown,
With a floor of tumbled locusts,
And along the country lane
Isabel dances dressed in red
Erect, thinking aloud,
Framed against sudden cloud
And its bold promise of much-needed rain.

CRUCIBLES OF LOVE

From where do poems come?
From workshops of the mind,
As do destructive armaments,
Philosophic calculations,
Schemes for man's betterment?

Or are poems born simply
From crucibles of love?
May not you and I together
Engrossed with each other
Assess their longevity?

For who else can judge merits
Or define demerits –
This remains a task for lovers
Held fast in love together
And for no others.

WOMAN POET AND MAN POET

Women poet and man poet
Fell in love each with the other.
It was unsafe for either
To count on sunny weather,
The body being no poet.

Yet it had been the woman
Who drew herself apart,
Cushioned on her divan,
And lent some bolder man
Her body, not her heart.

When seven long years were over
How would their story end?
No change of heart for either,
Mere changes in the weather,
A lover being no friend.

THE FIELD-POSTCARD

475 *Graves* (*Robert*) AUTOGRAPH POSTCARD signed (written in pencil), 1.R.W.Fus. B.E.F. Nov 27, '15 to Edward Marsh, autograph address panel on verso signed, Post Office and Censor's postmarks £30

'In the last few days I've been made a captain and shifted here. I won't get any leave till January at the earliest. . .'

Back in '15, when life was harsh
And blood was hourly shed,
I reassured Sir Edward Marsh
So far I was not dead.

My field-postcard duly arrived,
It seems, at Gray's Inn Square
Where Eddie, glad I still survived,
Ruffled his thinning hair . . .

A full half century out of sight
It lay securely hid
Till Francis Edwards with delight
Sold it for thirty quid.
But who retained the copyright,
The invaluable copyright?
In common law *I* did.

IF NO CUCKOO SINGS

And if no cuckoo sings,
What can I care, or you?
Each heart will yet beat true
While outward happenings
Kaleidoscopically continue.

Year in, year out, we lie
Each in a lonely bed
With vows of true love read
Like prayers, though silently,
To a well-starred and open sky.

Fierce poems of our past –
How can they ever die,
Condemned by love to last
Word for word and exactly
Under a wide and changeful sky?

MOUNTAIN LOVERS

We wandered diligently and widely
On mountains by the sea,
Greeting no *now* that was not *always,*
Nor any *I* but *we,*
And braved a turbulence of nights and days
From which no honest lover strays,
However stark the adversity.

THREE TIMES IN LOVE

You have now fallen three times in love
With the same woman, first indeed blindly
And at her blind insistence;

Next with your heart alive to the danger
Of what hers might conceal, although such passion
Strikes nobly and for ever;

Now at last, deep in dream, transported
To her rose garden on the high ridge,
Assured that there she can deny you
No deserved privilege,
However controvertible or new.

THE SENTENCE

Is this a sentence passed upon us both
For too ambitious love in separation:
Not as an alien intervention or intrusion
But as heaviness and silence,
As a death in absence?

We have lived these seven years beyond recourse,
Each other's single love in separation:
A whispered name before sleep overtakes us
And before morning wakes us
At some far-distant station.

Let us not hold that either drew apart
In weariness or anger or adventure,
Or the resolve to nurse a single heart. . . .
Call it an irresistible thunderbolt.
It was not my fault, love, nor was it your fault.

SPRING 1974

None yet have been good jocund days,
Clear dawning days,
Days of leisure and truth
Reflecting love's sharp gaze,
Being born, alas, in an evil month
By fetid marsh or by fouled river
Maligned in Hell, accursed in Heaven,
Always by love unshriven,
Void still of honest praise.

ADVENT OF SUMMER

You have lived long but over-lonely,
My grey-haired fellow-poet
Sighing for new melodies
In face of sullen grief,
With wanings of old friendship,
With sullen repetition –
For who can thrive in loneliness,
Accepting its cold needs?

Let love dawn with the advent
Of a cool, showery summer
With no firm, fallen apricots
Nor pods on any beanstalk,
Nor strawberries in blossom,
Nor cherries on the boughs.

Let us deny the absurdities
Of every true summer:
Let us never live ill-used
Or derided by new strangers;
Let us praise the vagrant thrushes
And listen to their songs.

THE UNPENNED POEM*

Should I wander with no frown, these idle days,
My dark hair trespassing on its pale brow –
If so, without companionship or praise,
Must I revisit marshes where frogs croak
Like me, mimicking penitential ways?

Are you still anchored to my slow, warm heart
After long years of drawing nightly nearer
And visiting our haunted room, timely
Ruffling its corners with love's hidden mop?
And still must we not part?

What is a poem if as yet unpenned
Though truthful and emancipated still
From what may never yet appear,
From the flowery riches of still silent song,
From golden hours of a wakeful Spring?

Approach me, Rhyme; advise me, Reason!
The wind blows gently from the mountain top.
Let me display three penetrative wounds
White and smooth in this wrinkled skin of mine,
Still unacknowledged by the flesh beneath.

A poem may be trapped here suddenly,
Thrusting its adder's head among the leaves,
Without reason or rhyme, dumb –
Or if not dumb, then with a single voice
Robbed of its chorus.

Here looms November. When last did I approach
Paper with ink, pen, and the half truth?
Advise me, Reason!

THE GREEN WOODS OF UNREST*

Let the weeks end as well they must
Not with clouds of scattered dust
But in pure certainty of sun –
And with gentle winds outrun
By the love that we contest
In these green woods of unrest.
You, love, are beauty's self indeed,
Never the harsh pride of need.

UNCOLLECTED POEMS

(1910–1974)

JUVENILIA: 1910–1914

A POT OF WHITE HEATHER

Thou, a poor woman's fairing, white heather,
Witherest from the ending
Of summer's bliss to the sting
Of winter's grey beginning.

Which is better, Dame Nature? A human
Woman's oft-uttered rapture
O'er thy dear gift, and the pure
Love that enshrines a treasure?

Or all the sweet plant loses, where grandly
A friendly mountain rises,
And a land of heather-trees
About its knees reposes?

THE MOUNTAIN SIDE AT EVENING

        Now even falls
And fresh, cold breezes blow
Adown the grey-green mountain side
Strewn with rough boulders. Soft and low
Night speaks, her tongue untied
Darkness to Darkness calls.

        'Tis now men say
From rugged piles of stones
Steal Shapes and Things that should be still;
Green terror ripples through our bones,
Our inmost heart-strings thrill
And yearn for careless day.

THE WILL O' THE WISP

See a gleam in the gloaming – out yonder
  It wand'reth bright flaming;
Its force – that is a fierce thing!
  It draweth men to drowning.

THE KING'S SON

Daintily stepped the son of the king
  Through the palace-gates flung wide,
He breathed of the fine fresh scents of Spring,
  As he walked by the river side;
But deep in his heart was blossoming
  The Tiger-lily of pride.

His eyes were a royal purple-grey,
  And his sweet lips harboured a smile,
As he dreamed of his kingdom far away,
  Of his wonderful Southern isle;
But evil lay in the purple-grey,
  And the smile was a tyrant's smile.

'The king, my sire, has given me
The fairest isle in all his lands;
Three-score stout vessels fringe her sands,
And seven-score guard the sea.

Thither I'll bid my captains bold
Bring droves of slaves, and thrice a day
A hundred heads I'll blow away
With my great gun of gold.

My squires will take the shattered skulls
And bind them with a golden chain,
To whiten in the sun and rain,
From my palace pinnacles.

O'er that fair isle my fancy roves,
She shall be clothed in majesty,
I'll pave her paths with ivory,
And gem-bedeck her groves.'

He mused by the river, foes forgot,
  While the wind in his love-locks blew;
But an hairy arm from the reeds upshot,
  And dragged him down by the shoe . . . .
The king's own brother plotted the plot,
  And the isle no boy-king knew.

THE MISER OF SHENHAM HEATH

A miser lived on Shenham Heath,
As lean and grey he was as death.
All children feared his long grey beard,
His toes peeped from the boots beneath.

Within the thatch he kept his store,
A thousand pounds of gold and more;
And every night by candle light
Would take and count them, o'er and o'er.

It chanced one chill November night,
He told the tale by candle light,
When sudden fled from heart and head
The lust for guineas round and bright.

He shivered, rose. Though he was old,
And though the waters glimmered cold,
A plunge he took in Shenham Brook
And washed away the taint of gold.

He cast his clouts and donned instead
A suit he'd worn when he was wed.
The cloth was new, of red and blue;
A feathered hat adorned his head.

He rose at dawning of the day,
That none might meet him on his way.
To Chert he went and money spent
But was not minded there to stay.

He bade a barber shave his chin,
And rode a-horse to Shenham Inn
In proper pride. The neighbours cried:
'A lord! A lord! but gruesome thin!'

Nor from that day forth did he cease
Feeding the countryside like geese:
He lavished gold on young and old –
Aye, even to his last gold piece!

A pauper lives on Shenham Heath,
As lean and grey he is as death;
All people fear to view him near,
His toes peep from his boots beneath.

RONDEAU

Word comes of a pursuing robber-band
From great Bokhara or from Samarkand.
    With tightened belly-girth and loosened rein
    The gallant, speedy dromedary-train
Pounds with broad feet the soft-embosomed sand;
And hearts are by such panic fear unmanned,
It hounds them onward while they yet can stand,
    With mingled snarl and cry and blow and strain,
        Southward away.

So, as I watch from my far Northern strand,
High o'er the waves sweep by on either hand
    Great gibbous cloud-beasts, merchandized with rain
    From chilly Northern seas to thirsty Spain,
Wind-chased in frightened rout o'er sea, o'er land,
        Southward away.

'AM AND ADVANCE: A COCKNEY STUDY

When we was wed my 'Erbert sed
  'Wot? Give 'em 'am? Good Lord!
Them wedding guests can beat their breasts,
  But 'am we can't afford.'

When 'Erbert died, Lord, 'ow I cried!
  But 'arf them tears was sham.
'At 'is bedside,' I thinks with pride,
  'The mourners they 'as 'Am.'

PEEPING TOM

I sat in my chamber yesternight;
I lit the lamp, I drew the blind,
And scratched with a quill at paper white;
With Mistress Bess was all my mind!
But stormy gusts had rent the blind
And you were peering from behind,
Peeping Tom in the skies afar –
Bold, inquisitive, impudent star!

Fair Bess was leaning o'er the well,
When down there dropped her store-room key.
A bucket lowered me where it fell;
Invisible, I yet could see
To blow her kisses secretly.
But down the shaft you laughed in glee,
Peeping Tom in the skies afar –
Bold, inquisitive, impudent star!

To-night I walk with Sweetheart Bess,
And love-glance follows love-glance swift;
I gather her in a soft caress,
With joy my eyes to heaven uplift.
But through the scudding vapour-drift
My mocker finds a fleeting rift,
Peeping Tom in the skies afar –
Bold, inquisitive, impudent star!

THE BALLAD OF THE WHITE MONSTER

We drave before a boisterous wind
For twenty days and three.
Stout was the barque wherein we sailed,
Shipmen from Normandie.

O carpenters, go take your tools
To patch the good ship's side.
Ceased is the wind whereon we drave;
The swelling waves subside.

The carpenters 'gan take their tools
To patch the good ship's side:
They caulked the gaping seams also,
To keep therefrom the tide.

But as they caulked the gaping seams
With mighty craft and care,
Writhed from the oily sea beneath,
White serpents everywhere.

Oh, be these worms or serpents strange
Thus rising from the sea?
Nay, 'tis a terrible monstér
Whose snaky arms they be.

The fish from out the oily waves
Heaved forth his vast bodie,
And seized the hapless carpenters
To pull them to the sea.

Come save us, save us, shipmates all,
Save us from this monstér
That hath seizèd us with his white, white arms,
An inch we may not stir.

'Tis they have ta'en their trusty swords
And fought right valiantlie,
The creature twined about the mast,
Most terrible to see.

The mariners 'gan smite and hack
  To save the carpenters,
And swore their blows they'd not abate
  For seven such monstérs.

They hacked away the slimy flesh
  And gared the monster flee,
Who took with him the carpenters
  To perish in the sea.

He sank beneath the yeasty waves,
  But erst a mariner
Had gougèd out with a bony thumb
  An eye of the monstér.

A wind arose, and back we sailed
  To France right merrilie,
And thanked the Saints we fed no fish
  At bottom of the sea.

THE FUTURE

Shepherd. 'Little Lamb of the Spring, in your pale-hued mountainy meadow,
By the rough wall bramble-bound mortarless couched in the shadow,
Lamb of the white hyacinthine fleece, give your heart to this saying:
Life for a lamb is a Year with his seasons. The Spring is for playing,
Summer for love, and the Colds for decaying.

'You will grow ere long, my delicate dainty creature –'
Lamb. 'As your Southdown Beast, not a sheep, but an insult to nature,
Loving the plains, large-trunked, foul, smutty-faced? I such another?'
Shepherd. 'No, little friend, but a ewe, slim, gentle and fair as your mother.'
Lamb. 'That would be good, to become like my mother.'

Shepherd. 'And the little white ram that is butting his fellow out yonder
Will be lover and lord in the Summer: beside him you'll wander
Out o'er the open summer-clad hills through harebell and heather . . . .
I will recall this day: I will laugh to behold you together.'
Lamb. 'Love? What is Love, thus to keep us together?'

ALCAICS ADDRESSED TO MY STUDY FAUNA

Mine eye commends thee, Japanese elephant,
Bright body, proud trunk, wrought by a silver-smith:
Thee too, O swart-cheeked elfin rider,
Bought for a couple of Greek Iambics.

Fair wooden doe-deer, chiselled in Switzerland,
Why starest sad-eyed down from my cup-board top?
'Once, lord, a stag ten-tyned, tremendous
Shielded my side – now the dust-cart holds him!'

Green china kit-cat, hailing from Chester-town,
Sweet mouthed thou smilest after the Cheshire way,
Plumb o'er my gas-globe poised. I shudder
Reckoning out what thy fall would cost me.

I boast a three-legged dusty old desert-ship,
Red terra-cotta, native Egyptian;
Unlike the real true living camel,
Never he bites at the hand that bred him.

Next Summer Quarter sorrowing Charterhouse
Knows me no longer. Then sell I all my goods,
And Noah's ark long years in Studies
Slowly will circulate till decay comes.

THE CYCLONE

On Friday night the wind came, fumbling at my window,
Like a baby tapping, shaking, rapping, drumming
With tiny white fingers, delicate and strengthless;
Striving to gain entrance at key-hole and chimney,
All intent to learn what was harboured within.
Little I expected, awaking on Saturday,
To find the babe already weaned, already
Grown to a boy-hood curious, sturdy-limbed.
Grown pagan-hearted, wild, unconscionable,
Tumbling down the poplar, huge limbs tearing
From age-honoured elm-tree, slates from every house-top
Boy-like, in wantonness and fury overthrowing
Now the rich-man's villa, now the huts of the poor.
And ere he abated his frenzy equinoctial,
Thronged were the city-streets, thronged the country-lanes,
With maimed men, with women shrieking above the blast.

THE APE GOD

Her young one dead, some mother of the grey
   Wise apes that haunt the jungle-swallowed fane,
Had stolen from his ayah's arms away
   A rescued man-child of the English slain.
Myself once spied the tiny midget-shape
   'Mid glossy leaves of a scarlet-berried tree
Far out of man's reach, clinging like an ape,
   Grave-eyed, stark naked, dangling dizzily.
He has grown to youth and taught the ape-men fear;
   Provoked, he stares their eyes to bestial fright:
Climbs to sick heights where never man clomb near
   And leaps amazing leaps from height to height.
A vision strange! Amid his temple towers,
The wild free ape-god, crowned with crimson flowers!

LAMENT IN DECEMBER

December's come and all is dead:
Weep, woods, for Summer far has sped,
And leaves rot in the valley-bed.

Grey-blue and gaunt the oak-boughs spread
Mourn through a mist their leafage shed.
December, season of the dead!

Brown-golden, scarlet, orange-red,
Autumn's bright hues, are faded, fled.
December, season of the dead!

The goblins Fog and Dulness, wed
Breed ugly children in my head
And thought lags by with feet of lead.
December, season of the dead!

MERLIN AND THE CHILD

(Adapted from an early Cornish poem)

Merlin went up the mountain side.
A young boy stood above him and cried:
'Merlin, Merlin, where are you bound
Early, so early, with your black hound?
Your rod of hazel, well shaped and thin,
Do magic powers lie closed within?'

Merlin put two hands to his head,
Hiding his eyes in a terror, said:
'Lamb of thunder, avenging dove,
Dealer of wrath, High-king of love,
To search the way and the ways I am come
For a round red egg to carry home,
Blood-red egg of an ocean snake
From the hollowed stone where bright waves break,
To search if ever the valleys hold
Green watercress, or grass of gold,
By a woodland fountain-side to lop
The highest cluster from oak-tree top.
My hazel twig is a magic wand –
Magic of earth, and a power beyond.'

Close to Merlin the young boy stood,
Stretched his hand to the slender wood:
'Merlin, Merlin, turn now again!
Unharmed let the cluster of oak remain,
The cress in the valley where fresh brooks run,
The gold grass dancing below the sun,
And the smooth egg of your ocean snake
In the hollow where dappled waters shake.
Turn again in the steps you have trod:
There is no diviner, but only God!'

A DAY IN FEBRUARY

This foul February day
Dims all colour with dead grey.
Save where stumps of the sawn willow
Mark with shields of orange-yellow
The brown windings of the Wey,
This foul February day
Like a painter lean and sallow,
Dims all colour with dead grey.

THE WASP

I arose at dawn with this end in mind
To display in the wide world everywhere
The sable and gold that alternate
My corselet of proof to beautify.
In a cluster of scented meadow-sweet,
Off right good nectar breakfasting
And too well drunk to be quarrelsome,
I heard the booming buzz of bees,
Big black boisterous bumble-bees,
'Ziz iz zo zweet' from the fuchsias.
Each filled to bursting his honey-bag,
An appendage I've never been troubled with,
Bore it away, up-ended it
And sailed again through the morning air
On a bee-line back to the fuchsias.
As I marvelled to view their industry,
One travelled past me, homeward bound,
Humming 'Ziz iz ze zirty zird
Ztuffed zack of zweet ambrozia!'
Which seemed to me far from credible
And would have provoked my waspishness,
But I dared not give him the lie direct
And name him a nectar-bibbing drone,
For a bee has the pride of a gentleman,
The honour and pride of a gentleman,
And I never did hold with duelling,
And a bumble-bee stings outrageous.

FIVE RHYMES

MY HAZEL-TWIG

My hazel-twig is frail and thin
Yet mighty magic dwells therein,
Black magic, potent in the night,
The master-sorcerer's delight;
Whenas my rival witch appears
This wand will grow him asses' ears;
My hazel-twig is frail and thin
Yet mighty magic dwells therein.

AFTER THE RAIN

Now Earth has drunk her fill of rain
The thirsty common lives again,
And raindrops quivering argentine
'Mid new-born needles of the pine,
As through and through a fresh wind soughs,
Drop shining down to nether boughs.
Now Earth has drunk her fill of rain
The thirsty common lives again.

ENVY

'Envy' I'm loth to call the blight
That cankers all my day and night,
Yet when I see a villain shine
In glory that is rightly mine,
And when he says his taunting say
To me, his better, Envy – nay!
'Envy' I'm loth to call the blight
That cankers all my day and night.

THE KING'S HIGHWAY

The King's Highway is all too wide:
For me, the narrow street and dark,
Where houses lean from either side,
Where robbers lurk at eventide;
There let me wander unespied,
To plot and counter-plotting hark –
The King's Highway is all too wide:
For me, the narrow street and dark.

THE GLORIOUS HARSHNESS OF THE PARROT'S VOICE

Hateful are studied harmonies
Where shrills the parrot as he flies
And cranes his painted neck. 'Oho!
Through towering Jungletown I go!
With green and gold my plumage gleams,
The World is nought to me,' he screams –
Hateful are studied harmonies
Where shrills the parrot as he flies.

TWO MOODS

Of old this universe was born
From sorrow travailing forlorn.
Its highest joys serve but as foil
To toil and pain, to pain and toil;
The serpent chokes us, coil o'er coil;
Blind Cupid heaps our head with scorn.
Of old this universe was born
From sorrow travailing forlorn.

The peach-tree blossoms out
Confirming Winter's rout
And everywhere
One song is heard from amorous bird
'My love is fair!'

To me a wondrous thing,
The thrushes brown yet sing
The notes they sung
From laced treetops of a birchen copse
When I was young.

We had forgotten this
That Life may all be bliss
Devoid of pain.
Which lesson then, my fellow-men,
Come, learn again!

THE BRIAR BURNERS

The round breasted hill above
  Glows like a lamp-lit dome,
As hither with the seeds of fire
  The briar burners come.

Youths with torches flaring yellow
  Kindle the thickets dry,
The flames waxing clearer, clearer,
  Nearer, yet more nigh.

A pillar of illumined smoke
  Wavering skyward, marks
The silvered purple of the night
  With starbright fire-red sparks.

The oak leaves that but yesterday
  Thrust from their pregnant spike
Quiver in the fire-flare cruel,
  Transparent jewel-like.

Exultant silhouetted dark
  Against the golden glow
From brake to brake with brands a-fire
  The briar burners go.

THE TYRANNY OF BOOKS

Spring passes, summer's young,
Yet mute has been my tongue.
This is the seventh week
I have not sung.
And now I hear the verdant hillside speak
Chiding me for this wrong
That I have celebrated not in song
The new-come colour on her faded cheek,
The sap that inly swells,
The rooks, the lush bluebells,
The meadow-grasses shooting strong.
Spring airs are pleasant and the day is long;
The year is young,
And yet have I not sung.
For by my elbow lies a pile
Of books, of stern insistent books,
Big, broad, stout books
Crammed full of knowledge. Though it looks
As if I'd finish in a little while,
Still grows the pile.
The more I read the more they breed:
Books wed to books
Bear bookish progeny that bids me heed,

Denies my pen over the page to speed.
Outside, the rooks
Circle in air and mate and feed,
But I must read and read.
Can I afford to find my books
Only in running brooks?

THE EXHAUST-PIPE

The selfish poet, falling sick
Heals his disorder double quick
By taking pen in hand and cursing
His birth, conception, breeding, nursing,
His education, the fell strife
Between his nature and his life,
His love affairs, religion, health,
His art, his friendship-commonwealth,
Till those who read the verses groan
To think his case most like their own,
To find their own life pain and sorrow,
To see no hopes for their to-morrow,
And weep – but he who caused their grief,
Has found expression and relief.
If I indulged my naughtiest mood
And fostered melancholy's brood
Of wingèd spites, and sat me down
With clattered pen and furious frown
And forelock round my fingers curled,
Resolved to satirize the world,
Then after meditation long
My fevered brain would cram my wrong
Into a tiny verse so hot,
So full, so poison-tipped, 'twould rot
Man's faith in living and provide
Excuse for general suicide.
But do I frame this pregnant plaint?
No, I do *not*, sir!
['What restraint!']

THE ORGAN GRINDER

Come along, gents: I'll play you a tune
That you won't 'ear twice in a blamed blue moon.
An' I bet that I'll simply give you fits
With me um-tum-tiddely twiddly bits.
I played this 'ere tune to a welchin' tout
An' a Baptist minister solemn an' swell:
One stood an' 'e laughed till 'is teeth shook out
An' 'tother one sang till 'e rang like a bell.
I played this 'ere tune to a jolly ole toff,
'Oo laughed an' quivered, and tears 'e shed
An' a smile went runnin' all round 'is 'ead
An' the upper 'alf of 'is face fell off . . . .
'Ey diddle diddle, the cat an' the fiddle!
I'll make you all giggle an' wriggle an' squiggle
An' stamp with your feet an' collapse in the middle!
Jingle jangle, 'ey diddle diddle!
You're 'oppin' about like peas on the griddle!
Tow row, rackety jangle – whirr!
That's the end of it.
Thank you, sir!

1918–1927

THE TWO BROTHERS

(An Allegory)

Once two brothers, Joe and Will,
   Parted each to choose his home,
Joe on top of Windy Hill
   Where the storm clouds go and come
All day long, but Will the other
   In the plain would snugly rest
Low and safe yet near his brother:
   Low and safe he made his nest
At the foot of Windy Hill,
Built a clattering Watermill.

In the winter Joe would freeze,
   Will lay warm in his snug mill;
Through the summer Joe's cool breeze
   Filled with envy burning Will.
Yet to take all times together
   Both were portioned their fair due,
Joe enjoyed the fine warm weather,
   Will could smile in winter too;
Neither troubled nor complained,
Each in his own home remained.

These two brothers at first sight
   Made a pair of Heavenly Twins,
Two green peas, two birds in flight,
   Two fresh daisies, two new pins:
Yet the second time you'd seen 'em,
   Seen 'em close and watched 'em well,
You would find there lay between 'em
   All the span of Heaven and Hell,
Spring and Autumn, East and West,
And I know whom I liked best.

Listen: once when lofty Joe
  Climbing down to view the mill,
Wept to find Will lived so low
  Would not stop to dine with Will,
Will climbed back through the cloudy smother
  Laughed to feel he stood so high,
Tossed his hat up, kissed his brother,
  Drank old ale, ate crusty pie . . .
Will had no high soul, but oh
Give us Will, we all hate Joe!

PEACE

When that glad day shall break to match
'Before-the-War' with 'Since-the-Peace',
And up I climb to twist new thatch
Across my cottage roof, while geese
Stand stiffly there below and vex
The yard with hissing from long necks,
In that immense release,
That shining day, shall we hear said:
'New wars to-morrow, more men dead'?

When peace time comes and horror's over,
Despair and darkness like a dream,
When fields are ripe with corn and clover,
The cool white dairy full of cream,
Shall we work happily in the sun,
And think 'It's over now and done',
Or suddenly shall we seem
To watch a second bristling shadow
Of armed men move across the meadow?

Will it be over once for all,
With no more killed and no more maimed;
Shall we be safe from terror's thrall,
The eagle caged, the lion tamed;
Or will the young of that vile brood,
The young ones also, suck up blood
Unconquered, unashamed,
Rising again with lust and thirst?
Better we all had died at first,
Better that killed before our prime
    We rotted deep in earthy slime.

BAZENTIN, 1916

(A Reminiscence – Robert and David)

R. That was a curious night, two years ago,
Relieving those tired Dockers at Bazentin.
Remember climbing up between the ruins?
The guide that lost his head when the gas-shells came,
Lurching about this way and that, half-witted,
Till we were forced to find the way ourselves?

D. Yes, twilight torn with flashes, faces muffled,
In stinking masks, and eyes all sore and crying
With lachrymatory stuff, and four men gassed.

R. Yet we got up there safely, found the trenches
Untraversed shallow ditches, along a road
With dead men sprawled about, some ours, some theirs –

D. Ours mostly, and those Dockers doing nothing,
Tired out, poor devils; much too tired to dig,
Or to do anything but just hold the ground:
No touch on either flank, no touch in front,
Everything in the air. I cursed, I tell you.
Out went the Dockers, quick as we filed in,
And soon we'd settled down and put things straight,
Posted the guns, dug in, got out patrols,
And sent to right and left to restore touch.

R. There was a sunken road out on the right,
With rifle-pits half dug; at every pit
A dead man had his head thrust in for shelter.

D. Dawn found us happy enough; a funny day –
The strangest I remember in all those weeks.
German five-nines were bracketting down our trenches
Morning and afternoon.

R. Why, yes; at dinner,
Three times my cup was shaken out of my hand
And filled with dirt: I had to pour out fresh.

D. That was the mug you took from the Boche gun.
Remember that field gun, with the team killed
By a lucky shot just as the German gunners
Were limbering up? We found the gunner's treasures
In a box behind, his lump of fine white chalk
Carefully carved, and painted with a message
Of love to his dear wife, and Allied flags,
A list of German victories, and an eagle.
Then his clean washing, and his souvenirs –
British shell-heads, French bullets, lumps of shrapnel,
Nothing much more. I never thought it lucky
To take that sort of stuff.

R. Then a tame magpie –
German, we guessed – came hopping into the trench,
Picking up scraps of food. That's 'One for sorrow'
I said to little Owen.

D. Not much mistaken
In the event, when only three days later
They threw us at High Wood and (mind, we got there!)
Smashed up the best battalion in the whole corps.
But, Robert, quite the queerest thing that day
Happened in the late afternoon. Worn out,
I snatched two hours of sleep; the Boche bombardment
Roared on, but I commended my soul to God,
And slept half through it; but as I lay there snoring
A mouse, in terror of all these wild alarms,
Crept down my neck for shelter, and woke me up

In a great sweat. Blindly I gave one punch
And slew the rascal at the small of my back.
That was a strange day!

R. Yes, and a merry one.

THE DANCING GREEN

Girl. What's that you're humming, gammer?
Grandmother. A silly old song,
They used to dance jigs to it in old Happy England
When *my* grandmother was young.

Girl. Where did they dance it, gammer?
Grandmother. Here where we stand,
Kicking up their heels on the green daisy carpet,
Girls and boys, hand in hand.

A blind man would make gay music
Perched on a cask,
And bent old folk brought currant-cake and cider
Dancers never had to ask.

Girl. Why did the jig end, gammer?
None dance it now.
Grandmother. Ninety years ago it was sent out of fashion:
Dance? we have forgotten how.

Girl. Who was the spoilsport, gammer?
Who stopped our play?
Grandmother. The lawyers and the Mills and the base new gentry,
They stole our laughter away.

THE PERSONAL TOUCH

Cunning indeed Tom Fool must be to-day
For us, who meet his verses in a book,
To cry 'Tom Fool wrote that . . . I know his way. . . .
. . . Unsigned, yet eyed all over with Tom's look. . . .
Why see! It's pure Tom Fool, I'm not mistook. . . .
Fine simple verses too; now who's to say
How Tom has charmed these worn old words to obey
His shepherd's voice and march beneath his crook?'
Instead we ponder 'I can't name the man,
But he's been reading Wilde', or 'That's the school
Of Coterie . . . Voices . . . Pound . . . the Sitwell clan . . . '
'*He* "knows his Kipling"' . . . '*he* accepts the rule
Of Monro . . . of Lord Tennyson . . . of Queen Anne . . . ';
How seldom, 'There, for a ducat, writes
TOM FOOL.'

SONG: THE RING AND CHAIN

Janet. *'Where are those treasures that you promised me*
If I should fetch and carry and bake your bread?
Two years beyond my time I have laboured free
And two on seven have worn me to a thread!'

Witch. *'Ay, these nine winters you have lived by me,*
No idler servant in the world than you:
Two more again from now you must labour free
And time shall bring reward if you serve me true.'

Janet. *'Where are those trinkets that you tokened me,*
The chain and ring if I should be your slave?
Four years beyond my time I have laboured free
And four on seven have brought me nigh the grave.'

Witch. *'Ay, four on seven you have lived here by me,*
But idler serving girl has never been mine;
Your ring and chain lie deep below the sea,
Where you may fish them up with hook and line.'

She was young and had a heart like steel,
And scarcely had she set her feet on sand,
When up a herring swam and a crownèd eel
And gave the jewels safe into her hand.

Janet has won the charm that makes unseen,
Janet has won a great gold wishing ring.
This child of beauty shall be England's queen,
And John the smith, her true-heart, shall be king.

THE OXFORD ENGLISH SCHOOL

1920

She's in the second row, see? No, not that one!
The girl in the green jersey, the pale fat one,
Taking few notes, sitting beatified,
Plump fingers locked, a large mouth open wide,
Eyes staring down. . . . Of course Professor Steel
Isn't a dried old haddock like Macneil,
The Chair of Anglo-Saxon, who'll admit
His period has no interest, not a bit,
Except to students ardent in research
For early records of our Laws or Church.
'Literature? No, nothing of the kind!
Still, Glosses need re-glossing you may find.' . . .
But Steel (Parks Road Museum at midday,
Tuesdays and Fridays) points a happier way.
(Ascetic chin, smooth hair, persuasive gesture,
Smile, gentle Oxford voice setting at rest your
Rebel's mistrust of mortar-board and gown.)
He quotes, smiles, pauses. Itching pens rush down
Chapter and verse; for we sit tier on tier,
A girl from Roedean there, a Serbian here,
Two Reds from Ruskin next the Meat-King's daughter,
A one-armed Brigadier returned from slaughter,
A young Babu, the Nun from Foxcombe way,
All in a row we crouch, scribbling away.
But She sits still, her notebook shut, her pen
Idling. Steel treats of Beowulf's death, and then
Wrings a deep sigh from her, almost a tear,

With 'That old tale, the Snows of Yester-year.'
. . . What was the joke? I missed it, but they laughed;
A map of Syria shuddered with the draught.
She dimpled up, she laughed, she's grave again.
The stops are changed, now a cathedral strain
Peals out: –
'This Norman influence brought in
Fresh themes of Poetry and we first begin
To meet a new word, sweetened by new rhyme,
The great word, Love.'
I looked away this time,
Green Jersey; after all what right had I
To twitch aside the curtains, to play spy?
Still I could feel the sudden burst of red
Drench your pale face when glancing up, he said
Quoting most reverently: 'A crowned "A"
And after, AMOR VINCIT OMNIA.'

THE STEPMOTHER AND THE PRINCESS

Through fogs and magic spells
All day I've guided you,
Through loud alarms and yells,
Through scent of wizard stew,
Through midday pools of dew,

Through crowds that moan and mock,
Ogres at human feast,
Blood-streams and battleshock,
Past phantom bird and beast,
Monsters of West and East.

But this calm wood is hedged
With the *set shape* of things;
Here is no phoenix fledged,
No gryphon flaps his wings,
No dragons wave their stings.

Nothing is here that harms,
  No toothed or spiny grass,
No tree whose clutching arms
  Drink blood when travellers pass,
  No poison-breathed Upas.

Instead the lawns are soft,
  The tree-stems grave and old:
Slow branches sway aloft,
  The evening air comes cold,
  The sunset scatters gold.

Nay, there's no hidden lair
  For tigers or for apes,
No dread of wolf or bear,
  No ghouls, no goblin shapes,
  No witches clad in capes.

My cloak, my ermine cloak,
  Shall keep you warm and dry;
Branches of elm I've broke
  To roof you as you lie
  Below the winking sky.

Sleep now and think no ill,
  No evil soul comes near.
The dreamy woods are still,
  Sigh, sleep, forget your fear,
  Sleep soundly, sleep, my dear.

CYNICS AND ROMANTICS

In club and messroom let them sit
At skirmish of ingenious wit;
Deriding Love, yet not with hearts
Accorded to those healthier parts
Of grim self-mockery, but with mean
And burrowing search for things unclean,
Pretended deafness, twisted sense,
Sharp innuendoes rising thence,
And affectation of prude-shame
That shrinks from using the short name.

We are not envious of their sour
Disintegrations of Love's power,
Their swift analysis of the stabs
Devised by virgins and by drabs
(Powder or lace or scent) to excite
A none-too-jaded appetite.
They never guess of Love as we
Have found the amazing Art to be,
Pursuit of dazzling flame, or flight
From web-hung blacknesses of night,
With laughter only to express
Care overborne by carelessness;
They never bridge from small to great,
From nod or glance to ideal Fate,
From clouded forehead or slow sigh
To doubt and agony looming by,
From shining gaze and hair flung free
To infinity and to eternity –
They sneer and poke a treacherous joke
With scorn for our rusticity.

RECORDS FOR WONDER

Once there came a mighty, furious wind
        (So old worthies tell).
It blew the oaks like nine-pins down,
And all the chimney-stacks in town
        Down together fell.
That was a wind – to write a record on,
                        to hang a story on,
                        to sing a ballad on,
        To ring the loud church bell!
But for one huge storm that cracks the sky
Come a thousand lesser winds rustling by,
And the only wind that will make me sing
Is breeze of summer or gust of spring,
But no more hurtful thing.

Once there came a mighty, thirsty drought
(So old worthies tell).
The quags were drained, the brooks were dried,
Cattle and sheep and pigs all died,
The Parson preached on Hell.
That was a drought – to write a record on,
to hang a story on,
to sing a ballad on,
To ring the loud church bell!
But for one long drought of world-wide note
Come a thousand lesser ones on man's throat,
And the only drought for my singing mood
Is a thirst for the very best ale that's brewed,
Soon quenched, but soon renewed.

Once there came a mighty, biting frost
(So old worthies tell).
It bound the never yet conquered lake
With ice that crow-bar scarce could break,
It froze the deep draw-well.
That was a frost – to write a record on,
to hang a story on,
to sing a ballad on,
To ring the loud church bell!
But for one black frost of strange alarm
Why, a thousand lesser ones bring no harm,
And the only frost that suits my strain
Is hoar-frost pattern on a latticed pane,
When Christmas comes again.

Once my sweetheart spoke an unkind word,
As I myself must tell,
For none but I have seen or heard
My sweetheart to such cruelty stirred
For one who loves her well.
That was a word – to write no record on,
to hang no story on,
to sing no ballad on,
To ring no loud church bell!
Yet for one fierce word that has made me smart
Ten thousand gentle ones ease my heart,
So all the song that springs in me
Is 'Never a sweetheart born could be
So kind as only she!'

OLD LOB-LIE-BY-THE-FIRE

Henceforth old Lob shall sweat for no man's hire
On winter nights knee-deep in snow or mire,
Split no hard logs, nor shoulder no huge burden,
Since he has seen his nightly favours harden
To obligation, his cream-brimming vat
Thin to mere whey, scarce quarter filled at that.
From god to blackleg labourer being sunk,
Instead of reverent dues, old Lob has drunk
Sour grudging minimum-wage, working so hard,
And farmer's wife keeps her warm kitchen barred;
Then weary Lob, his job complete, may stand
In the muckyard.
                                Oh, goodbye to this changed land!
To Canada or New Zealand or the Cape
He works his passage easily in the shape
Of a Dago stoker, or perhaps he hides
His matted shapelessness in a bale of hides.
Once over, he hopes cream and by some fire
To doze, yet shall he sweat for no man's hire,
Nor for ingratitude chore now never more.

MISGIVINGS, ON READING A POPULAR 'OUTLINE OF SCIENCE'

When man forswears *God* and dispels *taboo*
        Serving a butterfly expediency
        In ultimate anarchy,
Mating and murdering too
Regardless of who's who,
Only intent on doing what's to do –
        Will no one urge the sentimental plea
        For wise old savages like you and me,
His unsophisticated
Forbears of time undated?

THE TOADS

Do you wear away time
Over ballad and rhyme
Ecstatic in attic or basement,
Your difficult labours
The scorn of *Toad* neighbours
Who wink at your inky effacement?

O do you set Art
As a kingdom apart
Do you choose the sad Muses to bed with?
Then you shall have praise
At the close of your days
With bays to bedizen your head with.

But a *Toad* is a *Toad*
With so poisoned a mode
Of address that few dare to declare it.
He is crass, he is cruel,
He wears no hid jewel,
Despite worthy writers who swear it.

Your dearly bought fame
Will be dulled by the shame
Toads award any bard they call Master.
None such can go crowned
Or in purple robes gowned
But they spurt at him dirt and disaster.

For whatever your care
Or your secret despair
With scandal their hand'll unearth it.
Unlocking the locks
Of your intimate box
(Cry, pox on 'em! Is the praise worth it?)

They will prove that your brain
Never pleaded in vain
For cocaine-coloured dreams that enriched you,
That your wife was untrue
And your daughter a shrew
That a Jew and a Jesuit witched you.

They will show you complete
Lecher, liar and cheat,
A Job for ignoble diseases,
Ungentle, unwitty,
A sot without pity
Who preys and betrays as he pleases.

They will keep a sharp eye
On *Remains* when you die,
They will buy them for bagsfull of dollars.
Stray scraps that they find
Of old filth unrefined
They will bind up in books for the scholars.

They will oddly misquote
Whatsoever you wrote,
With a note on your 'exquisite manner':
And schoolmaster *Toads*
Will parade the long roads
With Centenary Odes and a banner.

And your unquiet ghost
Shall repent himself most
Of your boast for the bays and the laurels,
When Rose, Lily, Pink,
That in garlands you link
Shall stink of the *Toads* and their quarrels.

A HISTORY

The Palmist said: 'In your left hand, which shews your inheritance, the Line of Head dips steeply towards Luna. In your right hand, which shews your development, there is a determined effort to escape into less melancholy thinking.' I said nothing, but shewed him this sonnet: –

When in my first and loneliest love I saw
The sun swim down in tears to meet the sea,
When woods and clouds and mountains massed their awe
To whelm the house of torment that was me,
When spirits below the cromlech heard me pass,
Belling their hate with such malignant cries
That horror and anguish rustled through the grass
And the very flowers glared up with oafish eyes,

Then round I turned where rose the death-white Fay
And knew her well that exercised her wand,
That spurred my heart with rowellings day by day
To the very reach of madness, and beyond,
Thee, Moon, whom now I flout, by thought made bold,
Naked, my Joseph's garment in thy hold.

FOUR CHILDREN

As I lay quietly in the grass,
Half dreaming, half awake,
I saw four children barefoot pass
Across the tufted brake:
The sky was glass, the pools were glass,
And not a leaf did shake.

The autumn berries clustered thick,
Seldom I met with more;
I thought these children come to pick,
As many picked before;
Each had a long and crooked stick,
And crowns of ash they wore.

But not one berry did they take;
Gliding, I watched them go
Hand in hand across the brake
With sallies to and fro.
So half asleep and half awake
I guessed what now I know.

They were not children, live and rough,
  Nor phantoms of the dead,
But spirits woven of airy stuff
  By wandering fancy led,
Creatures of silence, fair enough
  No sooner seen than sped.

THE BARGAIN

The stable door was open wide:
I heard voices, looked inside.
Six candle-yellow birds were set
In a cage of silver net,
Shaking wing, preening feather,
Whistling loudly all together.
Two most ancient withered fairies
Bartered rings against canaries,
Haggled with a courteous cunning –
Hinting, boasting, teasing, punning
In a half-remembered tongue.
'Too low an offer!' 'Times are bad.'
'Too low!' 'By far the best you have had.'
'Raise it!' Then what a song was sung:
'Dicky is a pretty lad!
Dicky is a pretty lad!'
But diamonds twinkled with light flung
By twelve impatient golden wings,
The younger merchant took the rings,
Closed his bargain with a sigh,
And sadly wished his flock 'Goodbye.'
Goodbye, goodbye, in fairy speech
With a sugar-peck for each
Unsuspecting bright canary.
'Fare you well.'
                A sudden airy
Gust of midnight slammed the door.
Out went the lights: I heard no more.

IN THE BEGINNING WAS A WORD

The difficulty was, it was
Simple, as simple as it seemed;
Needing no scrutinizing glass,
No intense light to be streamed

Upon it. It said what it said
Singly, without backthought or whim,
With all the strictness of the dead,
Past reason and past synonym.

But they, too dull to understand,
Laboriously improvised
A mystic allegory, and
A meaning at last recognized:

A revelation and a cause,
Crowding the cluttered stage again
With saints' and sinners' lies and laws
For a new everlasting reign.

THE BAIT

My wish, even my ambition
(For such ambition spells no diminution
Of virtue, strict in self-possession),
Is not, to deaden the mind
To be resigned
To take the insistent bait
To be hauled out, hooked and hulking;
Is not, to refuse the bait,
To be angry, to go hungry,
To lodge in the mud, to be sulking:
It is, I would surge toward these troubles
Trailing a row of easy bubbles;
Would gulp the bait, the hook, rod, reel,
Fisherman and creel,
Converting even the landing-net's tough mesh,
The spaced and regular knots, to wholesome flesh;
And would subside again, resume my occupation,

With 'yes and no' for what showed blank negation:
So, would remain just fish.
That, or something of that, is my wish.

AN INDEPENDENT

The warring styles both claim him as their man
  But undisturbed, resisting either pull
He paints each picture on its own right plan
  As unexpected as inevitable.

They while admitting that this treatment is
  Its own justification, take offence
At his unmodish daily practices:
  Granting him genius, they deny him sense.

He grinds his paints in his own studio,
  Has four legitimate children (odd!) and thinks
Of little else; he dresses like a crow,
  Keeps with his wife and neither smokes nor drinks.

When painting is discussed, he takes no part,
  Pretends he's dull; and who can call his bluff?
The styles protest, while honouring his art,
  He will not take Art seriously enough.

[THE UNTIDY MAN]

There was a man, a very untidy man,
  Whose fingers could nowhere be found to put in his tomb.
He had rolled his head far underneath the bed:
  He had left his legs and arms lying all over the room.

1934–1939

MIDSUMMER DUET†

First Voice

O think what joy that now
Have burst the pent grenades of summer
And out sprung all the angry hordes
To be but stuttering storm of bees
On lisping swoon of flowers –
That such winged agitation
From midge to nightingale astir
These lesser plagues of sting and song
But looses on the world, our world.

O think what peace that now
Our roads from house to sea go strewn
With fast fatigue – time's burning footsounds,
Devilish in our winter ears,
Cooled to a timeless standstill
As ourselves from house to sea we move
Unmoving, on dumb shores to pledge
New disbelief in ills to come
More monstrous than the old extremes.

Second Voice

And what regret that now
The dog-star has accomplished wholly
That promise April hinted with
Faint blossom on her hungry branches,
And pallid hedgerow shoots?
Exuberance so luscious
Of fruit and sappy briar
Disgusts: midsummer's passion chokes
'No more!' – a trencher heaped too high.

† The First Voice is Laura Riding.

And O what dearth that now
We have sufficient dwelling here
Immune to hopes gigantical
That once found lodgement in our heart.
What if less shrewd we were
And the Dog's mad tooth evaded not –
But quick, the sweet froth on our lips,
Reached at fulfilments whose remove
Gave muscle to our faith at least?

First Voice

Let prophecy now cease
In that from mothering omens came
Neither the early dragon nor the late
To startle sleeping errantries
Or blaze unthinkable futures.
The births have not been strange enough;
Half-pestilential miseries
At ripeness failed of horrid splendour.
Our doomsday is a rabbit-age
Lost in the sleeve of expectation.

Let winter be less sharp
In that the heats of purpose
Have winter foreflight in their wings,
Shaking a frostiness of thought
Over those aestive fancies
Which now so inwardly belie
(Their fury tepid to our minds)
The outward boast of season –
We need not press the cold this year
Since warmth has grown so honest.

Second Voice

Let talk of wonders cease
Now that outlandish realms can hold
No prodigies so marvellous as once
The ten-years-lost adventurer
Would stretch our usual gaze with.
The golden apple's rind offends
Our parks, and dew-lapped mountaineers
Unbull themselves by common physic.
There comes no news can take us from
Loyalty to this latter sameness.

Let the bold calendar
Too garrulous in counting
Fortunes of solar accident
Weary, and festive pipes be soft.
Madness rings not so far now
Around the trysting-oak of time;
Midsummer's gentler by the touch
Of other tragic pleasures.
We need not write so large this year
The dances or the dirges.

First Voice

But what, my friend, of love –
If limbs revive to overtake
The backward miles that memory
Tracks in corporeal chaos?
Shall you against the lull of censoring mind
Not let the bones of nature run
On fleshlorn errands, journey-proud –
If ghosts go rattling after kisses,
Shall your firmed mouth not quiver with
Desires it once spoke beauty by?

And what of beauty, friend –
If eyes constrict to clear our world
Of doubt-flung sights and ether's phantom spaces
Cobwebbed where miserly conceit
Hoarded confusion like infinity?
If vision has horizon now,
Shall you not vex the tyrant eyes
To pity, pleading blindness?

Second Voice

But what, my friend, of death,
That has the dark sense and the bright,
Illumes the sombre hour of thought,
Fetches the flurry of bat-souls?
Shall you not at this shriven perfect watch
Survey my death-selves with a frown
And scold that I am not more calm?
Shall you not on our linking wisdoms
Loathe the swart shapes I living wear
In being dead, yet not a corpse?

And what of jest and play –
If caution against waggishness
(Lest I look backward) makes my mood too canting?
Shall you not mock my pious ways,
Finding in gloom no certain grace or troth,
And raise from moony regions of your smile
Light spirits, nimbler on the toe,
Which nothing are – I no one?

First Voice

Suppose the cock were not to crow
At whitening of night
To warn that once again
The spectrum of incongruence
Will reasonably unfold
From day's indulgent prism?

Second Voice

Suppose the owl were not to hoot
At deepening of sleep
To warn that once again
The gospel of oblivion
Will pompously be droned
From pulpit-tops of dream?

First Voice

And shall the world our world have end
In miracles of general palsy,
Abject apocalyptic trances
Wherein creature and element
Surrender being in a God-gasp?

Both Voices

Or shall the world our world renew
At worn midsummer's temporal ailing,
Marshal the season which senescence
Proclaimed winter but we now know
For the first nip of mind's hereafter?

MAJORCAN LETTER, 1935†

This year we are all back again in time -
For a year: excellent: in our zeal
We had abandoned, like new converts,
Certain practices which serve good sense
Under all cosmic flags. The later mind,
For instance, has a need of News as constant
As the earlier; strangers inhabit
Every liveable condition, and we cannot
Regulate our own affairs without at least
Such distancing (if not entire annulment)
Of theirs as with the reading of our papers
We had learnt to exert on foreign conduct.
A talent not to let lapse: the years
Increased the alien volume, few matters
Remained domestic. The need of privacy
Is as strong as ever, nor to be satisfied
Without a public universe to wall
The central reservations. Excellent then,
Those habits of concern with wars, politics,
Impromptu heroes, successes, tragedies,
All weather-mystic to the personal heart,
Substance of outer flush and evanescence;
Scientific rediscoveries of truths
Long known by natural names and numbers;
Theories of God, Finance, Verse and Diet
Called 'modern' because indeed many but now
First reflect on these primitive subjects,
As if wisdom had ceased to descend
And life were the amazed infant again.
It is well to look out from our discreet windows
With a still curious eye. It is well
To look upon the stale wonders and tumults
And, knowing the recent for ancient,
Remember how we are surrounded ever
As yesterday and once by the remote
Great populations of infinity;
And to keep advised how small-immediate
The space of final conference remains.

† With Laura Riding.

Communism is a mighty plan
For turning bread into a doctrine.
And each shall have as much doctrine
As bread: what could be simpler?
Religion was never so accurate.
But haven't they forgotten the wine?
Perhaps, after all, as they say,
Drinking is a lost art.
One still sees interesting recipes
For soups, but on the whole
The world is a drier place.
Ships do not merely no longer splash:
The very ocean has become
An abstraction whereon hotels
Convey the traveller to hotels
In the true spirit of competition,
Whose devices are more humane
Than Nature's, which after all
Is too literal-minded
For the comfortable accommodation
Of man's ubiquitous imagination.
In fact, water is an extinct element
Save for the quaint trickle in the taps
Wherewith they lay the ghosts
Of former hygienes, puny
To the present genii
Of vapours, creams and lotions.
Drinking is a lost art,
Baptism a lost rite,
Water a lost element.
Seaside balsam soothes away
The wetness sustained
In the exorcizing of wetness,
With the assistance of the sun.
And, the waves having by argument
Of logical progress from wet to dry
Undergone vigorous evaporation,
The world-at-large takes to the air-at-large,
In more generous fulfilment
Of the historic farewell
Governing the scattering of peoples
And senses: with a goodbye

More absolute than the mariner's
Salt tear and world-ho.
We are perfectly informed, you see,
In the character and manner
Of life as it is now lived
Around us and around us
And now and now and now
Along the ever-widening
Periphery of this modest
Memorial to coherence
Wherein ourselves have domicile.
(The three elements involved
In questions of this kind,
Our lawyer tells us,
Are Nationality, Residence
And Domicile. By Nationality
Is meant the political relationship
Existing between ourselves
And the sovereign states to which we owe –
But we, and our respective states,
Consider these formalities
Sacred to unpleasant incidents
Abroad, where our Consuls maintain us
In the liberty of feeling at home
Wherever the birth-days guaranteed
Mortal by our respective states
Find us in our post-national age.
Residence merely implies
The place we happen to dwell in
At a particular moment:
A word for the body absent
On the body's errands –
'A purely physical fact'
Our lawyer explicitly avows.
Each sleeps in many beds
During a lifetime of acquiring
Command over the limbs,
Till we are able, without regret,
To exact that permanence
Which our lawyer calls 'Domicil' –
He spells it without 'e', please note,
Terribly, insisting the spirit

Of the law before the letter.
'Domicil is a combination
Of facts and intention.'
We intend to remain thus
Resident in definite us
'For an indefinite time' –
Time, after the legal years
Have been passed, the numbers crossed out,
And no new counting can be done,
Becomes 'an indefinite time',
Which is to say we may safely
At any time go back, to consult
Our newspapers, lawyers or doctors,
Without being reported missing
From ourselves. Such is the credit
Of the extreme word 'Domicil'.)

And Anthony Eden is, we know,
A clever young man who, without
Other resources than tact and
A virile English education
And a flattering way of
Being at ease among the great
(So that the great exert themselves
To be greater, so that Anthony
May be still more at ease among them),
Has established the superior
Virtue of that which is charming.
In other times this would have caused
A complete paralysis of
Activity, not to mention wars,
All joining in the exaltation
Of the personal attractiveness
Of Anthony Eden. . . . Perhaps,
If he had been a woman . . . .
But the world has grown suspicious of
Solutions, everyone is anxious
For simple ways out of
Complicated situations
And simple ways back again:
Lest the trick of history-making
Be lost and life become the burden

Of those alive rather than, always,
The intact inheritance of
The unborn generation.
We know, you see, what is going on.
It is not as if we were living
On a desert island. When it is
A question of distance in time
Rather than in geography
It is easy to keep well-informed.
And there are no distances now
But in time, and time is a matter
Of print, we read neither by maps
Nor by dates; the works of T.S. Eliot
Are in no greater hurry to be read
Than the works of Homer –
It is this waiting-power, this
Going to sleep of the author
In the work, to be wakened after
An indefinite time, which makes
Literature the darling of
Leisure. 'Domicil' combines
The facts, intention, and leisure,
Homer is the God of leisure,
And T.S. Eliot its Christ.
One does not hesitate to mention
Homer heartily, he delights
In dozing off and hearing his name
Thunder, like a small boy letting
Sleep roll up the voice of breakfast.
But one is inclined to call softly on
T.S. Eliot, one is inclined, that is,
Not to wake him, to give him sleep
Of much soft calling; one feels
He would make breakfast a further
Occasion for martyrdom.
He is, you see, the Christ not risen
Of literature, leisure or domicil,
Whose glory is not to get up
Ever – thus the small boy becomes
The poet. We realize, you see,
The necessity of being
Back in time, at least for a year,

During which, of course, much may grow
Permanently unfit for interest;
Nevertheless, we mean not to lose
Interest. It is important
To cease looking, when one does,
Not merely because one is tired,
But because memory has succeeded
Observation by the ultimate
Yielding of contemporary
Life to the economic
Crisis: the expense of maintaining
A news-producing universe
For our benefit is gigantic,
Beyond the imagination
Of financiers, whose good-will depends
On the reasonable fantasticness
Of the investment. We do not,
Truly, require this lavish
Apparatus for impressing
On our minds what in any case
Our minds flash topically upon
The ever-paling screen of time:
It is a nice question whether
The whole dispatch of journalism
Is not, as far as we are concerned,
A work of supererogation.

Our regards to various people
Who may happen to read this verse,
(We dare not make it much better
For fear it may read much worse),

To the rich man in his castle
And the poor man at the Spike,
And the patriot Lady Houston
Whom personally we like,

And the new blue gentleman-bobby
With his microscopes and such,
A radio-set in his helmet,
And fluent in Czech and Dutch,

And fearless Admiral Philips –
  When the traffic light went red
He clapped his glass to his sightless eye
  And 'I can't see it,' he said,

And Number One Trunk-murderer
  And likewise Number Two,
And the fellow who left his legs behind
  In the train at Waterloo,

And the sixteen-year-old girl student
  Who wrote, with never a blot:
'The land of my birth is the best on Earth' –
  Which wasn't saying a lot,

And the hostesses of Mayfair
  Who do nothing out of season,
And the miners of the Rhondda
  Who are rebels within reason,

And men who fly to business,
  And women who fly to the Cape,
(But not that Viscount Castlerosse:
  We disapprove of his shape),

And the ex-ex-Rector of Stiffkey
  Who crouched in a barrel cozily,
And the ex-wild-life of Whipsnade
  And ex-Sir Oswald Mosley,

And almost-our-favourite author
  Who moderates loves and crimes
For *Shorter Notices: Fiction*
  In the supplement of the *Times*,

And W.H. Day-Spender,
  Who tries, and tries, and tries,
And the poet without initials –
  The Man with the Staring Eyes,

And the riveters of the Clyde
   And the coracle-men of Dee,
And the nightingale in the shady vale
   Who sings for the B.B.C. –

Now kindest regards to these
   And our love to all the rest,
And our homage to Mr. Baldwin
   (A Tory retort's the best),
And a warning frown to each little bird
   In somebody else's nest.

ASSUMPTION DAY

What was wrong with the day, doubtless,
Was less the unseasonable gusty weather
Than the bells ringing on a Monday morning
For a church-feast that nobody could welcome –
Not even the bell-ringers.

The pond had shrunk: its yellow lilies
Poked rubbery necks out of the water.
I paused and sat down crossly on a tussock,
My back turned on the idle water-beetles
That would not skim, but floated.

A wasp, a humble-bee, a blue-fly
Uncoöperatively at work together
Were sucking honey from the crowded blossom
Of a pale flower whose name someone once told me –
Someone to be mistrusted.

But, not far off, our little cow-herd
Made mud-cakes, with one eye on the cattle,
And marked each separate cake with his initials.
I was half-tempted by the child's example
To rescue my spoilt morning.

THE MOON ENDS IN NIGHTMARE

I had once boasted my acquaintance
With the Moon's phases: I had seen her, even,
Endure and emerge from full eclipse.
Yet as she stood in the West, that summer night,
The fireflies dipping insanely about me,
So that that the foggy air quivered and winked
And the sure eye was cheated,
In horror I cried aloud: for the same Moon
Whom I had held a living power, though changeless,
Split open in my sight, a bright egg shell,
And a double-headed Nothing grinned
All-wisely from the gap.

At this I found my earth no more substantial
Than the lower air, or the upper,
And ran to plunge in the cool flowing creek,
My eyes and ears pressed under water.
And did I drown, leaving my corpse in mud?
Yet still the thing was so.

I crept to where my window beckoned warm
Between the white oak and the tulip tree
And rapped – but was denied, as who returns
After a one-hour-seeming century
To a house not his own.

1952–1959

THE HOUSING PROJECT

Across the strand of no seaside
Will two waves similarly glide;
And always, from whatever strand,
The long horizon's drawn freehand.

Yet nature here must yield to art:
Look, these ten houses, kept apart
By the same exact interval,
Magnificently identical,
Whose ten same housewives, having now
Kissed ten same husbands on the brow
And sent them arm in arm away
To clock in, work, and draw their pay
At the same factory, which makes
Countless identical plum cakes,
Heave a light sigh in unison
And back to their same parlours run
With synchronized abandon, there
To put soap operas on the air.

ADVICE TO COLONEL VALENTINE

Romantic love, though honourably human,
Is comic in a girl or an old man,
Pathetic in a boy or an old woman.

'But counts as decent for how long?' Our nation
Allows a woman thirty years, tacks on
Ten more for men resolved on procreation.

Your decent years, alas, have lapsed? The comic
Come crowding, yet love gnaws you to the quick
As once when you were fifteen and pathetic?

What? Dye your hair, you ask? Dress natty,
Swing an aggressive cane, whistle and sigh?
No: that would be true comicality.

Honour your grey hairs, keep them out of fashion –
Even if a foolish girl, not yet full grown,
Confronts you with a scarcely decent passion.

HIPPOPOTAMUS'S ADDRESS TO THE FREUDIANS

(He quotes Plutarch's OF ISIS AND OSIRIS *32, pleading for the revision of the misnomer 'Oedipus Complex', which should be 'Hippopotamus Complex'. His own acts, unlike those of the Theban King Oedipus, were not committed in error, he asserts, but prompted by a genuine infantile libido.)*

Deep in Nile mire,
   Jam etiam:
'I slew my sire,
   I forced my dam.
Plutarch's *Of Isis*
Dwells on my vices,
   Shameless I am:
Free from repression
Or urge to confession,
   Freud's little lamb.
I slew my sire,
In frantic desire
   I forced my dam –
I and not Oedipus,'
Roars Hippopotamus,
'You have confounded us
   Jam etiam!'

TWIN TO TWIN

Come, ancient rival, royal weird,
Who each new May must grip my beard
Till circling time shall cease to be:
Ground your red lance and mourn with me,
Though it were briefly –

Mourn that our wild-flower-breasted Fate,
Who locked us in this pact of hate,
Cuckolds us both as here we stand
And with unmagic mars the strand
Of her own island.

Yet, once again, your heart being true,
Our interrupted strife renew:
Reach for my beard with heaving breast
To roar: 'You lie! She loved me best',
And fight your fiercest.

CONSIDINE

'Why', they demand, 'with so much yet unknown
Anticipate the final colophon
Where the book fails among appendices
And indices?

'To count the tale almost as good as done
Would be intimidation by the Sun,
That tap-house bully with his mounting score
Chalked on the door.

'Look at Sam Shepherd, ruinously white,
With marrow in his bones to leap all night!'
Yet Considine sits dead from the neck down,
With not a tooth lost and a beard still brown,
Curse of the town.

THE JUGGLER

(for Henry Ringling North)

Posturing one-legged on a slack wire,
He is no illusionist (nor I a liar)
When his free foot tosses in sequence up,
To be caught confidently by the joggled head,
Saucer, cup,
                        saucer, cup,
                                                saucer, cup,
                                                                        saucer, cup,
Each to fall fair and square on its mounting bed.
Wonder enough? Or not?
                                                Not:
                                                        for a teapot
Floats up to crown them; item, following soon,
Supererogatory lump-sugar, and spoon.

Thus the possible is transcended
By a prankster's pride in true juggling,
Twice daily for weeks at Ringling's ring,
Until the seasonal circuit's ended –
An act one degree only less absurd
Than mine: of slipperily balancing
Word
            upon word
                                upon word
                                                upon word,
Each wanton as an eel, daft as a bird.

THE YOUNG WITCH

The moon is full,
   Forget all faith and me,
Go your own road,
   If your own road it be;
Below the girdle women are not wise.

Hecatë hounds you on,
   You dare not stay,
Nor will she lead you home
   Before high day –
Here is the truth, why taunt me with more lies?

BIRTH OF A GREAT MAN

Eighth child of an eighth child, your wilful advent
   Means, as they say, more water in the stew.
Tell us: why did you choose this year and month
   And house to be born into?

Were you not scared by Malthusian arguments
   Proving it folly at least, almost a sin,
Even to poke your nose around the door –
   Much more, come strutting in?

Yet take this battered coral in proof of welcome.
   We offer (and this is surely what you expect)
Few toys, few treats, your own stool by the fire,
   Salutary neglect.

Watch the pot boil, invent a new steam-engine;
   Daub every wall with inspirational paint;
Cut a reed pipe, blow difficult music through it;
   Or become an infant saint.

We shall be too short-handed for interference
   While you keep calm and tidy and never brag –
But evade the sesquipedalian school-inspector
   With his muzzle and his bag.

TO MAGDALENA MULET, MARGITA MORA & LUCIA GRAVES

Fairies of the leaves and rain,
One from England, two from Spain,
You who flutter, as a rule,
At Aina Jansons' Ballet School,
O what joy to see you go
Dancing at the **Lírico**:
Pirouetting, swaying, leaping,
Twirling, whirling, softly creeping,
To a most exciting din
Of French horn and violin!

These three bouquets which I send you
Show how highly I commend you,
And not only praise the bright
Brisk performance of tonight
(Like the audience), but far more
The practising that went before.
You have triumphed at the cost
Of week-ends in the country lost,
Aching toes from brand-new points,
Aching muscles, aching joints,
Pictures missed and parties too,
And suppers getting cold for you
With homework propped beside the plate,
Which meant you had to sit up late.
From dawn to midnight fairies run
To please both Aina and the Nun.

THE PUMPKIN

You may not believe it, for hardly could I –
I was cutting a pumpkin to put in a pie,
And on it was written most careful and plain:
'You may hack me in slices, but I'll grow again.'

I hacked it and sliced it and made no mistake
As, with dough rounded over, I set it to bake:
But down in the garden when I chanced to walk,
Why, there was my pumpkin entire on the stalk!

MAX BEERBOHM AT RAPALLO

The happiest of exiles he, who shakes
No dust from either shoe, who gently takes
His leave, discards his opera hat, but stows
Oxford and London in twin portmanteaux,
To be unpacked with care and loving eyes
Under the clear blue of Ligurian skies,
And becomes guardian of such excellence
As cannot fade nor lose its virtue!
                                    Hence,
After their long experience of decay
And damage, which had sent all wits astray,
The rueful English to Rapallo went;
Where Max, unaltered by self-banishment
Welcomed them to his vine, then (over tea)
Taught them what once they were, and still might be.

THE GRANDFATHER'S COMPLAINT

A Broadsheet Ballad

When I was ten years old
  And Grandfather would complain
To me and my two brothers –
  Would angrily maintain:
That beer was not so hearty,
  Nor such good songs sung,
Nor bread baked so wholesome
  As when himself was young,
Nor youth so respectful,
  We made no contradiction,
Though Grandfather was mistaken –
  Or we held that conviction.

Now fifty years have passed,
   But when likewise I complain
To my three rude young grandsons,
   And angrily maintain
That beer is not so hearty,
   Nor such good songs sung,
Nor bread baked so wholesome
   As when myself was young,
Nor youth so respectful,
   I meet with contradiction –
Though with fact, and solid fact,
   To support my conviction.

You may call me a liar,
   Grandchildren, without fear . . .
Yet ask your nearest brewer
   If he still brews honest beer,
Or ask your nearest baker
   If he still bakes honest bread,
Then come back here to-morrow
   To tell me what they said;
Or sing me whatever
   You may think is still a song,
And I'll make no contradiction
   But leave you in the wrong.

SONG: A BEACH IN SPAIN

Young wives enjoy the statutory right
To slam the door, whether by day or night;
Young husbands, too, are privileged to spend
Long hours in bars, each with a chosen friend.
But tell me can such independence prove
More than a simple lack of love,
More than a simple lack of love?
O how can you regain
Love lost on honeymoon in sunny Spain?

Or though the nuptial contract, that deters
Adulteresses and adulterers,
May sweetly mortalize the venial sin
Of beach flirtation after too much gin,
Can such experiments in marriage prove
More than a simple lack of love,
More than a simple lack of love?
O how can you regain
Love lost on honeymoon in sunny Spain?

And if your OPERATION JEALOUSY
Should end with corpses tossing in the sea,
Both of you having sworn in hell's despite
Never to panic or break off the fight,
Can such heroic beach-head battles prove
More than a simple lack of love,
More than a simple lack of love?
O how can you regain
Love lost on honeymoon in sunny Spain?

BATHUNTS AT BATHURST

(Australian fantasy provoked by a Spanish compositor's end-of-line hyphens)

Bat-
hurst's famed bath-
unts are led uph-
ill by
    Swart bat-
    hat-
    tendants, bold Jehos-
    hop-
    hats,
Toph-
eavily toffed up in tall toph-
ats,
    Who, in the sooth-
    ung top-
    het (where bats fly),

Clutc-
hing bath-
andles with poth-
unting glee,
   Hoth-
   eadedly do lat-
   her bats with bats.

TO A CARICATURIST, WHO GOT ME WRONG

Every gentleman knows
Just when to wear the wrong clo'es,
And naturally that
Will include the wrong hat.
Merchants (the bright ones)
Always wear the right ones;
As do also those asses,
The professional classes.
Beggars have no choice,
Convicts no voice,
Cads and kings go dressed
Always in their best;
And as for me
In my dubious category
Which, yes,
You need hardly press,
I wear (or do not wear)
Whatever I dare,
Or whatever comes to hand,
Sometimes pretty grand,
Sometimes just so,
Sometimes scare-crow,
But was never seen to choose
Either sandals or suede shoes,
No, sir, not I –
Nor an Old Carthusian tie.

IN JORROCKS'S WAREHOUSE

One hundred years ago, hard-riding Mr Jorrocks
Came an almighty purler at a five-barred gate,
Lapsed into science-fiction, and forgot his date.

Afterwards, in the warehouse, superficially healed
With a pair of bloody steaks, vinegar and brown paper,
Jorrocks addressed Bob Dubbs, sportsman and linen-draper:

'At Jorrocks's Super-Logistical Universo Mart
Sales traffic has been canalized, as from today;
Watch out for the amber-light, buyers, and on your way!

'Follow the desired illuminated moving band –
I 10 for Marine Insurance, I 12 for Isotopes –
All goods displayed from Samoyedes to Edible Soaps.

'No supererogatory thank you, welcome, or goodbye.
Our assistants are deaf mutes, robots, zombies and such;
Your duty is to choose, point, pay and never touch.

'Goods found defective cannot, of course, be replaced –
See *Conditions of Jorrocks's Universo Mart.*
Customers are warned to realistically play their part.

'Band C 305 will convey them to *Complaints,*
If they find the stock we carry is not, in fact, their meat,
And a greasy slide will deposit them, bonk! in the street.'

Bob Dubbs the linen-draper listened in wide-eyed horror.
It made worse sense than the Reverend Silas Phipp's
Dominical Exegesis of the Apocalypse.

Though I could, no doubt, invent a whip-crack ending,
This simple moral, reader, should be enough for you:
'Never charge at a five-barred gate on a broken-winded screw.'

A FEVER

Where the room may be, I do not know.
It is beamed and parquetted,
With yew-logs charring on a broad hearth,
Curtains of taffeta, chairs of cherry,
And a rough wolfskin to lie at ease upon
Naked before the fire in half-darkness;
The shadowy bed behind.

Who she may be I do not know,
Nor do I know her nation.
She is truthful, she is tender,
In everything a woman, but for the claws:
Her skin moon-blanched, her arms lissom,
Her tawny tresses hanging free,
Her frown eloquent.

What we do together, that I know;
But when, eludes me;
Whether long ago, one night, or never . . .
Meaning? Meaning in some recess of Time,
Untemporal yet sure . . .
Why should it irk me? Now I must sleep –
She says so with her frown.

AUGEIAS AND I

Now like the cattle byre of Augeias
   My work-room, Hercules, calls for the flood
Of Alpheus and Peneius, green as glass,
   To hurtle down in catastrophic mood
And free me from accumulated piles
Of books, trays, journals, bulging letter-files.

In memory often, I remount the stairs
   To that top room where once a sugar-case
Served me for chair – the house was poor in chairs –
   A broken wash-stand lent me writing space,
And one wax-candle cast a meagre light;
Where all I wrote was what I itched to write.

Augeias, though, if he had dunged the trees,
   Cornland, and pot-herb garden studiously,
Would not have needed help from Hercules;
   We stand accused of careless husbandry
When nothing less than floods or cleansing fire
Can purge my work-room and his cattle byre.

IS IT PEACE?

'What peace,' came Jehu's answering yell,
'While Jezebel is Jezebel?' –
But when the hungry pariahs cease
To gnaw her bones, will that bring peace?

Why (harlot though she were, or worse)
Could he not leave her to God's curse?
Rather than pamper their unclean
Bellies with blood of a live queen?

Two wars, world wars. I lost in one
My cousins; in the next, a son –
That scarcely finished with, I heard
Dismal prognoses of a third.

Yet – since no signed memorial,
Nor bannered march, nor crowded hall
Our Jehus can, it seems, restrain
From bawling 'Jezebel!' again –

Unrealistically (or not?)
I cultivate my garden plot
Where peppers, corn and sea kale sprout
Careless of strontium fallout.

FINGERS IN THE NESTING BOX

My heart would be faithless
If ever I forgot
My farm-house adventure
One day by the fowl run
When Phoebe (of the fringe
And the fairy-story face)
Incited me to forage
Under speckled feathers
For the first time.

Fabulous I thought it,
Fabulous and fateful
(Before familiarity
With the fond pastime
My feelings blunted),
To clasp in frightened fingers
A firm, warm, round . . .
'Phoebe, dear Phoebe,
What have I found?'

BARABBAS'S SUMMER LIST

Barabbas, once a publisher
But currently Prime Minister,
Writes – not of course in his own fist –
'May we include you in our List'
(Across the *Times* in glory spread
With Baths and Garters at its head)?
'Your graceful lyric work,' says he,
'Fully deserves a C.B.E.'

I ask my agents, Messrs. Watt,
Whether I should accept or not.
Few agents are so tough as these
At battling with Barabbases:
The mongoose in his cobra-war
Provides a perfect metaphor.
'Barabbas ought to raise his price
By five per cent,' is Watt's advice.

STABLE DOOR

Watch how my lank team-fellow strains
        Home up the last incline!
His joints creak, but his heart remains
        As obdurate as mine.

Our crib may well contain no feed,
        The skies may be our roof,
Yet should two foundered horses need
        To clack an angry hoof

In their death-dream of oats and hay,
        A dry, well-littered floor,
And Sam the ostler, whistling gay,
        Drunk by the stable door?

FLIGHT REPORT

To be in so few hours translated from
Picking blood-oranges, mandarins, mimosa,
Roses and violets in my Spanish garden,
Where almonds also bloom like old men's polls
And olive twigs bow under wrinkled berries –
To be in so few hours translated here
Three miles above the frantic, chill Atlantic,
Is something monstrous.
                                        Tell me, how should I act?
Bored (as do my seasoned fellow-birds),
Recalling equally sensational flights
I have taken in my mind's own empyrean?
Or should I register rustic amaze?

The captain in his cockpit tilts the craft
To enchant us with what Coleridge never saw:
An iceberg, towering up from grey pack ice,
Through which the sun, whose dawn we long delayed,
Shines green as emerald – or greener, even.

Fasten your belts! And down we drop at Gander,
In a snowstorm, among firs of Newfoundland,
Then battle against head-winds five hours more
To New York, is it?
                              And this all began
Monstrously at a Barcelona counter
Where a suave clerk, his mind on smaller things,
Sold me my round-trip-ticket, with disdain
Checking the banknotes as I paid them out,
And grudged me even a formal *bon voyage!*

SCHOOL HYMN FOR ST TRINIAN'S

Allegro Come, playmates, lift your girlish hands
    In prayer to sweet St Trinian.
With eyes like fiery brands, he stands –
    Cleft hoof and bat-like pinion!
He fosters all your little deeds
    Of maidenly unkindness;
His foul intentions flower like weeds;
    He smites the Staff with blindness.
With ink and stink-bomb be content,
    Likewise the classroom rocket,
His more conventional armament.
    (An H-bomb bags the pocket.)

CHORUS
Maestoso *Learning to be a be-utiful lay-aydee*
    You can *if you try;*
Learning to be a be-utiful lay-aydee
    In the sweet by - and - by.

1960–1974

A PIEBALD'S TAIL

Fame is the tail of Pegasus
(A piebald horse with wings),
One thought of which away will twitch
The luck his colour brings.

It follows logically, of course,
That poets always fail
Who try to catch their piebald horse
By snatching at his tail.

THE INTRUDERS

I ask the young daughter
Of Jetto, a painter,
(Disclosing three faces,
Two bold and one fainter,
On Jetto's *Moon Chart*):
How dare these scapegraces,
These odd bodikins,
Who would once hide their grins
Among wall-paper roses
Or carved lambrequins,
Flaunt pantomime noses
And Carnival chins
In abstractionist art?

But Jetto's young daughter
Has drawn me apart
And pleads for the faces:
'Don't show them to Father!
He'll turn black as thunder
To see their grimaces –
He'll bury them under
Whole tubefuls of madder,
He'll widow my heart.'

TEIRESIAS

Courtship of beasts
And courtship of birds:
How delightful to witness
In fullness of Spring
When swallows fly madly
In chase of each other,
Prairie-dogs tumble,
Wild ponies cavort,
And the bower-bird proffers
Spectacular gifts
To the hen of his choice!

But as for the stark act
That consummates courtship:
Are not dusky rock-caverns
And desolate fastnesses,
Tangle of jungle
And blackness of night,
The refuges chosen
By all honest creatures
That pricked by love's arrow
Perform the said act?

Then despite curs or roosters,
Bulls, ganders or houseflies,
Or troops in sacked cities
Forgetful of shame,
It is surely a duty
Entailed in our beasthood
To turn and go dumbly
Averting the eye,
Should we blunder on lovers
Well couched in a forest
Who thought themselves free?

Courtship of beasts
And courtship of birds:
How delightful to witness
In fullness of Spring!
But be warned by Teiresias,
Thebes' elder prophet,
Who saw two snakes coupling
And crept up behind.
He for six years or seven
Was robbed of his manhood
But feigned to care nothing
And ended stark blind.

SONG: THE SMILE OF EVE

Her beauty shall blind you,
   Long as you live;
She will reap and grind you,
   Bolt you in a sieve,

Will blink her merry eyes,
   Set your brain a-fire,
Be womanly and wise,
   Thwart your desire.

Will trample you, skin you,
   Tear your flesh apart,
Slice nerve and sinew,
   Nestle at your heart.

Though her aspect alters
   Your pangs are the same;
Ready reason falters
   At sound of her name.

No serpent in his guile
   Nor no goatish man
Can rob her of the smile
   That with Eve began.

[VERSE COMPOSED OVER THE TELEPHONE]

Bullfight critics ranked in rows
   Crowd the enormous Plaza full;
But only one is there who *knows*
   And he's the man who fights the bull.

[FIR AND YEW]

Fir, womb of silver pain,
Yew, tomb of leaden grief –
Viragoes of one vein,
Alike in leaf –
With arms up-flung
Taunt us in the same tongue:
'Here Jove's own coffin-cradle swung'.

SONG: GARDENS CLOSE AT DUSK

City parks and gardens close
   Before day has ended,
To discourage crime for which
   They were not intended.

Yet when moonlight lawns resume
   The private peace they merit,
Why are boys and girls in love
   Told they may not share it?

MATADOR GORED

A breeze fluttered the cape and you were caught:
One thrust under your jaw, one in the belly,
A third clean through the groin. Nevertheless,
As you lie stretched on the familiar slab
Comfort yourself by swearing to live on
In bloody vengeance on all bulls. It is
The heifer's horns that defy surgery.

CONFITEOR UT FAS

Alienae civitates
Quas inspexit voster vates,
Etsi tanto procul jacent,
Non tantum regresso placent
Quam (confiteor, ut fas)
Mitis Universitas
De qua nusquam linguae tacent,
Qua dicendi libertas.

NEW MOON THROUGH GLASS

I shall wrap myself in a many-coloured cloak
Where the moon shines new on Castle Crystal,
But make no boast of a passage forced
Through red flames, choking blizzard and black fog.
The extremest courtesy of love is silence.

DYNAMITE BARBEE

Dynamite Barbee, no clo'es on,
Rode on a lion whose name was John –
Dynamite Barbee, no! man, no!
She'll make trouble wherever she go.
'Short life only and a long time dead,
Got to be practical,' Barbee said.

Judged old lion was nigh to death,
Changed to a jackal, corpse on his breath –
Stink of corpse on her hands and hair,
Dynamite Barbee, she don't care:
'Short life only and a long time dead,
Got to be practical,' Barbee said.

Dynamite Barbee never got rich –
Things she done for that son of a bitch!
Pawned her ear-rings, pawned her fur,
And big gold watch that Lion gave her:
'Short life only and a long time dead,
Got to be practical,' Barbee said.

Sunk to the bottom, we guessed she would:
Three times down and she's gone for good.
Dynamite Barbee, no! man, no!
That mean jackal never let her go –
'Short life only and a long time dead,
Got to be practical,' Barbee said.

WHEN A NECKLACE BREAKS

Two lovers sat together under a tree
When suddenly he spoke in a loveless voice –
She answered him as a true woman should,
And the dog howled at their feet.

When a necklace breaks and the beads spill,
Bouncing and rolling across the parquet floor
That is no fatal sign, only a warning
To gather, count, rethread.

Common danger can knit together in love
Almost any desperate human pair;
But the danger gone, they will part silently,
To forget each other's names.

You are good, you are indeed a good sword,
True steel welded and tempered without flaw,
Fit only for a King at his coronation –
Must my scabbard wear a worse?

Up rose the sun, blazing in at the window:
If you honour me as you say, why do you spend
All night in talk and, at my first appearance
Sleep almost till I set?

A QUEEN

Let other women wrangle with their dooms,
A queen is doomed to self-sufficiency;
Shown herself at whatever age she will,
Tempestuous child, grand lady, gruesome hag,
Shifting her mask and dress continually;
Scatters benignant smiles on common folk
Who neither envy or impugn her powers;
Scoffs at all vauntings of nobility;
Summons to table jugglers, cardinals,
Assassins, dancing women, generals,
From whom she learns resource of policy;
And scars her chosen lover's innocent breast
With wounds that testify her royalty.

IF LOVE BECOMES A GAME

If love becomes a game the sweet young fool,
   Now both player and prize,
Learns to resist a gentlemanly rule,
   Against unsporting lies,

That draws her far-from-ladylike attack
   When, as a last resort,
She's kicked the table down, scattered the pack
   And turned to other sport –

To sport, alas, with some gay gambling boy
   Who, judging it no sin
Her sweet, young, foolish licence to enjoy,
   Can never help but win.

QUEEN SILVER AND KING GOLD

Queen Silver and King Gold for untold years
Held planetary sway
Over such common clay
As led its life in eulogy of theirs –

And are still fawned upon even today,
By Voucher, most astute of Ministers
With Town, Court, Bourse and Army in his pay,
Who, if he had his way . . .

LEARN THAT BY HEART

If there's a poem in this book
  To which I've put my name
And Teacher growls: 'Learn that by heart!',
  Don't let *me* bear the blame.

Tell Teacher there are certain things
  No one should ever do –
Say that I write to please myself,
  Not just to torture you.

Press Teacher's nose against the wall,
  Try not to seem unkind,
But say: 'Stop there till he forgives
  The deed you had in mind.'

SONG: ONE IN MANY

To be loved by many and to love many
Is never to die, is to live purely,
Never to lack for noble company;

But to be loved by many, and to love many
Is to be singled out by one only,
Of all those many, who can love truly.

'My doors are barred, my blinds are drawn; for surely
This is the end of love. I loved her wholly –
Now she is lost to me among the many.'

What! In despair for one whom you loved wholly,
You who love many and are loved by many,
Have you no eyes for her who lives purely,

With eyes unhooded, with no hate nor envy,
Singling you out to love wholly and surely
Nor ever lacks for noble company?

A LATE DAFFODIL FOR THE PRINCE OF GWYNEDD

Thrice fortunate is he who winneth
As heir to Maelgwyn Pendragon
Grand welcome at the heart of Gwynedd:
Setting his princely feet upon
Those golden streets of Sinadon
And guarded against evil will
By Dewi Sant's own daffodil.

1999

These are the good old days: appreciate them!
    Hope has been lost, of course, but don't forget
We're still three to a bunk, beer is still drunk,
    And ten bob buys a genuine cigarette.

ANGRY GARDENER

Gentle wild flowers, each with its own strange, twisting,
Graceful habit of growth and innocent aspect,
Find careless welcome to waste garden-corners.
Yet should some honey-gathering go-between
Dare to inaugurate miscegenation
On your parterres or even in waste-corners,
With what blind rage you tear the bastards out!

SONG: WEATHER

What rules the weather for your lover
  Is neither wind nor rain nor mist;
Nor does his private climate alter,
  Since the proud night when first you kissed;
    For still the pulsing of his blood –
    Young manhood awed by womanhood –
Makes love his weather-vane and weather
  With neither wind, nor rain, nor mist.

FIERY ORCHARD

Will she ever need to fetch him home again
To man's beginnings, to that fiery orchard
Where frantic Adam lost himself in Eve?
Once in distress they drew together there,
Gasping, confused and blind,
Clasping and clasped in desperate make-believe;
Yet rose entire, each with a whole mind.

DEFEAT OF TIME

The omens being less than sympathetic,
    Love had recourse to its own magic
For the defeat of time.

This consummation (Love ruled briefly)
    Lies beyond all denial where both hearts burn
As in a single body.

Whether in distant past or future
    Who cares? Together sealed
Beyond all temporal favour.

SIX BLANKETS

How long is love, or how short is love,
        And what's the length of a string?
Nothing to something and back to nothing
        And around a small gold ring.

But to you I shall never, alas, be wed
        Though long I may mourn for you:
Across your bed six blankets are spread
        And I choke under more than two.

THE NOTE

And though your hasty note be bare
But for the secret sign you use,
I need no more – the essential news
Being instantly deciphered there:
That still you laugh, dance, dream and live,
That all you gave me you still give.

THE HEDGEPIG

The letter that you wrote me in your head,
   Last week, arrived at last by pigeon post,
Crumpled and smudged, but legible. It read:
   'Of all my countless worries I hate most
Pretending that your tickly-prickly foe
Sends you his love . . . He died three weeks ago.'

The nightmare flew me to you. First I hovered
   Over your bed, then I dropped into the shed
Where, with a smile of triumph, I discovered
   That you were wrong. Your hedgepig was not dead,
But hibernating in that cosy ball
Which all fat hedgepigs use when the leaves fall.

WHEN HE SAT WRITING

(Song for Shakespeare's Birthday, 1972)

When Will sat forging plays with busy friends
   He wrote no worse than they;
When he sat writing for his loves, and us,
   Such play outshone all play –
   And still it does today.

Comparisons are foolish: love alone
   Established Shakespeare's fame.
There's many a poet, laurelled on a throne,
   For whom the critics claim
   A like poetic flame.

Reject all rivals, even those richly blessed
   With histrionic art . . .
For groundlings he might jest, like all the rest,
   But suffered grief apart
   Mourning with his whole heart.

FOUR POEMS FROM *DEYA: A PORTFOLIO (1972)*

[OURS HAS NO BEARING ON QUOTIDIAN LOVE]

Ours has no bearing on quotidian love
And indeed how could it, while we live above
Quotidian circumstance, fitfully meeting,
Communing fitfully? Nor is ours bound
Like other loves to any common ground.

This is no marriage, nor must ever be –
We were both born more than free,
But our discovery of togetherness
Earned us a weight of silence, our charmed eyes
Lost in astonishment at such excess.

Silence, love's discipline by night or day –
Each time we meet, the occasion calls for silence
As at some unbelievable coincidence,
And, unbelievably, tomorrow will be Sunday:
Silence all but mistakable for absence.

[LOVE MAKES POOR SENSE IN EITHER SPEECH OR LETTERS]

Love makes poor sense in either speech or letters:
Its final truth cannot be told with words,
Only with grave and lengthening silences –
Such as might greet discoveries of truth.

Why then should I fall sick if weeks elapse
Without even a hasty scrawl from you?
Does this denote some fault in me, or merely
A woman's freedom from the snares of time?

And if I ceased to write, would you still love me?

[IS THERE ANOTHER MAN?]

Is there another man
Can claim what you deny me?
Is there another man?
The letters that you write me
Come seldom and invite me
To love you while I can –
Is there another man?

If there's another man
For whom you guard your beauty,
If there's another man,
Send no more letters to me
With kisses to renew me –
What kisses ever can,
If there's another man?

Yet where's the other man
Who loves you for your virtue,
Or where's the other man
Whose kiss of life can cure you?
Then let your pulse assure you
That there's no other woman
With me for other man.

[CONFESS, SWEETHEART, CONFESS]

Confess, sweetheart, confess
You cannot marry me:
Ours is no wedlock nor could ever be,
Though both live more than free –
Our childish greeting of togetherness
Grown to this weight of magic: our charmed eyes
Lost in bewilderment at love's excess.

Nor can we ever become otherwise
Than what love on the hillside made of us:
We scanned each other with close eyes,
We read fateful togetherness:
The door, the key, the power,
The unfolding flower.

And still we brood, our fingers twitch,
Nor can we yet prognosticate
The climax of our fate –
The occasion when, the country which –
Determined only that this brooding season
Of timeless love, this tremulous obsession,
Has its own fateful reason.

THE NOOSE

This is my own clear voice:
Sweetheart, keep faith with me.
A noose hangs from the rope;
I do not bring blind hope
But love in certainty.
Choose, for you have no choice:
Sweetheart, stand fast by me.

THE MORAL LAW

The moral law, being male, need not apply
To a true-hearted woman, though its breach
By such a woman wounds the male pride
Even of a lover loyal and wise enough
To condone her innocence –
Then proudly let him differentiate
Between tormented flesh and troubled spirit,
Resigned to nothingness in her defence.

BODIES ENTRANCED

Where poems, love also;
Where love, likewise magic
With powers indomitable,
Powers inexpendable,
Seasoned in love.

Whence come all true poems,
Their power and their magic
Of two souls as one?
From slow recognition
Of bodies entranced.

Which entrancement of bodies
Will rise from no impulse
To blind propagation,
But claim recognition
Of truth beyond love.

WHO MUST IT BE?

And if I suddenly die, will she have killed me,
   And must the wide world know it,
Gasping at mention of her name,
   My fellow poet,
Therefore the first to blame?

The child who years ago had mercy on me,
   Dragging me from the briars,
Thrusting this pen back in my hand,
   Hugging me close
For Love to understand?

And if I live will it be she who saved me
   From the tiger and the bear,
A reckless child among tall trees
   Balm on her fingers,
Her warm heart at ease?

THIS IS THE SEASON

This is the season
Of useless hunger,
Of strengthened reason,
Of more than danger,
Of endless drought,
Which Death, the stranger,
Has brought about.

This is the ending
Of promised plenty,
Of docile standing
Before God's throne,
The Goddess hidden
Beyond man's midden,
Proud and alone.

UNCO

The unco-guid and unco-ordinated
Walk hand in hand, closely related,
Being from birth so fated.

UNPUBLISHED AND POSTHUMOUSLY PUBLISHED POEMS

A Selection

JUVENILIA: 1910–1914

THE FIRST POEM

No, not for me the lute or lyre!
A knight, I'll ride my thoughts of fire
And fly on wings for ever and aye
Through an unresisting starry sky,
Where the gleaming aether turns and sings
Its strange slow song of the Birth of Things.
And I cry: 'Oh, if I had never known
The cares of this petty world! Alone,
Alone I'd fly, unfettered, free,
Through the Garden of God, Infinity.'
    And there lie paths that none have trod
    And none again shall tread,
    But I alone, with Rapture shod
    With Triumph garlanded –

NIGHTMARE

Oh, some warlock's spell has bound me,
Myriad torches flare around me.
The warlock's shroud,
A misty cloud,
Swims before me. Sudden, loud,
In my ear some creature cries,
Something flutters in my eyes.
Up stands my hair,
I clutch at air,
I must wake. It's the nightmare!
No, some warlock's spell has bound me,
Creatures hop around, around me,
Hop and scream – it is a dream.
Dream and Life like brothers seem.
I must make the holy sign:
Warlocks waste away and pine
At the sign – they waste and pine.

Are these fingers thine or mine?
Move, you fingers, do my will;
Mark the sign for good or ill,
On my breast the crosses make.
At the sign, they waste, they pine.
God be praised! I am awake.

THE DRAGON-FLY

Who'd drag the yet unopened lily-bud
  Slim stalk far-trailing, from the lake-floor up,
  To desecrate the gold and silver cup
With oozy slime and black befouling mud?

Not I, by Hera! Like the dragon-fly
  In blue and sable would I skim instead
  Where lap the waves around the lily-bed,
Desiring nought but only to be nigh.

BOY-MORALITY

I have apples in a very pleasant orchard
  But I may not eat thereof.
I have shining fish in a blue-watered lake:
They are easily taken in the meshes of a net,
  But their flesh is poison.
I have deer in a scented pine-forest
It is good sport hunting them with bows:
Their venison is tender as the flesh of young lambs,
  But whoso eateth, dyeth.

The load that I dragged uphill has slipped backward:
The rope has run scorching through my hands.
I must now return to the hill's very bottom,
And the toil upward will be harder than ever before.
When to this spot I have again dragged my burden,
I shall remember my former folly, and all that ensued.
I shall strengthen my heart with a high endeavour,
And with my hands shall I take a surer hold.

I have apples in a very pleasant orchard,
I have shining fish in a blue-watered lake,
I have deer in a pine-scented forest,
  But I may not eat lest I die.

THE CORACLE

The youngest poet launched his boat
  A wattle-laboured coracle,
He sang for joy to feel it float:
  'A miracle! A coracle!
I have launched a boat, I feel it float,
And all the waves cry miracle.

'I wrenched the wattles from their tree
  For the weaving of my coracle,
I thumped the slimy clay, and see!
  A miracle! A coracle!
I have built a boat, I feel it float,
And all the land cries miracle.

'With patient care her ribs I wove,
  My beautiful new coracle,
With clumsy fingers taught by love –
  A miracle, my coracle!
I have built a boat, I feel it float,
And all the air cries miracle.'

1915–1919

THE LAST DROP

The fires are heated, watch Old Age
   Crowd up to hear the torture-cry:
In sacrifice for private rage
   He has sentenced Youth to die.
But Youth in love with fire and smoke
   Hugs the hot coals to his heart,
And dies still laughing at the joke
   That his delight shall make Age smart.
A moral, gentle sirs, who stop
At home and fight to the last drop!
For look, Old Age weeps for the dead,
Shivers and coughs and howls 'Bread, Bread!'

TRENCH LIFE†

Fear never dies, much as we laugh at fear
   For pride's sake and for other cowards' sakes,
And when we see some new Death, bursting near,
   Rip those that laugh in pieces, God ! it shakes
Sham fortitude that went so proud at first,
   And stops the clack of mocking tongues awhile
Until (o pride, pride!) at the next shell-burst
   Cowards dare mock again and twist a smile.

Yet we who once, before we came to fight,
   Drowned our prosperity in a waste of grief,
Contrary now find such perverse delight
   In utter fear and misery, that Belief
Blossoms from mud, and under the rain's whips,
Flagellant-like we writhe with laughing lips.

THROUGH THE PERISCOPE†

Trench stinks of shallow-buried dead
   Where Tom stands at the periscope,
Tired out. After nine months he's shed
   All fear, all faith, all hate, all hope.

Sees with uninterested eye
   Beyond the barbed wire, a gay bed
Of scarlet poppies and the lie
   Of German trench behind that red: –

Six poplar trees . . . a rick . . . a pond
   A ruined hamlet and a mine . . .
More trees, more houses and beyond
   La Bassée spire in gold sunshine.

The same thoughts always haunt his brain,
   Two sad, one scarcely comforting,
First second third and then again
   The first and the second silly thing.

The first 'It's now nine months and more
   Since I've drunk British beer' the second
'The last few years of this mad war
   Will be the cushiest, I've reckoned'

The third 'The silly business is
   I'll only die in the next war,
Suppose by luck I get thro' this,
   Just 'cause I wasn't killed before.'

Quietly laughs, and at that token
   The first thought should come round again
But crack!
                    The weary circle's broken
And a bullet tears thro' the tired brain.

MACHINE GUN FIRE: CAMBRIN
(September 25 1915)

The torn line wavers, breaks, and falls.
'Get up, come on!' the captain calls
'Get up, the Welsh, and on we go!'
(Christ, that my lads should fail me so!)
A dying boy grinned up and said:
'The whole damned company, sir; it's dead.'
'Come on! Cowards!' bawled the captain, then
Fell killed, among his writhing men.

THE FUSILIER – (For Peter)

I left the heated mess-room, the drinkers and the cardplayers
My jolly brother officers all laughing and drinking
And giving them goodnight, I shut the door behind me
Stepped quickly past the corner and came upon the wind.
A strong wind a steady wind a cool wind was blowing
And flowed like a waterflood about the steamy windows
And washed against my face, and bore on me refreshfully:
Its good to step out into the beautiful wind!
But giving goodnight to that gallant hearty company
And walking all alone through the greyness of evening
The sparkle of wine and the quick fire went out of me
My gay whistle faded and left me heavy hearted
Remembering the last time I'd seen you and talked with you –
(Its seldom the Fusilier goes twice across the parapet
Twice across the parapet, returning safe again)
   Yet Life's the heated messroom and when I go under
That cool wind will blow away the Fusilier, the furious
The callous rough ribald-tongue the Fusilier captain
The gallant merry Fusilier that drank in the messroom
He'll drain his glass, nod good-night and out into the wind,
While the quiet one the poet the lover remaining
Will meet you little singer and go with you and keep you
And turn away bad women and spill the cup of poison
And fill your heart with beauty and teach you to love.
Forget, then, the Fusilier: you'll never understand him,
You'll never love a Regiment as he has learned to love one
Forget the Fusilier: there are others will remember him
In the jolly old mess-room, the pleasant idle messroom
But for you let the strong sea wind blow him away.

O

What is that colour on the sky
   Remotely hinting long-ago,
That splendid apricot-silver? Why,
   That was the colour of my 'O' –
It's strange I can't forget –
In my first alphabet.

TO MY UNBORN SON†

A Dream

Last night, my son, your pretty mother came
Bravely into the forest of my dreams:
I laughed, and sprang to her with feet of flame,
And kissed her on the lips: how queer it seems
That the first power of woman-love should leap
So sudden on a grown man in his sleep!

She smiled, and kissed me back, a lovely thing
Of slender limbs and yellow braided hair:
She set my slow heart madly fluttering,
Her silver beauty through the shadowed air.
But oh, I wish she'd told me at first sight,
Why she was breaking on my dreams last night!

For tears to kisses suddenly succeeded,
And she was pleading, pleading, son, for you:
'Oh, let me have my little child,' she pleaded,
'Give me my child, as you alone can do.'
And, oh, it hurt me, turning a deaf ear,
To say 'No, no!' and 'No, no, no!' to her.

I was most violent, I was much afraid
She'd buy my freedom with a kiss or curl,
And when she saw she'd die a sad old maid,
She wept most piteously, poor pretty girl –
But still, if Day, recalling Night's romance
Should write a sequel, child, you've got a chance.

RETURN

'Farewell,' the Corporal cried, 'La Bassée trenches!
No Cambrins for me now, no more Givenchies,
And no more bloody brickstacks – God Almighty,
I'm back again at last to dear old Blighty.'

But cushy wounds don't last a man too long,
And now, poor lad, he sings this bitter song:
'Back to La Bassée, to the same old hell,
Givenchy, Cuinchey, Cambrin, Loos, Vermelles.'

THE SAVAGE STORY OF CARDONETTE†

To Cardonette, to Cardonette,
  Back from the Marne the Bosches came
With hearts like lead, with feet that bled
  To Cardonette in the morning.

They hurry fast through Cardonette:
  No time to stop or ask the name,
No time to loot or rape or shoot
  In Cardonette this morning.

They hurry fast through Cardonette,
  But close behind with eyes of flame
The Turco steals upon their heels
  Through Cardonette in the morning.

And half a mile from Cardonette
  He caught those Bosches tired and lame,
He charged and broke their ranks like smoke
  By Cardonette in the morning.

At Cardonette, at Cardonette,
  He taught the Bosche a pretty game:
He cut off their ears for souvenirs
  At Cardonette in the morning.

DIED OF WOUNDS†

And so they marked me dead, the day
That I turned twenty-one?
They counted me as dead, did they,
The day my childhood slipped away
And manhood was begun?
Oh, that was fit and that was right!
Now, Daddy Time, with all your spite,
Buffet me how you can,
You'll never make a man of me
For I lie dead in Picardy,
Rather than grow to man.
Oh that was the right day to die
The twenty-fourth day of July!
God smiled
Beguiled
By a wish so wild,
And let me always stay a child.

SIX POEMS FROM 'THE PATCHWORK FLAG' (1918)

FOREWORD†

Here is a patchwork lately made
Of antique silk and flower-brocade
Old faded scraps in memory rich
Sewn each to each with featherstitch.
But when you stare aghast perhaps
At certain muddied khaki scraps
And trophy fragments of field-grey
Clotted and stained that shout dismay
At broidered birds and silken flowers;
Blame these black times: their fault, not ours.

LETTER TO S.S. FROM BRYN-Y-PIN†

Poor Fusilier aggrieved with fate
That lets you lag in France so late,
When all our friends of two years past
Are free of trench and wire at last
Dear lads, one way or the other done
With grim-eyed War and homeward gone
Crippled with wounds or daft or blind,
Or leaving their dead clay behind,
Where still you linger, lone and drear,
Last of the flock, poor Fusilier.
Now your brief letters home pretend
Anger and scorn that this false friend
This fickle Robert whom you knew
To writhe once, tortured just like you,
By world-pain and bound impotence
Against all Europe's evil sense
Now snugly lurks at home to nurse
His wounds without complaint, and worse
Preaches 'The Bayonet' to Cadets
On a Welsh hill-side, grins, forgets.
That now he rhymes of trivial things
Children, true love and robins' wings
Using his tender nursery trick.
Though hourly yet confused and sick
From those foul shell-holes drenched in gas
The stumbling shades to Lethe pass –
'*Guilty*' I plead and by that token
Confess my haughty spirit broken
And my pride gone; now the least chance
Of backward thought begins a dance
Of marionettes that jerk cold fear
Against my sick mind: either ear
Rings with dark cries, my frightened nose
Smells gas in scent of hay or rose,
I quake dumb horror, till again
I view that dread La Bassée plain
Drifted with smoke and groaning under
The echoing strokes of rival thunder
That crush surrender from me now.
Twelve months ago, on an oak bough

I hung, absolved of further task,
My dinted helmet, my gas mask,
My torn trench tunic with grim scars
Of war; so tamed the wrath of Mars
With votive gifts and one short prayer.
'Spare me! Let me forget, O spare!'
'*Guilty*' I've no excuse to give
While in such cushioned ease I live
With Nancy and fresh flowers of June
And poetry and my young platoon,
Daring how seldom search behind
In those back cupboards of my mind
Where lurk the bogeys of old fear,
To think of you, to feel you near
By our old bond, poor Fusilier.

NIGHT MARCH†

Evening: beneath tall poplar trees
  We soldiers eat and smoke and sprawl,
Write letters home, enjoy our ease,
  When suddenly comes a ringing call.

'Fall in!' A stir, and up we jump,
  Fold the love letter, drain the cup,
We toss away the Woodbine stump,
  Snatch at the pack and jerk it up.

Soon with a roaring song we start,
  Clattering along a cobbled road,
The foot beats quickly like the heart,
  And shoulders laugh beneath their load.

Where are we marching? No one knows,
  Why are we marching? No one cares.
For every man follows his nose,
  Towards the gay West where sunset flares.

An hour's march: we halt: forward again,
  Wheeling down a small road through trees.
Curses and stumbling: puddled rain
  Shines dimly, splashes feet and knees.

Silence, disquiet: from those trees
  Far off a spirit of evil howls.
'Down to the Somme' wail the banshees
  With the long mournful voice of owls.

The trees are sleeping, their souls gone,
  But in this time of slumbrous trance
Old demons of the night take on
  Their windy foliage, shudder and dance.

Out now: the land is bare and wide,
  A grey sky presses overhead.
Down to the Somme! In fields beside
  Our tramping column march the dead.

Our comrades who at Festubert
  And Loos and Ypres lost their lives,
In dawn attacks, in noonday glare,
  On dark patrols from sudden knives.

Like us they carry packs, they march
  In fours, they sling their rifles too,
But long ago they've passed the arch
  Of death where we must yet pass through.

Seven miles: we halt awhile, then on!
  I curse beneath my burdening pack
Like Sinbad when with sigh and groan
  He bore the old man on his back.

A big moon shines across the road,
  Ten miles: we halt: now on again
Drowsily marching; the sharp goad
  Blunts to a dumb and sullen pain.

A man falls out: we others go
   Ungrudging on, but our quick pace
Full of hope once, grows dull, and slow:
   No talk: nowhere a smiling face.

Above us glares the unwinking moon,
   Beside us march the silent dead:
My train of thought runs mazy, soon
   Curious fragments crowd my head.

I puzzle old things learned at school,
   Half riddles, answerless, yet intense,
A date, an algebraic rule,
   A bar of music with no sense.

We win the fifteenth mile by strength
   'Halt!' the men fall, and where they fall,
Sleep. 'On!' the road uncoils its length;
   Hamlets and towns we pass them all.

False dawn declares night nearly gone:
   We win the twentieth mile by theft.
We're charmed together, hounded on,
   By the strong beat of left, right, left.

Pale skies and hunger: drizzled rain:
   The men with stout hearts help the weak,
Add a new rifle to their pain
   Of shoulder, stride on, never speak.

We win the twenty-third by pride:
   My neighbour's face is chalky white.
Red dawn: a mocking voice inside
   'New every morning', 'Fight the good fight'.

Now at the top of a rounded hill
   We see brick buildings and church spires.
Nearer they loom and nearer, till
   We know the billet of our desires.

Here the march ends, somehow we know.
The step quickens, the rifles rise
To attention: up the hill we go
Shamming new vigour for French eyes.

So now most cheerily we step down
The street, scarcely withholding tears
Of weariness: so stir the town
With all the triumph of Fusiliers.

Breakfast to cook, billets to find,
Scrub up and wash (down comes the rain),
And the dark thought in every mind
'To-night they'll march us on again.'

POETIC INJUSTICE†

A Scottish fighting man whose wife
Turned false and tempted his best friend,
Finding no future need for life
Resolved he'd win a famous end.

Bayonet and bomb this wild man took,
And Death in every shell-hole sought,
Yet there Death only made him hook
To dangle bait that others caught.

A hundred German wives soon owed
Their widows' weeds to this one man
Who also guided down Death's road
Scores of the Scots of his own clan.

Seventeen wounds he got in all
And jingling medals four or five.
Often in trenches at night-fall
He was the one man left alive.

But fickle wife and paramour
Were strangely visited from above,
Were lightning-struck at their own door
About the third week of their love.

'Well, well' you say, 'man wife and friend
   Ended as quits' but I say not:
While that false pair met a clean end
   Without remorse, how fares the Scot?

THE SURVIVOR COMES HOME†

Despair and doubt in the blood:
Autumn, a smell rotten-sweet:
What stirs in the drenching wood?
What drags at my heart, my feet?
What stirs in the wood?

Nothing stirs, nothing cries.
Run weasel, cry bird for me,
Comfort my ears, soothe my eyes!
Horror on ground, over tree!
Nothing calls, nothing flies.

Once in a blasted wood,
A shrieking fevered waste,
We jeered at Death where he stood:
I jeered, I too had a taste
Of Death in the wood.

Am I alive and the rest
Dead, all dead? sweet friends
With the sun they have journeyed west;
For me now night never ends,
A night without rest.

Death, your revenge is ripe.
Spare me! but can Death spare?
Must I leap, howl to your pipe
Because I denied you there?
Your vengeance is ripe.

Death, ay, terror of Death:
If I laughed at you, scorned you, now
You flash in my eyes, choke my breath . . .
'Safe home.' Safe? Twig and bough
Drip, drip, drip with Death!

THE PUDDING

'Eat your pudding Alexander.'
''Tis too sour to eat.'
'Take it quickly, Alexander.'
'Now 'tis far too sweet.'
And now 'tis thin and slippy-sloppy
And now 'tis tough as leather,
Now too hot and now too cold,
And now 'tis all together.

MOTHER'S SONG IN WINTER

The cat is by the fire,
    The dog is on the mat:
The dog has his desire,
    So also has the cat.
The cat is white
    The dog is black,
The year's delight
    Will soon come back.
The kettle sings, the loud bell rings
And fast my baby clings.

TO JEAN AND JOHN

What shall we offer you, Jean and John?
The softest pillows to sleep upon,
The happiest house in the whole of Wales,
Poodle puppies with wingle tails,
Caldicott pictures, coloured toys
The best ever made for girls or boys
Plenty to drink, plenty to eat
A big green garden with flowers complete
A kind Scotch nurse, a Father and Mother
Doesn't this tempt you?
                                        All right, don't bother.

1920s–1930s

FROM AN UPPER WINDOW

Dark knoll, where distant furrows end
In rocks beyond the river-bend,
  I make my visionary stand
  In your secure well-wooded land
Where idle paths of idle fancy tend.

The charts that threaten all things free
With bondage of geography
  That loop you with a road way round
  Or pin you to some parish bound
Cannot withdraw your loveliness from me.

Nor though I went with hound and stick
With compass and arithmetic
  To gain myself a closer view
  Could I in space come up with you
Your glades with moving shades and colours quick.

You are remote in space and time
As inenarrable in rhyme,
  Yet by this very rareness doubt
  That you are you is blotted out –
Hill of green hopes with slopes no foot may climb.

DRINK AND FEVER

In fever the mind leaps three paces forward;
In drink the mind draws back the same three paces.

It turns about and sees the face twitching;
Stares ahead and sees the back stiffening.

It hears the voice auguring monstrously;
Hears the voice arguing meticulously.

Man is located then as man sleep-walking
Midmost between delirious and drunken.

So drink and fever touch and are combined
In the clear space where should be man's mind.

VESTRY

My parents were debtors,
And flung out of doors,
My brothers were eunuchs,
My sisters were whores;
If I tell the whole story,
You'll laugh till you cry,
That I am what I am
None knows better than I.

My breath smelt of garlic,
My body was lean,
My lovelocks were lousy,
My garments not clean;
When I strolled in the desert
Or dozed by the sea,
There was no one gainsaid me
In all Galilee.

I was all things to all men
But death to the rich;
I coaxed the dung-fire
And made cakes in the ditch;
My proverbs came pat,
And my features were flame,
And I paid the tax-penny
When quarter-day came.

I drove my disciples
With daily advice
About rubies and talents
And pearls of great price,
About laying up treasure
And profit and loss.
It was what my mind ran on
From manger to cross.

When my hearers went hungry
I bade them sit down,
And I fed them with fables
Of white bread and brown,
Of old wine and new wine,
Of herrings and salt;
And what happened after
Was never my fault.

THE END

Who can pretend
To spy to the very end
The ultimate confusion
Of belief and reason,
Perfection of all progress?
But I say, nevertheless:
That when instead of chairs
The altars of the martyrs
Are taken by philosophers
As vessels of reality;
When Cardinals devoutly
Canonize *in curia*
Some discarded formula
Of mad arithmetician
Or mad geometrician
Now seated in a swivel-chair
Widowed of its philosopher,
In that General Post
Down will come Pepper's Ghost
And proclaim Utopia,
The final synthesis,
With a cornucopia
And halitosis.

The dogs will bark,
The cats will cry,
And the Angel of Death go drumming by.

THE SAND GLASS

The sand-glass stands in frame both ways the same,
Single broad based; but so enclosed the glass
Alters in action, most revengeful, trickling
Minute by minute, minute-minus-moment,
By broken minute, nervous time,
Narrowing time,
Nearly time,
No time,
Time!
Upend,
Equilibrize
Eyes near maddened,
Sand-roped nonsensically:
Now sense, sight, sand, no nonsense.
Turn, suicide, from the wasp-waist, while time runs
A new five minutes: then view once more with calm
The base root-firm, each base, solid in time.

THIS WHAT-I-MEAN

A close deduction about close deduction.
Or, starting at an earlier point than that
With any pavement-rainbow after rain,
First, the experience of an easy pleasure,
Then the close observation 'filmed with oil',
Then qualification of that easy pleasure,
Then close deduction about doubtful pleasure,
Then close deduction about close deduction.

How to outgo this vistaed close deduction,
To find if anything is behind or not?
If not, no matter; no matter either way.
We are not collecting worms for the Museum.

And we are not taking Cat's Cradle, say,
Beyond the ninth, or is it the nineteenth, stage,
The last stage that the oldest experts know.
(That would be physical and scientific,
A progress further into the same close vista)

And we are not leaping the unknown gap;
Any poor fugitive does that with razor
Or lysol as the spring-board, and he knows
One brink of the gap at least before he jumps.

This what-I-mean is searching out the gap
Under all closeness and improving on it
And the new gaps above and every which way,
Gradually loosening everything up
So nothing sticks to anything but itself –
A world of rice cooked Indian fashion
To be eaten with whatever sauce we please.

THE FINGERHOLD

He himself
Narrowed the rock shelf
To only two shoes' width,
And later by
A willing poverty
To half that width and breadth.

He shrank it then
By angry discipline
To a mere fingerhold,
Which was the occasion
Of his last confusion:
He was not so bold
As to let go
At last and throw
Himself on air that would uphold.

He wept
Self-pityingly and kept
That finger crooked and strained
Until almost
His life was lost
And death not gained.

THEN WHAT?

If I rise now and put my straw hat on
   Against the strong sun lying in wait outside
Scorching the flowers and over the flat stone
   Making the air dance – what? The prospect's wide:
The sea swimming to nowhere, the near hills
   Incredible of ascent and horned with crags,
The blank sky darted through with the sun's quills,
   The pleasant poplar grove where the eye drags.
Then what? The path curves to the gate, from which
   A dusty road curves to my neighbour's gate:
Stroll past it, pausing at the boundary ditch
   Then turn, slowly, as granting leave to fate
To exploit this chance in grossness of event,
Then what? Then gladly home with nothing spent.

HISTORICAL PARTICULARS

And if at last the anecdotal world
Records my name among ten million more
In the long-drawn-out story of itself
(O tediousness) and far from the last page? –
'English poet and miscellaneous writer,
Eccentric of the Later Christian era,
Sometime a subject of King George the Fifth,
(While the ninth, eighth and seventh Popes of Rome
Before the last were reigning). It was the time
Of the World War – he served throughout – the time
Of airships and top-hats and communism,
Passports and gangsters, breach of promise cases,

When coal was burned in grates and gold coin minted,
When radio was a novelty and horses
Still ran with vans about the city streets . . . '
And if with such quaint temporal statistics
They date me in their books and bury me,
Could I protest an honest alibi
Who dreamed ill dreams one night and woke, staring,
In those too populous and wealthy streets
And wandered there, as it were dreaming still,
Out at heels and my heart heavy in me,
And drank with strangers in the bright saloons
And gossiped there of politics and futures?

My alibi's the future: there I went
And in the idle records found my record,
And left my spectre fast between the pages
As a memorial and a mockery
Where they shall find it when they come to be.
And as I am, I am, the visit over.
What name, what truth? Unbiographical.
The fixity of one who has no spectre.
I learn slowly, but I may not wander.

ADDRESS TO SELF

Our loves are cloaked, our times are variable,
We keep our rooms and meet only at table.

But come, dear self, agree that you and I
Shall henceforth court each other's company

And bed in peace together now and fall
In loving discourse, as were natural,

With open heart and mind, both alike bent
On a just verdict, not on argument,

And hide no private longings, each from each,
And wear one livery and employ one speech.

I worked against you with my intellect,
You against me with folly and neglect,

Making a pact with flesh, the alien one:
Which brought me into strange confusion

For as mere flesh I spurned you, slow to see
This was to acknowledge flesh as part of me.

PROSPERITY OF POETS

Several instances in time occur
When, numbers reckoned, there appears a quorum
Sufficient to explain the way of the world
To the world, in plural singularity.
The agenda, often, has been mass conversion
From sin, often mass resort to reason,
Rarely poems, and then what an array
Of unrelated beauties marshalled!
Mutual indulgence, each to each,
Among these poets being the arbiter
Of what shall stand. The world, noting
A harmless literary renascence,
Snatches up certain poems (as a sample)
Where the indulgence has been strained
To exclude poetry and include world,
And flutes them under academic escort
To that Glass Palace where the Great consort.

1940s–1950s

DIOTIMA DEAD

Diotima's dead – how could she die?
Or what says Socrates, now she is dead?
Diotima's wisdom he might credit
While still she looked at him with eyes of love:
He could his life commit to Diotima,
Clear vessel of the Word's divinity,
Until she cloaked herself in deathward pride
And ruin courted by equivocation –
Did he not swear then, she had always lied?

Scholars, the truth was larger than herself.
The truth it was she had told Socrates
(Though peevish in her immortality
And starving for what meats the God forbade)
Until her vision clouded, her voice altered,
And two lives must have ended, had he stayed.

THE HEARTH

The cat purrs out because it must,
   So does the cricket call;
The crackling fire in which they trust
   Cares not for them at all.

Though cat-and-cricket-like we cry
   Around a fatal fire,
And give 'because we must' for 'why',
   As children of desire,

Care is our reading of that glow
   Which to repay is wise:
Who will not yet his distance know
   For his own folly fries.

IN THE LION HOUSE

That chance what traveller would not bless
   In midday glare to see
Lion and tawny lioness
   At lust beneath a tree?

Here, superannuated bones
   Of leathery bull or horse,
An ailing panther's muffled moans
   And Monday's dismal course –

Who would not turn his head aside
   From this connubial show
Of *Felis Leo* and his bride,
   Half-hearted, smug and slow?

AN APPEAL

Though I may seem a fool with money, Lord,
To spend and lend more than I can afford,
Why should my creditors and debtors scoff
When tearfully I urge them to pair off,
Yet booze together at one bar; and why
Should all sport newer coats and hats than I?

A GHOST FROM ARAKAN

He was not killed. The dream surprise
Sets tears of joy pricking your eyes.
      So cheated, you awake:
A castigation to accept
After twelve years in which you've kept
      Dry-eyed, for honour's sake.

His ghost, be sure, is watching here
To count each liberated tear
And smile a crooked smile:
Still proud, still only twenty-four,
Stranded in his green jungle-war
That's lasted all this while.

1960s–1970s

ROBIN AND MARIAN

He has one bowstring, and from the quiver takes
An only shaft. Should Robin miss his aim
He cannot care whether that bowstring breaks,
Being then undone and Sherwood put to shame.
Smile, Marian, smile: resolve all doubt,
Speed Robin's goosequill to the clout.

NEVER YET

For History's disagreeable sake
I could review the year and make
A long list of your cruelties
As they appear in the world's eyes
(And even, maybe, in your own),
Until it shamed me to have grown,
By culling so much strength therefrom,
The sagest fool in Christendom.
But what would the world think if I
Declared your love for me a lie,
Courting renown in my old age
As Christendom's least foolish sage?
Or if in anger, close to hate,
Your truth you dared repudiate –
A truth long fastened with a fine
Unbreakable red thread of mine –

And called what seemed a final curse
Upon the tottering universe?
Nothing can change us; you know this.
The never-yet of our first kiss
Prognosticated such intense
Perfection of coincidence.

TANKA

Apricot petals on the dark pool fallen
Tassel both flanks of a broken cane:
Our Poet Emperor himself extols them
In five brief lines confounding
All foolish commentary.

HOUSE ON FIRE

The crowd's heart is in the right place:
Everyone secretly backs a fire
Against massed murderous jets of water
Trained on a burning house by the city's hoses –
While he still swears it cannot spread to his.

THE LILAC FROCK

How I saw her last, let me tell you. I heard screams
In a dream, four times repeated. It was Grimaut Castle.
She wore a lilac frock, her diamond ring,
Gold beads and the dove brooch.
'Escape!' she whispered.
'Emilio's mad again.'
He came from behind her
Flourishing a sharp Mexican machete.

Nonchalantly, I turned my back on him
And asked her: 'Could a young witch, taking the veil,
Count on the Mother Superior's connivance
If she kept a toad-familiar in her cell?'

She faltered: 'Yesterday I tried to join you –
I had even bought my ticket and packed my bags
But seeing a mist of sorrow cloud his eyes
How could I desert him? He had a painful boil.
I decided to eat beans with Emilio
Rather than suffer happiness with you . . .
So keep my paint box and my paint brushes,
I shall never have occasion to use them now:
Women born under Cancer lead hard lives.'

Sun blotted out sun, dogs howled, and a silver coffin
Went sailing past over the woods and hedges
With a dead girl inside. The man who saw it
Pointed in which direction the coffin flew,
Should I ever be drawn to pilgrimage.

DEPARTURE

With a hatchet, a clasp-knife and a bag of nails
He walked out boldly to meet the rising sun.
His step was resolute and his hair white.

Granted, death was lurking under that roof
And his funeral planned, down to the last speech.
But why not face it honourably, in comfort?

Neighbours looked glum, grandchildren whimpered.
'He has no right to leave us,' everyone said,
'He belongs here, our most familiar landmark.'

Visitors had flocked from a great distance
To inspect the forge and watch him tirelessly
Beating red-hot iron on his anvil.

It was hoped to keep it up, when he had died,
As a museum, with a small entrance fee,
And the grave, of course, would be refreshed with flowers.

Why did he defy them? And yet his bearing
Suggested no defiance – on the contrary,
He wore an innocent and engaging smile.

'I have given your own town back to you,'
Said he, 'though I had not thought myself the thief,
And with no choice but to start work elsewhere.'

NORTH SIDE

On the north side of every tree
   Snow clings and moss thrives;
The Sun himself can never see
   So much of women's lives;
But we who in this knowledge steer
Through pathless woods find the way clear.

A-

va Gardner brought me á
One winged angel yesterday
To kneel beside me when I pray
And guide me through the U.S.A. –
With one wing she won't fly away
Thank you, dearest Ava!

SONG: JOHN TRUELOVE

The surnames from our parents had
   Are seldom a close fit:
There's Matthew Good who's truly bad,
   And Dicky Dull's a wit.

There's Colonel Staid who's far from staid,
   There's glum old Farmer Bright
And Parson Bold who's much afraid
   Of burglars in the night.

So though my name be John Truelove,
Take warning, maidens all,
I shall keep true to none of you
Unless the worst befall.

REQUIREMENTS FOR A POEM†

Terse, Magyar, proud, all on its own,
Competing with itself alone,
Guiltless of greed
And winged by its own need.

THE ATOM

Within each atom lurks a sun,
Which if its host releases,
Opening a foolish mouth for fun,
The world must fly in pieces.

THE CUPID

A cupid with a crooked face
Peered into Laura's jewel-case:
'Emerald, diamond, ruby, moonstone,
Jacinth, agate, pearl, cornelian,
Red and black garnet, sapphire, beryl,
Topaz, amethyst and opal,
Pure rock-crystal.'

'These are hers, Cupid, for instruction
In love's variety, to have and hold.
No common glass intrudes among them
And all are set in gold.'

'But if she fails you?' asks the mannerless cupid.
'Will she return them? Will she sell them?
Will they be mine when sold?'

Dear God, how stupid can a cupid be,
Asking such mercenary questions of me?

OLIVES OF MARCH

Olives of March are large and blue, but few,
Peering like sapphires from the thick grass,
Yet none has ever known them to take root.

Pallas Athene sent an owl to wrench
A grey-green sprig from the sole Nubian stock:
Grafting it on an ancient oleaster
At her Acropolis, for distribution
Of olive-grafts by the Archimorius
To every city of Greece. Who dares neglect
An olive harvest must incur despair,
Starvation, haplessness and rootlessness.

THE UNDYING WORM

'The damned in their long drop from Earth to Hell,
   Meaning no fewer than ten thousand miles
At headlong speed – Hell may be nowhere
Yet friction of the fall causes rope-burns –
   Take only a few hours,' our verger smiles.

Return by Act of Mercy takes far longer
And though an angel's kiss is often praised
   As balm for penitents, you may be sure
That those red scars will glow again in sullen
   Resentment of their cure.

The damned are rendered down eventually
To clinker or a fine white ash. Yet what
  Of throats from which no cry of guilt is wrenched?
Can it be there that the worm dieth not
  And the fire is not quenched?

SONG: THOUGH TIME CONCEALS MUCH

Though time conceals much,
Though distance alters much,
Neither will ever part me
From you, or you from me,
However far we be.

So let your dreaming body
Naked, proud and lovely –
There is no other such,
So wholesome or so holy –
Accept my dream touch.

One kiss from you will surely
Amend and restore me
To what I still can be –
Though distance alters much,
Though time conceals much.

ALWAYS AND FOR EVER

Come, share this love again
Without question or pain,
Not only for a while
With quick hug and sweet smile
But always and for ever
In unabated fever
Without guess, without guile.

ACROSS THE GULF (1992)

THE SNAPPED ROPE†

When the rope snaps, when the long story's done
Not for you only but for everyone,
These praises will continue fresh and true
As ever, cruelly though the Goddess tricked you,
And lovers (it may be) will bless you for
Your blindness, grieved that you could praise no more.

THE GOLDSMITHS†

And yet the incommunicable sea
Proves less mysterious to you and me
Than how, through dream, we run together nightly
And hammer out gold cups in a dancing fury
Patterned with birds of prey, with tangled trees,
Lions, acanthus, wild anemones;
And that these cups are master-works is proved
By the deep furrows on our foreheads grooved;
And to sip wine from them is to be drunk
With powers of destiny, this mad world shrunk
To bean or walnut size, its ages flown
To enlarge the love-hour that remains our own.

ADAM IN HELL†

From the pit of Hell a whisper of pure love
Rises through crooked smoking crannies
To the lawns of Paradise.

Adam lies fettered by his basalt pillar:
A lodestone of male honour,
A moral for the damned.

So proud a lover, suffering no woman
To endure the torments that are his:
It was not Eve who sinned but the bright Serpent
Conspiring against man –
Tomorrow she will bruise her enemy's head
And raise up Adam from the loveless dead.

THE CARDS ARE WILD†

Tell me, how do you see me? Ring the changes
On father, lover, brother, friend and child –
A hand is dealt you, but the cards are wild.

You spoil me with a doubled span of years;
Having already overspent my due
Should I, or should I not, be grateful to you?

This cruel world grows crueller day by day,
And you more silent, more withdrawn and wise.
I watch its torments mirrored in your eyes –
Sweetheart, what must I say?
With you still here I dare not move away.

UNLESS†

Ink, pen, a random sheet of writing paper,
A falling inescapably in love
With you who long since fell in love with me . . .
But where is the poem, where my moving hand?

And if I am flung full length on a bed of thorns
How can I hope to retrieve lost memory,
Lost pride and lost motion,
Unless, defying the curse long laid upon me,
You prove the unmatchable courage of your kind?

THE POISED PEN†

Love, to be sure, endures for ever,
    Scorning the hour
That ends untimely in a hurried kiss
    And a breach of power.

Must I then sit here still, my pen poised
    As though in disgrace,
Plotting to draw strength from the single grief
    That we still dare face?

Or must I set my song of gratitude
    In a minor key,
To confess that you and I compound a truth
    That is yet to be?

[FRAGMENT]†

A smoothly rolling distant sea,
A broad well-laden olive tree,
A summer sky, gulls wheeling by
With raucous noise, and here sit I
For seven years, not yet set free.

[HOW IS IT A MAN DIES?]†

How is it a man dies
  Before his natural death?
He dies from telling lies
  To those who trusted him.
He dies from telling lies –
  With closed ears and shut eyes.

Or what prolongs men's lives
  Beyond their natural death?
It is their truth survives
  Treading remembered streets
Rallying frightened hearts
  In hordes of fugitives.

GREEN FLASH†

Watch now for a green flash, for the last moment
When the Sun plunges into sea;
And breathe no wish (most wishes are of weakness)
When green, Love's own heraldic tincture,
Leads in the mystagogues of Mother Night:
Owls, planets, dark oracular dreams.
Nightfall is not mere failure of daylight.

PEISINOË†

So too the Siren
Under her newly rounded moon
Metamorphoses naked men
To narwhale or to dolphin:
Fodder for long Leviathan
Or for his children
Deep in the caves of Ocean.

ACROSS THE GULF†

Beggars had starved at Dives' door
   But Lazarus his friend
Watched him lose hope, belayed a rope
   And flung him the loose end,
Sighing: 'Poor sinner, born to be
Proud, loveless, rich and Sadducee!'

TO HIS TEMPERATE MISTRESS†

You could not hope to love me more,
   Nor could I hope to love you less,
Both having often found before
   That I was cursed with such excess,
Even the cuckold's tragic part
Would never satisfy my heart.

FOOT-HOLDER-ROYAL†

As Court foot-holder to the Queen of Fishes
I claim prescriptive right
To press the royal instep when she wishes
And count her toes all night.
Some find me too assiduous in my task.
That is for her to say; they need but ask.

THE PRESSURE GAUGE†

Quoth the King of Poland
To his gipsy Roland:
'Wretch, go fetch my idle pages –
Ask them where my pressure-gauge is!'
Hurrah, hurrah, hurrah!

'Sire,' replied the gipsy,
'Thou art wondrous tipsy,
In these Polish Middle Ages
No one's heard of pressure-gauges – '
Hurrah, hurrah, hurrah!

BIBLIOGRAPHICAL AND TEXTUAL NOTES

Listed below are abbreviations for the books by Robert Graves in which poems in this volume appear, and for other works and manuscript collections cited in the notes.

These are followed by an alphabetical list giving publication details for each poem; and notes on the poems.

ABBREVIATIONS

Robert Graves: Poetry and Prose

For books in which Graves first published poems in this volume, the month as well as the year of publication is given; these dates are based on Higginson (see 'Bibliography', below).

5PH	*5 Pens in Hand* (New York: Doubleday, 1958).
10PM	*Ten Poems More* (Paris: Hours Press (limited edition), 1930).
16P	*Sixteen Poems* (Oxford: Oxford College of Technology (limited edition), 1967).
17PMLR	*Seventeen Poems Missing from 'Love Respelt'* (Barnet: Stellar Press (privately printed), June 1966).
AG	*At the Gate* (Hatfield: Stellar Press (privately printed), Dec. 1974).
AHH	*Ann at Highwood Hall: Poems for Children*, illustrated by Edward Ardizzone (London: Cassell, Oct. 1964; New York: Doubleday, 1964).
ATG	*Across the Gulf: Late Poems*, edited by Beryl Graves, Lucia Graves and Dunstan Ward (Deyá, Mallorca: New Seizin Press (limited edition), 1992).
BG	*Beyond Giving* (Hatfield: Stellar Press (privately printed), Oct. 1969).
CLR	*Colophon to Love Respelt* (Barnet: Stellar Press (privately printed), July 1967).
CP38	*Collected Poems* (London: Cassell, Nov. 1938; New York: Random House, 1939).
CP61	*Collected Poems* (New York: Doubleday, July 1961).
CP65	*Collected Poems 1965* (London: Cassell, Sept. 1965).
CP75	*Collected Poems 1975* (London: Cassell, Sept. 1975); *New Collected Poems* (New York: Doubleday, 1977).
CrP	*The Crowning Privilege* (London: Cassell, 1955).
CS	*Country Sentiment* (London: Secker, 1920; New York: Knopf, 1920).
CSS	*Complete Short Stories*, edited by Lucia Graves (Manchester: Carcanet, 1995).
CWP	*Collected Writings on Poetry*, edited by Paul O'Prey (Manchester: Carcanet, 1995).

DP	*Deyá: A Portfolio* (London: Motif Editions (limited edition), Nov. 1972).
DQEA	*Difficult Questions, Easy Answers* (London: Cassell, 1972; New York: Doubleday, 1973).
FC	*Food for Centaurs* (New York: Doubleday, May 1960).
FF	*Fairies and Fusiliers* (London: Heinemann, 1917; New York: Knopf, 1918).
GD	*Goliath and David* (London: Chiswick Press (privately printed), 1916).
GM	*The Greek Myths* (Harmondsworth: Penguin, 1955; second edition, 1960). References are to the second edition.
GSV	*The Green-Sailed Vessel* (Hatfield: Stellar Press (privately printed), Aug. 1971).
GTAT	*Good-bye to All That* (editions below).
GTAT29	*Good-bye to All That: An Autobiography* (London: Cape, 1929).
GTAT57	*Goodbye to All That*, revised edition (New York: Doubleday, 1957; London: Cassell, 1957).
HM	*Hebrew Myths: The Book of Genesis*, with Raphael Patai (New York: Doubleday, 1964; London: Cassell, 1964).
LFNR	*The Less Familiar Nursery Rhymes*, Augustan Books of English Poetry, second series, 14 (London: Benn, Nov. 1927).
LR	*Love Respelt* (London: Cassell (limited edition), July 1965).
LR66	*Love Respelt* (New York: Doubleday, April 1966).
LRA	*Love Respelt Again* (New York: Doubleday, 1969).
MBG	*Mammon and the Black Goddess* (London: Cassell, 1965; New York: Doubleday, 1965).
MBH	*Mock Beggar Hall* (London: Hogarth Press, 1924).
MDC	*The More Deserving Cases: Eighteen Old Poems for Reconsideration* (Marlborough: Marlborough College Press (limited edition), Feb. 1962).
MDWI	*Man Does, Woman Is* (London: Cassell, April 1964; New York: Doubleday, Nov. 1964.
MP61	*More Poems 1961* (London: Cassell, May 1961).
NMG	*No More Ghosts: Selected Poems* (London: Faber, 1940).
NP62	*New Poems 1962* (London: Cassell, Oct. 1962; New York: Doubleday, 1963).
OAP	*Oxford Addresses on Poetry* (London: Cassell, 1962; New York: Doubleday, 1962).
OB	*Over the Brazier* (London: Poetry Bookshop, 1916.)
OEP	*On English Poetry: Being an Irregular Approach to the Psychology of This Art, from Evidence Mainly Subjective* (New York: Knopf, 1922; London: Heinemann, 1922).
OP	*On Poetry: Collected Talks and Essays* (New York: Doubleday, 1969).
P14-26	*Poems (1914-26)* (London: Heinemann, 1927; New York: Doubleday, Doran, 1929).

P14-27	*Poems (1914-27)* (London: Heinemann (limited edition), 1927).
P29	*Poems 1929* (London: Seizin Press (limited edition), 1929).
P30-33	*Poems 1930-1933* (London: Barker, 1933).
P38-45	*Poems 1938-1945* (London: Cassell, 1945; New York: Creative Age Press, 1946).
P53	*Poems 1953* (London: Cassell, 1953).
P65-68	*Poems 1965-1968* (London: Cassell, July 1968; New York: Doubleday, 1969).
P68-70	*Poems 1968-1970* (London: Cassell, Oct. 1970; New York: Doubleday, 1971).
P70-72	*Poems 1970-1972* (London: Cassell, Nov. 1972; New York: Doubleday, 1973).
PAL	*Poems About Love* (New York: Doubleday, Feb. 1969; London: Cassell, Nov. 1969).
PAW	*Poems About War*, edited by William Graves (London: Cassell, 1988; Mt. Kisco, New York: Moyer Bell, 1990.)
PBFS	*The Poor Boy Who Followed His Star* (London: Cassell, Spring 1968).
PCP	*Poetic Craft and Principle* (London: Cassell, 1967).
PF	*The Penny Fiddle: Poems for Children*, illustrated by Edward Ardizzone (London: Cassell, Nov. 1960; New York: Doubleday, 1961).
P-G	*The Pier-Glass* (London: Secker, 1921; New York: Knopf, 1921).
PS51	*Poems and Satires 1951* (London: Cassell, 1951).
S	*Steps* (London: Cassell, 1958).
SL 1	*In Broken Images: Selected Letters of Robert Graves 1914-1946*, edited by Paul O'Prey (London: Hutchinson, 1982).
SL 2	*Between Moon and Moon: Selected Letters of Robert Graves 1946-1972*, edited by Paul O'Prey (London: Hutchinson, 1984).
TB	*Treasure Box* (London: Chiswick Press (privately printed), 1919).
TM	*Timeless Meeting* (Hatfield: Stellar Press (privately printed), June 1973).
TWE	*To Whom Else?* (Deyá: Seizin Press (limited edition), 1931).
W	*Whipperginny* (London: Heinemann, 1923; New York: Knopf, 1923).
WG52	*The White Goddess: A Historical Grammar of Poetic Myth*, second edition (London: Faber, 1952; New York: Vintage, 1958).
WG61	*The White Goddess: A Historical Grammar of Poetic Myth*, third edition (London: Faber, 1961); revised edition, ed. Grevel Lindop (Manchester: Carcanet, 1997; London: Faber, 1999).
WH	*Welchman's Hose* (London: The Fleuron (limited edition), 1925).
WIH	*Work in Hand* (London: Hogarth Press, 1942).

Bibliography

Higginson	Fred H. Higginson, *A Bibliography of the Writings of Robert Graves*, second edition, revised by William Proctor Williams (Winchester: St. Paul's Bibliographies, 1987).

Biography

RPG 1	Richard Perceval Graves, *Robert Graves: The Assault Heroic 1895-1926* (London: Weidenfeld and Nicolson, 1986).
RPG 2	Richard Perceval Graves, *Robert Graves: The Years with Laura 1926-1940* (London: Weidenfeld and Nicolson, 1990).
RPG 3	Richard Perceval Graves, *Robert Graves and the White Goddess 1940-1985* (London: Weidenfeld and Nicolson, 1995).

Manuscripts

Berg	The Henry W. and Albert A. Berg Collection at the New York Public Library.
Buffalo	The Robert Graves Collection in the Poetry/Rare Books Collection, University Libraries, State University of New York at Buffalo.
Canelluñ	The collection at Robert Graves's house, Canelluñ, at Deyá, Mallorca.
Carbondale	The Morris Library, Southern Illinois University at Carbondale.
Diary	Robert Graves's diary, February 1935-May 1939, at the University of Victoria, British Columbia, Canada; and his 1956-1965 diaries at Canelluñ, Deyá, Mallorca.
Eton	College Library, Eton College, Windsor.
JS	The collection of Julia Simon, London.
RWF	The Royal Welch Fusiliers Regimental Museum, Caernarvon.
Texas	The Harry Ransom Humanities Research Center, the University of Texas at Austin.
Tulsa	The McFarlin Library, University of Tulsa, Oklahoma.
Victoria	University Library, University of Victoria, B.C.

THE POEMS: PUBLICATION DETAILS

This list summarizes the publication history of the poems in this volume from Graves's books of verse. After each title, the data is given as follows: where first publication was in a periodical or anthology, the month and year; the book by Graves in which the poem first appeared; and other books by him in which it was reprinted, if any. For abbreviations and dates of first book publication, see above. (The reader is referred to Higginson – on which the list is based – for other publication details.) For uncollected and posthumously published poems, publication details are given in the notes on each poem.

Above the Edge of Doom, *LR, CP65, LRA, PAL, CP75*
Absent Crusader, *P70-72, CP75*
Accomplice, The, Sept. 1970, *P68-70, CP75*
Acrobats, *NP62, CP65, PAL, CP75*
Advent of Summer, Spring 1975, *CP75*
Advice from a Mother, *GSV, P70-72, CP75*
After the Flood, Jan. 1963, *MDWI, CP65, CP75*
Against Witchcraft, *BG, P68-70, CP75*
Age Gap, Nov. 1971, *P70-72, CP75*
Ageless Reason, *P70-72, CP75*
Alabaster Throne, The, *NP62*
All Except Hannibal, Oct.-Dec. 1966, *P65-68, CP75*
All I Tell You From My Heart, Winter 1964, *MDWI, CP65, PAL, CP75*
Always, Sept. 1972, *P70-72, CP75*
Ambience, *LR, CP65, LRA, PAL, CP75*
Ambrosia of Dionysus and Semele, The, Jan. 1962, *NP62, CP65, CP75*
Ample Garden, The, Oct. 1963, *MDWI, CP65, CP75*
Anchises to Aphrodite, Jan. 1961, *MP61, CP61*
Ann at Highwood Hall, *AHH*
***Antorcha y Corona, 1968*; Torch and Crown, 1968,** *BG, P68-70, CP75*
Apple Island, Jan. 1961, *MP61, CP61, CP65, 16P, CP75*
Ark, The, *P65-68, CP75*
Armistice Day, 1918, *BG, P68-70, CP75*
Arrears of Moonlight, *LR66, 17PMLR, P65-68, LRA, PAL, CP75*
Arrow on the Vane, *GSV, P70-72, CP75*
Arrow Shots, *P65-68, CP75*
As a Less Than Robber, *AG, CP75*
As All Must End, Jan. 1973, *TM, CP75*
As When the Mystic, *P70-72, CP75*
Astymelusa, Autumn 1966, *P65-68, CP75*
At Best, Poets, Oct. 1963, *MDWI, CP65, PAL, CP75*
At Seventy-Two, *PBFS*
At the Gate, *AG, CP75*
At the Well, May 1970, *P68-70, CP75*
Awakening, The, *P68-70, CP75*

Bank Account, *MDWI, CP65, CP75*
Basket of Blossom (*Song*), *BG, P68-70, CP75*
Batxóca, *LR, CP65, LRA, PAL, CP75*
Beatrice and Dante, Sept. 1972, *P70-72, CP75*
Beds of Grainne and Diarmuid, The, *MDWI, CP65, PAL, CP75*
Beggar Maid and King Cophetua, The, July 1967, *P65-68, CP75*

Between Hyssop and Axe, *LR, CP65, LRA, PAL, CP75*
Between Moon and Moon, June 1962, *NP62, CP65, PAL, CP75*
Between Trains, Nov. 1963, *MDWI, CP65, PAL, CP75*
Beware, Madam! Feb. 1962, *NP62, CP65, PAL, CP75*
Beyond Giving (*Song*), *BG, P68-70, CP75*
Bird of Paradise, *MDWI, CP65, PAL, CP75*
Birth of a Goddess, *P70-72, CP75*
Birth of Angels, *17PMLR, P65-68, LRA, PAL, CP75*
Bites and Kisses, July 1967, *CLR, P65-68, PAL, CP75*
Black, *LR, CP65, LRA, PAL, CP75*
Black Goddess, The, *MDWI, CP65, PAL, CP75*
Blackening Sky, July 1967, *CLR, P65-68, CP75*
Blanket Charge, Summer 1969, *BG, P68-70, CP75*
Blessed Sun, *CLR, P65-68, CP75*
Blind Arrow, A, May 1963, *MDWI, CP65, CP75*
Blow, The, *LR, LRA, PAL*
Bower-Bird, *CLR, P65-68, PAL, CP75*
Bracelet, A, *CLR, P65-68, PAL, CP75*
Breakfast Table, *P70-72, CP75*
Brief Reunion, April 1970, *P68-70, CP75*
Broken Compact, *P70-72, CP75*
Broken Girth, The, *NP62, CP65, PAL, CP75*
Broken Neck, *MDWI, CP65, CP75*
Burn It! Sept. 1960, *MP61, CP61*

Carol of Patience, Dec. 1969, *P68-70, CP75*
Casse-Noisette, *GSV, P70-72, CP75*
Catkind, July 1959, *FC*
Change, *LR, CP65, LRA, PAL, CP75*
Charm for Sound Sleeping, A, Sept. 1974, *CP75*
Cherries or Lilies (*Song*), *P65-68, PAL, CP75*
Child with Veteran, May 1970, *P68-70, CP75*
Circus Ring, *P70-72, CP75*
Cliff and Wave, *GSV, P70-72, CP75*
Cliff Edge, The, *NP62, CP65, CP75*
Clocks of Time, The, (*Song*), *BG, P68-70, CP75*
Clothed in Silence, *17PMLR, LRA*
Cock in Pullet's Feathers, *17PMLR, P65-68, LRA, PAL, CP75*
Colophon, *P70-72, CP75*
Colours of Night, The, *MDWI, CP65, CP75*
Come, Enjoy Your Sunday! (*Song*), April 1960, *MP61, CP61, CP65, CP75*
Compact, *BG, P68-70, CP75*
Complaint and Reply, *GSV, P70-72, CP75*
Confess, Marpessa, *GSV, P70-72, CP75*
Conjunction, *LR, CP65, LRA, PAL, CP75*

Consortium of Stones, *MDWI, CP65, CP75*
Coronet of Moonlight, *P70-72, CP75*
Court of Love, A, *LR, CP65, LRA, PAL, CP75*
Crab-Tree, The, *GSV, P70-72, CP75*
Crane, The, *CLR, P65-68, PAL, CP75*
Crown of Stars (*Song*), July 1967, *P65-68, PAL, CP75*
Crucibles of Love, *CP75*
Crystal, The, *CP75*
Cure, The, Jan. 1961, *MP61, CP61, CP65, 16P, CP75*

Dance of Words, Autumn 1963, *MDWI, CP65, CP75*
Dancing Flame, *LR66, 17PMLR, P65-68, LRA, PAL, CP75*
Dangerous Gift, The, Feb. 1961, *MP61, CP61, CP65, PAL, CP75*
Dans un Seul Lit, *P65-68, CP75*
Dazzle of Darkness, *MDWI, CP65, PAL, CP75*
De Arte Poetica, *P65-68, CP75*
Dead Hand, *17PMLR, P65-68, LRA, CP75*
Death Grapple, The, Jan. 1961, *MP61, CP61, CP65, 16P, PAL, CP75*
Deed of Gift, *MDWI, CP65, CP75*
Deliverance, *LR, CP65, LRA, PAL, CP75*
Depth of Love, *P70-72, CP75*
Descent into Hell, *CP65, CP75*
Desert Fringe, *P70-72, CP75*
Dew-drop and Diamond (*Song*), *P65-68, PAL, CP75*
Dilemma, The, July 1972, *P70-72, CP75*
Discarded Love Poem, The, Jan. 1974, *AG, CP75*
Double Bass, *CP65, CP75*
Dream of Frances Speedwell, A, Dec. 1971, *P70-72, CP75*
Dream of Hell, A, *CLR, P65-68, PAL, CP75*
Dream Recalled on Waking, *P70-72, CP75*
Dream Warning (*Song*), *BG, P68-70, CP75*
Dreaming Children, *GSV, P70-72, CP75*
Druid Love, *GSV, P70-72, CP75*

Eagre, The, *17PMLR, LRA*
Earlier Lovers, Sept. 1974, *AG, CP75*
East Wind, An, *MDWI, CP65, CP75*
Ecstasy of Chaos, *17PMLR, P65-68, LRA, PAL, CP75*
Elsewhere, *CP75*
Encounter, The, Spring 1964, *P70-72, CP75*
Endless Pavement, April 1963, *MDWI, CP65, PAL, CP75*
Envoi, *TM, CP75*
Established Lovers, July 1959, *FC, MP61, CP61*
Eurydice, *MDWI, CP65, CP75*
Everywhere Is Here, *LR, CP65, LRA, PAL, CP75*
Expect Nothing, Oct. 1963, *MDWI, CP65, PAL, CP75*

Fact of the Act, Aug. 1967, *P65-68, PAL, CP75*
Falcon Woman, The, Jan. 1961, *MP61, CP61, CP65, 16P, PAL, CP75*
Far Side of Your Moon, The, (*Song*), *LR, CP65, LRA, PAL, CP75*
Fast Bound Together, Dec. 1973, *AG, CP75*
Fetter, The, June 1965, *LR, CP65, LRA, PAL, CP75*
Field-Postcard, The, *CP75*
Fig Tree in Leaf (*Song*), *P65-68, CP75*
Fire Walker, *MDWI, CP65, CP75*
First Love, *P68-70, CP75*
Five; *Quinque*, *GSV, P70-72, CP75*
Flowering Aloe, The, *P70-72, CP75*
Food of the Dead, *MDWI, CP65, PAL, CP75*
Fools, June 1971, *GSV, P70-72, CP75*
For Ever, *P65-68, PAL, CP75*
Fortunate Child, Nov. 1965, *LR66, 17PMLR, P65-68, LRA, PAL, CP75*
Fragment, Jan. 1961, *MP61, CP61, CP65, PAL, CP75*
Freehold, *CLR, P65-68, CP75*
Friday Night, *P70-72, CP75*
Frog and the Golden Ball, The, *LR, CP65, LRA, PAL, CP75*
From Otherwhere or Nowhere (*Song*), Feb. 1973, *AG, CP75*

Garden, The, Spring 1971, *GSV, P70-72, CP75*
Gateway, The, *GSV, P70-72, CP75*
Gentleman, The, *GSV, P70-72, CP75*
Gift of Sight, *LR, CP65, LRA, CP75*
Gold and Malachite, *LR, CP65, LRA, PAL, CP75*
Gold Cloud, *BG, P68-70, CP75*
Golden Anchor, Jan. 1962, *NP62, CP65, PAL, CP75*
Good Night to the Old Gods, July 1965, *CP65, CP75*
Gooseflesh Abbey, Nov. 1966, *P65-68, CP75*
Gorge, The, *LR66, 17PMLR, P65-68, LRA, PAL, CP75*
Gorgon Mask, *GSV, P70-72, CP75*
Grace Notes, *CP65, PAL, CP75*
Green Castle, The, *MDWI, CP65, PAL, CP75*
Green Woods of Unrest, The, *CP75*
Green-Sailed Vessel, The, March 1971, *GSV, P70-72, CP75*
Growing Pains, *P70-72, CP75*

H, Sept. 1970, *P68-70, CP75*
Hag-Ridden, Jan. 1961, *MP61, CP61, CP65, 16P, CP75*
Half-Finished Letter, The, *P70-72, CP75*
Hazel Grove, The, *P70-72, CP75*
Hearth, The, *MDWI, CP65, PAL, CP75*
Heaven, *P70-72, CP75*
Hedges Freaked with Snow, *NP62, CP65, PAL, CP75*
Her Beauty, *P70-72, CP75*

Her Brief Withdrawal, July 1967, *CLR, P65-68, PAL, CP75*
Here Live Your Life Out! March 1959, *FC, MP61, CP61*
Hero, The, *PBFS, BG, P68-70, CP75*
Heroes in Their Prime, May 1959, *FC*
Hidden Garden, The, *LR, CP65, LRA, PAL, CP75*
Hide and Seek, *PBFS*
History of the Fall, July 1974, *CP75*
Home-Coming, The, *P65-68, CP75*
Hooded Flame, *CLR, P65-68, PAL, CP75*
Hoopoe Tells Us How, The, (Dedicatory), *GSV, P70-72, CP75*
Horizon, Nov. 1961, *NP62, CP65, PAL, CP75*
How Can I Care? (*Song*), *P65-68, CP75*
How It Started, *P68-70, CP75*
Hung Wu Vase, The, *MDWI, CP65, PAL, CP75*

I Have a Little Cough, Sir, *LFNR, AHH*
I Will Write, *MDWI, CP65, PAL, CP75*
I'd Die For You (Postscript), *LR, CP65, LRA, PAL, CP75*
Iago, *BG, P68-70, CP75*
Ibycus in Samos, June 1962, *NP62, CP65, CP75*
If and When, *PAL*
If No Cuckoo Sings, March 1974, *CP75*
Imminent Seventies, The, *P68-70, CP75*
Impossible, The, *LR, CP65, LRA, PAL, CP75*
Impossible Day, The, *TM, CP75*
In Disguise, Winter 1964, *MDWI, CP65, PAL, CP75*
In Her Only Way *NP62, CP65, PAL, CP75*
In Her Praise, Nov. 1961, *NP62, CP65, PAL, CP75*
In Perspective, Oct. 1966, *CLR, P65-68, PAL, CP75*
In the Name of Virtue, *BG, P68-70, CP75*
In the Vestry, July 1969, *P68-70, CP75*
In Time, Winter 1964, *MDWI, CP65, PAL, CP75*
In Time of Absence, *MDWI, CP65, PAL, CP75*
In Trance at a Distance, Jan. 1962, *NP62, CP65, CP75*
Injuries, *CLR, P65-68, PAL, CP75*
Inkidoo and the Queen of Babel, *NP62, CP65, PAL, CP75*
Intrusion, The, Jan. 1961, *MP61, CP61, 16P*
Invitation to Bristol, Sept. 1970, *P68-70, CP75*
Iron Palace, *LR, CP65, LRA, PAL, CP75*
Is Now the Time? July 1967, *P65-68, CP75*

Joan and Darby, Dec. 1959, *FC, MP61, CP61, CP65, CP75*
Jock o' Binnorie, Aug. 1926, *PF*
Joseph and Jesus, Jan. 1964, *AHH*
Joseph and Mary, *MDWI, CP65, PAL, CP75*
Judgement of Paris, Winter 1962, *MDWI, CP65, PAL, CP75*

Judges, The, April 1970, *P68-70, CP75*
Jugum Improbum, May 1968, *P65-68, PAL, CP75*
July 24th, *MDC*
Jus Primae Noctis, April 1971, *GSV, P70-72, CP75*
Just Friends (*Song*), *P65-68, CP75*

Knobs and Levers, *GSV, P70-72, CP75*

La Mejicana, *MDWI, CP65, PAL, CP75*
Lack, *NP62, CP65, CP75*
Lamia In Love, *MDWI, CP65, PAL, CP75*
Last Fistful, The, *P70-72, CP75*
Last Poem, A, *MDWI, CP65, CP75*
Late Arrival, A, April 1963, *MDWI*
Laugh, The, Jan. 1961, *MP61, CP61, CP65, 16P, CP75*
Leap, The, Winter 1964, *MDWI, CP65, PAL, CP75*
Like Owls, July 1967, *CLR, P65-68, CP75*
Lion Lover, May 1962, *NP62, CP65, PAL, CP75*
Lion-Gentle, *CLR, P65-68, PAL, CP75*
Logic, Sept. 1970, *P68-70, CP75*
Lost World, A, April 1961, *MP61, CP61, CP65, PAL, CP75*
Love and Night, Aug. 1970, *P68-70, CP75*
Love as Lovelessness, *TM, CP75*
Love Charms, *AG, CP75*
Love Gifts, *P68-70, CP75*
Love Letter, The, *AG, CP75*
Loving True, Flying Blind, Jan. 1966, *LR66, 17PMLR, P65-68, LRA, PAL, CP75*
Lure of Murder, Jan. 1966, *LR66, 17PMLR, P65-68, LRA, PAL, CP75*
Lyceia, Aug. 1960, *MP61, CP61, CP65, PAL, CP75*

Man Does, Woman Is, Winter 1964, *MDWI, CP65, PAL, CP75*
Man of Evil, Oct. 1970, *P68-70, CP75*
Mankind and Ocean, *P68-70, CP75*
Measure of Casualness, A, Oct. 1963, *MDWI, CP65, PAL, CP75*
Meeting, The, June 1962, *NP62, CP65, PAL, CP75*
Metaphor, The, *MDWI, CP65, PAL, CP75*
Miller's Man, The, *MDC, NP62, CP65, CP75*
Miracle, The, *GSV, DP*
Mist, Nov. 1966, *CLR, P65-68, PAL, CP75*
Moon's Last Quarter, The, *TM, CP75*
Moon's Tear, The, March 1974, *AG, CP75*
Motes, The, *BG*
Mountain Lovers, Oct. 1974, *CP75*
My Ghost (The Co-Walker), *P68-70, GSV, P70-72, CP75*
Myrrhina, Dec. 1963, *MDWI, CP65, PAL, CP75*

Name, *AG, CP75*
Name Day, June 1962, *NP62, CP65, CP75*
Narrow Sea, The, July 1967, *P65-68, PAL, CP75*
Near Eclipse, The, *17PMLR, P65-68, LRA, PAL, CP75*
Necklace, The, Sept. 1966, *CLR, P65-68, PAL, CP75*
New Eternity, The, *CP75*
New Year Kisses (*Song*), *BG*
Nightfall at Twenty Thousand Feet, Nov. 1960, *MP61, CP61*
Nightmare of Senility, *P70-72, CP75*
No Letter, *MDWI, CP65, PAL, CP75*
Non Cogunt Astra, April 1964, *MDWI, CP65, PAL, CP75*
None the Wiser, *P65-68, CP75*
Not at Home, May 1962, *NP62, CP65, PAL, CP75*
Not to Sleep, *MDWI, CP65, PAL, CP75*
Nothing Now Astonishes, *LR, CP65, LRA, PAL, CP75*

O, March 1962, *MDWI, CP65, CP75*
Of Course (*Song*), *P65-68, CP75*
Old World Dialogue, March 1959, *FC*
Oleaster, The, *MDWI, CP65, PAL, CP75*
Olive Tree (*Song*), June 1970, *P68-70, CP75*
Olive-Yard, The, July 1968, *P65-68, PAL, CP75*
On Giving, *17PMLR, P65-68, LRA, PAL, CP75*
Once More (*Song*), Sept. 1970, *P68-70, CP75*
Our Self, *CLR, P65-68, PAL, CP75*
Ours Is No Wedlock, Sept. 1974, *AG, CP75*
Ouzo Unclouded, *NP62, CP65, PAL, CP75*

Pact, The, *P70-72, CP75*
Palm Tree, The, (*Song*), Dec. 1966, *CLR, P65-68, PAL, CP75*
Pandora, Aug. 1970, *P68-70, CP75*
Pardon, The, *CP65, CP75*
Patience, Jan. 1961, *MP61, CP61, CP65, 16P, CP75*
Pearl, The, Oct. 1963, *MDWI, CP65, CP75*
P'eng that was a K'un, The, *CLR, P65-68, CP75*
Penny Fiddle, The, Aug. 1926, *PF*
Perfectionists, July 1967, *CLR, P65-68, PAL, CP75*
Person from Porlock, The, Oct. 1959, *FC, MP61, CP61*
Personal Packaging, Inc., *P65-68, CP75*
Phoenix Flame, A, (*Song*), (Morning Phoenix), *TB, P-G, MDWI, CP65, CP75*
Picture Nail, The, May 1959, *FC*
Pity, *P70-72, CP75*
Poem: A Reminder, *BG, P68-70, CP75*
Poet's Curse, The, *TM, CP75*
Point of No Return, *CP65, CP75*

Septuagenarian, The, April 1963, *MDWI, CP65, CP75*
Serpent's Tail, *GSV, P70-72, CP75*
Seven Fresh Years (*Song*), Sept. 1974, *AG, CP75*
Seven Years (Where Is the Truth?), *TM, CP75*
Sharp Ridge, The, Jan. 1961, *MP61, CP61, CP65, 16P, PAL, CP75*
She Is No Liar, Oct. 1963, *MDWI, CP65, PAL, CP75*
She to Him, *P65-68, PAL, CP75*
Shift of Scene, A, *CP65, LR66, CP75*
Should I Care? *TM, CP75*
Sigil, The, (*Song*), *P68-70, CP75*
Silent Visit, Sept. 1972, *P70-72, CP75*
Simpleton, The, June 1960, *MP61, CP61*
***Sincèrement*,** *P65-68, CP75*
Singleness in Love, *AG, CP75*
***Sit Mihi Terra Levis*,** *P65-68, CP75*
Six Badgers, The, 1955, *PF*
Snap-Comb Wilderness, The, *LR, CP65, LRA, PAL, CP75*
Snapped Thread, The, (The Tangled Thread), Jan. 1966, *LR66, 17PMLR, P65-68, LRA, PAL, CP75*
Solomon's Seal, May 1970, *P68-70, CP75*
Something to Say, *P68-70, CP75*
***Son Altesse*,** *LR, CP65, LRA, PAL, CP75*
Spite of Mirrors, *CLR, P65-68, PAL, CP75*
Spring 1974, *CP75*
St Antony of Padua, Sept. 1972, *P70-72, CP75*
St Valentine's Day, Feb. 1964, *AHH*
Starred Coverlet, The, Jan. 1961, *MP61, CP61, CP65, 16P, PAL, CP75*
Stolen Jewel, Jan. 66, *17PMLR, P65-68, LRA, PAL, CP75*
Strangeness, *CLR, P65-68, PAL, CP75*
Strangling in Merrion Square, The, June 1970, *P68-70, CP75*
Strayed Message, The, *BG, P68-70, CP75*
Sundial's Lament, The, (*Song*), *BG, P68-70, CP75*
Sun-Face and Moon-Face, Nov. 1966, *CLR, P65-68, PAL, CP75*
Superman on the Riviera, Jan. 1959, *FC*
Superstition (Leave-Taking), *BG, P68-70, CP75*
Surgical Ward: Men, Jan. 1960, *MP61, CP61, CP65, CP75*
Sweet-Shop Round the Corner, The, Summer 1965, *CP65, CP75*
Sword and Rose (*Song*), April 1964, *MDWI, CP65, PAL, CP75*
Symptoms of Love, Jan. 1961, *MP61, CP61, CP65, 16P, PAL, CP75*

Testament, *GSV, P70-72, CP75*
That Other World, *MDWI, CP65, CP75*
That Was the Night, *TM, CP75*
Theme of Death, The, *P68-70, CP75*
This Holy Month, *LR, CP65, LRA, PAL, CP75*
Those Blind from Birth, May 1971, *GSV, P70-72, CP75*

Those Who Came Short, June 1965, *LR, CP65, LRA, PAL, CP75*
Though Once True Lovers (*Song*), *P65-68, CP75*
Three Locked Hoops, *GSV, P70-72, CP75*
Three Rings for Her (*Song*), *P65-68, CP75*
Three Songs for the Lute, *NP62, CP65, PAL, CP75*
Three Times In Love, Sept. 1972, *CP75*
Three Words Only, *AG, CP75*
Three Years Waiting, *AG, CP75*
Three-Faced, The, *MDWI, CP65, PAL, CP75*
Through a Dark Wood, July 1969, *P68-70, CP75*
Tilth, May 1971, *P70-72, CP75*
Time of Waiting, A, Oct. 1963, *MDWI, CP65, PAL, CP75*
Timeless Meeting, *TM, CP75*
Title of Poet, The, March 1972, *P70-72, CP75*
To a Rose (*Song*), *BG, P68-70, CP75*
To Be In Love, *P65-68, PAL, CP75*
To Be Poets, *GSV, P70-72, CP75*
To Become Each Other (*Song*), *P70-72, CP75*
To Beguile and Betray, Autumn 1963, *MDWI, CP65, CP75*
To Come of Age, Sept. 1974, *CP75*
To Myrto About Herself, Winter 1964, *MDWI, CP65, CP75*
To Myrto of Myrtles, Jan. 1961, *MP61, CP61*
To Ogmian Hercules, July 1967, *P65-68, PAL, CP75*
To Put It Simply, *P68-70, CP75*
To Tell and Be Told, *P68-70, CP75*
To the Teumessian Vixen, Autumn 1963, *MDWI, CP65, PAL, CP75*
Toast to Death, A, *P70-72, CP75*
Tolling Bell, *BG, P68-70, CP75*
Tomorrow's Envy of Today, *LR, CP65, LRA, CP75*
Touch My Shut Lips, *TM, CP75*
Tousled Pillow, *P65-68, CP75*
Tower of Love, The, *AG, CP75*
Traditionalist, The, Sept. 1972, *P70-72, CP75*
Trial of Innocence, *BG, P68-70, CP75*
Troublesome Fame, April 1969, *BG, P68-70, CP75*
Troughs of Sea, Jan. 1961, *MP61, CP61, CP65, 16P, PAL, CP75*
True Evil, *TM, CP75*
True Joy, June 1965, *LR, CP65, LRA, PAL, CP75*
True Magic, *AG, CP75*
Truth Is Poor Physic, *NP62, CP65, PAL, CP75*
Turn of the Moon, Jan. 1961, *MP61, CP61, CP65, PAL, CP75*
Twice of the Same Fever, Jan. 1960, *FC, MP61, CP61, CP65, PAL, CP75*
Twinned Heart (*Song*), *P68-70, CP75*
Twins, Oct.-Dec. 1966, *P65-68, CP75*
Two Children (The Young Goddess), Dec. 1959, *FC, MP61, CP61*
Two Crucial Generations, *CP75*

Two Disciplines, *AG, CP75*
Two Rhymes About Fate and Money, Sept. 1960, *PF* **(How and Why),** *MP61*
Two Witches, The, *MP61, CP65, CP75*

Ugly Secret, The, *AG, CP75*
Uncalendared Love, May 1962, *NP62, CP65, CP75*
Uncut Diamond, The, March 1970, *P68-70, CP75*
Undead, The, *MDWI, CP65, PAL, CP75*
Under the Olives, Jan. 1961, *MP61, CP61, CP65, 16P, PAL, CP75*
Unnamed Spell, The, *NP62, CP65, CP75*
Unpenned Poem, The, May 1975, *CP75*
Unposted Letter (1963), *P70-72, TM, CP75*
Until We Both, *GSV, P70-72, CP75*
Utter Rim, The, Nov. 1966, *CLR, P65-68, CP75*

Victims of Calumny (*Song*), *P68-70, CP75*
Virgin Mirror, *P68-70, CP75*
Virus, The, *GSV, P70-72, CP75*
Visitation, The, Jan. 1961, *MP61, CP61, CP65, 16P, PAL, CP75*
Vow, The, *LR, CP65, LRA, PAL, CP75*

Wall, The, Sept. 1972, *P70-72, CP75*
Wand, The, *GSV, P70-72, CP75*
Watch, The, Nov. 1961, *NP62, CP65, CP75*
Wedding, The, *LR, CP65, LRA, CP75*
Were-Man, The, Feb. 1960, *FC, MP61, CP61*
What Can We Not Ask? *CP75*
What Did You Say? *17PMLR, P65-68, LRA, PAL, CP75*
What Is Love? *BG, P68-70, CP75*
What We Did Next, Summer 1969, *BG*
What Will Be, Is, *LR, CP65, LRA, CP75*
When and Why, *TM, CP75*
When Love Is Not, July 1969, *P68-70, CP75*
Wherever We May Be (*Song*), *BG, P68-70, CP75*
Whole Love, *LR, CP65, LRA, PAL, CP75*
Why of the Weather, The, April 1963, *MDWI, CP65, PAL, CP75*
Wigs and Beards, June 1967, *P65-68, CP75*
Wild Cyclamen, *LR, CP65, LRA, PAL, CP75*
Window Pane, The, *TM, CP75*
Winged Heart, The, *NP62, CP65, PAL, CP75*
With a Gift of Rings, *GSV, P70-72, CP75*
With No Return (*Song*), *MDWI*
With the Gift of a Lion's Claw, *P65-68, CP75*
Within Reason, *P65-68, PAL, CP75*
Woman of Greece, *MDWI, CP65, CP75*
Woman Poet and Man Poet, *CP75*

Women and Masks (translation), Autumn 1970, *P70-72, CP75*
Word, The, July 1967, *CLR, P65-68, PAL, CP75*
Work Drafts, May 1970, *GSV, P70-72, CP75*
Work Room, July 1967, *P65-68, CP75*
Wreath, The, June 1962, *NP62, CP65, CP75*

Yesterday Only (*Song*), *BG, P68-70, CP75*
Yet Unsayable, The, *P65-68, PAL, CP75*
Young Sibyl, The, *P70-72, CP75*

NOTES ON THE POEMS

The arrangement of the notes corresponds to that of the poems, with a brief introduction to each of Graves's books of verse.

Textual notes are keyed to the text by stanza (*st.*), section (*sect.*) and line numbers.

As in the text, single quotation marks have been adopted.

Data on the poems in this volume is given as follows:

i) Background information, with quotations from and/or references to other poems, letters, and prose works. When *The White Goddess* is cited, the abbreviation *WG61* is followed by the page reference to the 1961 edition, and then, after an oblique stroke, to the revised edition.

ii) First publication (uncollected poems; for poems from books, see 'Publication Details', above).

iii) 'Text': the source – book(s), periodical/newspaper, manuscript(s) and/or typescript(s) – of the last version as printed in the text of this edition. If revisions have been incorporated from a book in Graves's library, the abbreviation is followed by *Lib*.

iv) Previous titles in books and (uncollected poems) periodicals.

v) 'Emendations': the emendation is given first, followed by a closing square bracket; the unemended text is then quoted to the right of the bracket. Where an earlier reading has been preferred, the source is indicated. *Ed.* denotes an editorial correction.

vi) For poems from books and uncollected poems, lists under 'Variants' (or 'Other variants') are preceded and/or followed by any omitted material, together with other details about different versions. In the lists, the version in this edition is quoted on the left, followed by a closing square bracket (as with 'Emendations'); to the right of the bracket is the reading in the first edition or first publication (unless otherwise specified). When a whole line has been revised, only the line in the first edition/publication is given. For successive quotations from the same text, the source only appears after the initial quotation, to avoid undue repetition.

vi) For unpublished poems, information about other versions is followed by posthumous publication details (where applicable), and evidence for dates of composition.

FOOD FOR CENTAURS (1960)

Food for Centaurs was the last of four books in which Graves included poems together with prose pieces, the other three being *The Crowning Privilege* (1955), *5 Pens in Hand* (1958) and *Steps* (1958).

Published in the United States on 6 May 1960 by Doubleday, *Food for Centaurs* contains twenty poems in its fifth and final section (after 'Stories', 'Talks on Poetry', 'Studies in History' and 'Critiques of New Books'). The thirteen new poems are indicated by an asterisk in the following list ('Heroes in Their Prime', 'Cat-Kind', 'Superman on the Riviera' and 'The Picture Nail' were published in England only in magazines, and 'Old World Dialogue' not at all):

Trudge, Body!; The Christmas Robin; Twice of the Same Fever*; Nothing; Call It a Good Marriage; Read Me, Please!; The Twin of Sleep; Established Lovers*; The Quiet Glades of Eden*; Heroes in Their Prime*; Catkind*; The Young Goddess*; Here Live Your Life Out*; Joan and Darby*; Superman on the Riviera*; The Picture Nail*; Old World Dialogue*; The Were-Man*; The Person from Porlock*; Around the Mountain.

The poems are preceded by a 'Preface to a Reading of Poems' given at the University of Michigan on 12 February 1958 (also printed in *Steps*; see the note in *Complete Poems*, Volume II, for an extract).

Established Lovers

Text: *CP61*.
Variant:

st.3 l.5	the *CP61*] that *FC*

The Quiet Glades of Eden

Text: *CP75*.
Variants:

st.1 l.4	Classic *CP75*] noble *FC*
st.2 l.2	protest] protest,
st.4 l.1	agreed,] indeed,
l.2	pure] hot

Heroes in Their Prime

This poem was written on 21-23 August 1958 (Diary), while Graves was working on *The Anger of Achilles* (New York: Doubleday, 1959; London: Cassell, 1960), his translation of the *Iliad*. 'Nestor, Homer's favourite butt after Agamemnon, can never refrain from boasting of his youthful prowess', he writes in the Introduction, describing him as 'droning on' instead of attending to his wounded comrade Machaon in Book XI – here 'Homer's humour is at its dryest' (pp.21-2 (American edition)/xx-xxi

(English edition)); see pp.199/164-5, 201-6/167-71, 235-6/200-1, and Ronald Searle's illustration facing p.168 in the American edition.

See also *GM*, for sts.1-2: 96.*b,c,d,k*, 98, 104.*f,g*; sts.3-4: 75; sts.5-6: 148, 152.*a-i*, 157.*b*; sts.7-8: 80.*g*, 139.*e,f*.

Text: *FC*.

Two Children

Text: *CP61*.

Previous title: 'The Young Goddess' (*FC*).

Here Live Your Life Out!

Originally called 'The Mulberry Tree', this poem was written on a train journey from Barcelona to Geneva.

Text: *CP61*.

Variants:

sect.1 l.7	Hills, hay-fields, orchards, mills – *CP61*] Hills, mills, hayfields, orchards – *FC*

In *FC* the title does not have an exclamation mark.

Joan and Darby

Text: *CP75*.

Variants:

st.3 l.4	Like *CP75*] As *FC*
	in their] share a
l.5	Who] But

In the copy of *MP61* with his revisions for *CP65*, Graves has cancelled st.1 with three diagonal lines (Canelluñ).

Old World Dialogue

Text: *MP61* proof (Canelluñ).

In a proof copy of *MP61* date-stamped 10 January 1961 (Canelluñ), 'Old World Dialogue' is printed on p.38; over it is pasted a carbon typescript of 'The Two Witches', which replaced it. The text differs from *FC* as follows: in st.1 in *FC*, the closing inverted comma at the end of l.1 is missing, l.3 does not have a comma after 'But' and 'hush!', and l.4 'Much' is in roman; in st.2, l.4 has 'blind' in place of 'red'. (An indent in st.1 l.4 and an extra space after the line-break in the proof are evidently errors.)

The Person from Porlock

'The Person from Porlock' was first published in *Papeles de Son Armadans*, 15 (Oct. 1959), 50, and issued as an offprint – fifty signed copies of a four-page booklet containing the text, a reproduction of the manuscript, and a Spanish translation by Camilo José Cela.

Text: *CP61*.

Graves has shortened and slightly adapted the extract from Coleridge's note.

THE PENNY FIDDLE (1960)

The publication by Cassell on 10 November 1960 of *The Penny Fiddle: Poems for Children*, illustrated by Edward Ardizzone, was the realisation of a project dating back to 1918.

The original *Penny Fiddle*, a collection of rhymes for children (see the note on *Treasure Box* in *Complete Poems*, Volume I), had illustrations by Graves's first wife, Nancy Nicholson, and songs set to music by H.R. Heath. 'We have been two years making the book perfect', Graves wrote in 1920 when he sent it to his agent, who was, however, unable to get it published.[1]

The 1960 volume contains twenty-three poems; eighteen of them appeared in books of verse in 1916-1930, and of the rest, four are revised versions of uncollected poems from the same period or include some early material (see the notes below). The one completely new poem, 'How and Why', was revised and republished as the second of 'Two Rhymes About Fate and Money' in *More Poems 1961*, and is printed in this version in the present edition.

The following list gives the complete contents:

The Penny Fiddle; Allie (*CS*); Robinson Crusoe; The Six Badgers; One Hard Look (*CS*); Jock o' Binnorie; What Did I Dream? (*TB*); Lift-Boy (*10PM*); Henry and Mary (*TB*); Dicky (*CS*); Love Without Hope (*WH*); The Hills of May (*P-G*); In the Wilderness (*OB*); 'The General Elliott' (*W*); Vain and Careless (*CS*); The Forbidden Play (*CS*); The Bedpost (*W*); The Well-Dressed Children (*CS*); The Magical Picture (*P-G*); The *Alice Jean* (*CS*); A Boy in Church (*FF*); How and Why; Warning to Children (*P29*).

The Penny Fiddle

Text: *PF*.

This poem was first published in *Collins' Children's Annual* (London: Collins, 1926), p.12, with st.1 as in *PF*, and these two further stanzas:

If I had but saved up the halfpennies
  That I spent upon buns and plums,
A shilling would have bought real music,
  But now the whisper comes.

I shall sell my boots to buy a fiddle,
  And walk about with ankles bare,
I shall laugh in the falling snow-flakes,
  For what should a fiddler care.

A manuscript (Buffalo) of this version (inscribed 'For Collins') has 'But

[1] Graves to E. Pinker, 18 May [1920]; Berg.

now not a whisper comes.' in place of st.2 l.4 as printed, which is defective both in sense and metre; and a question mark after 'care' in st.3 l.4. A version similar to the one in *PF* appeared in *The Merry-Go-Round: A Collection of Rhymes and Poems for Children*, edited by James Reeves (London: Heinemann, 1955),[2] p.133; differences from *PF* include 'A little red man' in place of 'A gipsy girl' in st.2 l.1, and 'guineas' for 'shillings' in st.3 l.3.

Robinson Crusoe

Text: *PF*.

For st.3 ll.3-4, cf. an unpublished early typescript poem of twenty lines entitled 'Pig' (Buffalo), with the headnote 'A Scene From the Mabinogian':[3]

> Unto Math, Mathonwy's son,
> Spoke the wizard Gwydion.
>
> 'To the Southward I divine
>   The appearance of a beast,
> Like no beast, O Math, of thine –
>   Good for hunting, good for feast.

The wizard ends:

> With the Pig as staff and stay
>   Thou shalt journey in no doubt
> Bacon ushers in new day,
>   Pork! shall put thy candle out.'

The last four lines above also appear in a slightly different version in another eight-line manuscript poem called 'Pig', dated 'Sept 1913' (Buffalo):

> Silver pigs
> Carven fair,
> Potent prove
> To chase dull care.
> With the pig as staff and stay
> Man need journey in no doubt:
> Bacon ushers in his day,
> 'Pork!' should put his candle out.[4]

---

[2] The anthology is not recorded in Higginson. See the note on 'The Six Badgers' (*PF*), below.

[3] From the tale 'Math the Son of Mathonwy', in the edition of Lady Charlotte Guest's translation in Graves's library (London: Dent, 1906), pp.61-80; the 'scene' is on p.62.

[4] This version is from the 'Juvenilia' typescript (see the note on 'A Pot of White Heather' ('Uncollected Poems')); in the manuscript, 'care' in l.4 has a capital 'C' and there is a full stop after 'doubt' in l.6.

(The final line refers to extinguishing a candle by saying 'Pork!' at the flame instead of blowing on it.)

The Six Badgers

Text: *PF*.

This was one of several unpublished rhymes 'of 1923-24 vintage' that Graves came across while 'rummaging idly in the attic' at Canelluñ and sent to James Reeves in 1950.[5] Reeves printed 'The Six Badgers' (with some differences from *PF* in wording, punctuation and layout) and another unpublished rhyme, 'The Pumpkin' ('Uncollected Poems'), in his 1955 Heinemann anthology for children, *The Merry-Go-Round*,[6] pp.135, 141, and also in a later children's anthology, *A Golden Land* (London: Constable, 1958), pp.260, 286.

Jock o' Binnorie

Text: *PF*.

An earlier version of sts.1 and 3, entitled 'The King's Story Teller', was included in the typescript of Graves's unpublished 1918 collection 'The Patchwork Flag' (Berg) (see 'Unpublished Poems'). It was printed as 'The Story Teller' in *Collins' Children's Annual* (London: Collins, 1926), p.11, with changes in wording, punctuation and layout; 'King Andrew' becomes 'King Stephen', and the story-teller 'Andrew' instead of 'Philip'. James Reeves put a similar version with the title 'King Stephen' in *The Merry-Go-Round* (1955).[7] The following also appears as no.36 in *LFNR* (1927), p.16:

> I'll tell you a story of Jock o' Binnorie,
>   And now my story's begun;
> I'll tell you another of Jock and his brother,
>   And now my story's done.

MORE POEMS 1961 (1961)

More Poems 1961 was published by Cassell on 11 May 1961. The 'Foreword' states: 'This is a supplement to *Collected Poems, 1959*; hence the section numbers XI and XII. Four poems, *Fragment, In Single Syllables, The Laugh,* and *A Lost World* are early ones revised.' There is also a fifth, 'Under the Olives' (see the note below).

Graves placed four of them in section XI, among poems written in June-November 1960.[8] The twenty-two-poem section begins a sequence,

---

[5] See Graves to Reeves, 14 Dec. 1950, *SL2*, p.83; also Graves to Reeves, n.d. [1952], *SL2*, p.105.

[6] See the note on 'The Penny Fiddle' (*PF*), above.

[7] See the previous note.

[8] Diary.

continued in *New Poems 1962* and *Man Does, Woman Is* (1964), in which he 'ventured to dramatize, truthfully and factually, the vicissitudes of a poet's dealings with the White Goddess, the Muse, the perpetual Other Woman':[9]

> By ancient tradition, the White Goddess becomes one with her human representative – a priestess, a prophetess, a queen-mother. No Muse-poet grows conscious of the Muse except by experience of a woman in whom the Goddess is to some degree resident; just as no Apollonian poet can perform his proper function unless he lives under a monarchy or a quasi-monarchy. A Muse-poet falls in love, absolutely, and his true love is for him the embodiment of the Muse. As a rule, the power of absolutely falling in love soon vanishes; and, as a rule, because the woman feels embarrassed by the spell she exercises over her poet-lover and repudiates it; he, in disillusion, turns to Apollo who, at least, can provide him with a livelihood and intelligent entertainment, and reneges before his middle 'twenties [*sic*]. But the real, perpetually obsessed Muse-poet distinguishes between the Goddess as manifest in the supreme power, glory, wisdom and love of woman, and the individual woman whom the Goddess may make her instrument for a month, a year, seven years, or even more. The Goddess abides; and perhaps he will again have knowledge of her through his experience of another woman.[10]

'In Single Syllables', a revised version of 'This Is Noon' (*P14-26*) (see *Complete Poems*, Volume I, pp.316-17, and the note on p.420) follows 'The Death Grapple' in *More Poems 1961* and *Collected Poems 1961*, after which it

---

[9] 'Intimations of the Black Goddess' (1963), *MBG*, p.151; in the 'Foreword' to *MDWI* he refers to it as 'a three-book sequence dramatizing the vicissitudes of poetic love' (see the note below). 'Factually', the sequence concerns Graves's relationship with Margot Callas, his 'muse' in 1960-63; they met at Deyá on 10 June 1960 (see *RPG 3*, pp.308, 311, *et seq*.).

[10] 'Postscript 1960', *WG61*, pp.490/481. Graves added the 'Postscript' when he was revising *WG52* for the third edition, from 24 March to 17 June 1960 (Diary). It comprises extracts from his 1957 lecture 'The White Goddess' (in *5PH*, pp.54-72, and *S*, pp.86-105; the text in *S* is included in the 1997 revised edition of *WG61*, pp.489-504). The passage above was reprinted with one change: in *5PH* and *S* the first sentence begins 'By ancient religious theory'. Cf. *MBG*, p.151: 'On consulting the Oxford English Dictionary, to discover from its dated quotations what English poet had first written of an inspiratory Muse possessing a particular woman, I was surprised to find no such concept mentioned, though it has lately become a literary commonplace. [. . .] Though I have believed in a personal Muse for so long that I cannot recall her first entry into my heart, I would feel far happier to know that some other poet – Raleigh or Coleridge or Keats, for instance, all of whom record their visions of the Muse-goddess – had anticipated me in this usage.' (See *WG61* (1997), Introduction, pp.xi-xii.)

was suppressed (but see the note on 'The Intrusion', below).

'A Lost World' is in the other section, XII. Of its eighteen poems, eight were published in America a year earlier, in *FC*; these are indicated with an asterisk in the following contents list:

XI
Lyceia; Symptoms of Love; The Sharp Ridge; Under the Olives; The Visitation; Fragment; Apple Island; The Falcon Woman; Troughs of Sea; The Laugh; The Death Grapple; In Single Syllables; The Starred Coverlet; The Intrusion; Patience; The Cure; Hag-Ridden; Turn of the Moon; The Secret Land; Seldom Yet Now; To Myrto of Myrtles; Anchises to Aphrodite

XII
Two Children*; A Lost World; The Dangerous Gift; Twice of the Same Fever*; Surgical Ward: Men; Nightfall at Twenty Thousand Feet; The Simpleton; The Were-Man*; Two Rhymes About Fate and Money; The Two Witches; The Person from Porlock*; Established Lovers*; The Quiet Glades of Eden*; Here Live Your Life Out!*; Burn It!; Joan and Darby*; Song: Come, Enjoy Your Sunday!

Lyceia

See *WG61*, pp.222/216, 390/381-2; and *GM*, 22, 114.*h*.

Text: *CP75*.

Emendation:

st.7 l.3 hope, *MP61*, *CP61*] hope. *CP75*

Symptoms of Love

Text: *CP75*.

Variant:

st.5 l.2 Could *CP75*] Can *MP61*

Under the Olives

Text: *CP75*.

Graves adapted 'Under the Olives' from an unpublished twenty-one line poem in blank verse, 'Scarves', among the manuscripts acquired in 1959 by the State University of New York at Buffalo, which he visited in May 1960 for the inaugural exhibition:

> At Buffalo I was shown three or four 1930-35 ms poems from the bundle I sent them, and asked if they had ever been published, and if not, why not. They looked O.K. and surmise that Laura asked me to suppress them. I'll get copies sent me, and see if they pass muster. It may have been, of course, that I forgot about them when I snatched up my handbag and caught the last destroyer back to England in 1936. It's rather like finding a buried blackened silver spoon (Hester Bateman) in a flower

bed the other day.[11]

The Visitation

See *WG61*, pp.192/187-8.

Text: *MP61/CP75*.

Fragment

Text: *MP61/CP75*.

'Fragment' was originally st.1 of 'The Kiss' (*TB*) (see *Complete Poems*, Volume I). This version first appeared in the 'Foreword' to *CP38*, p.xxi (Graves has written the title 'Fragment' above the stanza in the bound proof copy in his library); it differs slightly in punctuation from the printings in *TB* and *P-G*, and the indents in the even-numbered lines have been suppressed.

Apple Island

See *WG61*, pp.254-8/246-50 and 292/283-4; 310/302 and 312-13/304; 374/365, 385-6/376-8 and 395/386; 447-8/438-9; and *GM*, 11. See also 'The Felloe'd Year' (*TWE*), and 'To Juan at the Winter Solstice' (*P38-45*) and 'The White Goddess' (*PS51*), with the notes to these two poems and to 'The Battle of the Trees' (*CP14-47*), in *Complete Poems*, Volume II.

Text: *MP61/CP75*.

Troughs of Sea

Text: *CP75*.

Variant:

st.4 l.2 walls, *CP75*] waves, *MP61* (*misprint*)

The Laugh

Text: *MP61/CP75*.

The first six lines of 'The Laugh' are adapted from st.1 of an unpublished manuscript poem in four six-line stanzas, 'Love in Absence' (Buffalo) (ll.2-6 have only three changes: l.2 'grew' and 'would' in place of 'was made' and 'was', and l.5 'manageable' for 'governable'). The title 'Love in Absence' appears, cancelled, in a draft list of contents for *P30-33* (Buffalo). This is evidently another of the poems Graves was shown in Buffalo in May 1960:[12] see the note on 'Under the Olives' (*MP61*), above.

The Death Grapple

Text: *CP75*.

---

[11] Graves to James Reeves, 6 June 1960; Texas. On 25 Sept. 1960 he recorded in his diary, 'Working on poems from Buffalo[,] The Lost World – & Under the Olives – '. See the notes on 'The Laugh' and 'A Lost World' (both *MP61*).

[12] He mentions it in his diary on 19 Sept. 1960 – 'Going over old poem now called *The Laugh*' – and again the next day.

Variant:
sect.1 l.1 between *CP75*] below *MP61*

The Starred Coverlet

See *WG61*, pp.262/254.
Text: *MP61/CP75*.

The Intrusion

See *GM*, 88.*8*.
Text: *MP61/CP61*.

Like 'In Single Syllables' (*P14-26*) (see the note on *MP61*, above), 'The Intrusion' was omitted from section XI after *CP61*, but reprinted in a selection from this section which was published as a limited edition, *Sixteen Poems*, by students of the Oxford College of Technology in 1967. In both poems there is a word that differs from the *MP61* text: 'The Intrusion' has 'comfort' in place of 'consolation' in sect.3 l.1, evidently an error; similar discrepancies occur in poems reprinted, according to the colophon in *16P*, from *CP65* ('Symptoms of Love', st.5 l.2 'pain' for 'grief'; 'The Visitation', st.5 l.1 'dispels' for 'scatters'; 'The Falcon Woman', st.3 l.3 'farther' for 'faster'). The text of 'The Intrusion' in the present edition has, therefore, been taken from *MP61* and *CP61* (identical), even though *16P* is later.

Hag-Ridden

For the 'Hag of the Mill' – 'another name for the White Goddess' – see Graves's account of the medieval Irish tale *The Madness of Suibne*, which 'must be the most ruthless and bitter description in all European literature of an obsessed poet's predicament', in *WG61*, pp.450-5/441-6 (p.455/446),[13] with his versions of extracts from three of the poems incorporated in the tale.[14]
Text: *MP61/CP75*.

Turn of the Moon

See *GM*, pp.13-14, and 21.*10*, 22.*2*.
Text: *MP61/CP75*.

The Secret Land

'If I die in a state of grace, my timeless paradise will be the secret garden of the woman I love best.'[15]
Text: *CP75*.

---

[13] An extract, slightly revised, from 'Sweeney Among the Blackbirds', in *S*, pp.120-6, *FC*, pp.112-18, and *CWP*, pp.276-81.

[14] He used the original Irish Text Society edition of the tale, translated and edited by J.G. O'Keeffe (London: David Nutt, 1913).

[15] 'Lecture Three, 1965', *PCP*, p.177, republished as 'Ecstasy', *CWP*, p.511.

Emendations:

st.5 l.3 palm; *CP61*] palm. *MP61, CP75*

st.6 l.2 hollowed *MP61, CP61*] hallowed *CP75* (*misprint*)

(The 1988 American issue of *CP75* (New York: Oxford University Press) has the second emendation.)

Seldom Yet Now

Text: *CP75*.

Variant:

st.1 l.2 fierce *CP75*] wild *MP61*

To Myrto of Myrtles

See *WG61*, p.262/254.

Text: *MP61/CP61*.

Anchises to Aphrodite

See *GM*, 18.*f,g,3*; and (for the 'knot-of-wisdom', st.1 l.2) 'The Personal Muse', *OAP*, p.77, and *CWP*, p.350.

Text: *MP61/CP61*.

A Lost World

Text: *MP61/CP75*.

'A Lost World' is the revised version of another of the '1930-35' manuscript poems Graves obtained from Buffalo; see the note on 'Under the Olives' (*MP61*), above. (The manuscripts and typescript have the titles 'It was so, it was true' and 'Tears for Old Love'.)

The Dangerous Gift

Text: *CP75*.

Variant:

st.1 l.2 that *CP75*] the *MP61*

In his library copy of *CP61* Graves has cancelled 'For' in st.2 l.3 and written 'And'; this change appears in 'Intimations of the Black Goddess', *MBG*, p.153, and *CWP*, p.391, but not elsewhere.

Surgical Ward: Men

Following a prostatectomy at St Thomas's Hospital, London, on 7 September 1959, Graves suffered haemorrhaging which necessitated two further operations, the last, on 22 September, 'after some memorable pain'.[16] See *RPG 3*, pp.295-6.

Text: *CP75*.

---

[16] Diary (Graves dictated the entry for 22 Sept. to his wife); he wrote the poem in six drafts on 20-26 October.

Two Rhymes About Fate and Money

Text: *MP61*.

The second rhyme was published as one of the 'Poems for Children' in *PF* (1960), with the title 'How and Why'.

Variant:

st.2 l.4 But *MP61*] Yet *PF*

The Two Witches

See the note on 'Old World Dialogue' (*FC*).

Text: *CP75*.

Variant:

st.1 l.4 of years *CP75*] of all years *MP61*

Burn It!

Text: *MP61*/*CP61*.

Graves's diary records that he worked daily on a 'Piece for 65th birthday' (24 July 1960) from 30 June to 5 July 1960, when he 'decided to abandon it'. The next day he noted, 'To Palma[;] worked in the flat and cafes on *Burning a Manuscript*', and on 7 July he wrote the tenth draft.

Song: Come, Enjoy Your Sunday!

See 'Lecture Three, 1965', *PCP*, pp.178-9, republished as 'Ecstasy', *CWP*, pp.511-12:

> A few years ago, after an emotional crisis, I wrote a poem advising myself to be content with the mild pleasures of old age and inaction: ['*Song:* Come, Enjoy Your Sunday!' quoted]. But it was already another Monday morning; the Moon being insistent in her demands: ['Between Moon and Moon' (*NP62*) quoted].

Text: *CP75*.

This poem was first published in the *London Magazine*, 7 (April 1960), 29, as 'Song: A Month of Sundays', with a different word at the beginning of the fourth line in each stanza: 'Fool,', 'And', 'Then', 'Come,', 'So' (the fourth and fifth lines are in italics).

COLLECTED POEMS 1961 (1961)

Published on 21 July 1961 by Doubleday, *Collected Poems 1961* was the American edition of *Collected Poems 1959*, augmented by sections XI and XII from *More Poems 1961*, which Graves termed 'a supplement' to the previous volume. The 'Foreword' is from *Collected Poems 1959*, updated and slightly adapted (see note, *Complete Poems*, Volume II).

There are 272 poems in *Collected Poems 1961*. The first ten sections are as in *Collected Poems 1959*, with the following changes: in section II, a revised version of an earlier poem, 'The Coronation Murder' (*P-G*) (see *Complete Poems*, Volume I, pp.134-5 and 370-2), appears between 'Ancestors' and 'Children of Darkness', while another revised earlier poem, 'A Lost World' (*MP61*), transferred from section XII, follows 'The Bards'; and four poems are omitted:

III: 'Saint'. IX: 'With the Gift of a Ring'. X: 'The Enlisted Man'; 'Read Me, Please!'

Graves made further changes in the two sections from *More Poems 1961*. In section XI, 'The Cure' follows 'Hag-Ridden' instead of preceding it, while the last four poems are re-ordered thus: 'Seldom, Yet Now' (the comma was removed in *Collected Poems 1965*); 'Anchises to Aphrodite'; 'The Secret Land'; 'To Myrto of Myrtles'. He omitted in section XII 'Two Rhymes About Fate and Money' and 'The Two Witches' (the latter was restored in *Collected Poems 1965*), and placed the one new poem, 'Ruby and Amethyst', after 'Joan and Darby'. The volume closes with 'Leaving the Rest Unsaid'.

Ruby and Amethyst

See 'Intimations of the Black Goddess', *MBG*, pp.147-51, and *CWP*, pp.387-90:

> There are two distinct, but complementary, orders of women, both of them honoured by poets. First, the ideal woman of patriarchal civilization whom the Greeks deified as the Goddess Hestia, the Lahns as Vesta; and who is represented in Christianity as the Virgin Mary – heroine of all old-fashioned songs and stories. Beautiful, tender, true, patient, practical, dependable: the woman whom Solomon described as 'more precious than rubies' – the guardian of the sacred hearth, the wife-to-be, dreamt of by romantic soldiers in desert bivouacs.
>
> Then the other woman: the multitudinously named White Goddess, a relic of matriarchal civilization or (who knows?) the harbinger of its return. She scorns any claim on her person, or curb on her desires; rejects male tutelage, hates marriage, and demands utter trust and faithfulness from her lovers – treating love not as a matter of contract, but as a sudden, unforeseeable miracle. She punishes the pride of any suitor who dares hope that he will one day make her his wife. [. . .]
>
> [. . .] The difference between these complementary characters is presented in: ['Ruby and Amethyst' quoted]. The Muse and Vesta rule different worlds. Yet few rubies are unflawed. The sacred hearth fire is often left unattended, and to marry even the Virgin Mary herself did not make a poet of Saint Joseph . . . In fact, more poems spring from a realization that domestic love has cooled or died than from resolute praises of domesticity; and the Muse, the perpetual Other Woman, always inspires them. Nevertheless, there are settled marriages over which the White Goddess has no power. She will smile if the husband

writes his faithful wife a well-turned ode on their silver wedding anniversary, and pass on with a disdainful shrug.

For st.5 l.2 'garden', see 'The Poet in a Valley of Dry Bones', *MBG*, p.93, and *CWP*, p.380:

> Among the gaps in the *Oxford English Dictionary* is *garden*: a jeweller's term for the bright cloudiness in certain gems, caused by chemical impurities, but giving them individuality and character. I am told that such a *garden* now proves that it is a genuine stone: such chemists as can artificially produce genuine rubies, emeralds, sapphires and the rest, have not yet got round to making any but flawlessly translucent ones: [st.5 quoted].

Text: *CP75*.

THE MORE DESERVING CASES (1962)

'Wonderful what the excision of bad lines will do for an old poem', Graves commented on *The More Deserving Cases: Eighteen Old Poems for Reconsideration*, which was published in a limited edition (400 copies) by the Marlborough College Press on 1 February 1962.[17]

The 'Foreword' states:

> I am sometimes asked to reconsider long-discarded poems, and have kept a mental list of these, from which I recently picked out the more deserving cases. Many of them needed drastic abridgement as well as general amendment; others had been let go for personal reasons that no longer seemed cogent.
> Eighteen of them are here resurrected, for however brief a new life, by the kindness of my great-nephew Martin Freeth, Master of the Chapel at Marlborough College, and his fellow-printers.

Of the eighteen poems, fifteen had been published previously (see the notes in *Complete Poems*, Volumes I and II): 'Sullen Moods' (later '*Song:* Sullen Moods') (*W*); 'The Dialecticians' (*W*); 'A Village Feud' (*W*); 'The Clipped Stater' (*WH*); 'Epitaph on an Unfortunate Artist' (*W*); 'The Corner Knot' (*P14-26*); 'Death of the Farmer' (*WH*); 'Virgil the Sorcerer' (*P14-26*); 'Pygmalion to Galatea' (*P14-26*); 'Diplomatic Relations' (*MBH*); 'The Philatelist-Royal' (*P14-27*); 'To Be Less Philosophical' (later '*Song:* To Be Less Philosophical') (*P14-27*); 'Variables of Green' (previously 'Green

[17] Graves to James Reeves, 29 May 1961; *SL 2*, p.203. The book was produced by Graves's great-nephew with a group of fellow pupils. There was another issue of 350 copies.

Loving') (*CP38*); 'Devilishly Provoked' (previously 'Devilishly Disturbed') (*TWE*); 'The Blotted Copy-Book' (*P53*). The last poem is preceded by three earlier poems published for the first time, 'The Miller's Man, 'July 24th' and 'Safe Receipt of a Censored Letter' (see the notes below).

The most 'drastic abridgement' was undergone by 'Virgil the Sorcerer', which lost nine of its twenty stanzas, and by 'Death of the Farmer', reduced from sixteen stanzas to seven.

The Miller's Man

Cf. *WG61*, pp.140/135.

Text: *CP75*.

Graves records in his diary that he wrote 'The Miller's Man' on 16-17 May 1938. At this time he was going over his poems for *CP38* with Laura Riding, and presumably she rejected it. In the 'Contents' in *MDC* it is dated '1934'; it may have been among the copies of '1930-35' manuscript poems sent from Buffalo in 1960 (see the note on 'Under the Olives' (*MP61*), above). The poem was reprinted later the same year in *NP62*.

For the title, cf. no.59 in *LFNR*, p.23:

> God made the bees,
> And the bees make honey.
> The miller's man does all the work,
> But the miller makes the money.

July 24th

In the 'Contents' of *MDC* this poem is dated '1942' (see st.8 l.3).

Text: *MDC*.

Emendation:

st.4 l.3 Sweden *Ed.*] Sweeden *MDC* (*misprint*)

Safe Receipt of a Censored Letter

Though dated '1942' in *MDC*, this poem was in fact written in London on 11-13 January 1938. The letter, which arrived via Mallorca on 10 January, had been sent by Ernest Neale, the postman in the village of Islip, near Oxford, where Graves lived in 1921-26.[18]

In his diary on 10 January 1938 Graves noted: 'Letter from Mr Neale - – a year & a half old – about a year after his death[,] forwarded from Palma.'[19] The letter must have reached Palma not long after Graves and Laura Riding left Mallorca on 2 August 1936, following the outbreak of the Spanish Civil War.

---

[18] Graves dedicated his 'Ballad-Opera' *John Kemp's Wager* (Oxford: Basil Blackwell, 1925) 'To my friend Ernest Neale of the Islip Post Office' (the villain in the play is the village postman, Harry Dee).

[19] The next day's diary entry ends, 'Poem: *A letter from Ernest Neale*'; two more drafts were recorded on 12 Jan., and a further two (with the final title) the following day.

'Safe Receipt of a Censored Letter' was replaced by 'The Fallen Signpost' in the proofs of *CP38*.[20]

Text: *MDC*.

NEW POEMS 1962 (1962)

> Have just got the proofs of my *New Poems* which will be published in October. They come as a shock because the cumulative effect of so many particular instances is far greater than I had thought; publication at the beginning of the Michaelmas term will put me in an odd position – they are *not* the sort of poems that a professor writes, and the nearest I have ever got to saying what I mean.[21]

New Poems 1962 was published by Cassell on 18 October 1962,[22] a few days before Graves began his second series of lectures as Professor of Poetry at Oxford. He had in fact already included two of these poems in a lecture the previous December, and more from this book and the next were to be examined in his 1963 Oxford lectures.[23] A paradoxical verse[24] introduces *New Poems 1962*:

FOREWORD

Privacy finds herself a nook
In bold print of an open book
Which few have eyes to read; the rest
(If studiously inclined) will look
For cypher or for palimpsest.

On the dust-jacket Graves asks: 'What can I say of these poems? That there are more than I publish most years? That they must not be taken for academic exercises? That they have been unusually hard to write? Let them speak for themselves.'

The 'Foreword' concludes: 'The two parts of this book, like those of *More Poems 1961*, are numbered as continuations of *Collected Poems 1959*.' In part XIII, 'Ruby and Amethyst' is from *Collected Poems 1961*, and 'Variables of Green' is the revised version from *The More Deserving Cases* (1962) of 'Green

[20] Diary, 11 Sept. 1938; see the note on 'The Fallen Signpost' (*CP38*), *Complete Poems*, Volume II, p.317.

[21] Graves to Rab Shiell, 11 May 1962; St John's College, Oxford.

[22] The second edition, in Feb. 1963, is not mentioned in Higginson, which does record, however, a 'second impression' in Aug. 1963, making over 8000 copies in Britain and America.

[23] See 'The Personal Muse', *OAP*, pp.55-81 (pp.79-80), and *CWP*, pp.336-53 (pp.351-2); and 'Intimations of the Black Goddess', *MBG*, pp.141-65, and *CWP*, pp.384-99.

[24] First published as 'Privacy', *New Yorker*, 37 (21 Oct. 1961), 52.

Loving' (*CP38*); another poem from *The More Deserving Cases*, 'The Miller's Man', is in XIV. The remaining thirty poems were making their first book appearance. All except 'The Alabaster Throne' were reprinted in the 1965 and 1975 *Collected Poems*.

The complete contents are as follows:

XIII

Ruby and Amethyst; Recognition; Variables of Green; The Watch; Name Day; Uncalendared Love; The Meeting; Lack; Not at Home; Horizon; Golden Anchor; Lion Lover; Ibycus in Samos; Possessed; The Winged Heart; In Trance at a Distance; The Wreath; In Her Praise; The Alabaster Throne; A Restless Ghost; Between Moon and Moon

XIV

Beware, Madam!; The Cliff Edge; The Miller's Man; Acrobats; Ouzo Unclouded; The Broken Girth; Inkidoo and the Queen of Babel; Three Songs for the Lute: Truth Is Poor Physic, In Her Only Way, Hedges Freaked With Snow; The Ambrosia of Dionysus and Semele; The Unnamed Spell

The Watch

An earlier version of this poem was published in the *Saturday Evening Post*, 234 (11 Nov. 1961), 93, with the title 'Trance'.

Text: *CP75*.

Uncalendared Love

See *WG61*, pp.94-5/90, and 387-8/378-9, 392-3/383-4; *GM*, 1.*a,b,c,2*, 4.*2*; and *HM*, 6.*f*, 12.*a,b,c,9,15*. See also *PCP*, p.98, and *CWP*, pp.460-1. For st.3 l.4, cf. Genesis 3. 15.

Text: *NP62/CP75*.

Lack

'She [i.e. the White Goddess] is represented as making alternate love first with the creative, impassioned demi-God of the Waxing Year, and then in pity with his murderer, the luckless demi-God of the Waning year, named Lack, Drought and Envy.'[25]

Text: *NP62/CP75*.

Horizon

See 'Intimations of the Black Goddess', *MBG*, p.154, and *CWP*, pp.391-2. For st.3 l.4, cf. Psalm 41. 9, and 'The Personal Muse' *OAP*, p.63, and *CWP*, p.340.

Text: *CP75*.

Variant:

st.3 l.2 which *CP75*] that *NP62*

[25] 'Lecture One, 1965', *PCP*, p.108, republished as 'The Duende', *CWP*, p.467.

Lion Lover

See 'Intimations of the Black Goddess', *MBG*, p.155, and *CWP*, pp.392-3, where, after quoting st.3 of 'Inkidoo and the Queen of Babel', Graves states that 'Ishtar, Queen of Babylon, was the original Virgin of the Zodiac, who appears on steles, naked and riding a lion, the poet's zodiacal sign: ['Lion Lover' quoted]'. Graves, whose birthday was 24 July, was himself a Leo.

See also *WG61*, pp.379-80/370-1, 404/395; *GM*, 7.*8*, 11.*1*, 97.*4*; and *SL 2*, pp.222-3.

Text: *NP62/CP75*.

Ibycus in Samos

See *WG61*, pp.234/228.

Text: *NP62/CP75*.

The Winged Heart

'Wings have long emblemized freedom and exaltation; and the sensation of having the heart sprout feathers is a common phenomenon among lovers.'[26]

Text: *CP75*.

Variant:

st.5 l.1 has *CP75*] had *NP62*

In Trance, at a Distance

Text: *CP75*.

Variant:

st.2 l.5 a while *CP75*] awhile *NP62*

The Wreath

For l.4, cf. 'To Juan at the Winter Solstice' (*P38-45*), st.7 l.6.

Text: *NP62/CP75*.

In Her Praise

See *WG61*, pp.490-1/481, quoted in the note on *MP61*, above:

'[. . .] the real, perpetually obsessed Muse-poet distinguishes between the Goddess as manifest in the supreme power, glory, wisdom and love of woman, and the individual woman whom the Goddess may make her instrument for a month, a year, seven years, or even more. The Goddess abides; and perhaps he will again have knowledge of her through his experience of another woman.'

'In Her Praise' is quoted in 'The Personal Muse', *OAP*, p.80, and *CWP*, p.352; and in 'Intimations of the Black Goddess', *MBG*, pp.156-7, and *CWP*,

[26] 'Lecture One, 1965', *PCP*, p.100, and 'The Duende', *CWP*, p.462.

pp.393-4.

See also, for ll.2-3: 'Intimations of the Black Goddess', *MBG*, p.145, and *CWP*, pp.385-6; ll.6-7: *WG61*, pp.85-6/81-2; l.12: *WG61*, pp.88-9/84-5, 216-7/211, 413/404, and cf. 'The Sibyl' (*W*), *Complete Poems*, Volume I, pp.173-4.

Text: *NP62/CP75*.

The first published version, in the *Saturday Evening Post*, 234 (11 Nov. 1961), 93, has 'betray' in l.5 in place of 'gainsay'.

The Alabaster Throne

See *WG61*, pp.53/48, 369/360; and *GM*, 11, 67.*d,f,2*, 100.*1*.

Text: *NP62*.

Between Moon and Moon

See the note on '*Song:* Come, Enjoy Your Sunday!' (*MP61*), above.

Text: *NP62/CP75*.

Beware, Madam!

'Have written several more poems, including one beginning "Beware, Madam, the Witty Serpent" – which will make the hair rise on some lovely necks.'[27]

See also 'The Personal Muse', *OAP*, pp.79-80, and *CWP*, pp.351-2.

Text: *NP62/CP75*.

Ouzo Unclouded

Graves wrote the original version, 'Ouzo: At Nonacris', in the plane on the way back from his first visit to Greece, in August 1961.[28] He described it in a letter to Eleni Straton as 'A selenic poem: I hope. With nine lines in Selene's honour – as you know *Non*acris is her seat above the Styx [. . .]. *Unclouded* is the key word.'[29] See *RPG 3*, pp.336-7.

See *GM*, 14.5.

Text: *NP62/CP75*.

Inkidoo and the Queen of Babel

Of this poem, 'cast in seventeenth-century ballad form', Graves states:

> The original of these stanzas was written more than four thousand years ago – the hero Enkidu's address to the Love-goddess Ishtar. I have translated them word for word from the Babylonian *Gilgamesh Epic*, though omitting to name the 'callant born far hence' – in the original, he figured as 'Tammuz'; for the Greeks he was Adonis. Enkidu's refusal

---

[27] Graves to James Reeves, 29 May 1961; *SL 2*, p.203.

[28] He recognized Greece 'at once' as 'the true cultural centre of the Mediterranean'; see 'The Greek Tradition', *DQEA*, p.124.

[29] Graves to Eleni Straton, 27 Aug. 1961; Canelluñ.

to trust Ishtar a seventh and last time, earned him the punishment of death without resurrection.

See 'Intimations of the Black Goddess', *MBG*, pp.148-9, and *CWP*, pp.387-8 (p.388). See also the note on 'Lion Lover' (*NP62*), above.
Text: *CP75*.

The Ambrosia of Dionysus and Semele
This poem originated in Graves's experience when he took the Mexican hallucinogenic mushroom *psilocybe* on 31 January at the New York apartment of the mycologist R. Gordon Wasson.[30] Afterwards, he was

> startled to find that the deities in charge of the Paradise that I visited – the appearances of which is [*sic*] authenticated by Mexican legends and works of art – namely Tlalóc and Chalciolithicue, correspond exactly with the Greek God Dionysus and his mother Semele (another name for Proserpine or Persephone). It seems that the ritual eating of the Mexican mushroom had its Greek counterpart in the eating of the divine food *ambrosia* ('not for mortals'), and that the autumnal *Ambrosia*, sacred to Dionysus, were sacramental feasts in which the divine flesh of the bitter mushroom was eaten. Dionysus and Tlalóc – to whom the toad is sacred – were both born from a flash of lightning and their divine characteristics are identical – the alleged eating of infant boys ascribed to both apparently refers to the *hombrecitos* ('little men') as the mushrooms are called in Mexico.[31]

For Graves's argument identifying *ambrosia* as the 'fly-cap' mushroom *amanita muscaria*, see 'Centaur's Food' in *FC*, pp.257-82 (especially pp.258-70), republished as 'What Food the Centaurs Ate' in *S*, pp.319-43 (see especially pp.319-31). See also *WG61*, pp.183-4/178-9, and *GM*, 'Foreword', pp.9-10. The correspondences between Tlalóc and Dionysus and their sacred mushroom rites – and the Christian Eucharist – are set out in 'The Poet's Paradise', *OAP*, pp.109-29. This essay examines the 'traditional pattern' followed by the paradises of different cultures, and suggests that 'a common drug causes the paradisal visions and provides

---

[30] R. Gordon Wasson (1898-1986), American mycologist and banker. His Russian wife, Valentina Wasson, co-author of *Mushrooms, Russia and History* (New York: Pantheon, 1957), wrote to Graves in January 1949 about the cause of the death of the Emperor Claudius; see *SL 2*, pp.52-6, and 'New Light on an Old Murder', in *FC*, pp.201-8, and *S*, pp.312-18. Graves's relations with Gordon Wasson – and his contributions to his theories – can be traced in the letters and the linking commentary in *SL 2*; see also 'The Two Births of Dionysus', *DQEA*, pp.104-12, his review of Wasson's *Soma: Divine Mushroom of Immortality* (New York: Harcourt, Brace and World, 1968).

[31] 'Lecture Three, 1965', *PCP*, pp.153-79 (p.171), republished as 'Ecstasy', *CWP*, pp.495-512 (p.507); the poem is quoted in full.

the remarkable mental illumination described as "perfect wisdom"'. It also contains Graves's detailed account (pp.122-6) of his 'wholly good'[32] experience of *psilocybe*; sects.3 and 4 of 'The Ambrosia of Dionysus and Semele' follow passages in this closely. There is also a brief résumé of the account in a revised version of the essay, 'The Universal Paradise', *DQEA*, pp.77-103; and further analysis of it in a later essay summarizing Graves's various findings, 'Mushrooms and Religion', *DQEA*, pp.94-103: see p.99, and also pp.96-7.

See also *WG61*, pp.44-5/40, and *GM*, 14.*c*, 27.*h*,*k*,*11*.

Text: *NP62/CP75*.

The Unnamed Spell

For the references to mistletoe ('All heal') in sts.5-8, see *WG61*, pp.57/52, 65-6/60-1, 105/101, 125/120, and (especially) 249-50/242-3. See also Graves's Introduction to Idries Shah's *The Sufis* (New York: Doubleday, 1964), p.xvi, quoting a letter from Shah: 'unimpaired honour is, with love, one of the two main pillars of Sufism'.[33]

Text: *CP75*.

Variants:

st.5 l.3	above earth: *CP75*] above the earth: *NP62*
st.8 l.3	themselves sometimes] themselves have sometime

MAN DOES, WOMAN IS (1964)

'*Man Does, Woman Is* closes a three-book sequence dramatizing the vicissitudes of poetic love', Graves writes in the 'Foreword' to the book, which was published by Cassell on 17 April 1964.

> Because such love walks on a knife-edge between two different fates, Parts XV and XVI – these numbers stand for additions to my *Collected Poems*, 1959, and to the 1961 and 1962 supplements – supply alternative endings to the sequence. Part XVII contains miscellaneous poems mostly written under less emotional tension.

Part XVI could also be regarded as the beginning of another sequence, centred on a new 'muse',[34] with the Black Goddess emerging as tutelary divinity. (See the notes on 'The Hearth' and 'The Black Goddess', below.)

---

[32] p.127.

[33] Graves met the Afghan writer and authority on Sufism, Idries Shah (1924-1996) in Mallorca in January 1961; through him, Sufism became a significant element in Graves's work.

[34] Cindy Lee (Aemilia Laraçuen), his 'muse' in 1963-66. They first met in Deyá on 15 August 1958; see *RPG 3*, pp.283-4 *et seq*.

In a 1965 Oxford lecture Graves provides this comment on the title, *Man Does, Woman Is*:

> Ideally women *are*, meaning that they possess innate magic; sometimes they also *do*, but theirs is not doing in the male sense. Whenever men achieve something magically apt and right and surprising, their *duende* has always, it seems, been inspired by women. Whatever they attempt in male pride, by the ingenious use of intellect or fancy, is sorcery rather than magic. ['At Best, Poets' (*MDWI*) quoted (without title).] Right doing by men is achievement. Right doing by women is a simple by-product of being; quiet, unemphatic, non-competitive, but breathtaking.[35]

Of the sixty-two poems in the book, all are new except '*Song:* A Phoenix Flame', a revised version of an early poem, 'Morning Phoenix' (*TB*); see the note below. Only three were not reprinted in the 1965 and 1975 *Collected Poems*: 'Rain of Brimstone', 'A Late Arrival', and '*Song:* With No Return'.

The complete contents are as follows:

XV
A Time of Waiting; Expect Nothing; No Letter; The Why of the Weather; In Time; Fire Walker; Deed of Gift; At Best, Poets; She Is No Liar; A Last Poem; The Pearl; The Leap; Bank Account; Judgement of Paris; Man Does, Woman Is; The Ample Garden; To Myrto About Herself; The Three-Faced; Dazzle of Darkness; Myrrhina; Food of the Dead; Eurydice; To Beguile and Betray; I Will Write

XVI
Bird of Paradise; The Metaphor; *Song:* A Phoenix Flame; Secrecy; Joseph and Mary; An East Wind; Dance of Words; A Blind Arrow; The Oleaster; The Septuagenarian; *Non Cogunt Astra*; *Song:* Sword and Rose; Endless Pavement; In Disguise; A Measure of Casualness; In Time of Absence; The Green Castle; Not to Sleep; The Hearth; That Other World; The Beds of Grainne and Diarmuid; Rain of Brimstone; Consortium of Stones; The Black Goddess

XVII
Broken Neck; O; Woman of Greece; The Colours of Night; Between Trains; The Teumessian Vixen; The Hung Wu Vase; *La Mejicana*; Lamia In Love; After the Flood; A Late Arrival; *Song:* With No Return; All I Tell You From My Heart; The Undead

[35] 'Lecture One, 1965', *PCP*, pp.114-15, republished as 'The Duende', *CWP*, p.472.

A Time of Waiting

Graves describes the creative process that supplied 'caul' in sect.1 l.5 in his 1962 Oxford lecture 'The Poet in a Valley of Dry Bones', *MBG*, pp.88-91, and *CWP*, pp.377-9.

Text: *MDWI/CP75.*

The Why of the Weather

Cf. Laura Riding, 'The Why of the Wind',[36] sect.1 ll.1-3:

> We have often considered the wind,
> The changing whys of the wind.
> Of other weather we do not so wonder.

and sect.4 ll.3-5:

> We are not the wind.
> We are not every vagrant mood that tempts
> Our minds to giddy homelessness.

See Graves's diary, 26 March 1935: 'I went to village with poem of Laura *Why of Wind* to type'.

Text: *CP75.*

At Best, Poets

See the note on *MDWI*, above.

Text: *MDWI/CP75.*

She Is No Liar

'That was written not in anger: I was merely echoing the text of Proverbs XXX, 20.' ['Such is the way of an adulterous woman; she eateth, and wipeth her mouth, and saith, I have done no wickedness.'][37]

Text: *MDWI/CP75.*

A Last Poem

Lines 5-6 appear in a slightly different form in 'New Moon Through Glass' ('Uncollected Poems'), ll.1-2. See *WG61*, pp.109/105.

Text: *MDWI/CP75.*

The Pearl

Text: *CP75.*

Variant:

l.8 Such *CP75*] True *MDWI*

---

[36] Laura Riding, *Collected Poems* (London: Cassell, 1938; reprinted Manchester: Carcanet, 1980), pp.329-30 and 292-3.

[37] 'Genius', *DQEA*, p.20.

Judgement of Paris

See 'Lecture One, 1965', *PCP*, p.119, republished as 'The Duende', *CWP*, p.475:

> The theme of complementary love does not occur in Classical literature, even by Homer. Although the Siege of Troy is provoked by Helen's fatal elopement with Paris, the physical attraction between this pair is all that we are allowed to see, and she calls herself a bitch for having deserted her husband Menelaus and caused so many deaths. The domestic affection between Hector and his wife Andromache is endangered only by the sense of male honour which sends him to his death at Achilles' hands; but the blind overwhelming power which took Helen to Troy has been sanctified in poetry at the expense of all other emotions, despite the eventual defeat of both lovers. ['Judgement of Paris' quoted (without title).]

See also *GM*, 159 *et seq*.
Text: *MDWI*/*CP75*.

Man Does, Woman Is

See the note on *MDWI*, above.
Text: *CP75*.

The Ample Garden

For st.1, cf. *WG61*, pp.24/20: 'The Goddess [. . .] will suddenly transform herself into sow, mare, bitch, vixen, she-ass, weasel, serpent, owl, she-wolf, tigress, mermaid or loathsome hag.'
Text: *MDWI*/*CP75*.

Myrrhina

For Myrrhina, see *WG61*, pp.394-6/386-7, and for Eve, pp.257/249-50.

There is an earlier poem with this title in *MBH* (1924); see *Complete Poems*, Volume I, pp.206-7.
Text: *MDWI*/*CP75*.

Food of the Dead

For Graves's own detailed explication of this poem, see 'Intimations of the Black Goddess', *MBG*, pp.157-9, and *CWP*, pp.394-6. See also *GM*, 28.
Text: *MDWI*/*CP75*.

Eurydice

See Graves's commentary on 'Eurydice', which follows on from that on the previous poem, 'Food of the Dead' (see above), in 'Intimations of the Black Goddess', *MBG*, pp.160-1, and *CWP*, p.396:

> Arabs, when down-trodden, robbed or cheated, often refrain from

curses, since these are apt to boomerang back. They merely cry instead: '*Maslum, Maslum, Maslum!*', which means 'I am oppressed, I am oppressed, I am oppressed!' and leave the avenging of their injury, if undeserved, to God or Fate. So should the poet refrain from cursing Eurydice, however ill she has used him: ['Eurydice' quoted].

Text: *CP75*.

To Beguile and Betray

See 'Intimations of the Black Goddess', *MBG*, pp.155-6, and *CWP*, p.393. For 'the mandalot', see *Paris Review*, 47 (Summer 1969), p.123: 'I invented the word, from the Greek; it comes from *mandalós* (which is the bolt you put in the socket) and means the tongue-kiss or by dictionary definition "a lecherous and erotic kiss"'.

Text: *MDWI/CP75*.

Bird of Paradise

Text: *MDWI/CP75*.

This poem was printed on Doubleday's 1963 Christmas card, with a drawing of a bird of paradise by Leonard Baskin.

Song: A Phoenix Flame

Text: *MDWI/CP75*.

Though not designated as such, this is a revised version of a four-stanza poem first published in 1919, 'Morning Phoenix' (*TB*); see *Complete Poems*, Volume I, p.65.

Variants:

st.1 l.1 heart a phoenix *CP75*] body lives a *TB*
l.2 Flame that burns me all the day,
l.3 Should] When
do] does
l.4 die] am charred

Sts.2 and 3 are in the reverse order in *TB*.

st.2 l.1 Caves I long for and cold rocks,
l.2 Minnow-haunted mountain] Minnow-peopled country
l.3 Blustering] Blundering
l.4 Sunless valley-nooks.
st.3 l.1 boast] keep
careless] smiling
l.2 Doubly roasted,] Roasted so in
l.3 Sun's] sun's
l.4 Scorched by love inside?

St.4 in *TB*:

Daily so I might restore
   Calcined heart and shrivelled skin,

A morning phoenix with proud roar
  Kindled new within.

Secrecy

Text: *CP75*.

Variants:

st.3 l.3 world *CP75*] word *MDWI* (*misprint*)

st.5 l.2 brazenly] brazonly (*misprint*)

Dance of Words

See 'Intimations of the Black Goddess', *MBG*, p.147, and *CWP*, p.386-7:

Poetry is a way of thought – non-intellectual, anti-decorative thought at that, – rather than an art. Would-be poets today experiment in new loveless Apollonian techniques, taking pictorial abstractionism as their model, all working 'objectively' – that being for them a term of praise – and unprepared to accept the poetic trance with its fantastic co-ordination of sound, rhythm and meaning. Poets who serve the Muse wait for the inspired lightning flash of two or three words that initiate composition and dictate the rhythmic norm of their verse. ['Dance of Words' quoted.]

Text: *CP75*.

The Oleaster

For sect.2 l.3, see *WG61*, pp.438-9/429-30. See also 'Olives of March' ('Unpublished Poems') and note.

Text: *MDWI*/*CP75*.

In Disguise

Text: *CP75*.

Variant:

st.1 l.4 veteran *CP75*] soldier *MDWI*

Not to Sleep

See Graves to James Reeves, 2 May 1963; *SL 2*, p.225:

– As a matter of record: I have never been so happy in my life as now: all the unhappiness of three years has peeled away. I wrote a poem two days ago beginning: 'Not to sleep all night long, for pure joy . . .' which is one of the few poems of utter happiness ever written.

Text: *MDWI*/*CP75*.

The Hearth

See 'Intimations of the Black Goddess', *MBG*, pp.162-4, and *CWP*, pp.397-9:

> [. . .] Ishtar [the Love-goddess],[38] though the most powerful deity of her day, did not rule alone. At Hierapolis, Jerusalem and Rome she acknowledged a mysterious sister, the Goddess of Wisdom, whose temple was small and unthronged. Call her the Black Goddess: Provençal and Sicilian 'Black Virgins' are so named because they derive from an ancient tradition of Wisdom as Blackness. This Black Goddess, who represents a miraculous certitude in love, ordained that the poet who seeks her must pass uncomplaining through all the passionate ordeals to which the White Goddess may subject him.
>
> The *Orphic Fragments* tell how Night mothered a Love-god named Phanes, who set the Universe in motion. Night, for the Orphics, appeared in triad as Blackness (namely, Wisdom), Order and Justice. Before her cave sat the inescapable Rhea – the White Goddess – beating a brazen drum and compelling man's attention to Night's oracles. Throughout the Orient, Night was regarded as a positive power, not as a mere absence of daylight; and Black as a prime colour, not as absence of colour, was prized for capturing the Sun's virtue more than any other. [. . .]
>
> Night had a dove's head, and Phanes, God of Love, was hatched from a silver egg that she laid. There is no more ancient emblem of love than the turtle-dove; or of spiritual re-birth than the phoenix. Shakespeare's strange prophetic line 'The Phoenix and turtle fled in a mutual flame from hence', carries a world of meaning. The phoenix, according to the Egyptians, was born as a worm from the ashes of its self-consumed predecessor and, after four years, grew to a chick: ['The Hearth' quoted].
>
> Poetry, it may be said, passes through three distinct stages: first, the poet's introduction, by Vesta, to love in its old-fashioned forms of affection and companionship; next, his experience of death and recreation at the White Goddess's hand; and lastly a certitude in love, given him by the Black Goddess, his more-than-Muse.

For the phoenix, see *WG61*, pp.412-13/403-4, 'An Eminent Collaborationist', in *5PH*, pp.113-14, and 'The Pentagram of Isis', in *DQEA*, pp.174-5.

See also 'Lecture Two, 1965', *PCP*, pp.134-5, republished as 'Muntu, Mammon, Marxism', *CWP*, p.483:

> The subject of poetry is the certitude that, despite all possible doubts and difficulties, true lovers will one day reconcile lunar with solar time, imagination with reason, intuition with planning, honour with freedom; the male with the female mind. This happens only in a timeless *now*, which must not, however, be dismissed as a fanciful *then* by its participants: it is the *now* of wisdom, the poetic *now*, the *now* of the Black Goddess – of Wisdom as Night.

Text: *MDWI*/*CP75*.

[38] See the notes on 'Lion Lover' and 'Inkidoo and the Queen of Babel' (*MDWI*).

That Other World

See 'Intimations of the Black Goddess', *MBG*, pp.162-3, and *CWP*, pp.397-8.

Text: *MDWI/CP75*.

The Beds Of Grainne and Diarmuid

For the legend of the flight of Grainne and Diarmuid across Ireland, see *WG61*, pp.210/205 and 211/206; and 'Lecture Two, 1965', *PCP*, pp.149-50, republished as 'Muntu, Mammon, Marxism', *CWP*, p.494.

Text: *MDWI/CP75*.

Consortium of Stones

For stones as 'human souls' (sect.1 l.5), cf. Graves's short story 'The Shout'.[39]

Text: *MDWI/CP75*.

The Black Goddess

See the note on 'The Hearth' (above), and 'Intimations of the Black Goddess', *MBG*, p.164, and *CWP*, pp.399:

> The Black Goddess is so far hardly more than a word of hope whispered among the few who have served their apprenticeship to the White Goddess. She promises a new pacific bond between men and women, corresponding to a final reality of love, in which the patriarchal marriage bond will fade away. Unlike Vesta, the Black Goddess has experienced good and evil, love and hate, truth and falsehood in the person of her sister; but chooses what is good: rejecting serpent-love and corpse flesh. Faithful as Vesta, gay and adventurous as the White Goddess, she will lead man back to that sure instinct of love which he long ago forfeited by intellectual pride.

See also, for st.3 ll.1-2, *WG61*, pp.75/71, 167-8/162-3, 183/178, 214/208, 369/360; *GM*, 27.*12*; and 'Instructions to the Orphic Adept' (*P38-45*), sect.3 ll.2-3.

Text: *MDWI/CP75*.

To the Teumessian Vixen

See *GM*, 89.*h*,*8*.

Text: *MDWI/CP75*.

The Hung Wu Vase

Text: *MDWI/CP75*.

Emendation:

st.2 l.6 forgot *Ed.*] forget *MDWI*, *CP75*

---

[39] *The Shout* (London: Elkin Mathews and Marrot, 1929), reprinted in *CSS*, pp.7-22.

Lamia In Love

See *GM*, 61.

Text: *MDWI/CP75*.

PAL has '(*revision*)' after the title (and in l.4 'of' for 'in'); a corresponding earlier version of the poem has not been traced.

After the Flood

Text: *CP75*.

Emendation:

st.3 l.3 mud, *MDWI*] mud. *CP75*

ANN AT HIGHWOOD HALL (1964)

Following the success of *The Penny Fiddle* (1960), which sold some 20,000 copies, Graves and his illustrator Edward Ardizzone produced a second book of 'Poems for Children', *Ann at Highwood Hall*, published by Cassell on 8 October 1964. It is dedicated 'To my grandchildren | Georgina and David Graves | with love'.

Of the seven poems, two are revised versions of poems from the 1920s: 'George II and the Chinese Emperor', an extensively reworked version of 'Diplomatic Relations', published in 1924 in *Mock Beggar Hall* and revived in *The More Deserving Cases* (1962), and 'The Sewing Basket', two stanzas of the twelve-stanza poem in *Whipperginny* (1923) (see *Complete Poems*, Volume I); while 'Caroline and Charles' is a revised version of 'Mike and Mandy', from *Steps* (1959) (see *Complete Poems*, Volume II).

The contents of the book are:

Ann at Highwood Hall; St Valentine's Day; George II and the Chinese Emperor; I Have a Little Cough, Sir; The Sewing Basket; Joseph and Jesus; Caroline and Charles

I Have a Little Cough, Sir

Text: *AHH*.

Six lines in this poem – st.1 ll.1-2 and 5-8 – were published (untitled and unsigned) in 1927 as no.58 in *The Less Familiar Nursery Rhymes*.

Variants:

st.1 l.5 And every *AHH*] Every *LFNR*

l.7 cough, sir:] cough, cough,

In a typescript of children's rhymes (Buffalo), its title is 'A Rhyme My Nurse Taught Me'.

Joseph and Jesus

Text: *AHH*.

The original Spanish verse, from a Christmas carol, is as follows:[40]

[40] The verse, with a small illustration of the Nativity, is on part of a page apparently torn from a religious leaflet; Canelluñ.

La Virgen va caminando

La Virgen va caminando . . .
por una montaña oscura . . .
al vuelo de la perdiz . . .
se le ha espantado la mula . . .
San José al Niño Jesús . . .
un beso le dio en la cara . . .
y el Niño Jesús le dice . . .
que me pinchas con las barbas . . .
Al Niño le dieron sopas . . .
y no las quiso comer . . .
como estaban calentitas . . .
se las comió San José . . .

LOVE RESPELT (1965)

Entirely in facsimile of Graves's handwriting, with illuminations by Aemilia Laraçuen – the poems concern Graves's relationship with her – *Love Respelt* was published by Cassell on 16 July 1965 in a limited edition (280 copies, 250 of them for sale).

All but one of the thirty-three poems were included in the 1965 and 1975 *Collected Poems*; 'The Blow' was reprinted only in *Love Respelt Again* and *Poems About Love*, and 'A Shift of Scene' (*CP65*) was inserted before 'Change'. Other modifications to the sequence: '*Son Altesse*' was moved up to twelfth place, after 'Between Hyssop and Axe'; 'Everywhere Is Here' and 'What Will Be, Is' appear in the reverse order; and 'Postscript', retitled 'I'd Die For You', was transferred to section II (see note).

A typeset edition of *Love Respelt*, with seven poems added, was published in America on 4 April 1966 by Doubleday (see the note on *Seventeen Poems Missing from Love Respelt*, below).[41]

[41] The eighty-poem *Love Respelt* sequence involved five books:

1) *Love Respelt* (London: Cassell, 1965), limited edition of thirty-three poems in facsimile of Graves's handwriting.

2) *Love Respelt* (New York: Doubleday, April 1966), typeset trade edition of *LR* with seven additional poems.

3) *Seventeen Poems Missing from 'Love Respelt'* (London: Bertram Rota, June 1966), privately printed limited edition including the seven poems added to *LR66*.

4) *Colophon to 'Love Respelt'* (London: Bertram Rota, 1967), privately printed limited edition of twenty-eight poems.

5) *Love Respelt Again* (New York: Doubleday, 1969), 1000-copy edition of the fifty poems from *LR* (1965) and *17PMLR*, in facsimile of Graves's handwriting.

Further details are given in the notes on these volumes. The sequence forms sections XVIII, XIX and XX in *CP75*.

Wild Cyclamen

Text: *CP75*.

Emendation:

sect.2 l.1 forehead, *LR, CP65*] forehead *CP75*

Variants:

sect.2 l.1 O the *CP75*] o, the *LR*

l.2 task –] task! –

Gift of Sight

For l.7, cf. 'Green Loving' (*CP38*), st.2 l.4: 'True sky was never seen until to-day'; see the note on 'Variables of Green', *Complete Poems*, Volume II, p.312.

Text: *CP75*.

Variants:

l.1 wood, *CP75*] forest, *LR*

l.3 Knew] Also

Batxóca

'Batxóca (with the *x* pronounced as *ch*) is a Majorcan word meaning "bean-like" or "over-imaginative" as beans run crazily up their poles.'[42]

Text: *CP75*.

Variants:

l.1 high-bosomed, *CP75*] high-breasted, *LR*

In *LR* there is no extra space after l.14 (which has a dash after the exclamation mark; there is no dash at the end of l.9).

Change

Text: *CP75*.

Variant:

st.2 l.3 wrong, *CP75*] wrong. *LR*

Gold and Malachite

See Graves's account of his experience of taking the hallucinogenic mushroom *psilocybe*, cited in the note on 'The Ambrosia of Dionysus and Semele' (*NP62*).

Text: *CP75*.

Variants:

sect.1 l.7 how; and which *CP75*] how, which *LR*

sect.2 l.3 unwisdom;] unwisdom

The Vow

Text: *CP75*.

Variants:

st.1 l.1 No *CP75*] The *LR*

---

[42] 'Foreword', *LR66*.

ever] never
st.2 l.1 be yourself?] be for yourself?
st.4 l.2 not to the] not the
st.5 l.1 uninstructible] indestructible

This Holy Month

For ll.16-17, see *GM*, 82.4.
Text: *CP75*.

The Blow

Text: *PAL*.
Variant:
st.1 l.3 your *PAL*] that *LR*

The Fetter

Text: *CP75*.
Variant:
st.4 l.1 we only *CP75*] we, only, *LR*

Iron Palace

Text: *CP75*.
Variant:
st.2 l.3 would *CP75*] could *LR*

True Joy

See 'Lecture Three, 1965', *PCP*, p.173, republished as 'Ecstasy', *CWP*, p.508:

> I was never saved from drowning, but many of those who have been saved record that their forcible resuscitation was far more painful than the experience. The result of the lungs being filled with water is that the brain becomes deoxygenated. Sailors have a name for the drowners' paradise, from which few return to tell the tale. It is Fiddler's Green, sometimes called merely 'The Green', where they find perpetual dancing, drinking and jollity. According to the *Folk Lore Record* 1881, Cornish sailors describe it as an Isle of the Blest. Kirkby's dictionary of West Yorkshire dialect words places it 'ten miles 'tother side of Hell Square' – and I suppose this quotation reflects the difference between a sailor who drowns in a state of grace and one who drowns with a sin-laden conscience. I have written on this subject in a poem: ['True Joy' quoted].

Text: *CP75*.

Tomorrow's Envy of Today

For sect.2 ll.8-9, cf. Graves's description of his visions after taking the hallucinogenic mushroom *psilocybe*: 'The song-notes became intricate links of a round golden chain that coiled and looped in serpentine fashion among jade-green bushes: the only serpent I met in Eden. . . .'[43]

Text: *LR/CP75*.

What Will Be, Is

Text: *CP75*.

Variant:

st.3 l.2 for *CP75*] with *LR*

Son Altesse

See 'The Word "Romantic"', *PCP*, pp.181-95, especially pp.188-90.

Text: *CP75*.

Everywhere Is Here

For sect.2 ll.3-5, cf. *WG61*, pp.412-13/403-4.

Text: *CP75*.

Variant:

sect.2 l.5 in *CP75*] on *LR*

Song: The Far Side of Your Moon

Text: *CP75*.

Emendation:

st.2 l.4 openly, *LR*] openly *CP75*.

Deliverance

See *WG61*, pp.179/174, 383-5/374-6, 485/475-6.

Text: *LR/CP75*.

Conjunction

See *WG61*, pp.441/432.

Text: *CP75*.

Nothing Now Astonishes

Text: *CP75*.

Emendation:

st.1 l.2 Lights *LR*] lights *CP75*

I'd Die For You

Text: *CP75*.

Previous title: 'Postscript' (*LR*).

In *CP65* and *CP75* this poem is placed in section II, among poems from the 1920s, though the drafts (Carbondale) indicate that it was written in 1965 (one is dated 'March 5 1965').

---

43 'The Poet's Paradise', *OAP*, pp.124-5; see the note on 'The Ambrosia of Dionysus and Semele' (*NP62*).

COLLECTED POEMS 1965 (1965)

'Standards rise while poems multiply', claims the 'Foreword' to *Collected Poems 1965*, published by Cassell on 23 September 1965: Graves 'discarded' fifty-two of the poems in *Collected Poems 1959*, while including virtually all of his recent love poetry.

Of the 343 poems in *Collected Poems 1965*, 157 are from books published in the last six years. Though ten poems in *Food for Centaurs* (1960) are omitted, and six in *More Poems 1961*, he retained all but one of the thirty-three in *New Poems 1962*, fifty-nine of the sixty-two in *Man Does, Woman Is* (1964), and thirty-two of the thirty-three in *Love Respelt* (1965).

The following poems in *Collected Poems 1959* were rejected:[44]

> To Calliope. I: 'The General Elliott'; Unicorn and the White Doe[45]; The Country Dance; An English Wood; The Bedpost; Mermaid, Dragon, Fiend. II: The Witches' Cauldron. III: Callow Captain; Saint; Traveller's Curse After Misdirection; The Last Day of Leave. IV: Galatea and Pygmalion; Sergeant-Major Money; Vision in the Repair-Shop; Act V, Scene 5; Midway; Recalling War; Hotel Bed at Lugano; History of the Word; Defeat of the Rebels; The Fallen Signpost; The China Plate. V: Alexander and Queen Janet. VI: The Worms of History; The Glutton; The Rock at the Corner; Cold Weather Proverb. VII: At the Savoy Chapel; Dream of a Climber; The Eugenist; A Civil Servant; Gulls and Men; Conversation Piece; General Bloodstock's Lament for England; '¡Wellcome, to the Caves of Artá!'; I'm Through with You For Ever; The Sacred Mission; Poets' Corner. VIII: Amergin's Charm; The Battle of the Trees; The Sirens' Welcome to Cronos; Intercession in Late October; The Jackals' Address to Isis; The Destroyer. IX: With the Gift of a Ring; The Mark; Reproach to Julia; Dethronement. X: The Coral Pool; The Enlisted Man; Read Me, Please!

This, the last of Graves's successive poetic purges,[46] left little more than a third of his pre-1960 work in the canon, and narrowed its range. The main reason for 'discarding' poems, he declares in the 'Foreword', 'should be that one suspects lovelessness':

> These *Collected Poems* are due to appear on my seventieth birthday, after four similar recensions in 1926, 1938, 1947 and 1959. Each time I have left out whatever dissatisfied me, though playing fair with my younger, clumsier selves; the lack of any radical break or change in this half-century sequence suggests that I always aimed at writing more or less as I still do.

---

[44] Four had already been excluded from *CP61*; see note.

[45] Restored in *CLR*; see note.

[46] See *Complete Poems*, Volume I, Introduction.

Standards rise while poems multiply; it becomes easier with the years to recognize the derivative, the over-clever, the flawed, the repetitious, the didactic, the irrelevant. These gradually fade on the page. And the main reason for discarding them should be that one suspects lovelessness. Whenever a poem reads memorably, this is almost always because a living Muse has directed its need and, however individual the poet's choice of words and rhythms, impressed her secret image on them. If such an image is unapparent, I question the poem's validity, which prevents me from ever feeling the least authorial pride. Who can regard himself as the originator of lines which move readers no less than he was himself moved to write them? Granted, numerous poems of simple male parentage (the Apollonian sort) are widely honoured; but they do not concern me.

A light-hearted region lies around this; and at times the satiric left hand of poetry displaces the lyric right hand. Occasional jokes and satires have therefore been included here. While trying to avoid topical references, I cannot deny my place in the late Christian epoch of two World Wars and their horror-comic aftermaths. And since I never took refuge in the fictitious Arcadia of Classical verse, my recourse at times to obsolescent words means simply that no exact contemporary equivalent occurred to me.

Some of these poems were written in England, Wales, France, Switzerland, Greece, Mexico and the United States; one, *Beware, Woman!* [*sic*], in flight across the Atlantic; but by far the most at Deyá, Majorca, which has been my home since 1929.

My main theme was always the practical impossibility, transcended only by a belief in miracle, of absolute love continuing between man and woman.

R.G.

Deyá
Majorca
Spain

The eight new poems in *Collected Poems 1965* (in sections XVII and XVIII) are indicated with an asterisk in the following contents list:

I

In the Wilderness; The Haunted House; Reproach; The Finding of Love; Rocky Acres; Outlaws; One Hard Look; A Frosty Night; Allie; Henry and Mary; Love Without Hope; What Did I Dream?; The Troll's Nosegay; The Hills of May; Lost Love; Vain and Careless; The Pier-Glass; Apples and Water; Angry Samson; Down

II

In Procession; Warning to Children; Alice; Richard Roe and John Doe; I'd Die For You; Ancestors; The Coronation Murder; Children of Darkness;

The Cool Web; Love in Barrenness; Song of Contrariety; The Presence; The Land of Whipperginny; In No Direction; The Castle; Return; The Bards; Nobody; The Progress; Full Moon; Vanity; Pure Death; Sick Love; It Was All Very Tidy

III
Thief; The Furious Voyage; *Song:* Lift-Boy; The Next Time; Ulysses; The Succubus; The Reader Over My Shoulder; The Legs; Gardener; Front Door Soliloquy; In Broken Images; Trudge, Body!; The Christmas Robin; On Rising Early; Flying Crooked; Fragment of a Lost Poem; Brother

IV
The Devil's Advice to Story-Tellers; Sea Side; Wm. Brazier; Welsh Incident; Interruption; Hell; Leda; Synthetic Such; The Florist Rose; Lost Acres; At First Sight; Down, Wanton, Down!; A Former Attachment; Nature's Lineaments; Time; The Philosopher; On Dwelling; Ogres and Pygmies; Single Fare; To Walk on Hills; To Bring the Dead to Life; To Evoke Posterity; Any Honest Housewife; Never Such Love; Certain Mercies; The Cuirassiers of the Frontier; The Laureate; A Jealous Man; The Cloak; The Foreboding; With Her Lips Only; The Halls of Bedlam; Or to Perish Before Day; A Country Mansion; Lovers in Winter; Advocates

V
On Portents; The Terraced Valley; The Chink; The Ages of Oath; New Legends; Like Snow; End of Play; The Climate of Thought; The Fallen Tower of Siloam; The Great-Grandmother; No More Ghosts

VI
A Love Story; Dawn Bombardment; The Shot; The Thieves; Lollocks; To Sleep; Despite and Still; The Suicide in the Copse; Frightened Men; The Oath; Language of the Seasons; Mid-Winter Waking; The Beach; The Villagers and Death; The Door; Under the Pot; Through Nightmare; To Lucia at Birth; Death by Drums; She Tells Her Love While Half Asleep; Theseus and Ariadne; Penthesileia; The Death Room; To Juan at the Winter Solstice; To Be Called a Bear

VII
My Name and I; 1805; The Persian Version; The Weather of Olympus; Apollo of the Physiologists; The Oldest Soldier; Grotesques i, ii, iii, iv, v, vi; Beauty in Trouble; Sirocco at Deyá; From the Embassy

VIII
The White Goddess; The Song of Blodeuwedd; Instructions to the Orphic Adept; Lament for Pasiphaë; Return of the Goddess

IX
Counting the Beats; The Young Cordwainer; Your Private Way; The

Survivor; Questions in a Wood; Darien; The Portrait; Prometheus; The Straw; Cry Faugh!; Hercules at Nemea; Dialogue on the Headland; Liadan and Curithir; The Sea Horse; Cat-Goddesses; The Blue-Fly; A Lost Jewel; The Window Sill; Spoils; Rhea

X

The Face in the Mirror; Gratitude for a Nightmare; Friday Night; The Naked and the Nude; Woman and Tree; Forbidden Words; A Slice of Wedding Cake; A Plea to Boys and Girls; Nothing; Call It a Good Marriage; The Second-Fated; The Twin of Sleep; Around the Mountain; Leaving the Rest Unsaid

XI

Lyceia; Symptoms of Love; The Sharp Ridge; Under the Olives; The Visitation; Fragment; Apple Island; The Falcon Woman; Troughs of Sea; The Laugh; The Death Grapple; The Starred Coverlet; Patience; The Cure; Hag-Ridden; Turn of the Moon; The Secret Land; Seldom Yet Now

XII

A Lost World; The Dangerous Gift; Twice of the Same Fever; Surgical Ward: Men; The Two Witches; The Quiet Glades of Eden; Joan and Darby; *Song:* Come, Enjoy Your Sunday!

XIII

Ruby and Amethyst; Recognition; Variables of Green; The Watch; Name Day; Uncalendared Love; The Meeting; Lack; Not at Home; Horizon; Golden Anchor; Lion Lover; Ibycus in Samos; Possessed; The Winged Heart; In Trance at a Distance; The Wreath; In Her Praise; A Restless Ghost; Between Moon and Moon

XIV

Beware, Madam!; The Cliff Edge; The Miller's Man; Acrobats; Ouzo Unclouded; The Broken Girth; Inkidoo and the Queen of Babel; Three Songs for the Lute: Truth Is Poor Physic, In Her Only Way, Hedges Freaked With Snow; The Ambrosia of Dionysus and Semele; The Unnamed Spell

XV

A Time of Waiting; Expect Nothing; No Letter; The Why of the Weather; In Time; Fire Walker; Deed of Gift; At Best, Poets; She Is No Liar; A Last Poem; The Pearl; The Leap; Bank Account; Judgement of Paris; Man Does, Woman Is; The Ample Garden; To Myrto About Herself; The Three-Faced; Dazzle of Darkness; Myrrhina; Food of the Dead; Eurydice; To Beguile and Betray; I Will Write

XVI

Bird of Paradise; The Metaphor; *Song:* A Phoenix Flame; Secrecy; Joseph and Mary; An East Wind; Dance of Words; A Blind Arrow; The Oleaster; The Septuagenarian; *Non Cogunt Astra*; *Song:* Sword and Rose; Endless Pavement; In Disguise; A Measure of Casualness; In Time of Absence; The Green Castle; Not to Sleep; The Hearth; That Other World; The Beds of Grainne and Diarmuid; Consortium of Stones; The Black Goddess

XVII
Broken Neck; O; Woman of Greece; The Colours of Night; Between Trains; To the Teumessian Vixen; The Hung Wu Vase; *La Mejicana*; Lamia In Love; After the Flood; All I Tell You From My Heart; The Undead; Grace Notes*; Good Night to the Old Gods*; The Sweet-Shop Round the Corner*; Double Bass*; Descent into Hell*; The Pardon*; Point of No Return*

XVIII
The Red Shower; Above the Edge of Doom; Wild Cyclamen; Gift of Sight; *Batxóca*; The Snap-Comb Wilderness; A Shift of Scene*; Change; A Court of Love; Black; Between Hyssop and Axe; *Son Altesse*; Gold and Malachite; Ambience; The Vow; The Frog and the Golden Ball; Those Who Came Short; Whole Love; This Holy Month; The Impossible; The Fetter; Iron Palace; True Joy; Tomorrow's Envy of Today; The Hidden Garden; The Wedding; Everywhere Is Here; What Will Be, Is; *Song:* The Far Side of Your Moon; Deliverance; Conjunction; Nothing Now Astonishes

Grace Notes

'Grace Notes' was inspired by Isla Cameron, folk-singer and friend of Graves's.

Text: *CP65/CP75*.

The Sweet-Shop Round the Corner

This poem was first published in *Joan*, 1 (Summer 1965), p.3.

Text : *CP65/CP75*.

SEVENTEEN POEMS MISSING FROM 'LOVE RESPELT' (1966)

This is the first of six privately printed, large-format books, published in limited editions by Bertram Rota, in which Graves's late work appeared in 1966-74 before being gathered into the regular volumes produced by Cassell and Doubleday. The other five are *Colophon to 'Love Respelt'* (1967), *Beyond Giving* (1969), *The Green-Sailed Vessel* (1971), *Timeless Meeting* (1973), and *At the Gate* (1974).[47]

[47] The printer was Bill Hummerstone of the Stellar Press, at Barnet and, later, Hatfield. The series was conceived and organized by the novelist Selwyn Jepson, Graves's close friend and adviser (they met in 1950). Graves wrote this inscription

Seventeen Poems Missing from 'Love Respelt' was published on 6 June 1966, in an edition of 330 copies (300, numbered and signed, for sale).

Seven of the poems had been included in the American trade edition of *Love Respelt*, published two months earlier: 'The Gorge', 'Arreas of Moonlight', 'The Snapped Thread' ('The Tangled Thread'), 'Lure of Murder', 'Fortunate Child', 'Loving True, Flying Blind', 'Dancing Flame'.

Graves intended the seventeen poems to complete the sequence, as he explains in the 'Foreword':

> The contents of *Love Respelt*, a limited edition of thirty-three poems illuminated by Aemilia Laraçuen, now form a section of my *Collected Poems, 1965*; but the sequence had not been rounded off when I published the book. This is its conclusion.
>
> Aemilia Laraçuen, whose essential presence in both parts will be evident, has supplied the Fragmenting Sun on page 7; the similarity of the poem and the illumination being coincidental. Once more, my theme is metaphorical of experiences which, as in Classical Persian Poetry, transcend ordinary physical circumstance.
>
> R.G.
>
> *Deyá, Majorca*

A year later, however, he was to add a further twenty-eight poems with *Colophon to 'Love Respelt'* (see the 'Foreword' in the note, below). The penultimate poem in *Seventeen Poems Missing from 'Love Respelt'*, 'Clothed in Silence', became st.3 of 'Strangeness' in *Colophon to 'Love Respelt'* (see note).

The original handwritten *Love Respelt* was republished together with the seventeen 'missing' poems (but not the *Colophon*) in 1969 by Doubleday, in America, under the title *Love Respelt Again*.

Cock in Pullet's Feathers

Text: *CP75*.

Variant:

l.3 crowing *CP75*] crowning *17PMLR* (*misprint*)

---

in Jepson's copy of *17PMLR* (William Graves collection):

To Selwyn Jepson | who arranged for the | publication of this book | and saw it through –

The Grand Climacteric that Brings
A Parsimony and Tightening of Purse Strings
Has Passed Him by: the Longer SELWYN Lives,
The More, it Seems, He Finds to Give; and Gives

R.G.

Deyá Sept 5
1966

Arreas of Moonlight

Text: *CP75*.

Variant:

l.3 terrestrial *LR66, CP75*] terrestial *17PMLR* (*misprint*)

Lure of Murder

Text: *CP75*.

Variant:

sect.1 l.3 Awed *CP75*] Tamed *LR66, 17PMLR*

The Gorge

' – But I always know where I am; if only on a bridge I cannot see, going over a canyon; I feel it under my feet.'[48]

Text: *CP75*.

Variants:

l.1 hopes *17PMLR, CP75*] hope *LR66*

l.3 howl phantoms] two howl ghosts

Ecstasy of Chaos

See Graves's discussion of the effects of marihuana, and of LSD and other psychedelic drugs, in 'Lecture Three, 1965', *PCP*, pp.161-5; cf. his reconsidered views in the revised text, 'Ecstasy', *CWP*, pp.500-2.

Text: *CP75*.

Variant:

l.5 that *CP75*] the *17PMLR*

This poem is quoted (without its title) in *PCP*, p.165, and *CWP*, p.502, with 'the royal vow' in place of 'that royal love' in l.5, and 'truly, can restore' for 'certainly, restores' in l.6.

Stolen Jewel

Text: *CP75*.

An earlier version entitled 'What Do We Fear?' was published in the *New Republic*, 154 (1 Jan. 1966), 31.

Emendation:

sect.1 l.1 whole-heartedly – *P65-68 proof (Canelluñ)*] whole heartedly– *P65-68, CP75*

Variant:

sect.2 l.1 took *CP75*] stole *17PMLR*

The Eagre

This poem and 'Clothed in Silence' were republished only in *LRA*; see the note on 'Strangeness' (*CLR*).

Text: *LRA*.

Variant:

l.1 Suddenly *LRA*] . . . Suddenly *17PMLR*

---

[48] Graves to Selwyn Jepson, 7 Jan. 1965; *SL 2*, p.245.

The Snapped Thread

See 'Lecture One, 1965', *PCP*, pp.105-7, republished as 'The Duende', *CWP*, pp.465-6.

Text: *CP75*.

Previous title: 'The Tangled Thread' (*LR66*).

Variant:

sect.3 l.6	miracle snapped? *17PMLR, CP75*] miracle tangled, not snapped. *LR66*

Loving True, Flying Blind

See 'Lecture Two, 1965', *PCP*, pp.136-9, republished as 'Muntu, Mammon, Marxism', *CWP*, pp.485-6.

Text: *CP75*.

Variants:

st.3 l.3	bear *17PMLR, CP75*] cleave *LR66*
l.4	With] To

The Near Eclipse

Text: *CP75*.

Variant:

l.1	Out shines *CP75*] Outshines *17PMLR*

Dancing Flame

Text: *CP75*.

Variants:

l.3	gambols, *17PMLR, CP75*] frolics, *LR66*
	song;] cries,

LR66 does not have ll.4-5, added in *17PMLR*.

COLOPHON TO 'LOVE RESPELT' (1967)

Graves introduces *Colophon to 'Love Respelt'*, which was published by Rota on 10 July 1967 in a privately printed limited edition of 386 copies (350 for sale), thus:

FOREWORD

'Colophon' has, of late, come to mean a publisher's device, having previously meant an ornament announcing the end of a book or manuscript and giving the bibliographical information now as a rule found on the title page. In Greek it was the finishing stroke put to any work; and this is the sense in which I have used it here. Some record that the word commemorates the Lydian city of Colophon whose cavalry were renowned for their irresistible charges.

When I sent *Love Respelt* and *Seventeen Poems Missing from Love Respelt* to the printers I twice deceived myself into thinking that this particular poetic battle had ended; in each case, another charge was needed.

Now, I can withdraw my forces awhile and see whether 'Respelt' should have read 'Mis-spelt'; for the battlefield seems deserted for a while.[49] Perhaps, though, in Theocritus's words, misquoted by Coleridge in his introduction to *Kubla Khan*:

"Ἐγὼ δ'ὔμμιν καὶ ἐς ὕστερον ἅδιον ᾄσῶ.'
'And henceforth I shall sing to you even more sweetly.'
Who knows?

R.G.

Deyá, Majorca

The fifth of the book's twenty-eight poems (i.e. placed after 'The Utter Rim') is a substantially revised version of 'Unicorn and the White Doe' (*W*), dated '(1920 – recast 1966)': see *Complete Poems*, Volume I, pp.143-4 and 374-6.

Graves's changes on a set of galley proofs of *Colophon to 'Love Respelt'* were not inserted by the printer, and only one (correcting a misprint) is among the revisions in *Collected Poems 1975* which Graves made for *Poems 1965-1968*; he may have overlooked the others. They include 'dark' for st.7 l.4 'chequered' in 'Unicorn and the White Doe'; the rest are recorded in the notes below.

The P'eng that was a K'un

Text: *CP75*.

In *CLR* and *P65-68* (and the corresponding typescripts and manuscripts (Victoria)) the closing quotation mark in sect.2 is at the end of l.4.

Like Owls

Text: *CLR/CP75*.

In the proofs (Canelluñ), l.2 'obscure' has been changed to 'unnamed'.

The Utter Rim

For Graves's views on taking hallucinogenic drugs, see the note on 'Ecstasy of Chaos' (*17PMLR*).

Text: *CLR/CP75*.

The version of 'The Utter Rim' quoted in 'Lecture Three, 1965', *PCP*, p.164, and 'Ecstasy', *CWP*, p.502, has 'What if my Cerberus, the mind' in place of 'But if that Cerberus, my mind' in l.1; 'wild-eyed' for 'wide-eyed' in l.4; 'Jumbled' for 'Endless' in l.6; and four differences in punctuation.

Mist

Text: *CLR/CP75*.

In the proofs (Canelluñ), l.4 'guard' has been changed to 'fast'.

---

[49] Proofs (Canelluñ): 'deserted at last.'

The Word

Text: *CP75*.

Variant:

st.1 l.5 inaudibly. *CLR proofs (Canelluñ), P65-68, CP75*] inaudibly *CLR* (*misprint*)

Perfectionists

Text: *CP75*.

Variant:

sect.1 l.3 proud *CP75*] stern *CLR*

Prison Walls

Text: *CP75*.

Variants:

st.2 l.4 My *CP75*] A *CLR*

st.3 l.1 a] the

st.5 l.6 you let fall] that you shed

Bites and Kisses

For st.3 ll.4-6, cf. 'The Dragon-Fly' (1913) ('Unpublished Poems').

Text: *CP75*.

Variant:

st.2 l.2 Way, *CP75*] way, *CLR* (*misprint*)

Freehold

Text: *CLR/CP75*.

In the proofs (Canelluñ), a comma has been inserted after l.1 'past'.

The Necklace

Text: *CP75*.

Variant:

l.7 cross-quarter-days *CP75*] cross-quarter days *CLR*

Blackening Sky

Text: *CP75*.

Variant:

st.2 l.2 always *CP75*] ever *CLR*

Song: The Palm Tree

See *WG61*, pp.190/185, 395/386, and *HM*, 12.*i*, 51.*6*.

Text: *CP75*.

Variant:

st.3 l.4 a *CP75*] this *CLR*

In *P65-68* and *CP75* Graves moved this poem to the next section, XXI, as the fifth of a group of eleven songs.

Spite of Mirrors

Text: *CP75*.

Variants:

sect.1 l.12	cheerful *CP75*] passionate *CLR*
l.13	No] Nor
	no] nor
l.14	No] Nor
sect.2 l.1	How, with a mirror,] And how, with mirrors,

Pride of Love

Text: *CP75*.

The first word in l.2 was previously 'Astonished', but Graves decided that 'Resentful' was 'more honest': see Graves to Selwyn Jepson, 14 Nov. 1966; *SL 2*, p.256.

Injuries

Text: *CP75*.

Variants:

l.5	So *CP75*] Then *CLR*
	must] need

Her Brief Withdrawal

Text: *CP75*.

Variant:

l.14	had passed *CP75*] had long passed *CLR*

Strangeness

Text: *CLR/CP75*.

St.3 was first published separately as 'Clothed in Silence', the sixteenth poem in *17PMLR*, with 'Yet' in place of 'But' in l.3, and a semi-colon in place of the colon in l.4.

THE POOR BOY WHO FOLLOWED HIS STAR (1968)

In addition to the title story, there are three 'children's poems' in *The Poor Boy Who Followed His Star*, which Cassell published, with illustrations by Alice Meyer-Wallace, in the spring of 1968.

The first two poems precede the story and 'At Seventy-Two' follows it.

The Hero

Text: *PBFS/CP75*.

There is another poem with this title in *P53*.

POEMS 1965-1968 (1968)

The reviews of *Poems 1965-1968* were generally unfavourable; Graves's response was that it made him 'laff'[50] (he had similarly been 'rather amused' to receive his first 'really cordial batch' since 1916 for *Poems 1938-1945*).[51] He dismissed the critical reaction, after ten years of lavish praise, as predictable.

Poems 1965-1968 was published by Cassell on 25 July 1968. It contains eighty-four poems, divided into four sections. Half are from *Seventeen Poems Missing from 'Love Respelt'* (section XIX; 'The Eagre' and 'Clothed in Silence'[52] are omitted) and *Colophon to 'Love Respelt'* (section XX; '*Song:* The Palm Tree' is placed in a group of eleven songs in section XXI).

The other forty-two poems, states the 'Foreword', 'are, with a few exceptions, more recent'. A number are addressed to Graves's new (and last) 'muse', the focus of his poetry for the remainder of his life.[53]

The 'exceptions' include '*Song:* Sullen Moods'(*W*), first published in 1921 (see *Complete Poems,* Volume I, pp.145 and 376), and 'Possibly' (*CrP*) (see *Complete Poems,* Volume II, pp.230 and 360), both in section XXI.

The complete contents are as follows:

XIX
Cock in Pullet's Feathers; Dead Hand; Arrears of Moonlight; What Did You Say?; Lure of Murder; The Gorge; Ecstasy of Chaos; Stolen Jewel; The Snapped Thread; Fortunate Child; Loving True, Flying Blind; The Near Eclipse; Dancing Flame; Birth of Angels; On Giving

XX
The P'eng that was a K'un; Like Owls; In Perspective; The Utter Rim; Unicorn and the White Doe; Bower-Bird; Mist; The Word; Perfectionists; Prison Walls; A Dream of Hell; Our Self; Bites and Kisses; Sun-Face and Moon-Face; Freehold; The Necklace; A Bracelet; Blackening Sky; Blessed Sun; Lion-Gentle; Spite of Mirrors; Pride of Love; Hooded Flame; Injuries; Her Brief Withdrawal; The Crane; Strangeness

XXI
Song: How Can I Care?; *Song:* Though Once True Lovers; *Song:* Cherries or Lilies; *Song:* Crown of Stars; *Song:* The Palm Tree; *Song:* Fig Tree in Leaf;

[50] Graves to Isla Cameron, 28 Sept. 1968; Victoria. See also Graves to Ruth Fainlight ('"shabby, peeling, Georgian stucco" (*Listener*) is hard to beat'), 13 Jan. 1969; *SL 2,* p.277.

[51] Graves to Lynette Roberts, n.d. ['c. May' 1946], *Poetry Wales,* 19, no.2 (1983), 92-3; *SL 1,* p.344. See the note on *P38-45, Complete Poems,* Volume II, p.325.

[52] See the note on 'Strangeness' (*CLR*).

[53] Julia (Juli) Simon, daughter of Graves's friends George and Joanna Simon, who was seventeen when she became his 'muse' in October 1966; see *RPG 3,* pp.433-4 *et seq.*

Song: Dew-drop and Diamond; *Song:* Sullen Moods; *Song:* Just Friends; *Song:* Of Course; *Song:* Three Rings for Her; *Sincèrement*; *Dans un Seul Lit*; Possibly; Is Now the Time?; Twins; Sail and Oar; Gooseflesh Abbey; The Home-Coming; With the Gift of a Lion's Claw; Wigs and Beards; Personal Packaging, Inc.; Work Room; The Ark; All Except Hannibal; The Beggar Maid and King Cophetua; For Ever; *Jugum Improbum*; *De Arte Poetica*; *Sit Mihi Terra Levis*

XXII
Astymelusa; Tousled Pillow; To Be In Love; Fact of the Act; To Ogmian Hercules; Arrow Shots; She to Him; Within Reason; The Yet Unsayable; None the Wiser; The Narrow Sea; The Olive-Yard

Song: How Can I Care?

Of a later group of songs, Graves declared that 'to readers who cannot invest them with an imagined melody they must suggest unframed canvases leaning against a studio wall'.[54]

Text: *P65-68*/*CP75*.

Song: Crown of Stars

See *WG61*, pp.386/377-8:

> [. . .] it must never be forgotten that the Triple Goddess, as worshipped for example at Stymphalus, was a personification of primitive woman – woman the creatress and destructress. As the New Moon or Spring she was girl; as the Full Moon or Summer she was woman; as the Old Moon or Winter she was hag.

See the note on 'To Juan at the Winter Solstice' (*P38-45*), *Complete Poems*, Volume II, pp.329-31.

See also the note on 'Lion Lover' (*NP62*); and cf. 'The Wreath' (*NP62*). For l.9, cf. Luke 2. 35.

Text: *P65-68*/*CP75*.

Song: Fig Tree in Leaf

For st.2 ll.1-2, cf. Mark 13. 28, 37.

Text: *P65-68*/*CP75*.

Song: Dew-drop and Diamond

Cf. 'A Dewdrop' (*W*), ll.1-2, *Complete Poems*, Volume I, p.183, and see the note on p.387.

Text: *P65-68*/*CP75*.

---

[54] 'Foreword', *BG* (1969); see the note, below.

Gooseflesh Abbey

Graves refers to 'witches of Western Europe who kept toads and snakes as diabolic "familiars"' in 'The Poet's Paradise', *OAP*, pp.115-16, revised as 'The Universal Paradise', *DQEA*, p.82.

Text: *P65-68/CP75*.

Jugum Improbum

This poem was first published as 'Ad Pyrrham' in *Isis* (1 May 1968), 23, with a prose translation:[55]

> A careful translation by ROBERT GRAVES, Wadham and St. John's, our late Professor of Poetry, from the above reproachful Latin hexameter epigram, recovered from a palimpsest of the middle first century B.C., runs as follows:
>
> TO PYRRHA
> So it has come to this, has it, Pyrrha? You are yolking a calf with a lion (in the shafts of your chariot). You may be fond of him, but does the poor frightened creature deserve to be savagely whipped forward to his death in the heart of your fire?
>
> NOTE: apparently Pyrrha, which means 'Fire-woman' in Greek, had started a liaison with a rich (?) young fool but did not let him know that she was still in love with the jealous leonine poet – who here warns her that she is playing with fire.

Text: *CP75*.

Emendation:

l.3 ignem? *Isis, PAL*] ignem. *P65-68, CP75*

Astymelusa

Sir Hugh Lloyd-Jones, Regius Professor of Greek at Oxford, recalled after Graves's death how this poem came to be written:

> When he was ill in St. Thomas' Hospital [in Oct. 1966] and I came to see him, he asked me what had come up in the papyri lately. I remembered some beautiful lines of Alcman about a girl dancing in a religious ceremony, and he made me write them down. The very next morning, there came in the post a superb translation, which he later published.[56]

---

[55] In *Isis* there are two misprints, 'vitulam' for l.1 'vitulum' and 'moniturus' for l.3 'moriturus'; the poem (and the introductory sentence) follow Graves's translation instead of preceding it. The page, headed 'Robert Graves | A new poem given to ISIS by the author', features a drawing of a stylized couple dancing.

[56] Hugh Lloyd-Jones to Beryl Graves, 22 Jan. 1986; Canelluñ. In this letter he also records: 'Robert was for forty years the living poet whom I most admired, and even before I began to read his poetry his other books meant a good deal to me. The

'Astymelusa' first appeared, with the Greek text, in the *Oxford Magazine*, 6 (Michaelmas [Autumn] 1966), 94.

Text: *P65-68*/*CP75*.

To Be In Love

Graves told the poet John Montague that in 'To Be In Love' he was referring to the medieval Irish tale of Suibne Geilt.[57] See 'Sweeney Among the Blackbirds', in *S*, pp.120-6, and *CWP*, pp.276-81; and *WG61*, pp.450-5/441-6:

> The flying madness [with which St Ronan cursed Suibne] is described as making his body so light that he could perch in the tops of trees, and leap desperate leaps of a hundred feet or more without injury. (Mediaeval Latin philosophers described the condition as *spiritualizatio*, *agilitas* and *subtilitas*, and applied it to cases of levitation by ecstatic saints.)[58]

See also the note on 'Hag-Ridden' (*MP61*).
Text: *P65-68*/*CP75*.

To Ogmian Hercules

This poem is 'addressed to the Celtic Hercules known to the Greek historian Lucian as Ogmian Hercules. The early Irish *ollamhs*, or master-poets, called him Ogma Sun-Face. He was their patron, under the Triple Muse-Goddess Brigit, inventor of their sacred Ogham alphabet, and represented as white-haired'.[59]

See *WG61*, pp.113/108, 133-4/128-9, 141/136, 232/225-6; and *GM*, 52.*4*, 125.*1*, 132.*3*, and 118-145.

Sect.1 l.3 is a quotation from Laura Riding's 'Fragments', 5:[60]

> Here is escape then, Hercules, from empire:
> Where Zero the Companionable
> Consoles unthinkable lusts.

Text: *PAL*.

Graves made several punctuation changes in 'To Ogmian Hercules' at

---

Claudius books had a good deal to do with my becoming a classical scholar; Robert was amused to learn that I had answered a question in Greats about the arrangements Augustus made for his succession entirely from my memories of what I had learned from his two novels.'

[57] Graves to John Montague, 1 March 1969 (draft); Canelluñ.

[58] *WG61*, pp.451/442.

[59] 'Foreword', *PAL*, p.7.

[60] *Poems: A Joking Word* (London: Cape, 1930), p.159.

the end of the 'Foreword' to *PAL* (see note), but evidently overlooked them when preparing *CP75*, which reprints the *P65-68* version; in the latter, sect.1 l.1 ends with a semi-colon in place of the comma, 'threshing-floor' in sect.2 l.2 is not hyphenated, and sect.3 has a comma in place of the semi-colon at the end of l.1 and a comma in place of the full stop at the end of l.2.

The Olive-Yard

For st.1 ll.3-5, cf. 'O' ('Unpublished Poems'), written in 1916.
Text: *P65-68/CP75*.

BEYOND GIVING (1969)

Beyond Giving was published by Rota on 19 October 1969 in a limited edition of 536 copies, 500 of them, numbered and signed, for sale.

'All my verse goes through several manuscript drafts before publication, and then years pass before I can be sure how much, if any, of it to include in my periodically pruned *Collected Poems*', Graves writes in the 'Foreword'. Only three of the thirty poems were, in the event, not reprinted in *Collected Poems 1975*: 'What We Did Next' and 'Song: New Year Kisses' from Part I, and 'The Motes' from Part II.

The foreword continues:

> Songs are the trickiest to decide about: to readers who cannot invest them with an imagined melody they must suggest unframed canvases leaning against a studio wall.
>
> The first part of this volume is concerned with love. The second contains, among other miscellaneous pieces, *Troublesome Fame*, a self-satire, and *The Sundial's Lament*, a throw-back to the jocose early nineteenth-century tradition of my Anglo-Irish family. Also *Armistice Day 1918*, a street-ballad written when I was a twenty-two-year-old infantry captain with a disability pension; it had been unprintable until last year's Jubilee celebration.
>
> I recited my Spanish *Antorcha y Corona*, with its English translation, at the Mexican Cultural Olympics in November 1968. This was dedicated to the Señorita Enriqueta de Basilio, the first woman athlete ever privileged to put a torch to the Olympic fire. I persuaded her to attend the Olympic Village Poetry Recital, for organizing which, despite its boycott by a group of politically-oriented poets, the Cultural Committee was good enough to award me a gold medal.
>
> R.G.
>
> *Deyá, Majorca*

Song: Dream Warning

Text: *CP75.*

'*Song*' was added to the title in *P68-70.*

Variants:

l.5 with *CP75*] in *BG*
l.6 legs] claws
in] with

Trial of Innocence

Text: *CP75.*

Variants:

l.3 Troubled by fear *CP75*] Beset by awe *BG*
l.4 Or of temporal] Or temporal

Superstition

Text: *CP75.*

Previous title: 'Leave-Taking' (*BG*).

Variants:

The first three lines in *BG*:

Sweetheart, be patient with my foolishness
Born only from blind superstition
Or long despair of earlier loves

st.1 l.4 stood *CP75*] stand *BG*
l.5 your] a
st.2 l.2 ugly history for my wild] all uncharitably attendant
l.3 own] set
st.3 l.6 its] the

In the Name of Virtue

Text: *CP75.*

Variant:

st.3 l.7 again *CP75*] once more *BG*

What We Did Next

See 'The Poet's Paradise', *OAP*, pp.109-29, especially pp.113-15 and 124-5.

Text: *BG.*

Compact

Text: *CP75.*

Variants:

st.2 l.4 sour *CP75*] restless *BG*
st.3 l.3 review] all revision
l.5 a purity] virginity

Song: The Clocks of Time

Text: *CP75*.

'Song' was added to the title in *P68-70*.

Variants:

st.1 l.3 No need to *CP75*] No one need *BG*

st.3 l.6 closeness] courtship,

Gold Cloud

For Graves's theory that 'We plan our own births' (st.1 l.2), see the text of an interview with Edwin Newman on American radio on 15 February 1970, 'Speaking Freely', *DQEA*, pp.206-7:

> [. . .] I have come to agree with my advanced mathematic friends who now agree that time is only a convenience, having no absolute sense. [. . .] People often plead, 'It was not my fault' – blaming their parents for giving them a difficult childhood, and so on. I take sole responsibility for having been born. My parents never chose me, because they knew nothing about me and had no idea which of their own genes I'd choose, what I'd look like, what sort of life I'd live. . . . Then who *did* know? It's no good saying 'God' because God is surely a mere question mark? So I say: 'I arranged it all myself!' Now, to make yourself responsible for your entire life, with all your stupidities, successes, ill luck, joys and sufferings, puts you in a very strong position, because you can blame nobody else. But the question arises: when were these decisions taken? Obviously you didn't exist *before* your time, although you can mentally go back in time and forward in time, which is quite a common experience among clairvoyants. Then precisely when did I make myself? . . . At the moment of my death. [. . .] That's the only time when one's life is complete. And of course, when you're dying, your whole past life is said to come flooding in with precise memories. Very well! That gives you a neat package all tied up. Yet it has not yet happened, and from the point of view of people living in other solar systems it won't happen until millions of years hence.

Text: *CP75*.

Variants:

st.2 l.3 Whether *CP75*] Either *BG*

l.4 Paradise,] this Great Park,

For 'Great Park', see the note on 'Until We Both . . .' (*GSV*).

Song: Basket of Blossom

Text: *CP75*.

'Song' was added to the title in *P68-70*.

Variants:

st.1 l.4 blossoms *CP75*] blossom *BG*

st.2 l.2 honour's] passion's

Song: Wherever We May Be

Text: *CP75*.

'*Song*' was added to the title in *P68-70*.

Variants:

st.1 l.6	plus, there *CP75*] plus and there *BG*
st.2 l.5	going,] presence,
	coming,] absence,

What Is Love?

Text: *CP75*.

Variants:

st.1 l.1	dear heart, *CP75*] my love, *BG*
l.2	a] this
	A] This
st.2 l.2	The] A
	our] one's

Song: The Promise

Text: *CP75*.

Variant:

l.7	the *CP75*] a *BG*

Semi-Detached

'–I find myself writing nothing but *Songs*, of obsessional perfectionalism; though the other day there *was* an ordinary poem about neighbours in a semi-detached house, and how much got overheard and suspected.'[61]

Text: *CP75*.

Variants:

sect.3 l.6	as affront – *CP75*] as an affront – *BG*
l.20	who had] what

In *BG* there is a space after sect.3 l.13, making a fourth, seven-line section.

Against Witchcraft

For sect.2 ll.1-2, see *GM*, 170.*5*: 'Late Classical writers attached the name "moly" to a sort of garlic with a yellow flower which was believed to grow (as the onion, squill, and true garlic did) when the moon waned, rather than when it waxed, and hence to serve as a counter-charm against Hecate's moon-magic.'

A traditional custom is referred to in sect.2 l.6: placing a broom upside down to get an unwelcome visitor to leave. See also *WG61*, pp.173/168; and *GM*, 28.*4*, 31.*f*,*7*, 37.*1*.

Text: *CP75*.

---

[61] Graves to James Reeves, 16 Jan. [1968]; *SL 2*, p.268.

Tolling Bell

Text: *CP75*.

Variants:

l.6 childhood? *CP75*] childhood, *BG*

l.16 'Angered,] 'Angry,

Blanket Charge

Text: *CP75*.

Variants:

st.3 l.1 Law *CP75*] law *BG*

st.5 l.3 not some] no

Song: The Sundial's Lament

See the 'Foreword' to *BG*, above.

See also, for st.2, Isaiah 38. 1-8.

Text: *CP75*.

Emendation:

In *BG*, *P68-70* and *CP75*, st.1 ll.7-8 are printed as a single line, an error in the typescript (Canelluñ) which was not corrected.

Poem: A Reminder

Text: *CP75*.

BG does not contain the 'conventional' version, which was added in *P68-70*. In the other version, the title does not have a colon in *BG*, and there is a semi-colon after 'notprose'.

Antorcha y Corona, 1968

Text: *CP75*.

'1968' was added to the Spanish and English titles in *P68-70*.

Emendation:

st.1 l.1 caballero *BG*] cabellero *P68-70*, *CP75* (*misprint;* corrected in the 1988 Oxford University Press American reprint)

Variants:

st.1 l.1 Píndaro *CP75*] *accent omitted BG*

st.2 l.1 aquí] *accent omitted*

l.3 entrará] *accent omitted*

st.4 l.3 así] *accent omitted*

st.5 l.1 allí] *accent omitted*

st.6 l.1 fraternidad] fraternided (*misprint*)

st.11 l.1 Aquí] *accent omitted*

The footnote was added in *P68-70*.

Graves's written Spanish was not perfect; errors in the poem are listed below, with corrections to the right of the square bracket (these have not been made in the text, so as to preserve its character):

st.2 l.1 alaban las mujeres *CP75*] alaban a las mujeres

st.3 l.3	fué] fue
st.4 l.1	Hercules] Hércules
l.3	alentado] alentando
st.5 l.1	existia] existía
l.2	mas] más
l.3	presidia] presidía
st.6 l.2	Supero] Superó (more grammatically, 'Superaba')
	maxima] máxima
st.9 l.1	primeval] primeva
st.10 l.1	tres cientas] trescientas
l.2	Este] Éste
	nego] negó
l.3	Amenazandolas,] Amenazándolas,
	ai,] ¡ay,

Torch and Crown, 1968

Text: *CP75*.

Variants:

st.7 l.2	Atalanta, *CP75*] Atlanta, *BG* (*misprint*)
st.8 l.1	gold] golden
st.10 l.2	though] but

Armistice Day, 1918

See the 'Foreword' to *BG*, above.

When the war ended Graves was in North Wales, where he had been posted to train officer cadets: 'The news sent me out walking alone along the dyke above the marshes of Rhuddlan (an ancient battle-field, the Flodden of Wales) cursing and sobbing and thinking of the dead.'[62]

An early version of 'Armistice Day, 1918' was enclosed with other poems in a letter to Edward Marsh, which describes it as 'a little squib called Nov.11. thrown in for fun':[63]

Nov 11th

Why are they cheering & shouting
  What's all the scurry of feet
With little boys banging on kettle & can
  Wild laughter of girls in the street?

---

[62] *GTAT*, pp.342/246.

[63] Graves to Edward Marsh, 28 Nov. 1918; Berg. See *PAW*, p.91. Between sts.1 and 2 in the manuscript there is a short horizontal line, crossed in the centre by two small diagonal strokes; *PAW* states that this seems to indicate there were other verses, but identical lines appear between the stanzas in another of the poems enclosed, 'Pot and Kettle' (*CS*), which is complete, so Graves may have just forgotten to put them between sts.2 and 3 of the 'little squib'. Sts.1-2 reappear together in a later version (see below).

O those are the froth of the city
  The thoughtless & ignorant scum
Who hang out the bunting when war is let loose
  And for victory bang on a drum

But the boys who were killed in the battle
  Who fought with no rage & no rant
Are peacefully sleeping on pallets of mud
  Low down with the worm and the ant

'Nov 11th' reappears, revised, as 'XIV' in the notebook 'Wasters, Samples, Odd ends.' (Buffalo),[64] with an additional stanza between sts.2 and 3. This became st.7 of 'Armistice Day, 1918' and is the last stanza in a preceding eight-stanza version entitled 'Armistice Day in an Allied Capital' (Buffalo); William Nicholson, Graves's father-in-law, objected to its inclusion in a proposed edition of his collected works in the early 1920s.[65]

Text: *CP75*.

POEMS ABOUT LOVE (1969)

Of the 212 of his poems that Graves selected for *Poems About Love*, 150 are from books published in 1960-68. The one new poem, 'If and When', was not reprinted.

First published on 14 February 1969 in America by Doubleday,[66] *Poems About Love* was published by Cassell in Britain in November 1969.

In his foreword, Graves distinguishes between 'love poems' and 'poems about love'; and he warns that 'poetry should not be confused with autobiography':

FOREWORD

These poems chosen from more than twenty books published in the past half-century are here printed in roughly chronological order, most of them being variations on the main poetic problem: which is how to restore the lost age of love-innocence between men and women.

Civilization seems to have begun as an enhancement not only of mother love, but of personal love-pacts; which in time brought about the ritual foundation of gift-exchanging clans and tribes. Ancient nations decayed as soon as a weakening of its individual love-pacts and

[64] For other details of the notebook, see *Complete Poems*, Volume I, p.374, footnote 42.

[65] '*Must* you put in "Armistice Day in an Allied Capital"[?] Edie [Stuart-Wortley, his second wife] and I both think it very unworthy.' William Nicholson to Graves, n.d. [1923]; Carbondale.

[66] K. McCormick, Doubledays, to Graves, 1 Nov. 1968; Canelluñ. Higginson states 'late 1969'.

love-treaties made the central religious authority harden into impersonal law; after which religion itself slowly faded. Yet even nowadays an archaic sense of love-innocence recurs, however briefly, among most young men and women. Some few of these, who become poets, remain in love for the rest of their lives, watching the world with a detachment unknown to lawyers, politicians, financiers, and all other ministers of that blind and irresponsible successor to matriarch and patriarchy – the mechanarchy.

Poets understand love as the union of complementary souls, an ecstatic event which sets the world on fire and allows them to transcend the loveless limits of time, space and circumstance. Love poems perpetuate this mystic moment. Poems about love, as a rule, either sadly or satirically record its defeat by practical circumstance.

Poetic faith may be proved logically untenable, but poets are not logicians. Although aware that man-woman love began as sexual courtship, they cannot regard its physical consummation as more than a metaphor for love itself, and refuse to let courtship degenerate into marital routine. And although the birth of children, though greeted at first with delight, may force lovers apart and involve them as parents in unnatural obedience to the mechanarchy, yet poets cannot disown their children. Nor can they renounce physical union as irrelevant to mystic union; still less, while reserving spiritual love for the beloved, can they take random bedfellows to ease a physical frustration.

Nevertheless, poets look forward to a final reign of love-innocence when the so-called impracticable will once more become the inevitable, when miracles are accepted without surprise or question, and when the patently illogical Machine has at last performed its *reductio ad absurdum*, by disintegrating.

Omar Khayyam in a quatrain omitted by FitzGerald [*sic*] from his 'adaptation' of the *Rubaiyat* writes:[67]

> The Moon by her own nature prone to change
> Varies from animal form to vegetable.
> Destroy her form, you have destroyed nothing;
> For what she seems survives her not yet being.

The Moon here is Woman, with a temperament influenced by her menstrual period and by the Moon itself: she changes from the thin crescent moon which resembles a horn or tusk, to the full moon which

[67] Spelt as above, 'Khayyam' and '*Rubaiyat*'. For *The Rubaiyyat of Omar Khayaam*, translation and critical commentaries by Robert Graves and Omar Ali-Shah (London: Cassell, 1967; New York: Doubleday, 1968), and Omar and Idries Shah's dealings with Graves over their alleged 'twelfth-century manuscript', see *SL 2*, pp.253-4, 257, 263, 264, 280-3. See also 'Translating the *Rubaiyyat*', in *The Crane Bag and Other Disputed Subjects* (London: Cassell, 1969), pp.225-39, and *CWP*, pp.519-30.

suggests a melon or gourd; sometimes she shows fierce animal passion, sometimes she is easy-going and placid as a garden vegetable. She cannot in either condition be changed by male precept or persuasion. Khayyam's sharpest line is the last: he means that men believe in her love, and that this belief, although erroneous, remains active even when she has failed to love with the pure and faithful devotion offered her: because it secretly points to a time when women will not dissemble, lie or cheat in love. In Omar's day, the early twelfth century, Moslem women were, almost everywhere except in Berber countries, left uneducated, treated as chattels, and allowed no freedom in love. But Khayyam can do nothing about the general situation: he can only prophesy that she will one day BE in the true love sense.

Each of the love poems printed here commemorated a secret occasion and was written solely for whoever inspired it. Once these events had passed into history, the poems circulated and took on a life of their own, though still printed above my name; and I am embarrassed to take credit for work to which I can have only a partial, if nominal, claim. The numerous poems about lost love supply the thorny background, a warning of its intractability and, if it were not for the love poems, might well read as evidence of ingratitude to life – against which, however, because I myself chose to be born, I have never lodged any ingrateful protest. Since poetry should not be confused with autobiography I refrain from marking large groups with names of the women who inspired or provoked them. It would lead only to mischief.

My education has been Classical, and my family tradition Anglo-Irish; so here is an introductory poem addressed to the Celtic Hercules known to the Greek historian Lucian as Ogmian Hercules. The early Irish *ollamhs*, or master-poets, called him Ogma Sun-Face. He was their patron, under the Triple Muse-Goddess Brigit, inventor of their sacred Ogham alphabet, and represented as white-haired: ['To Ogmian Hercules' (*P65-68*) quoted, without the title; see note].

ROBERT GRAVES

Deyá, Mallorca, Spain, 1968

POEMS 1968-1970 (1970)

'Having more to say, no continued need to earn my living by writing historical novels, and fewer children around my knees, has for some years now swelled the yearly number of poems I write,' Graves declares in the 'Foreword' to *Poems 1968-1970*, which was published by Cassell on 12 October 1970.

The book contains forty-four new poems, together with twenty-seven from *Beyond Giving* (though not in the same order). *Collected Poems 1975* incorporates *Poems 1968-1970* in its entirety, with only two changes in the arrangement: 'My Ghost' (previously 'The Co-Walker') and 'Research and

Development: Classified' are moved to section XXVII.

The complete foreword is as follows:

FOREWORD

Collected Poems 1965, in sections numbered from I to XVIII, had superseded five similar collections since 1926, each in turn rejecting a large number of previous choices in favour of new ones. This was followed by *Poems* 1965-1968 in sections numbered from XIX to XXII, and here is *Poems* 1968-70, the sections continuing to XXV. There is a further section of occasional verse. Having more to say, no continued need to earn my living by writing historical novels, and fewer children around my knees, has for some years now swelled the yearly number of poems I write, though each must still go through a long series of drafts before being either suppressed or accepted on probation. In one's seventy-fifth year it is easy to plagiarize oneself, but I have done my best to weed such plagiarisms out; no legitimate pack of cards should contain more than one Jack of Diamonds or Ace of Hearts.

Poets have for centuries used the childbirth metaphor of a poem's appearance after difficult labour. Yet, just as in true childbearing the mother has admitted alien genes to her blood-stream, a tolerance markedly affecting her thoughts, desires and behaviour throughout gestation, so also in the poet's birth-metaphor. The poem of which he is brought to bed must have alien genes: borrowed, at the best, from the woman with whom he is in love, and at the worst from the whore of contemporary fashion.

Deyá 1970 R.G.

The following list gives the complete contents (new poems are indicated with an asterisk):

XXIII

Song: Dream Warning; *Song:* Beyond Giving; *Song:* The Sigil*; *Song:* Basket of Blossom; *Song:* Yesterday Only; *Song:* Twinned Heart*; *Song:* Olive Tree*; *Song:* Once More*; *Song:* The Promise; *Song:* Victims of Calumny*; *Song:* To a Rose; *Song:* The Clocks of Time; *Song:* Wherever We May Be

XXIV

Gold Cloud; Compact; Trial of Innocence; Love Gifts*; Mankind and Ocean*; Poisoned Day; Virgin Mirror*; What Is Love?; Secret Theatre*; How It Started*; Brief Reunion*; The Judges*; Love and Night*; Child with Veteran*; Superstition; Purification*; Powers Unconfessed*; Pandora*; Solomon's Seal*; To Put It Simply*; In the Name of Virtue; To Tell and Be Told*; The Theme of Death*; At the Well*

XXV

Logic*; Robbers' Den*; The Accomplice*; First Love*; Through a Dark

Wood*; In the Vestry*; When Love Is Not*; The Reiteration*; Semi-Detached; Iago; Against Witchcraft; Man of Evil*; The Raft*; Tolling Bell; The Hero; Blanket Charge; The Uncut Diamond*; The Strayed Message; The Co-Walker*; The Risk*; Something to Say*; Troublesome Fame
OCCASIONALIA
Research and Development: Classified*; The Imminent Seventies*; Carol of Patience*; H*; Invitation to Bristol*; The Primrose Bed*; Poem: A Reminder; The Strangling in Merrion Square*; *Song:* The Sundial's Lament; *Antorcha y Corona, 1968,* Torch and Crown, 1968; The Awakening*; Armistice Day, 1918

Love and Night

Canelluñ, the Mallorquin name of Graves's house on the outskirts of Deyá, means 'The Far House' (cf. st.9 l.1).

For st.10, see 'The Sufic Chequer-board', in *Difficult Questions, Easy Answers* (cf. st.9 l.2), p.185: 'The Orphic mystics of the Northern Aegean worshipped a black goddess, known as Mother Night, representing order, justice and wisdom, and distinguished her from the white orgiastic love-and-battle goddess.' See also the note on 'The Hearth' (*MDWI*).

Text: *P68-70*/*CP75*.

Purification

See *GM*, 11.*a*,*1*, 18.*c*.

Text: *P68-70*/*CP75*.

Powers Unconfessed

See 'Genius', *DQEA*, pp.5-22, especially pp.7, 19-20.

Text: *P68-70*/*CP75*.

Pandora

See *GM*, 39.*h*,*j*,*8*; and 'Pandora's Box and Eve's Apple', *5PH*, pp.93-9, where Graves discusses Hesiod's 'libellous anecdote of Pandora and her jar' and concludes that 'Pandora has long been an ambivalent character, whom poets and artists are at liberty to use in contrary senses: as the world's ruin, or the world's delight, according to the ebb and flow of the sex-war' (pp.98-9).

Text: *P68-70*/*CP75*.

Solomon's Seal

See 'Solomon's Seal', *DQEA*, pp.176-9:

> Solomon's Seal [. . .] consists of a circle surrounding two superimposed equilateral triangles [. . .]. It is also called, by Jews, the 'Star of David' [. . .].
>
> [. . .] When examined closely it proves to be a statement of man's dependence on woman for his well-being, most applicable wherever

man is equated with the Sun as power and energy, and woman with the Moon as wisdom and healing.

An ancient Egyptian architectural rule insisted, we are told, that every pyramid should rest on an inverted one of the same proportions. This concealed pyramid plainly represented the power of the Great Goddess by whose divine mercy each Pharaoh reigned [. . .]. (pp.176-7)

Text: *P68-70*/*CP75*.

Logic

Text: *P68-70*/*CP75*.

Emendation:

sect.2 l.6 peace, *mss (Eton)*] peace *ts.(Eton), CP75*

Man of Evil

Text: *P68-70*/*CP75, P68-70Lib.*

Emendation:

st.3 l.3 tears. *ms.(Eton), P68-70Lib.*] tears, *P68-70, CP75*

The comma has been cancelled (in ink) in Graves's library copy of *P68-70* and a full stop inserted in the margin.

My Ghost

Text: *CP75*.

Previous title: 'The Co-Walker' (*P68-70*).[68]

Emendation:

st.4 l.1 newspapers, *P68-70*] newspapers *CP75*

Variants:

st.1 l.2 When *CP75*] While *P68-70*

l.4 my] those

In *P68-70*, ll.3 and 4 are in the reverse order; l.3 is not in parentheses, with 'comparison' followed by a full stop and an ellipsis.

st.2 l.1 Passage] Slow lapse

l.2 near-affection, for] slow acceptance, of

l.4 kept] still

st.3 l.1 thus to be] to be well

l.2 my own ghost] a co-walker

much to my disquiet,] eventually

l.4 Came to identify and certify

l.5 including] distorting

st.4 l.1 should] when

l.2 on] in

large get-togethers,] State banquets,

l.3 disregard] disavow

foolish capers;] clumsy capers:

[68] For 'co-walker', see 'General Bloodstock's Lament for England' (*PS51*), *Complete Poems*, Volume II, p.195.

l.5 table] table;
l.6 present] watchers

The revised version of the poem, 'My Ghost', was published in *GSV* and placed in section XXVII in *P70-72* and *CP75*.

Carol of Patience

In a radio interview, Graves gave an account of the origin of this 'old-fashioned' poem:

> I was asked the other day to write a carol for *The New York Times*,[69] and thought, 'That's a silly thing to do', and then I . . . you see, I now spend a lot of my time picking up olives. It's the season, and picking is very good for the back, and keeps your fingers greasy. Also it keeps your mind working, because half the time you don't have to think. [. . .] So I found myself writing a carol as I was picking olives.[70]

Text: *P68-70/CP75*.

The Primrose Bed

Text: *P68-70/CP75*.

'The Primrose Bed' was first published as 'The Lily Bed' in the *New Statesman*, 79 (27 March 1970), 449.

THE GREEN-SAILED VESSEL (1971)

The Green-Sailed Vessel was published by Rota on 2 August 1971, in an edition of 536 copies, of which 500, numbered and signed, were for sale.

The 'Foreword' is as follows:

> Now well into my seventy-sixth year, I am more concerned than ever before with poetic problems akin to those of mathematics and physics. They deal particularly with what may be called the magical powers of thought. These powers, as interpreted for instance by the mediaeval Irish *ollamhs*, or master-poets – some women among them – and by their Middle-Eastern Sufic contemporaries, such as Khayaam and Rumi, over-ride and reinterpret simple love-entanglements to a point where physical absence supplies a living presence.[71] Alliances of this nature provide the strongest possible fulcrum for the gradual depression of

---

[69] *New York Times Magazine*, 21 Dec. 1969, p.5.

[70] See 'Speaking Freely', an interview with Edwin Newman on American radio, 15 Feb. 1970, in *DQEA*, pp.210-11.

[71] See the quotation from Rumi in 'Lecture Three, 1965', *PCP*, pp.167-8, republished as 'Ecstasy', *CWP*, pp.504-5.

public inhumanity, and for the re-elevation of natural law.

R.G.

Deyá

See the 'Foreword' to *Poems 1970-1972*, which, after a revised version of sentences 1-3 above, continues:

> These experiences occur not only in the fourth dimension, where prison walls are easily cheated – see the poem *A Reduced Sentence* – but in the fifth, where time proves as manipulable as is vertical or lateral space in the usual third dimension, and where seemingly impossible coincidences and so-called 'Acts of God' occur almost as a matter of course. In poetry, the fifth-dimensional coidentification of lovers is truth rather than idealistic fancy, and the phenomenon is here described – however inadequately – in *Five, Serpent's Tail, Testament, The Crab-Tree, Cliff and Wave, Three Locked Hoops* and subsequent pieces.

The Green-Sailed Vessel contains thirty-six poems: 'Dedicatory' (subsequently retitled 'The Hoopoe Tells Us How'), nineteen 'Love Poems' in Part I, and sixteen poems, 'Mainly Satires', in Part II. All, apart from 'My Ghost' (previously 'The Co-Walker'), are new; and all were included in *Collected Poems 1975* except 'The Miracle', which was reprinted in *Deyá: A Portfolio* (1972) (see 'Uncollected Poems', and the note below).

The Hoopoe Tells Us How

Text: *CP75.*

Previous title: 'Dedicatory' (*GSV);* the poem is placed between the 'Foreword' and Part I.

The Wand

For sect.3 l.7, cf. 'Against Witchcraft' (*BG*), sect.1 l.4.

Text: *CP75.*

Variants:

sect.3 l.1 while we *CP75*] while so we *GSV*

l.7 hatch?] hatch (*misprint*; corrected by Graves in his library copy)

Five

See 'The Pentagram of Isis', *DQEA*, pp.172-5.

Text: *CP75.*

Quinque

Text: *CP75.*

Variant:

l.1 luces *CP75*] *literae GSV*

In his library copy of *GSV*, Graves has cancelled *'literae'* and written '*stellae*' in the margin, then cancelled this and written '*luces*' above it.

The poem is in italics in *GSV*, but in roman, the title included, in *P70-72* and *CP75*; the title has been italicized in the present edition as all the other non-English titles are printed thus in *CP75*.

To Be Poets

Text: *CP75*.

Variants:

st.1 l.6 others *CP75*] they may *GSV*
l.7 a] the

The Prohibition

Text: *CP75*.

Variant:

st.2 l.4 daylight, *CP75*] daylight. *GSV*

Until We Both . . .

'Drayton Great Park' (sect.1 l.1) was the name Graves gave to the small garden behind the house of the Simon family at 12 Drayton Gardens, London SW10; see *RPG 3*, p.441.

Text: *CP75*.

Variants:

sect.1 l.5 enough ... *CP75*] enough.
sect.2 l.3 these] those

The Miracle

Text: *DP*.

This poem was reprinted only in *DP* (1972), in facsimile of Graves's handwriting, without a title.

Variants:

st.1. l.3 deep *DP*] lost *GSV*
l.4 scorched,] scorched
st.2 l 1 some] a

The Rose

Text: *CP75*.

Variant:

st.2 l.1 Fetch *C75*] bring *GSV*

Testament

Text: *CP75*.

Variants:

sect.1 l.5 Then *CP75*] So *GSV*
sect.2 l.4 it] it,

The Crab-Tree

See *WG61*, pp.246/239, 251-61/244-53, and *RPG*, p. 441.
Text: *GSV/CP75*.

Three Locked Hoops

Text: *CP75*.
Variant:

l.2 Lock *CP75*] Look *GSV* (*misprint*; corrected by Graves in his library copy)

Cliff and Wave

Text: *CP75*.
Variant:

l.6 Now *CP75*] Thus *GSV*

Those Blind from Birth

Text: *CP75*.
Variant:

st.2 l.4 mood, *CP75*] mood *GSV*

Fools

Text: *CP75*.
Variant:

st.1.l.3 reach *CP75*] teach *GSV* (*misprint*)

The Gentleman

Text: *CP75*.
Variant:

l.8 dumb *CP75*] pure *GSV*

Complaint and Reply

Text: *CP75*.
Variants:

sect.1 l.3 will *CP75*] can *GSV*
task,] task:
l.6 must] will
l.15 neatly?] neatly.
sect.2 l.2 scholars – yes.] scholars. Yes,

The Virus

Text: *CP75*.
Variant:

st.1 l.1 these *CP75*] those *GSV*

Druid Love

Text: *CP75*.
Variant:

sect.2 l.4 herself – ultimate *CP75*] herself. Ultimate *GSV*

Problems of Gender

Text: *CP75*.

Variant:

st.3 l.2 sex: *CP75*] sex; *GSV*

Confess, Marpessa

Cf. *GM*, 74.*a,e,f,4*; and *WG61*, pp.67/62, 188/183.

Text: *CP75*.

Variant:

st.2 l.3 steed *CP75*] horse *GSV*

Jus Primae Noctis

Text: *CP75*.

Variant:

l.7 clear: *CP75*] clear; *GSV*

Work Drafts

Text: *CP75*.

Variant:

st.3 l 2 work (or play)-drafts *CP75*] work-or-play-drafts *GSV*

POEMS 1970-1972 (1972)

'The poetic power to make things happen [. . .] raises simple love-alliances to a point where physical absence supplies living presence', Graves affirms in his 'Foreword' to *Poems 1970-1972*.

Published by Cassell on 16 November 1972, this is the last of the three interim collections which appeared between the 1965 and 1975 volumes of *Collected Poems*. It contains forty-three new poems, together with thirty-five from *The Green-Sailed Vessel*, plus 'Research and Development: Classified' (*P68-70*), moved from the 'Occasionalia' in section XXV to section XXVII.

The complete foreword is as follows:

FOREWORD

About half of these seventy-nine poems – sections XXVI and XXVII of my *Collected Poems* – have lately been published by Messrs Bertram Rota in *The Green Sailed Vessel* [*sic*] (1971), a signed limited edition. The series began in my *Collected Poems 1965* with eighteen sections, the first section containing a poem written as early as 1914. Section XXVI consists of love-poems; XXVII contains satire and contemporary comment.

Little need be added to my *Foreword* in *The Green Sailed Vessel*. I wrote there that, now well into my seventy-sixth year, I had become increasingly concerned with hidden powers of poetic thought, which raise and solve problems akin to those of advanced mathematics and physics. The word 'poetry' meant in Greek the 'act of making' – a sense that has survived in the old Scottish word for a poet, namely 'maker', though the Scots often spelt it *makar*. The poetic power to make things happen, as understood for instance by the early mediaeval Irish master-poets, and by their Middle Eastern Sufic contemporaries, raises simple love-alliances to a point where physical absence supplies living presence. These experiences occur not only in the fourth dimension, where prison walls are easily cheated – see the poem *A Reduced Sentence* – but in the fifth, where time proves as manipulable as is vertical or lateral space in the usual third dimension, and where seemingly impossible coincidences and so-called 'Acts of God' occur almost as a matter of course. In poetry, the fifth-dimensional coidentification of lovers is truth rather than idealistic fancy, and the phenomenon is here described – however inadequately – in *Five, Serpent's Tail, Testament, The Crab-Tree, Cliff and Wave, Three Locked Hoops* and subsequent pieces.

Recently in a broadcast I admitted my constant debt – with which I had, however, never been charged – to early Welsh prosody. In my boyhood at Harlech, North Wales, I was indoctrinated by 'Gwynedd' (the bardic name of our celebrated neighbour Canon Edwards) in *cynganedd* and other ancient metrical devices. In 1913 I even published an English *englyn* without transgressing too many of its ninety-five statutory rules. Briefly, the subsequent use I made of *cynganedd* was to strengthen my verse with complex half-concealed chains of alliteration. But I also borrowed the ancient Irish use of internal rhyme.

Prosody is now generally underrated by English and American writers, who fail to recognize it as a necessary means of hypnotizing the reader into the same dream-like mood – the top level of sleep – which the true poet himself must enter. English poetry is, I admit, complex enough without recourse to Welsh prosody; it combines the Anglo-Saxon metre of the tugged oar with the dancing metres of ancient Greece and with the resolute marching metre of the Roman legionaries – *Caesar Galliam subegit, Nicomedes Caesarem. . . .*[72]

Deyá R.G.
Majorca

The following list gives the complete contents of *Poems 1970-1972* (new poems are indicated with an asterisk):

XXVI
The Hoopoe Tells Us How*; The Wand; Five, *Quinque*; Arrow on the Vane;

[72] See Suetonius, *The Twelve Caesars*, translated by Robert Graves, revised edition (Harmondsworth: Penguin, 1979), p.35: 'Gaul was brought to shame by Caesar; / By King Nicomedes, he.'

Gorgon Mask; To Be Poets; With a Gift of Rings; *Casse-Noisette*; The Garden; The Green-Sailed Vessel; Dreaming Children; The Prohibition; Serpent's Tail; Until We Both . . .; The Rose; Testament; The Crab-Tree; Three Locked Hoops; Cliff and Wave; Her Beauty*; Always*; Desert Fringe*; The Title of Poet*; Depth of Love*; Breakfast Table*; The Half-Finished Letter*; The Hazel Grove*; Pity*; Silent Visit*; Coronet of Moonlight*; *Song:* To Become Each Other*; Heaven*; Growing Pains*; Friday Night*; The Pact*; Poor Others*; A Toast to Death*; The Young Sibyl*; Records*; The Flowering Aloe*; Circus Ring*; Ageless Reason*; As When the Mystic*; Unposted Letter (1963)*

XXVII
Birth of a Goddess*; Beatrice and Dante*; The Dilemma*; The Gentleman; The Wall*; Women and Masks (translation)*; Tilth*; The Last Fistful*; The Traditionalist*; The Prepared Statement*; St Antony of Padua*; Broken Compact*; A Dream of Frances Speedwell*; The Encounter*; Age Gap*; Nightmare of Senility*; Research and Development: Classified; Fools; Those Blind from Birth; The Gateway; Advice from a Mother; A Reduced Sentence; Absent Crusader*; Complaint and Reply; My Ghost; *Song:* Reconciliation; Knobs and Levers; The Virus; Druid Love; Problems of Gender; *Jus Primae Noctis*; Confess, Marpessa; Dream Recalled on Waking*; Work Drafts; Colophon*

The Hazel Grove

See *WG61*, pp.181-2/176-7.
Text: *P70-72/CP75*.

Silent Visit

Text: *P70-72/CP75*.
Emendation:
st.3 l.5 Aden *ms.(Eton), ts.(Canelluñ)*] Aden. *CP75*

Song: To Become Each Other

For st.2, see *WG61*, pp.387-8/378-80.
Text: *P70-72/CP75*.

Heaven

Text: *P70-72/CP75*.
The two stanzas were originally separate poems, 'The Rose' and 'Needle Point' (tss (Canelluñ)).

Friday Night

Text: *P70-72/CP75*.
There is another poem with this title in *5PH* (1958); see *Complete Poems*, Volume II. Both are included in *CP75*.

Poor Others

See the note on 'Gold Cloud' (*BG*).

Text: *P70-72/CP75*.

Emendation:

st.4 l.2 tremble, *ms.(JS)*] tremble. *CP75*

A Toast to Death

See the note on 'Gold Cloud' (*BG*).

Text: *P70-72/CP75*.

The Flowering Aloe

'In 1931 I planted an agave here; and not until this year did it flower, shooting up a 20-feet stem with flowers that were in full bloom on my birthday and that dripped honey by the pint over the steps leading to the grotto.'[73]

Text: *P70-72/CP75*.

Ageless Reason

Text: *P70-72/CP75*.

Cf. ['Confess, sweetheart, confess'], st.3, in *DP* ('Uncollected Poems').

Unposted Letter (1963)

Text: *TM*.

The *P70-72* version is reprinted in *CP75*, Graves evidently having overlooked the revisions he made for *TM*; the revised version has been adopted for the present edition.

Variants:

l.1 Do *TM*] Can *P70-72*, *CP75*
once having] having once

l.5 May] Will

Birth of a Goddess

See 'Goddesses and Obosoms', *DQEA*, pp.65-76, where Graves begins, after quoting 'Birth of a Goddess' (without the title), 'Poems should explain themselves, as I trust this does; but it seems correct for once to supply a detailed historical commentary'; in the course of the essay he summarizes 'what seems to be the first explanation of the Virgin birth that makes sense', the one provided by Graves and Joshua Podro in *The Nazarene Gospel Restored* (London: Cassell, 1953).

Text: *P70-72/CP75*.

The Dilemma

Text: *P70-72/CP75*.

There is another poem with this title in *PS51*; see *Complete Poems*, Volume II.

---

[73] Graves to Idries Shah, 2 Aug. 1967; *SL 2*, p.263.

The reduced indents in *P70-72* and *CP75* – the printers evidently misunderstood Graves's proof correction (*P70-72* proof (Canelluñ)) – have been adjusted in the present edition.

Women and Masks

Graves and the Hungarian poet, classical scholar and translator Gábor Devecseri (1917-1971) became close friends after they met in Budapest on 3 May 1968. Graves returned in 1970 and 1971, and Devecseri visited Graves in Majorca in 1970. They translated each other's poems, and Devecseri also helped to set up the Robert Graves Prize, funded with Graves's Hungarian royalties, for the best Hungarian poem of the year, and served as one of the jurors. See *Winged by Their Own Need*, edited by Miklós Vajda (Deyá, Mallorca: New Seizin Press, 1988), Introduction, 'Robert Graves and His Hungarian Prize', pp.11-16; and 'Requirements for a Poem' ('Unpublished Poems'), and note. See also Gábor Devecseri, 'In Robert Graves's Olive Grove', *New Hungarian Quarterly*, 40 (Winter 1970), 73-82, and Graves's 'Gábor Devecseri: Record of a Poetic Friendship', *New Hungarian Quarterly*, 45 (Spring 1972), 121-3; and Martin Seymour-Smith, *Robert Graves: His Life and Work*, revised edition (London: Bloomsbury, 1995), pp.533-4.

'Women and Masks' is one of five translations by Graves of poems by Devecseri in *Modern Hungarian Poetry*, edited by Miklós Vajda (New York: Columbia University Press, 1977), pp.126-9, the others being 'The World Awoke Me', 'The Bath in Pylos', 'His Life', and 'Odysseus in Phaeacia', reprinted from *New Hungarian Quarterly*, 31 (Autumn 1968), 170-1 and 38 (Summer 1970), 81-2; see also 'Deyá', *Arion 5* (1970), 151. For Graves's translation, with Thelma Dufton, of Devecseri's sequence of thirty-three poems 'Lament for a Bull', see *Arion 5* (1972), 9-20 (with 'Gábor Devecseri: Record of a Poetic Friendship', pp.7-8).

Text: *CP75*.

Emendations:

The spelling of Gábor Devecseri's name, 'Devesceri' in *CP75*, has been corrected, and the accent inserted.

In *P70-72*, sect.3 l.10 is at the bottom of the page (p.54), and evidently as a consequence *CP75* has a space after it, creating a fourth section (also in *Modern Hungarian Poetry*); this space, which is not in typescripts of the poem (Canelluñ), has been suppressed in the present edition.

The Encounter

Text: *P70-72*/*CP75*.

There is another poem with this title in *P53*; see *Complete Poems*, Volume II.

TIMELESS MEETING (1973)

'This I find to be my fortieth volume of poems published since 1916, the year in which the first of them, *Over the Brazier*, appeared', Graves writes in *Timeless Meeting*, which was published by Rota on 22 June 1973 in an edition of 536 copies, 500 of them, numbered and signed, for sale.

The 'Foreword' continues:

> *Timeless Meeting* seems highly 'Gravesian': a dubious encomium contributed to the new edition of the *Oxford English Dictionary* by the late T.S. Eliot.[74] As a rule, poets cease writing after the age of 26, but though I have now reached my 78th year I cannot yet foresee retirement. There may be necessary poems waiting to be written – who knows? I am still in love and the palmists promise me a great, if boring, longevity. Two of my Graves ancestors, John and Richard, reached the age of one hundred and three and one hundred and eleven; but that happened in the still relatively unpolluted English 18th century. Moreover neither was a poet and both had, it seems, grown senile.
>
> R.G.
>
> *Deyá, 1973*

The book contains eighteen new poems, all of which were included in *Collected Poems 1975* as section XXVIII, and, after 'The Window Pane', a revised version of 'Unposted Letter (1963)' (*P70-72*).

Seven Years

Text: *CP75*.

Previous title: 'Where Is the Truth?' (*TM*).

Emendation:

l.7 far-striding, *ms.(JS)*] far-striding *TM*, *CP75*

The Moon's Last Quarter

Graves's death, on 7 December 1985, occurred in fact in the moon's last quarter, in the twelfth lunation of the year.

Text: *TM*/*CP75*.

That Was the Night

Text: *CP75*.

Variants:

sect.1 l.3 our *CP75*] my *TM*
intolerably,] intolerably. (*misprint*)

Sect.2 does not appear in *TM*. Graves intended to include the revised two-section version in *AG* but agreed to replace it with 'Love Charms',[75] putting it in *CP75* instead.

---

[74] Misprinted 'Elliot'.

[75] Selwyn Jepson to Graves, 10 Feb. and 24 Feb. 1974; Canelluñ.

AT THE GATE (1974)

The last of the six limited editions produced by the Stellar Press and Bertram Rota, *At the Gate* was published at the end of 1974;[76] of the 536 copies, 500, numbered and signed, were for sale.

The twenty poems in the book were all included in *Collected Poems 1975*, twelve in section XXIX and eight in XXX.

The 'Foreword' is as follows:

> The foreword to *Timeless Meeting* (Bertram Rota, 1973) shows it to have been my fortieth volume of poems published since 1916 – the year when I celebrated my twenty-first birthday by officially dying of wounds at High Wood on the Somme. Usually I am busied with a prose-book as well – the prose-poetry relation being ten to four; but this year my eyes have troubled me, and make 1974 an exception. *At the Gate* is dedicated to my fellow-poet Julie Simonne whose work I have admired since she was a sixteen-year-old dancer at the Royal Ballet School, and who remains my closest critic. It is always a surprise when a spell of poem-writing overtakes me, but at least I never repeat myself, and I have never yet been accused of imitating my contemporaries or predecessors.
>
> Robert Graves
>
> *Deyá, 1974*

Ours Is No Wedlock

Text: *CP75*.

Variant:

l. 1 could *CP75*] would *AG*

Two other versions of 'Ours Is No Wedlock' were incorporated into poems in *Deyá: A Portfolio* (1972): ['Ours has no bearing on quotidian love'], st.2, and ['Confess, sweetheart, confess'], st.1 ll.3-7; see 'Uncollected Poems'.

Earlier Lovers

Text: *CP75*.

Variant:

st.1 l.4 honour *CP75*] humour *AG* (*misprint*)

Three Words Only

Text: *CP75*.

Variant:

st.3 l.3 cruelty *CP75*] cruelty, *AG*

True Magic

Text: *CP75*.

Variant:

st.1 l.2 are *CP75*] were *AG*

---

[76] Selwyn Jepson to Beryl and Robert Graves, 18 Nov. 1974; Canelluñ.

At the Gate

During the preparations for publication, 'At the Gate' was substituted for 'The Field Postcard', which was printed in *CP75* instead.[77]

For the title (and st.2), cf. *GM*, 139.*1*, 170.*4*. Graves initially proposed *From Otherwhere or Nowhere* as a title for the book; this was considered too long, and he agreed to 'Love Charms' instead, but finally chose 'At the Gate'.[78]

Text: *CP75*.

Variants:

st.2 l.4 fire *CP75*] fire, *AG*
st.3 l.2 desire,] desire

The Moon's Tear

Text: *CP75*.

Variants:

st.1 l.1 recklessly: *CP75*] fatefully: *AG*
l.3 those feckless] such
l.5 Those] From
innocence.] innocence –

In *AG* the poem is not divided after l.5; the next two lines are:

His shame in sharing her disgrace
Being not unmerited . . .

st.2 l.1 Why should he] How could he hope to
strange] proud
l.2 elbow] elbow –

The last two lines were added in *CP75*.

Song: From Otherwhere or Nowhere

Text: *CP75*.

Emendations:

st.1 l.4 carefully, *AG*] carefully *CP75*
st.3 l.6 unintelligible, *AG*] unintelligible *CP75*

Two Disciplines

Text: *CP75*.

Emendation:

l.3 manège: *AG*] manége: *CP75* (*misprint*)

The Ugly Secret

Text: *CP75*.

Variant:

st.1 l.3 away, *CP75*] away. *AG* (*misprint*)

---

77 Selwyn Jepson to Beryl and Robert Graves, 10 Feb. 1974; Canelluñ.

78 See footnote 77; and Selwyn Jepson to Graves, 24 Feb. 1974; Canelluñ.

Three Years Waiting

Text: *CP75*.

Variants:

sect.2 l.2 secret *CP75*] close *AG*

sect.2 l.5 bowstring?] bowstring (*misprint*)

CP75 has an extra space, creating a new, third section, after the line break in sect.2 l.3; this does not appear in *AG* or in a revised typescript of the *CP75* version (JS), and has been suppressed in the present edition.

COLLECTED POEMS 1975 (1975)

Graves's last volume of poetry, *Collected Poems 1975* was published by Cassell in September 1975, when he was eighty.

This was his eighth *Collected Poems* (including two American collections) and, with 592 pages and 632 poems (plus a translation), easily the largest. A two-volume edition was envisaged, but by printing, where appropriate, more than one poem to a page, the publishers were able to reduce the 864 pages to 'something more manageable'.[79]

Collected Poems 1975 reprints all the 343 poems in *Collected Poems 1965*, and practically the entire contents of the ten books that followed it – 270 poems (only five are omitted: 'The Eagre' (*17PMLR*); 'What We Did Next', 'Song: New Year Kisses', 'The Motes' (*BG*); 'The Miracle' (*GSV*)) – together with twenty new poems.

Graves acknowledges in the 'Foreword' that in the last ten years he has 'written more poems and discarded fewer than at any other time'. Having earlier emphasized that each poem was 'on probation',[80] and that years passed before he could be sure how much verse, 'if any', to include in his 'periodically pruned *Collected Poems*',[81] when he came to prepare this final collection his health was failing, and he evidently felt that the task of further pruning was beyond him.

As a consequence, *Collected Poems 1975* does, in effect, comprise two volumes: one is a 'Collected Poems 1960-1975'; the other is a 'Selected Poems 1914-1959', since only 189 of the 536 poems that appeared in books before 1959 are reprinted.[82]

The complete 'Foreword' is as follows:

> These *Collected Poems* – due to appear after my eightieth birthday – will probably be my last. My first collection was published in 1926 and later collections in 1938, 1947, 1959 and 1965, and until this present

[79] Kenneth Parker, Editorial Director at Cassells, to Beryl Graves, 26 Feb. 1974, and to Beryl and Robert Graves, 23 Dec. 1974; Canelluñ.

[80] *P68-70*, 'Foreword'.

[81] *BG*, 'Foreword'.

[82] The figure of 189 includes revised versions of earlier poems published after 1959.

publication the volumes have not greatly increased in size. During each of the last ten years I have written more poems and discarded fewer than at any other time, with the exception of 1974 when I wrote only five. I notice, however, that the annual survival rate of new poems, prior to 1965 was in fact five,[83] and now in my eightieth year it is unlikely to rise significantly again.

Most of the new poems included in this volume have been read to audiences in Budapest and some to those in Warsaw and Crakow.

R.G.
1975

Deyá
Majorca
Spain

The following list gives the complete contents (new poems are indicated with an asterisk):

Sections I-XVIII are identical to those in *Collected Poems 1965* (see note).

XIX
Cock in Pullet's Feathers; Dead Hand; Arrears of Moonlight; What Did You Say?; Lure of Murder; The Gorge; Ecstasy of Chaos; Stolen Jewel; The Snapped Thread; Fortunate Child; Loving True, Flying Blind; The Near Eclipse; Dancing Flame; Birth of Angels; On Giving

XX
The P'eng that was a K'un; Like Owls; In Perspective; The Utter Rim; Unicorn and the White Doe; Bower-Bird; Mist; The Word; Perfectionists; Prison Walls; A Dream of Hell; Our Self; Bites and Kisses; Sun-Face and Moon-Face; Freehold; The Necklace; A Bracelet; Blackening Sky; Blessed Sun; Lion-Gentle; Spite of Mirrors; Pride of Love; Hooded Flame; Injuries; Her Brief Withdrawal; The Crane; Strangeness

XXI
Song: How Can I Care?; *Song:* Though Once True Lovers; *Song:* Cherries or Lilies; *Song:* Crown of Stars; *Song:* The Palm Tree; *Song:* Fig Tree in Leaf; *Song:* Dew-drop and Diamond; *Song:* Sullen Moods; *Song:* Just Friends; *Song:* Of Course; *Song:* Three Rings for Her; *Sincèrement*; *Dans un Seul Lit*; Possibly; Is Now the Time?; Twins; Sail and Oar; Gooseflesh Abbey; The Home-Coming; With the Gift of a Lion's Claw; Wigs and Beards; Personal Packaging, Inc.; Work Room; The Ark; All Except Hannibal; The Beggar Maid and King Cophetua; For Ever; *Jugum Improbum*; *De Arte Poetica*; *Sit Mihi Terra Levis*

---

[83] He presumably meant 1959; the average in 1960-65 was 26.

XXII

Astymelusa; Tousled Pillow; To Be In Love; Fact of the Act; To Ogmian Hercules; Arrow Shots; She to Him; Within Reason; The Yet Unsayable; None the Wiser; The Narrow Sea; The Olive-Yard

XXIII

Song: Dream Warning; *Song:* Beyond Giving; *Song:* The Sigil; *Song:* Basket of Blossom; *Song:* Yesterday Only; *Song:* Twinned Heart; *Song:* Olive Tree; *Song:* Once More; *Song:* The Promise; *Song:* Victims of Calumny; *Song:* To a Rose; *Song:* The Clocks of Time; *Song:* Wherever We May Be

XXIV

Gold Cloud; Compact; Trial of Innocence; Love Gifts; Mankind and Ocean; Poisoned Day; Virgin Mirror; What Is Love?; Secret Theatre; How It Started; Brief Reunion; The Judges; Love and Night; Child with Veteran; Superstition; Purification; Powers Unconfessed; Pandora; Solomon's Seal; To Put It Simply; In the Name of Virtue; To Tell and Be Told; The Theme of Death; At the Well

XXV

Logic; Robbers' Den; The Accomplice; First Love; Through a Dark Wood; In the Vestry; When Love Is Not; The Reiteration; Semi-Detached; Iago; Against Witchcraft; Man of Evil; The Raft; Tolling Bell; The Hero; Blanket Charge; The Uncut Diamond; The Strayed Message; The Risk; Something to Say; Troublesome Fame

OCCASIONALIA

The Imminent Seventies; Carol of Patience; H; Invitation to Bristol; The Primrose Bed; Poem: A Reminder; The Strangling in Merrion Square; *Song:* The Sundial's Lament; *Antorcha y Corona, 1968,* Torch and Crown, 1968; The Awakening; Armistice Day, 1918

XXVI

The Hoopoe Tells Us How; The Wand; Five, *Quinque*; Arrow on the Vane; Gorgon Mask; To Be Poets; With a Gift of Rings; *Casse-Noisette*; The Garden; The Green-Sailed Vessel; Dreaming Children; The Prohibition; Serpent's Tail; Until We Both . . . ; The Rose; Testament; The Crab-Tree; Three Locked Hoops; Cliff and Wave; Her Beauty; Always; Desert Fringe; The Title of Poet; Depth of Love; Breakfast Table; The Half-Finished Letter; The Hazel Grove; Pity; Silent Visit; Coronet of Moonlight; *Song:* To Become Each Other; Heaven; Growing Pains; Friday Night; The Pact; Poor Others; A Toast to Death; The Young Sibyl; Records; The Flowering Aloe; Circus Ring; Ageless Reason; As When the Mystic; Unposted Letter (1963)

XXVII

Birth of a Goddess; Beatrice and Dante; The Dilemma; The Gentleman; The Wall; Women and Masks (translation); Tilth; The Last Fistful; The

Traditionalist; The Prepared Statement; St Antony of Padua; Broken Compact; A Dream of Frances Speedwell; The Encounter; Age Gap; Nightmare of Senility; Research and Development: Classified; Fools; Those Blind from Birth; The Gateway; Advice from a Mother; A Reduced Sentence; Absent Crusader; Complaint and Reply; My Ghost; *Song:* Reconciliation; Knobs and Levers; The Virus; Druid Love; Problems of Gender; *Jus Primae Noctis*; Confess, Marpessa; Dream Recalled on Waking; Work Drafts; Colophon

XXVIII

The Promised Ballad; The Impossible Day; The Poet's Curse; Seven Years; Love as Lovelessness; The Scared Child; As All Must End; Touch My Shut Lips; The Moon's Last Quarter; True Evil; When and Why; The Window Pane; Pride of Progeny; That Was the Night; *Song:* The Queen of Time; Should I Care?; Timeless Meeting; Envoi

XXIX

Ours Is No Wedlock; The Crystal*; The Discarded Love Poem; A Charm for Sound Sleeping*; Earlier Lovers; Fast Bound Together; The New Eternity*; History of the Fall*; £. s. d.; Three Words Only; True Magic; The Tower of Love; The Love Letter; *Song:* Seven Fresh Years; Love Charms; Elsewhere*; As a Less Than Robber; What Can We Not Ask?*; Two Crucial Generations*; To Come of Age*

XXX

Singleness in Love; September Landscape*; Crucibles of Love*; At the Gate; Woman Poet and Man Poet*; The Field-Postcard*; If No Cuckoo Sings*; The Moon's Tear; *Song:* From Otherwhere or Nowhere; Name; Two Disciplines; The Ugly Secret; Mountain Lovers*; Three Times In Love*; Three Years Waiting; The Sentence*; Spring 1974*; Advent of Summer*; The Unpenned Poem*; The Green Woods of Unrest*

A Charm for Sound Sleeping

Text: *CP75*.

Emendation:

st.2 l.1 magic, *ms.(Eton), ts. (Canelluñ)*] magic *CP75*

What Can We Not Ask?

Text: *CP75*.

Emendation:

sect.3 l.3 prayers? *ms.(Eton)*] prayers. *CP75*

Two Crucial Generations

Text: *CP75*.

Emendation:

l.9 rage? *mss, tss (Eton)*] rage. *CP75*

In the final typescript (Eton), Graves may have overlooked the question mark at the end of l.7 when he substituted (in ink) 'Nor' for 'And' in l.3 and for 'Or how' in l.5.

To Come of Age

Text: *CP75*.

Variant:

st.3 l.1 none of us *CP75*] we never *Encounter*, 43 (Sept. 1974), 38.

The Unpenned Poem

Text: *CP75*.

Emendation:

st.3 l.4 song, *revised tss (Eton)*] song *CP75*

The Green Woods of Unrest

Text: *CP75*.

This is the last poem Graves published; he sent it at the end of January 1975 to be added to *CP75*.[84]

UNCOLLECTED POEMS

JUVENILIA: 1910–1914

A Pot of White Heather

See *GTAT*, pp.57-8/29-30.

Text: *CP38*, 'Foreword', p.xv; 'Juvenilia' ts. (Victoria).

Previous title: 'To a Pot of White Heather Seen in the Window of a House in a Mean Street' (*CP38*).

In the 'Juvenilia' typescript (see below), '(1913)' follows the title, but Graves states in the 'Foreword' to *CP38* (p.xv) that the poem was written in 1910; he quotes the first stanza as one of several early examples of his 'difficult technical experiments in prosody and phrasing' (see *Complete Poems*, Volume II, p.301).

Graves also discusses the poem in a 1943 letter to Lynette Roberts:

> I really am a very ignorant person but it happens that I was the first Englishman, so far as I know, to write a Welsh *englyn* according to the fixed ninety-odd rules. I did this when I was thirteen and the result is in my father's not very profound book *Welsh Poetry Old and New* (1913).[85] I found the consonantal sequences too oppressive for English and modified them, slightly only, in a set of four[86] sequent *englyns*

[84] Kenneth Parker to Graves, 12 Feb. 1975; Canelluñ. Graves's letter with the copy of the poem was dated 31 Jan. 1975.

[85] See the note on 'The Will o' the Wisp' ('Uncollected Poems'), below. The book was published in 1912.

[86] The fourth has not been traced.

> (consecutive in thought) when I was 14!
> They began, I remember: [st.1 quoted].
> This brought about my discovery of the useful trick of rhyming stressed with unstressed syllables, which I introduced into English poetry and which has since been copied by several poets; and of the use of assonance, which Wilfred Owen learned from me.[87]

'A Pot of White Heather' is one of seventeen early poems in a typescript that Graves sent in December 1958 to Neville Braybrooke, who was compiling an anthology of twentieth-century juvenilia.[88] Thirty years later the anthology was published: *Seeds in the Wind: Juvenilia from W.B. Yeats to Ted Hughes*, edited with an introduction by Neville Braybrooke (London: Hutchinson, 1989). Three of Graves's poems, 'The Dying Knight and the Fauns' (*OB*), 'The Miser of Shenham Heath' and 'Merlin and the Child' (see below), were included, among some hundred items – verse, prose and drawings.

Braybrooke had initially decided on an age-limit of eighteen, but lowered it to sixteen at Graves's suggestion. 'Graves reminded me that by eighteen many of his generation were soldiers in the trenches. He also gave me two pieces of advice: "Secure Pound, Eliot and Auden so as to make your book worthwhile (and saleable)," and "Give no consideration to how long it will take you to do."'[89]

Of the poems in the typescript, six were published in the *Carthusian*:[90] 'The King's Highway', 'The Glorious Harshness of the Parrot's Voice', 'Pan Set at Nought' (subsequently 'Faun' (*FF*)), 'Merlin and the Child', 'Rondeau', and 'Ghost Music'; see the notes on these poems below. For 'Pig', see the note on 'Robinson Crusoe' (*PF*); and for 'The First Poem', 'The Dragon-Fly' and 'The Coracle', see 'Unpublished Poems'.

The complete list is as follows:

> The First Poem; The King's Highway; The Glorious Harshness of the Parrot's Voice; Willaree (*OB*); The Dying Knight and the Fauns (*OB*); Pan Set at Nought; The Miser of Shenham Heath; The Dragon-Fly; A Pot of White Heather; Merlin and the Child; Pig; Rondeau; The Coracle; Ghost Music (*OB*); The Poet in the Nursery (*OB*); Star-Talk (*OB*); In the Wilderness (*OB*)

---

87 Graves to Lynette Roberts, 1 Sept. 1943; *SL 1*, p.317.

88 Graves to Neville Braybrooke, 4 Dec. 1958 (revised carbon ts.); Victoria. The typescript of the poems has a contents page headed 'Robert Graves – JUVENILIA' and eight numbered pages of poems, emended and corrected in ink, with a date after each title.

89 *Seeds in the Wind*, p.14; Braybrooke managed to 'secure' all three, and clearly followed Graves's other advice as well.

90 For the *Carthusian*, see the note on 'The Mountain Side at Evening', below.

Another poem from the *Carthusian*, 'My Hazel Twig' (see the note below), originally followed 'The First Poem', but has been cancelled in the typescript.

In his covering letter, Graves wrote:

> Here are some starry-eyed early poems, mostly written at Charterhouse. I end the series at the age of just nineteen, when I was a soldier waiting to join the B.E.F. in France.
>
> What may interest readers is my use of technical devices not generally exploited until some years later: the half-rhymes in *The Dying Knight and the Faun*[*s*] (1910), e.g. *roses-daisies; mosses-passes;* in *A Pot of White Heather*, the rhyming of an unstressed syllable with a stressed one, e.g. *beginning-sting; rapture-pure; rises-knees;* and, in *Ghost Music* and *In the Wilderness*, the near-rhymes *thunderous-tremulous, communion-pelican*, etc. These near-rhymes are also found in *A Pot of White Heather* – the metrical structure of which I based on the difficult Welsh *englyn* form.[91]
>
> *The Dying Knight and the Fauns* was a curious mythic anticipation of my fellow-boxer Raymond Rodakowski's death in Delville Wood, six years later; I was thinking of him when I wrote it.[92]

The Mountain Side at Evening

This was the first of twenty-nine of Graves's early poems to be published in the *Carthusian*, the Charterhouse school magazine (Graves was a pupil there from 1909-1914); it led to his joining the school Poetry Society.[93] He became assistant editor of the *Carthusian* in 1914, but was forced to resign, with the editor, on account of his unorthodox views.[94]

Most of his poems in the magazine are signed with the initials 'R.G.'; a few have 'Z' or are unsigned. Three were included in *OB* (1916), another five in *FF* (1917). The remainder were not reprinted. In 1958, however, Graves offered six of them for an anthology of juvenilia; see the note on 'A Pot of White Heather', above.

Text: *Carthusian*, 10 (June 1911), 425.

The 'Foreword' to *CP38* (p.xvi) quotes st.2 ll.4 and 6 as the end of the poem, omitting l.5, and with 'We' in place of 'And' in l.6; see *Complete Poems*, Volume II, p.302.

The Will o' the Wisp

Text: Alfred Perceval Graves, *Welsh Poetry Old and New* (London: Longmans, Green, 1912), p.139. See 'A Note on Welsh Metres', pp.138-9:

---

[91] See the note on 'The Will o' the Wisp' ('Uncollected Poems').

[92] See *GTAT*, pp.67-76/36-42.

[93] See *GTAT*, pp.68-9/37.

[94] See *GTAT*, pp.84-5/48-9, and *RPG 1*, pp.100-1. The Poetry Society was dissolved after a scandal in 1912; see *GTAT*, pp.83-4/47-8.

The *englyn* is the Welsh epigram, and is remarkable for the complexity of its structure. It has five varieties, but by far the most important is [. . .] [the] *englyn unodl union,* or direct single-rhymed englyn. Its chief characteristics [are] the highly organized consonantal framework, and the complicated vowel-harmonies [. . .].

For English readers I give an *englyn* in English wrought after the Welsh pattern by my son Robert. It will be observed that the first line is divided into two parts of seven and three syllables, respectively; that the second line consists of six, and the third and fourth of seven syllables, that the ends of the first division of the first line and of the second, third and fourth lines are rhymed, or rather have the same termination, but that the last word of the third line is and indeed must be monosyllabic. The harmonic scheme is completed by the combined accentual and alliterative nexus of *gleam, gloam,* OUT YONDER IT WAND'reth, I*ts* FORCE THA*t* is a FIERCE THing, I*t dra*weth men *to drow*ning. [The poem follows.]

See also the 'Foreword' to *P70-72*, paragraph 3.

The King's Son

Text: *Green Chartreuse* (July 1913), 3.

See *GTAT*, pp.80-1/45: 'George Mallory, Cyril Hartmann, Raymond [Rodakowski], and I published a magazine in the summer of 1913 called *Green Chartreuse*. It was only intended to have one number; new magazines at a public school always sell out the first number and lose heavily on the second.'

The Miser of Shenham Heath

Text: *Green Chartreuse* (July 1913), 13, 'Juvenilia' ts. (Victoria).

Braybrooke reproduces the version from *Green Chartreuse* in *Seeds in the Wind*; in the 'Juvenilia' typescript, however, Graves has made changes to wording and punctuation, and these have been incorporated in the text.

Emendation:

st.8 l.4 Aye, *Ed.*] Ate, *Juvenilia ts.* (*error*)

Variants:

st.1 l.4 the *'Juvenilia' ts.*] his *Green Chartreuse*
beneath.] uneath.[1]
st.4 l.1 Then, though that he was weak and old,
l.3 Brook] brook,
st.7 l.4 'Soothly a lord, but ghastly thin.'
st.8 l.1 Nor from] From
did he] he would not
l.2 Feeding] To feed
l.3 old –] old,
l.4 Aye, even to] Till he had spent
piece!] piece.
st.9 l.4 beneath.] uneath.[1]

Footnote in *Green Chartreuse*: [1] uneasily.

Rondeau

Text: *Carthusian*, 11 (Oct. 1913), 174, 'Juvenilia' ts. (Victoria).
Previous title: 'Rondeau: The Clouds' (*Carthusian*).
Date in 'Juvenilia' ts.: '(1913)'.
Emendations:

st.2 l.1 my far Northern *Carthusian*] my Northern *'Juvenilia' ts.* (*error (?)*)

The omission of 'far' would make the line metrically defective.

l.4 Northern *Carthusian*] northern *Juvenilia ts.*

'Am and Advance: A Cockney Study

Text: *Carthusian*, 11 (Nov. 1913), 188.

Peeping Tom

Text: *Spectator*, 111 (8 Nov. 1913), 758.
Emendations:

st.2 l.8 Bold, inquisitive, *ts.(Buffalo)*] Bold inquisitive, *Spectator*
star! *ts.(Buffalo)*[95]] star. *Spectator*

In his introduction to *CP38* (p.xiv), Graves refers to 'Peeping Tom' as 'my first poem, written in 1908 when I was thirteen years old.[96] This was about the mocking interruptions of a poet's privacy by a star'. He then quotes st.1, omitting l.4 and changing the wording as follows:

st.1 l.3 And I took my pen in hand to write; *CP38*

l.5 stormy gusts *Spectator*] boisterous winds

There are also four changes in punctuation: the semi-colon in l.1 becomes a comma; the comma at the end of l.2 is omitted; and the comma and dash at the end of ll.6 and 7 are reversed.[97]

As some of these revisions disrupt the stanza pattern in the poem as a whole, the previous text has been retained in the present edition.

The Ballad of the White Monster

Text: *Carthusian*, 11 (Dec. 1913), 205.

The Future

Text: *Carthusian*, 11 (Dec. 1913), 206.
Emendation:

st.1 l.5 *decaying. Ed.*] *decaying.' Carthusian*

Alcaics Addressed to My Study Fauna

Text: *Carthusian*, 11 (Dec. 1913), 206.

---

95 'Star' has a capital 's' in the typescript.

96 Cf. 'The First Poem' ('Unpublished Poems'), and note.

97 See *Complete Poems*, Volume II, p.301. On a manuscript fair copy of the poem at Buffalo, inscribed 'Harlech | April 1913', Graves has written '(I dislike these vers Academic [*sic*])'.

The Cyclone

Text: *Carthusian*, 11 (Dec. 1913), 207.

Emendation:

l.12 wantonness *ts.(Buffalo)*] wantoness *Carthusian, ms.(Buffalo)*

The Ape God

Text: *Carthusian*, 11 (Feb. 1914), 229.

Lament in December

Text: *Carthusian*, 11 (Feb. 1914), 231.

Merlin and the Child

See *WG61*, pp.39/34, 181-2/176-7, 248-9/241-2, 387-8/378-9.

Text: 'Juvenilia' ts. (Victoria).

Date in 'Juvenilia' ts.: '(1914)'.

Graves included 'Merlin and the Child' in the typescript of his unpublished 1918 collection 'The Patchwork Flag' (Berg) (see 'Unpublished Poems').

The 'Patchwork Flag' version does not have the headnote. In Braybrooke the information is given in a footnote (p.115), and 'aged 16' appears below the title, in place of the date; the text is otherwise that of the 'Juvenilia' typescript.

Variants:

sect.2 l.2 Hiding *'Juvenilia' ts.*] Biting *'Patchwork Flag' ts.*
eyes] lips

l.7 an] the

sect.3 l.1 boy] child

In 'The Patchwork Flag', sect.3 has an additional, concluding line:

Thus the boy spoke and Merlin broke his rod.

An earlier version of the poem was printed in the *Carthusian*, 11 (Feb. 1914), 233:

MERLIN THE DIVINER

(An incantation of the fifth century, from the original Cornish)

Merlin! Merlin! whither art bound
At dawn of day with thy great black hound?
Oi! oi! oi! oi! oi!, oi! oi! oi! oi! oi!
Oi! oi! oi! oi! oi!

To search the way am I hither come
For a blood-red egg to carry home,
A blood-red egg of the ocean-snake
From the hollowed stone where billows break:
To search if ever the valleys hold
Green water-cress and grass of gold:
By a woodland fountain-side to lop
The highest twig from an oak tree top.

Merlin! Merlin! Turn thee again!
Let the twig on the oak untouched remain:
The water-cress in the valley green,
With the fairy grass of golden sheen,
And the red egg of thine ocean-snake
In the stone where spumy billows break.
Turn thee! Tread in the steps thou hast trod!
There is no diviner but only God!

A Day in February

Text: *Carthusian*, 11 (March 1914), 247.

The Wasp

Text: *Carthusian*, 11 (March 1914), 248.

Emendations:

l.15 fuchsias. *ts.(Buffalo)*] fuchsias *Carthusian*

Graves considered putting 'The Wasp' in *OB*, and discussed several changes with Marsh: in l.3, deleting an unintended comma after 'alternate'; in l.7, '"Too well drunk" does not imply intoxication necessarily, if thats your idea. "Too full drunk"?'; and '"Zduffed," certainly', instead of l.19 'Ztuffed'.[98]

Five Rhymes

Text: *Carthusian*, 11 (March 1914), 252.

Graves included the fourth and fifth 'Rhymes' in the 'Juvenilia' typescript: his revisions have been incorporated in the present edition (see below).

The King's Highway

Text: *Carthusian*, 11 (March 1914), 252, 'Juvenilia' ts. (Victoria).

Previous title: 'Triolet: The King's Highway' (*Carthusian*).

Date in 'Juvenilia' ts.: '(1910)'.

Three punctuation changes in the 'Juvenilia' typescript have been incorporated.

The Glorious Harshness of the Parrot's Voice

Text: *Carthusian*, 11 (March 1914), 252, 'Juvenilia' ts. (Victoria).

Date in 'Juvenilia' ts.: '(1910)'.

Variants:

ll.2,8 parrot *'Juvenilia'*] Parrot *Carthusian*

l.3 And] He

There are five other changes in punctuation.

The 'Foreword' to *CP38* (p.xvi) quotes ll.1-3, with 'screams' for 'shrills' in l.2, and 'Craning' in l.3; see *Complete Poems*, Volume II, p.302.

[98] Graves to Marsh, 'St David's Day' [1 March] 1916; Berg.

Two Moods

Text: *Carthusian*, 11 (April 1914), 267-8.

Emendation:

st.4 l.4 lesson *Ed.*] lessen *Carthusian*

The Briar Burners

Text: *Carthusian*, 11 (June 1914), 286.

The Tyranny of Books

Text: *Carthusian*, 11 (July 1914), 311.

The Exhaust-Pipe

Text: *Carthusian*, 11 (July 1914), 313.

Emendation:

l.4 nursing, *ms., ts.(Buffalo)*] nursing *Carthusian*

This poem was published anonymously. Another version (in manuscript and typescript), entitled 'The Unselfish Poet' and dated 'June 1914', is in the notebooks of early poems at Buffalo; it has 'so' in place of 'most' in l.10, 'hope' for 'see' in l.12, 'the wrong' for 'my wrong' in l.22, 'national' for 'general' in l.26, and the final half-line is not in quotation marks or brackets.

The Organ Grinder

Text: *Greyfriar*, 6 (July 1914), 149.

1918–1927

The Two Brothers

Text: *Colour*, 8 (May 1918), 80.

'"Colour" asked me for some poems day before yesterday; I sent them two both bad to match the paper & they sent £3.0.0. by return – I laugh, I sing.'[99] (The other poem was 'Country at War' (*CS*).)

In the typescript of 'The Patchwork Flag' (Berg) (see 'Unpublished Poems'), 'The Two Brothers' has an additional stanza between sts.3 and 4:

Joe was righteous and austere,
  Always turned his other cheek.
Built a God of Faith and Fear
  Fasted for him thrice a week.
Will was just an honest drinker
  Loved old ale and country fun,
Never posed as a deep thinker,

[99] Graves to C.K. Scott-Moncrieff, 5 Feb. 1918; National Library of Scotland, Edinburgh.

Always gave two blows for one.
He was true to Joe, but never
Rivalled him in stern endeavour.

Other variants:

st.2 l.9 nor *Colour*] or *'Patchwork Flag' ts.*
st.4 l.1 Listen: once] Judge by this:
l.8 Filled a tankard, drained it dry . . .
l.9 high] pure

In *Colour* the subtitle is in small capitals; it has been printed in the present edition as in Graves's books.

Peace

Text: *New Statesman*, 11 (21 Sept. 1918), 493.

In the typescript of 'The Patchwork Flag' (Berg) (see 'Unpublished Poems'), this poem has two further lines in sts.1 and 2 (as in st.3), cancelled in pencil.

'Peace' was reprinted in *Cenotaph*, edited by Thomas Moult (London: Cape, 1923), p.52 (with 'earthly' in place of 'earthy' in st.3 l.11), and *PAW*, p.67.

Bazentin, 1916

Cf. Graves's prose account of the events in this poem in *GTAT*, pp.265-6/187-8, 269/190; for the attack on High Wood (ll.46-8) and Graves's reported death of wounds, see pp.272-82/193-201. See also 'Escape' (*GD*), *Complete Poems*, Volume I, p.31, and the note on pp.342-3.

Text: *Land and Water*, 2961 (6 Feb. 1919), 31.

'Bazentin, 1916' was included in 'The Patchwork Flag' (Berg) (see 'Unpublished Poems'). One of Sassoon's suggestions when he read the typescript in August 1918 was 'bloody' instead of 'merry' in the final line, which Graves said he had adopted.[100] In the typescript he has made the revision in pencil, and has similarly changed l.20 'got' to 'pushed', and l.21 'restore' to 'get some'. These revisions do not appear, however, in the version published in 1919; Graves may have overlooked them.

The poem was reprinted in *PAW*, pp.68-9.

The Dancing Green

Text: *Vineyard*, new series, 4 (Harvest 1919), 175.

The Personal Touch

See *OEP* (1922), Chapter XLVIII, 'Tom Fool', pp.111-12:

[100] Graves to Sassoon, 26 Aug. 1918; *SL 1*, p.101. For Graves's relationship with Sassoon, see *Complete Poems*, Volume II, p.270, footnote 1.

There is a saying that 'More people know Tom Fool than Tom Fool knows'; that may be all right if it means recognizing him in the street, but he has to be a wonder before he can, without eccentricity, make his work immediately recognized in print and be even distinguishable from the best efforts of imitators. This proverb was obviously in the head of the man or woman who wrote the following sonnet, in the *Spectator* (I think) about a year ago; I have lost the cutting and the reference, and ask to be pardoned if I misquote:– [the poem follows, without the title]. The writer evidently had a keen eye for the failings of others, but is convicted out of his own mouth, for I have met nobody who can identify this particular Tom Fool for me.

First published: *Spectator*, 124 (24 Jan. 1920), 110.
Text: *OEP*.
Emendations:

l.8	crook?' *Spectator*] crook? *OEP*
l.11	Coterie *Ed.*] Côterie *OEP*
l.13	Anne . . . '; *Ed.*] Anne' *OEP*
l.14	writes *Spectator*] writes, *OEP*
	FOOL.' *Spectator*] FOOL. *OEP*

Variants:

l.1	Cunning indeed *OEP*] A cunning man *Spectator*
l.2	us,] friends
	meet] find
	verses] poems

In ll.3-5 the *Spectator* version has semi-colons instead of ellipses (with no ellipsis at the beginning of l.4).

l.3	cry] swear:
	I] *italicized*
l.5	Why see!] See here,
l.7	worn] lame
l.8	shepherd's] shepherd
	march] flock

In the *Spectator* there is a space between the octave and the sestet.

l.9	ponder 'I can't name the man,] sigh: 'Heaven knows who wrote that stuff
l.10	Wilde', or 'That's the school] Swinburne'; or 'That man

ll.11-13:

> Is one, I can't say which, of the Sitwell school';
> Or 'Here's a Georgian made to Marsh's plan';
> Or 'She's some Oxford poetess, sure enough';

l.14	How] But

Song: The Ring and Chain

Text: *Voices*, 3 (Feb. 1920), 16.

The Oxford English School

Text: *Anglo-French Review*, 4 (Aug. 1920), 52-3, revised.

Previous title: 'The Lady Student | A Study in Norman Influences' (*Anglo-French Review*).

This edition incorporates Graves's revisions (in ink and pencil) on a copy of the poem in his library, two loose pages torn from the *Anglo-French Review*, as follows:

l.3	few] no
l.10	records] record
l.14	way.] way –
l.15	(Ascetic] Ascetic
l.17	gown.)] gown
l.21	Two Reds from Ruskin] Eton and Balliol
	Meat-King's] Vicar's
l.22	slaughter,] slaughter.
l.23	A] The
l.26	idling.] idling:
l.29	laughed;] laughed.
l.31	again.] again:
l.35	new word, sweetened by new] word unknown to earlier
l.37	had] have
l.39	could] must
l.41	reverently:] reverently

Two further lines are cancelled:

And turn aside I must to the far bench where sits
Your phantom Chaperone. She nods and knits.

The date '1920' has been inserted in ink below the poem.

Graves evidently revised the poem in several stages. Most of the substantive revisions appear in the version in the manuscript book of poems which he gave to Siegfried Sassoon for Christmas in 1925 (see the note on 'From an Upper Window' ('Unpublished Poems')). However, he apparently made subsequent revisions on the *Anglo-French Review* pages. In l.21, the 'Vicar's daughter' first becomes a 'baronet's' ('Baronet's' in the manuscript book) – making the line metrically anomalous – but this is then deleted and 'Steel King's' substituted, 'Steel' finally being replaced by 'Meat-'. The manuscript book version is entitled 'A Study in Norman Influences', the original subtitle, which is cancelled on the *Anglo-French Review* page (a new title, 'The Oxford English School | 1920' has been inserted in ink). There are, in addition, significant punctuation changes which have not been made in the manuscript book version. (The latter has some thirty differences in punctuation, over half of them the problematic omission of a comma – though one is added, after 'Still' in l.39.) For these reasons, the revised *Anglo-French Review* version has been preferred in this edition.

The text printed in the *Anglo-French Review* was republished without change in *Living Age*, 306 (11 Sept. 1920), 682.

The Stepmother and the Princess

Cf. *WG61*, pp.421/412.

The text in the present edition is from a printer's proof (or 'pull') which Graves presented to his great-nephew Simon Gough in 1975 at the birth of his third child, Daisy; it is inscribed (in ink) above the poem with the names of his two eldest children: 'For Tamasin and Samuel and ......', and signed below 'Robert Graves | June 1975'. The poem seems to have been laid out for a large format (or as a broadsheet), with the poet's name printed in capitals above the title; no corresponding appearance in a periodical or the press has been traced. On the reverse side of the proof Graves has written 'Pier-Glass | not pub in it'.

In May 1918 Graves enclosed the poem in a letter to Marsh: 'Also the Wicked Stepmother who isn't yet quite right. Wants cutting down do you think? Please give advice about her: she's promising.'[101] He included 'The Stepmother and the Princess' that summer in the unpublished collection 'The Patchwork Flag' (Berg) (see 'Unpublished Poems'), and a slightly revised version, 'The Wicked Stepmother and the Princess', in another collection, 'New Poems' (Buffalo), which eventually became *CS* (1920), but without the poem. In 1921 an incomplete text appeared in the *Oxford Fortnightly Review*, 2 (20 Jan. 1921), 95, as Part IV of 'Tasters and Wasters. (From the Notebook of Robert Graves)':[102] st.1, st.2 ll.4-5, sts.3-5, and st.7 (minus the first two words of l.1).

Having evidently decided against putting it in *P-G* (Feb. 1921), Graves finally recast the poem as 'An English Wood', reducing its forty lines to twenty-seven, fifteen of them from 'The Stepmother and the Princess', and published this in *W* (1923); 'An English Wood' stayed in the canon until *CP65*.

The version on the proof is close to that in the 'New Poems' typescript, with only four differences in wording. How Graves happened to have the proof to hand in 1975 is not known.

Cynics and Romantics

First published: *To-Day*, 8 (June 1921), 154.

Text: *Oxford Poetry 1921*, edited by Alan Porter, Richard Hughes and Robert Graves (Oxford: Blackwell, 21 Nov. 1921), p.21.

Emendation:

l.20 blacknesses *To-Day*] blackness *ms.(Buffalo), Oxford Poetry (misprint (?))*

---

[101] Graves to Marsh, 27 May 1918; Berg.

[102] See *Complete Poems*, Volume I, p.374, footnote 42.

As printed in *Oxford Poetry*, l.20 is metrically defective.

Variants:

l.9 And courteous punctuated shame *To-Day*
l.18 Art *Oxford Poetry*] art
l.24 or] and
Fate,] fate,

In *OEP* (1922), Chapter XLIV, 'Surface Faults, An Illustration', pp.103-6, Graves uses 'Cynics and Romantics' ('contrasting the sophisticated and ingenuous ideas of Love') to illustrate 'the conscious process of getting a poem in order': he takes the first four lines through six drafts, declaring after the sixth, 'It may be rotten, but I've done my best.'

In 1989 the earlier version of the poem was reprinted in an edition of 150 copies by the Gruffyground Press, Sidcot, Somerset.

Records for Wonder

Text: *Saturday Westminster Gazette*, 4 June 1921, p.10.

In *OEP* (1922), Chapter XXV, 'Putty', Graves describes how, having been interrupted during the composition of 'Records for Wonder', he had to finish it 'consciously' as best he could. 'This poem has been on my conscience for some time.'[103]

Sts. 1, 2 and 4 are quoted, with one difference in wording, 'loved' in place of 'loves' in st.4 l.5.

Old Lob-Lie-by-the-Fire

Text: *Spectator*, 128 (7 Jan. 1922), 15.

On a cutting from the *Spectator* Graves has cancelled the title of the poem and written above (in pencil) 'Never more'.[104]

Misgivings, on Reading a Popular 'Outline of Science'

Text: *Lyric*, 3, no.7 (July 1923), 1.

The Toads

First published: *Oxford Outlook*, 6 (Feb. 1924), 76-7.

Text: *London Mercury*, 14 (July 1926), 232-3.

Previous title: 'The Cost' (*Oxford Outlook*).

Variants:

In *Oxford Outlook* there is another stanza before st.1:

He who spite of the debt,
The squalor, the sweat
And the lather, would rather by far gain
Admission to sit
In the Chamber of Wit
Than be quit of this hazardous bargain.

---

[103] *OEP*, p.80.

[104] Buffalo.

st.1 l.1 He who frets out his time *Oxford Outlook*
l.4 Your *London Mercury*] His
l.5 *Toad*] his
l.6 your] his
st.2 l.1 He, I say, who sets Art
l.3 Do you choose the sad] Who chooses the
l.4 Then you] He
l.5 your] his
l.6 your] his
St.3 does not appear in 'The Cost'.
st.4 l.1 Your] But this
l.2 Will be dulled by] Is surcharged with
l.3 *Toads*] Men
any] to the
l.5 in purple robes] yet decently
st.5 l.2 Or your] Sir, or
l.3 their] some
l.6 praise] tale
st.6 l.1 prove that] show how
l.4 That] How
l.5 And your] Your one
l.6 That] How
Jesuit witched] juggler bewitched
st.7 l.1 show] sketch
ll.4-5:

A vile fount of Rumour
Sans honour, sans humour,

St.9 does not appear in 'The Cost'.
st.10 l.4 Lily, Pink,] Lily, and Pink
l.6 stink of the *Toads* and their] stink, even these, of old

A History

For sect.2 l.6, see Genesis 39. 1-20.

Text: *Decachord*, 1 (Nov.-Dec. 1924), 146.

Emendation:

l.8 eyes, *Ed.*] eyes. *Decachord* (*misprint (?)*)

Four Children

Text: *Spectator*, 135 (28 Nov. 1925), 972.

Graves took l.1 and adapted ll.2-3 from the corresponding lines in an eight-line, two-stanza poem, 'The Funeral', the last of a group of six rhymes in 'The Patchwork Flag' (Berg) (see 'Unpublished Poems').

'Four Children' was reprinted in *The Best Poems of 1926*, selected by Thomas Moult (London: Cape, 1927), p.1, and again in *The Merry-Go-Round*, edited by James Reeves (London: Heinemann, 1955), pp.268-9.

The Bargain

Text: *Spectator*, 135 (19 Dec. 1925), 1143.

This poem incorporates some material from 'The Funeral' in the typescript of 'The Patchwork Flag' (see the previous note).

In the Beginning Was a Word

Text: *Poetry*, 30 (April 1927), 16.

The Bait

Text: *Poetry*, 30 (April 1927), 17-18.

An Independent

Text: *Saturday Review of Literature*, 3, no.49 (2 July 1927), 939.

[The Untidy Man]

Text: *LFNR*, p.29, ms. (Buffalo).

Graves himself provided no fewer than eight of the 'less familiar nursery rhymes' in this 1927 collection, in which he numbered the rhymes without giving titles or authors' names; this is no. 82. The title 'The Untidy Man' has been taken from the manuscript of a slightly different version in 'New Poems', a collection of poems superseded by *CS* (1920); evidently one of 'Twenty Rhymes' concluding the collection, it follows 'The Vain Man' and 'The Careless Lady', recast as 'Vain and Careless' (*CS*).

1934–1939

Midsummer Duet

First published: *The Year's Poetry: A Representative Selection*, compiled by Denys Kilham Roberts, Gerald Gould and John Lehmann (London: Bodley Head, 4 Dec. 1934), pp.139-44, as 'Midsummer Duet 1934' by 'Laura Riding and Robert Graves', without a footnote.

Text: Laura Riding, *Collected Poems* (London: Cassell, 1938), pp.145-9.

A 'Note' in the 1980 edition of Riding's *Collected Poems* (Manchester: Carcanet), p.403, states that 'Midsummer Duet' was 'written *for' The Year's Poetry*. 'Since the conception, the spirit, the format, of the poem originated with me, and grew from the initiating two stanzas delivered by the First Voice, I had necessarily, in the duet-partnership, an invisible backstage editorial role. It was naturally agreed on between my duet-partner and myself, when we were planning each a 1938 *Collected Poems*, that the "Duet" should appear in mine.' Some 'incidental revisions' were 'made in partnership agreement'.

Graves's entry in his diary for 20 August 1937 begins: 'Laura not well: was revising our Midsummer Duet for her Collected Poems.' Of the twenty-one lines with revisions as listed below, nineteen lines were by

Graves (*Second Voice*).

The text of the poem in the 1980 edition (pp.141-4), not seen by Graves, has 'ten-year-lost' for 'ten-years-lost' (in the first two printings) in st.7 l.4, and a dash misprinted as a hyphen at the end of st.12 l.1.

Variants:

Second Voice:

st.3 l.1	And *Riding CP*] O *Year's Poetry*
l.3	That] What
l.5	shoots?] shoots.

First Voice:

st.6 l.2	heats of purpose] topic heats now
l.5	fancies] pleasures
l.8	boast] truth
	season –] seasons –

Second Voice:

st.8 l.2	Too] So
l.4	soft.] soft:
l.5	far] wide
l.7	gentler] wiser
l.8	tragic pleasures.] scenes and tempers.
st.11 l.5	perfect] lamplit
l.6	Survey my death-selves] Deny corruption
l.7	I am not more calm?] death lays not more low?
l.9	Loathe] Curse
l.10	yet not a corpse?] in being changed?
st.12 l.2	waggishness] waggishness,
l.3	look backward)] forget you)
l.4	mock my pious ways,] laugh my gloom aside,
l.5	gloom] piety
	no certain grace] no grace

The concluding stanza, st.16, is headed 'Second Voice' in *The Year's Poetry*, not 'Both Voices' as in the revised version.

st.16 l.5 For certitude of quiet after?

In *The Year's Poetry*, sts.1-4 have ll.2-3 and 6-7 indented; sts.5-8, ll.2-3 and 6-8; sts.9 and 11, ll.2-4 and 7; sts.10 and 12, ll.2-3 and 5. There are no indents in sts.13-16.

Majorcan Letter, 1935

Text: *Focus*, 4 (Dec. 1935), 1-9.

Emendation:

st.11 l.4 Eyes, *Ed.*] Eyes. *Focus* (*misprint (?)*)

Written in August 1935,[105] this was intended, like 'Midsummer Duet',

[105] See Diary, 20 Aug. 1935: 'Laura writing poem for anthology for me to cooperate with.' On 22 Aug. Graves recorded, 'Tried to write rhymes for end of L's anthology poem: did a few', and the next day, 'Finished rhymes for *Letter from Majorca*'.

for the anthology *The Year's Poetry* (see the previous note), but was rejected as too long; Riding and Graves refused to cut it and printed it in *Focus*, their circle's newsletter, instead.[106] It begins what proved to be the final issue of *Focus*, and is headed, like the other items, with the authors' first names – '*Laura and Robert:*'.

Assumption Day

'Assumption Day' was written while Graves and Riding, together with Beryl and Alan Hodge, were living at the Château de la Chevrie, near Rennes (see *Complete Poems*, Volume II, p.317, footnote 40). Graves's diary entry for 15 August 1938 begins: 'This is the day on which Hitler is supposed to be invading Czechoslovakia [. . .]. Anyhow, a bad day. Cold and cross.' On 16 August he records 'A poem about being cross', and on 18 August, 'I finished a poem in 3 drafts about Assumption Day'.

Text: ts. (Victoria).

The poem was printed in Martin Seymour-Smith, *Robert Graves: His Life and Work* (London: Hutchinson, 1982), p.315.

The Moon Ends in Nightmare

Graves inserted this poem in his 1935-39 diary before the last entry, for 6 May 1939. The references to the 'summer night' (sect.1 l.4) and the 'creek' (sect.2 l.3) indicate, however, that it was written after Graves moved in June from the farmhouse where he and Laura Riding were staying with Schuyler Jackson at New Hope, Pennsylvania, into a cottage on the property, which he shared with Beryl and Alan Hodge and David Reeves, and where Riding had a workroom. He left for England in August; Riding and Jackson were married in 1941. See *RPG 2*, pp.301-13.

The manuscript was reproduced with a transcript in a special issue for Graves's eightieth birthday of the *Malahat Review* (see below), published by the University of Victoria, British Columbia, which had acquired the diary.

On an earlier draft (Buffalo), one of the cancelled titles is 'Event'; cf. 'A Love Story' (*NMG*), st.5 l.6.

For sect.3, see 'Frightened Men' (*WIH*), sect.2 ll.6-8, *Complete Poems*, Volume II, p.137, and the note on p.324.

See also 'Diotima Dead' ('Unpublished Poems') and note.

Text: *Malahat Review*, 35 (July 1975), 8-9, ms. (Victoria).

Emendations:

sect.2 l.2 Than *ms.(Buffalo)*] That *ms.(Victoria)*[107]

l.4 water. *ms.(Victoria)*] water, *Malahat Review* (*error in transcription*)

---

[106] Diary, 27 Aug. 1935: 'Wire from Kilham Roberts wanting to use on[ly] the end part of Letter from Majorca. We replied, no, use small print if necess. but no cutting.' See also *Focus*, 4 (Dec. 1935), 55. For *Focus*, see the note on 'The Christmas Robin' (*CP38*), *Complete Poems*, Volume II, p.310.

[107] In the *Malahat Review* transcription, this error in the manuscript has been corrected silently.

1952–1959

The Housing Project

Text: *New Yorker*, 28 (17 May 1952), p.101.

In the *New Yorker* the poem is attributed to 'Trevor Sevarg'.

Advice to Colonel Valentine

First published: *New Yorker*, 28 (27 Dec. 1952), 26.

Text: *New Statesman*, 47 (13 Feb. 1954), 196.

Variants:

st.1 l.1	Romantic *New Statesman*] To fall in *New Yorker*
	honourably] classically
l.2	in] if
l.3	in] if
st.2 l.1	'But counts as] Love remains
	Our] The
l.2	a woman] each female
l.3	men resolved] males intent
st.3 l.1	alas,] you say,
st.4 l.1	What? Dye your hair, you ask?] Dye your hair, do you ask?
l.2	sigh?] lie?
l.3	That would indeed be to act comically.
st.5 l.1	Honour] Friend: honor
	keep them out] keep out

In 1979 a booklet entitled *Advice to Colonel Valentine*, containing the later version of the poem together with 'Hippopotamus's Address to the Freudians' (see the following note), was published in an edition of twenty-five copies by the Gruffyground Press, Sidcot, Somerset.

Hippopotamus's Address to the Freudians

The reference to the hippopotamus evidently caught Graves's attention when he was consulting Plutarch for Chapter 24 of *GM*, 'Demeter's Nature and Deeds', in which he cites 'On Isis and Osiris', 69;[108] one of the eight drafts of the poem is written on the back of a sheet of manuscript of this chapter, and three drafts on the typescript of the next chapter, concerning Athene.

Plutarch records that for the Egyptians the hippopotamus symbolizes 'impudence, because (as they say) he killeth his sire and forceth his dam'.[109]

See also 'An Eminent Collaborationist', in *5PH*, pp.109-10: 'Alas, for that Oedipus complex! How many millions of good dollars are annually paid out in its name by the sick, idle or credulous to diploma'ed head-shrinkers!' (p.109).

First published: *Hudson Review*, 5 (Winter 1953), 518.

---

[108] See *GM*, 24.*1*.

[109] *Plutarch's Miscellanies and Essays*, sixth edition, revised by William W. Goodwin, 5 vols (Boston: Little, Brown, 1889), IV, p.93 (in Graves's library).

Text: *Punch*, 225 (11 Nov. 1953), 568.

Variants:

l.2 *Jam etiam: Punch*] *Jamqu' etiam: Hudson Review*

l.12 desire] desire,

l.17 *Jam etiam*!'] *Jamqu' etiam!'*

See the note on 'Advice to Colonel Valentine', above.

Twin to Twin

Text: *Hudson Review*, 5 (Winter 1953), 519.

In 1977 this poem and 'Considine' were reprinted in a booklet entitled *Twin to Twin* by the Gruffyground Press, Sidcot, Somerset, in an edition of twenty-five copies.

Considine

Text: *Punch*, 225 (14 Oct. 1953), 457.

Emendation:

st.1 l.4 indices? *ms.(Buffalo)*] indices?' *Punch*

See the note on 'Twin to Twin', above.

The Juggler

Henry Ringling North, President of Ringling Bros. and Barnum & Bailey Combined Shows Inc., was a personal friend of Graves's.

First published: *Saturday Review of Literature*, 36 (17 Oct. 1953), 12.

Text: *Time and Tide*, 34 (5 Dec. 1953), 1575.

Emendation:

st.2 l.2 juggling, *Saturday Review of Literature*] juggling. *Time and Tide*

The Young Witch

'The male proverb "no woman is wise below the girdle" is, of course, a libellous exaggeration' ('Genius', *DQEA*, p.19); cf. st.1 l.5.

Text: *Atlantic*, 193 (Feb. 1954), 49.

Birth of a Great Man

This poem was written for the birth of Graves's youngest son, Tomás, on 27 January 1953, in Palma, Mallorca.

First published: *New Yorker*, 30 (10 April 1954), 30.

Text: *New Statesman*, 48 (4 Sept. 1954), 269.

Variants:

st.2 l.1 arguments *New Statesman, ms.(Buffalo)*] arguments, *New Yorker*

st.5 l.2 brag –] brag.

To Magdalena Mulet, Margita Mora & Lucia Graves

Graves wrote this rhyme for an end-of-year performance at the Teatro Lírico, Palma, on 4 May 1954. For the ballet-school background, see 'Flesh-coloured Net Tights', which dates from the same year,[110] in *CSS*, pp.94-7.

[110] *Punch*, 227 (4 Aug. 1954), 176.

Text: Privately printed leaflet.

Emendations:

sect.1 l.6 **Lírico** *Ed.*] *accent omitted*

sect.2 l.6 practising *Ed.*] practicing (*misprint*)

l.9 brand-new *Ed.*] brand-news (*misprint*)

The leaflet, printed in Palma, also has a Spanish translation.

The Pumpkin

See the note on 'The Six Badgers' (*PF*).

First published: *The Merry-Go-Round*, edited by James Reeves (London: Heinemann, 1955), p.135. Reprinted in *A Golden Land*, edited by James Reeves (London: Constable, 1958), p.286.

Text: ts. (Buffalo), a superseded version of *PF* entitled 'Twenty-One Children's Rhymes'.

For the typescript Graves has revised the published text, which has 'in letters most plain' for 'most careful and plain' in st.1 l.3; and in st.2 l.1 'seized' for 'hacked', 'put' for 'set' in l.2, 'soon' and 'as' for l.3 'down' and 'when', and 'that' and 'his' for l.4 'my' and 'the'.

Max Beerbohm at Rapallo

Max Beerbohm (1872-1956) died on 20 May 1956; the poem was written and posted on 11 June.[111]

For Graves's memories of Max Beerbohm, see his BBC eightieth birthday tribute, printed in the *Listener*, 48 (28 Aug. 1952), 338 (Part IV), in which he reminded Beerbohm of their first meeting:

> At the close of the 1914-18 war I became son-in-law to William Nicholson – Kid Nicholson – who kept a collection of discarded hats in his studio at Appletree Yard, St James's. At his request I hung up my steel helmet as an *ex voto* offering on the peg next to a certain superbly glossy top-hat. I had the curiosity to look at the lining. Inside was your visiting card. It commemorated your abandonment of London club life when you went to live in Italy. You had written:
>
> Once I used to perch on Max Beerbohm's pate,
> But now he's become Italianate;
> So here in contempt and disregard
> I moulder for ever at Appletree Yard.
>
> In 1920 I met you at last: at Nicholson's house in north Wales. And what were you and he doing that afternoon? Libellously embellishing a copy of *The Illustrated London News*: shading the photographic portraits with your busy pencils, giving the senior statesman a hypocritical leer, giving the bride of the year an imbecile squint, giving a group of visiting royalty crapulous simpers which recalled Goya's portraits of Fernando

[111] Diary.

VII and his frightful family. You were working very seriously and methodically with a delicate precision worthy of an even nobler cause.

They next met thirty years later at Rapallo. In his tribute Graves described Beerbohm as the only writer of the generation above him for whom he had kept 'the same whole-hearted admiration'.

See also Graves's letter to Alastair Reid, 1 June 1956, quoted in Martin Seymour-Smith, *Robert Graves: His Life and Work* (London: Bloomsbury, 1995), pp.421-2.

Text: *Punch*, 230 (27 June 1956), 755.

The Grandfather's Complaint

Text: *Punch*, 231 (8 Aug. 1956), 155.

Song: A Beach in Spain

Text: *Punch*, 231 (29 Aug. 1956), 251.

Bathunts at Bathurst

Text: Robert Graves, *¡Catacrok!: Mostly Stories, Mostly Funny* (London: Cassell, 8 Nov. 1956), p.203.

To a Caricaturist, Who Got Me Wrong

First published: *New Republic*, 135 (17 Dec. 1956), 27.

Text: *Time and Tide*, 38 (15 June 1957), 736.

In Jorrocks's Warehouse

Cf. 'O Jorrocks, I Have Promised' (*P14-27*), *Complete Poems*, Volume II, pp.4-6, and the note on p.272.

Text: *London Magazine*, 4 (March 1957), 13.

Emendation:

st.9 l.1 Though *Ed.*] Though, *ms.(Buffalo), London Magazine*

A Fever

First published: *Atlantic*, 199 (May 1957), 35.

Text: *New Statesman*, 54 (6 July 1957), 24.

Previous title: 'The Fever' (*Atlantic*).

Variants:

st.2 l.4 but for the *New Statesman*] but the *Atlantic*

st.3 l.6 sleep –] rest –

Augeias and I

See *GM*, 127.

Graves wrote 'Augeias and I' on 11-12 July 1957, evidently feeling the need for 'floods or cleansing fire' after giving up the family flat in Palma and moving the contents of his workroom into the one at Canelluñ.[112]

---

[112] Diary.

First published: *New Statesman*, 54 (14 Sept. 1957), 321.
Text: *Harpers*, 216 (June 1958), 35.
Variant:

st.2 l.1 In memory often, *Harpers*] Nostalgically, *New Statesman*

Is It Peace?

See II Kings 9. 21-2, 30-7.

'Is It Peace?' was written in June 1957;[113] earlier that year Graves was revising a poem in memory of the son mentioned in st.3 l.2, but he never published it: see 'A Ghost from Arakan' ('Unpublished Poems').

Text: *What's New*, 203 (Christmas 1957), 7.

Fingers in the Nesting Box

Text: *S* proofs (Canelluñ), *New Yorker*, 34 (29 March 1958), 98.

This poem was to have been republished later in 1958 in *Steps*, p.254, but Graves cancelled it in the proofs, and pasted over it a typescript of 'Trudge, Body!' (*P30-33*). There is one variant: 'farm-house' (st.1 l.3) is hyphenated in the proofs, as in the manuscripts (Buffalo), but not in the *New Yorker*.

Barabbas's Summer List

Harold Macmillan offered Graves the CBE in a letter dated 10 May 1957.[114] When Graves sent 'Barabbas's Summer List' to his literary agent the following month, W.P. Watt replied, 'I certainly did get a laugh, and was also flattered by your testimonial to our efficiency, BUT I don't think that you can possibly publish it.'[115] Nevertheless, Graves put it in a lecture, 'Sweeney Among the Blackbirds', given at the University of Texas on 17 February 1958, which was published in *Texas Quarterly*, 1 (Spring 1958), 83-102 (pp.92-3), and reprinted in *S* (1958), pp.106-28, *FC* (1960), pp.97-119, and in *OP*, pp.249-72 (p.60) and *CWP*, pp.265-82 (p.273) (with 'Pott' in place of 'Watt' in st.2 ll.1 and 8, except in *OP* and *CWP*). In the lecture he recounts the episode thus:

> Minor poets who happen also to be professors of literature, or museum curators, are sometimes made Commander of the British Empire, or C.B.E. A minor poet, whom I know very well, was offered one the other day because his name had so often appeared in our literary weeklies that the Establishment hoped he might eventually mature and qualify for a Companionship of Honour, or even an Order of Merit. However, he declined the honour on the ground that politicians have no right to distribute poetry prizes, even in the name of Her Gracious Majesty Queen Elizabeth II; and because he felt loth to deprive some retiring

---

[113] Diary, 13 and 17 June 1957.

[114] Canelluñ.

[115] W.P. Watt to Graves, 28 June 1957, replying to Graves's letter of 17 June; Canelluñ.

station-master, or Assistant Commissioner in Lunacy, of a reward earned by a lifetime of loyal public service. Virginia Woolf had set him a precedent: when offered a Dameship of the British Empire, she replied by postcard that her mother had once warned her never to accept candy from strange men.

Yes, indeed. The writing of poetry is a private and non-competitive task commissioned by the Muse herself; no board of poets has any right to award diplomas, still less has the English faculty of any university – and as for a Prime Minister, especially when he is a publisher by trade . . . ! Here is a minor poem that came out of the incident: ['Barabbas's Summer List' follows].

An offer of the Companion of Honour made by Margaret Thatcher in 1984 was also declined.[116]

The Queen's Gold Medal for Poetry was presented to Graves by Queen Elizabeth at Buckingham Palace on 6 December 1968 (see *RPG 3*, p.460).

Text: *OP*, p.260.

Stable Door

Text: *S* proofs (Canelluñ), *New Statesman*, 55 (17 May 1958), 640.

Previous title: 'The Stable Door' (*New Statesman*).

In the proofs of *Steps*, 'Stable Door' has been cancelled on p.261, and a typescript of 'The Twin of Sleep' has been pasted over it.

Variant:

st.2 l.3 should *S proofs*] do *New Statesman*

Flight Report

The first two drafts are pencilled on a TWA form for passengers' comments and on the back of in-flight drink and cigarette price-lists.

Text: *Saturday Review*, 41 (9 Aug. 1958), 30.

Emendations:

sect.1 l.4 polls *mss (Buffalo)*] pools *Saturday Review*

l.7 Three miles *mss (Buffalo)*] Three thousand miles *Saturday Review*

In the *Saturday Review* sects.1 and 3 are each divided into two sections by a space at the line break; this spacing is not in the manuscripts, and has been suppressed in the present edition.

School Hymn for St Trinian's

Text: *The St Trinian's Story*, compiled by Kaye Webb (London: Perpetua, 1959), p.49.

Graves wrote the 'Hymn' for his friends Kaye Webb and Ronald Searle. According to the Acknowledgements in *The St Trinian's Story* it was 'originally composed as a flamenco for the Deyá Girls' Choir'; it is printed with an illustration by Searle.

---

[116] Margaret Thatcher to Graves, 8 May 1984; Canelluñ.

1960–1974

A Piebald's Tail

First published: *Listener*, 63 (30 June 1960), 1135.

Text: *Ladies' Home Journal*, 78 (May 1961), 112.

The Intruders

This poem first appeared in the catalogue of an exhibition of paintings by Frank Hodgkinson at the Drain Gallery, London, which opened on 19 April 1960; Graves wrote it for Hodgkinson's daughter, Kate. It was subsequently published in the *Saturday Review*, 43 (2 July 1960), 31.

Text: *Listener*, 63 (25 Aug. 1960), 1290.

In the *Saturday Review* the poem is not divided.

Teiresias

See *GM*, 105.*h*.

Text: *New Statesman*, 60 (6 Aug. 1960), 191.

Song: The Smile of Eve

Text: *New Statesman*, 60 (8 Oct. 1960), 532.

[Verse Composed over the Telephone]

This verse was first published in the William Hickey column in the *Daily Express*, 17 Feb. 1961, p.3:

> Oxford's new Professor of Poetry, Robert Graves, had hardly heard the news of his election last night before he had composed a verse in honour of the event. He wrote it for me over the telephone from Spain in three minutes flat – dashing proof of his fitness to fill the chair recently vacated by W.H. Auden. The issue in the election – the liveliest for a poetry professor that Oxford has ever seen – was whether a poet or a critic should fill the post.
>
> Graves picked the controversy for his theme and, since he was in Madrid, wrapped it in a bullfighting image:– [the verse follows, in quotation marks].
>
> This he accomplished after a few creative grunts, and a pause to find a pencil.
>
> 'And,' he added unpoetically after reading it to me, 'a helluva bull it is.'

In his inaugural lecture, 'The Dedicated Poet', Graves observes:

> This Chair, the only elective one at Oxford, has been linked by statute with the School of English Language and Literature – albeit of far older foundation. The occupant is therefore expected to make no pronouncement irreconcilable with the view of poetry that tutors and examiners require from undergraduates. It may thus be called a Siege

Perilous: because Ben Jonson, of glorious memory, to whom the young wits of Oxford used to flock when in his old age he held forth at Great Tew, allowed poets alone the faculty of judging poems; and few English School tutors have been practising poets . . . As Domingo Ortega, the veteran bullfighter, remarked the other day (the translation is mine): [the verse follows].[117]

Text: 'The Dedicated Poet', *OAP*, p.4.
Variants:

l.1 Experts ranked in serried rows *Daily Express*
l.2 Crowd *OAP*] Fill
Plaza] plaza
l.3 *knows*] *roman*

In the *Daily Express* ll.2 and 4 are not indented.

[Fir and Yew]

According to *WG61*, Chapter XI, the vowels of the ancient Irish tree-alphabet, the Beth-Luis-Nion ('Birch-Rowan-Ash') make a 'seasonal sequence', representing 'stations in the year', the five corresponding trees being 'particularly sacred to the White Goddess':[118]

The first tree is the silver fir, [. . .] sacred in Greece to Artemis the Moon-goddess who presided over childbirth, and the prime birth-tree of Northern Europe, familiar in the Nativity context. [. . .] The silver fir has its station on the first day of the year, the birthday of the Divine Child, the extra day of the winter solstice.[119] [. . .] The fifth tree is the yew, the death-tree in all European countries, sacred to Hecate in Greece and Italy. [. . .] I place the station of the yew on the last day of the year, the eve of the Winter Solstice. Ailm the Silver-fir of Birth and Idho the Yew of Death are sisters: they stand next to each other in the circle of the year and their foliage is almost identical. Fir is to yew as silver is to poisonous lead. The mediaeval alchemists, following ancient tradition, reckoned silver to the Moon as presiding over birth, and lead to Saturn as presiding over death; and extracted both metals from the same mixed ore.[120] [The poem follows.]

Text: *WG61*, pp.194-5/190. The poem is untitled.

Song: Gardens Close at Dusk

Text: *Listener*, 65 (29 June 1961), 1127.

---

[117] *OAP*, pp.3-4; reprinted in *CWP*, p.303, with a footnote by the editor, Paul O'Prey: 'This was quoted by President Kennedy at his first press conference, but attributed in error to the Spanish philosopher Ortega y Gasset.'
[118] *WG61*, pp.189/184.
[119] *WG61*, pp.190-2/185-6.
[120] *WG61*, pp.193-4/189-190.

Matador Gored

Text: *Saturday Evening Post*, 234 (4 Nov. 1961), 53.

Confiteor Ut Fas

Text: *Oxford Magazine*, new series, 2 (15 March 1962), 255.

New Moon Through Glass

First published: *Atlantic*, 212 (Oct. 1963), 67.

Text: *New Statesman*, 67 (12 June 1964), 914.

Variants:

l.1 I *New Statesman*] He *Atlantic*
myself] himself

l.2 new on] horned through

The *Atlantic* version adapts ll.3-5 in two further sections:

And if the Queen walks quietly in to greet him
Beside the bubbling vat of her wide hall,
Let him remember how he forced a passage
Through gold flames and white blizzards and black fogs,
Leaving his corpse three times at the wayside
With a death melody vibrant in all ears.

And if she sets a harp between his knees,
Lays both his hands to the strings, and laughs,
Let him render her the courtesy of silence:
Hers is a love far beyond human song,
That three times without flinching took his life.

The first two lines also appear, in a slightly different form, in 'A Last Poem' (*MDWI*), ll.5-6.

Dynamite Barbee

'Dynamite Barbee' was written at the request of Susan Bealby Wright and recorded by the Barrow Poets (Fontana Records, 1968).

Text: *Arena*, 4 (Spring 1965), 1.

Emendation:

st.2 l.5 and a long *Ed.*] and long *Arena* (*misprint*)

When a Necklace Breaks

'Just back from Mexico where I went for a month with Aemile, and stayed there *incommunicado*, & the story is horror-fiction; but I'm here again. The necklace broke, the beads spilled.'[121]

See the note on 'Departure' ('Unpublished Poems').

Text: *New Republic*, 153 (16 Oct. 1965), 28.

[121] Graves to Spike Milligan, 22 April 1965; *Dear Robert, Dear Spike: The Graves-Milligan Correspondence*, edited by Pauline Scudamore (Stroud: Sutton, 1991), p.12.

Emendation:
st.3 l.4 each other's *Ed.*] each others' *New Republic*

A Queen

Text: *Adam*, 300 (1963-65), 60.

'*Adam* will soon be *50* and I should like to celebrate R.G.'s creativity and friendship for my journal by printing a couple of hitherto unpublished poems', wrote the editor, Miron Grindea.[122] In the special issue of *Adam* (published in 1965), a revised typescript of 'Bank Account' (*MDWI*) is reproduced above 'A Queen', which has 'Palma de Mallorca, August, 1963' below it in italics; Graves's diary records that he started 'A Queen' on 7 February 1963, wrote 'more drafts' on 10 and 11 February, and finished it on 12 February in fifteen drafts.

If Love Becomes a Game

First published: *Atlantic*, 218 (Aug. 1966), 93.
Text: *New Statesman*, 72 (19 Aug. 1966), 263.

Queen Silver and King Gold

First published: *New Statesman*, 72 (23 Sept. 1966), 453.
Text: *New Republic*, 155 (26 Nov. 1966), 19.

Learn That By Heart

Cf. 'A Plea to Boys and Girls' (*5PH*), *Complete Poems*, Volume II, p.246.
Text: *Winter's Tales for Children*, 3, edited by Kevin Crossley-Holland (London: Macmillan, 1967), p.42.
Emendation:
st.2 l.1 Teacher *Ed.*] teacher *Winter's Tales for Children*

Song: One in Many

Text: *Atlantic*, 220 (Dec. 1967), 66.

A Late Daffodil for the Prince of Gwynedd

This poem featured in a special number of the *Sunday Telegraph Magazine* commemorating the investiture of Prince Charles as the twenty-first Prince of Wales at Caernarvon Castle on 1 July 1969. With it Graves provided the following note:

> Gwynedd (pronounced 'Gwinneth' in Welsh) is the ancient name for North Wales, and gave its title to the Royal House. Prince Charles is descended by way of the Mortimers and King James I of England from the King Maelgwyn Gwynedd, a 6th-Century North Welsh monarch, who bore the title Pendragon, or Chief Dragon. This meant that he was Commander-in-Chief of the national forces and had sole right (like King

[122] Grindea to Beryl Graves, n.d. [1963?]; Canelluñ.

Arthur's father, King Uther Pendragon) to fly a red silk dragon banner. The banner had come to Britain from China by way of 5th-Century Byzantium and was a windsock in dragon shape.[123]

The Dia Goch, or Red Dragon, became the emblem of Gwynedd and was, in 1689, made the regimental badge of The Royal Welch Fusiliers, of which Her Majesty the Queen is now Colonel-in-Chief. One of her heralds, the 'Rouge Dragon Poursuivant', also takes his name from this emblem. Caernarvon, where the Royal Welch Fusiliers records are stored, in the Castle Museum, was founded by the Roman General Agricola (Tacitus's uncle) and named Seguntium, but called by the Welsh Caer Segeint or Caer Sant.

In the history of Nennius (8th-Century) it appears as Sinadon by confusion with Snaedune or Snowdon, the nearby mountain.

The daffodil is 'St David's Leek' – and he is familiarly known in Wales as Dewi Sant – and its stronger-smelling cousin has become the badge of Her Majesty's Welsh Guards (p.18).

Text: *Sunday Telegraph Magazine*, 6 July 1969, p.2.
Emendation:

l.2 As *Ed.*] as *Sunday Telegraph*

1999

Text: *Daily Telegraph Magazine*, 18 July 1969, p.25.

Angry Gardener

First published: *Mediterranean Review*, 1 (Fall 1970), 47.
Text: *Listener*, 84 (8 Oct. 1970), 481.

Song: Weather

Text: *Virginia Quarterly Review*, 47 (Spring 1971), 227.

Fiery Orchard

Text: revised ts. (Canelluñ).

A two-stanza version of 'Fiery Orchard' was published in the *Virginia Quarterly Review*, 47 (Spring 1971), 228. In a typescript of this version which Graves has revised in ink (Canelluñ), the second stanza has been cancelled (each line is heavily scored through, and the stanza is cancelled with two diagonal lines); there is a fair copy in a superseded version of *GSV*, 'New Poems 1970' (carbon ts., Canelluñ).

Variants:

st.1 l.5 Gasping *tss (Canelluñ), ms.(JS)*] Grasping *Virginia Quarterly Review* (*misprint (?)*)

---

[123] See 'The Cuirassiers of the Frontier' (*CP38*) *Complete Poems*, Volume II, pp.80-1, and the note on p.311.

l.7 rose entire, each with] rose with

The second stanza in the *Virginia Quarterly Review*:

Though common love will never long survive
Without recourse to its ancestral vent,
These two now sleep felicitously apart,
Breathing each other's names, heart against heart,
Enraptured and content.

On the preceding typescript sheet (Canelluñ) Graves has made the following revisions to this stanza, which are incorporated in the cancelled version: 'may' for 'will' in l.1, 'Save by' for 'Without' in l.2, and 'still' for 'now' in l.3. (In l.4 'each other's' is mispunctuated 'each others'' in the typescripts and was printed thus.)

Defeat of Time

Text: *Mademoiselle*, 74 (Nov. 1971), 70.

Emendation:

st.3 l.3 favour. *ms. (Canelluñ)*] favour *Mademoiselle*

Six Blankets

Text: *Malahat Review*, 21 (Jan. 1972), 9.

The Note

First published: *Listener*, 87 (13 Jan. 1972), 44. Reprinted in *New Poems 1972-73: A P.E.N. Anthology of Contemporary Poetry*, edited by Douglas Dunn (London: Hutchinson, 1973), p.70.

Text: carbon ts., revised ts. (Canelluñ).

In the revised typescript, the *Listener* version is revised in green crayon and three different inks; these changes are incorporated in the carbon typescript.

Variants:

l.1 hasty *tss (Canelluñ)*] smuggled *Listener*
l.2 you] we
l.3 the essential] a mint of
l.4 instantly] readily
l.5 That] How
laugh, dance, dream] laugh and dance
l.6 That] How

In the *Listener*, ll.2 and 4 are indented.

The Hedgepig

Text: *New Statesman*, 83 (25 Feb. 1972), 247.

When He Sat Writing

This poem was written at the invitation of Sam Wanamaker for a concert in Southwark Cathedral on 23 April 1972, where it was performed in a musical setting by Ramon Farran.

Text: *Poems for Shakespeare* (London: Globe Playhouse Trust Publications, 1972), p.63.

In *Poems for Shakespeare* the subtitle is printed in capitals.

***Four Poems from* Deyá: A Portfolio (1972)**

Deyá was a limited edition of seventy-five large portfolios (53.5 x 75.5 cm.) comprising five poems in facsimile of Graves's handwriting, incorporated within coloured lithographs by Paul Hogarth of scenes in and around Deyá. Printed in Paris by Mourlot, it was published by Motif Editions in London on 22 November 1972.

Paul Hogarth, a neighbour of Graves's, had previously illustrated his book of essays and stories *Majorca Observed* (London: Cassell, 1965).

The first lines of the five poems, which are untitled, are: 'Ours has no bearing on quotidian love'; 'Love makes poor sense in either speech or letters'; 'No one can understand our habit of love' (a slightly revised version of 'The Miracle' (*GSV*) (see note); 'Is there another man'; and 'Confess, sweetheart, confess'. The first poem was printed (typeset) and the second and third reproduced in facsimile with Hogarth's lithographs in an article in the *Daily Telegraph Magazine*, 8 Dec. 1972, pp.40-7.

Graves felt that the five belonged so closely to *P70-72* that he was reluctant to have them separated from the rest (for five years, under the publisher's contract).[124]

[Ours has no bearing on quotidian love]

Text: Daily Telegraph Magazine, 8 Dec. 1972, p.45.

DP has 'were born' in place of 'were both born' in st.2 l.2, and two differences in punctuation (a comma at the end of st.1 l.1, and no comma after 'it' in l.2).

Another version of st.2 appears in st.1 ll.3-7 of the last poem in *DP*, 'Confess, sweetheart, confess' (see below); and this material is reworked in 'Ours Is No Wedlock' (*AG*).

St.3 was originally a separate poem entitled 'Silence', with 'ours' in place of 'Sunday' in l.5 (ts.(Tulsa)).

[Love makes poor sense in either speech or letters]

Text: *DP*.

[Is there another man?]

Text: *DP*.

[Confess, sweetheart, confess]

Text: *DP*.

---

[124] Graves to Michael Horniman, A.P. Watt (his literary agents), 11 Jan. 1972 (draft); Canelluñ.

For st.1 ll.3-7, see the note above on 'Ours has no bearing on quotidian love'. A slightly different version of st.3 was published as 'Ageless Reason' in *P70-72* earlier the same month (Nov. 1972); variants are as follows:

l.1 And still we brood, *DP*] We laugh, we frown, *P70-72*
l.3 The climax of] How we shall learn
l.5 this brooding season] this season
l.6 Of timeless love, this] Of royal
l.7 Has] Shall find
own fateful] deathless

The Noose
Text: *Playboy*, 19 (Dec. 1972), 220.

The Moral Law
Text: *Listener*, 89 (8 Feb. 1973), 174.

Bodies Entranced
Text: *Listener*, 91 (24 Jan. 1974), 107.

Who Must It Be?
Text: *Listener*, 91 (21 March 1974), 355.

This Is the Season
Text: *Listener*, 91 (27 June 1974), 841.

Unco
Text: *Listener*, 92 (18 July 1974), 73.

UNPUBLISHED AND POSTHUMOUSLY PUBLISHED POEMS

JUVENILIA: 1910–1914

The First Poem
See 'The Poet in a Valley of Dry Bones', *MBG*, pp.85-6, and *CWP*, p.375:

As a young poet, I wrote my first serious poem in the summer of 1906, when I was eleven years old. I had been turned out of the family wagonette by my short-tempered grandfather, for having climbed aboard without my school cap; and so missed a picnic beside the river. I spent the afternoon working out a country-poem in rhymed couplets about a farmer who, so far as I recall, prudently harvested and carted his wheat just before a hailstorm flattened the crops of all his less industrious neighbours. The poem ended: 'The swain gave thanks at daybreak for God's grace; / At Kirk this morn I saw his smiling face.' I remember thinking that *swain* and *kirk* and *morn* were very elegant words; and that I had scored off my grandfather (to whom, on his return, I dedicated the poem) by showing how little I cared for family picnics. This was a false start. Three years later I felt a genuine afflatus, and wrote one moonlit night in June: [ll.1-6 of 'The First Poem' quoted, without a title, and with 'O' for 'No' in l.1, and 'I' for 'I'll' in l.2]. There was a difference in kind between these two failures: the first, an academic exercise, was sadly deficient in technique; the second, a personal statement, was equally deficient in craftsmanship – but my hand trembled as I wrote it down; nor did I parade it for public approval.

Text: ms., ts. (Buffalo), 'Juvenilia' ts. (Victoria). The Buffalo manuscript, in red crayon, is dated 'Jan 1910', with '(copied out later)' pencilled above this; the typescript is dated 'January, 1910'.

The Buffalo manuscript and typescript are in two notebooks of both published and unpublished poems. The first notebook contains autograph fair copies; the front cover is inscribed in ink: 'Verses | 1910-1914 [originally '1910-1916'] | Robert Graves.', with 'Poems written at | Charterhouse | 1910-1914' pencilled on the inside of the cover. The second notebook comprises bound carbon typescripts of these and other poems; on the front cover is pencilled 'Early poems | & poems included in *Over the Brazier* | *& Fairies & Fusiliers*'.

Other unpublished poems in the present edition with manuscripts and/or typescripts in these notebooks are: 'Nightmare', 'The Dragon-Fly', 'Pig', 'Boy-Morality', 'The Coracle', 'To My Unborn Son', 'Machine Gun Fire', 'Return'.

The text of 'The First Poem' in the 'Juvenilia' typescript (see the note on 'To a Pot of White Heather' ('Uncollected Poems')) is that of the Buffalo typescript, with the following punctuation changes, which have been incorporated in the present edition: in l.1, an exclamation mark in place of a full stop; a comma inserted after 'knight' in l.2, and omitted after 'fire'; a capitalized 'T' in l.6 'Things'; a colon in place of a comma after 'cry' in l.7; a comma inserted after 'fly' and 'free' in l.9, omitted after 'trod' in l.11, and inserted after 'tread' in l.12; in l.13, a comma inserted after 'alone' and omitted after 'shod'; after l.14 'garlanded', a dash (as in the manuscript) in place of a full stop.

Another manuscript version at Buffalo (in the same manuscript notebook), entitled 'Rhapsody' and inscribed 'Nov 1910 | Charterhouse', has a space after l.10 and three additional stanzas (with two extra lines in the last one), in which an unidentified 'he' is to fly with the speaker ('For love for Woman Fair is slight / when man is loved as he'); a later draft stanza (inserted after the first of these additional stanzas) states that 'he' was the only person 'To stretch a finger to the load / That was o'erpowering me'.

Nightmare

Text: ms., ts. (Buffalo); both are dated 'June 1910'.

The Dragon-Fly

Text: ms., ts. (Buffalo), 'Juvenilia' ts. (Victoria).

In the Buffalo manuscript and typescript the poem is dated September 1913; it has the sub-title 'A Protestation' (cancelled in the manuscript), and 'thy lily-bed' in place of 'the lily-bed' in st.2 l.3. Punctuation changes in the 'Juvenilia' typescript: a comma inserted after 'far-trailing' in st.1 l.2 and omitted after 'cup' in l.3.

Boy-Morality

The autograph fair copy (Buffalo) is inscribed 'Jan 1914 | Champéry'. Graves recounts in *GTAT*, pp.94-5/55, how he endangered his life by skiing down an ice-covered slope at this resort in Switzerland. See also *RPG 1*, pp.95-8.

Text: ms., ts. (Buffalo).

The Coracle

Text: ms., ts. (Buffalo), 'Juvenilia' ts. (Victoria).

In the Buffalo manuscript and typescript, the poem, dated 'July 1914', is entitled 'The Youngest Poet'. Two further stanzas in the manuscript have been cancelled.

In st.3 l.6 the 'Juvenilia' typescript restores the original reading, 'And all the air cries', cancelled in the manuscript and replaced by 'Earth, air and sea cry', which is also in the corresponding typescript.

Differences in punctuation between the Buffalo and 'Juvenilia' typescripts: at the end of each stanza a full stop replaces an exclamation mark, and closing quotation marks in sts.1 and 2 have been suppressed; a comma omitted at the end of st.1 l.1, and a colon at the end of l.3 in place of a comma; a comma inserted after st.2 l.3 'clay'; in st.3 l.4, a comma in place of an exclamation mark, with a lower-case 'm' in 'my' instead of a capital letter.

1915–1919

The Last Drop

Text: ts., Royal Welch Fusiliers Regimental Museum, Caernarvon.

Emendation:

l.2 torture-cry *ms.(RWF)*] torture cry *ts.(RWF)*

The RWF collection includes the manuscript of an earlier version entitled 'Jusqu'au bout', which is inscribed 'Havre 1915'; Graves left Liverpool for Le Havre on 12 May 1915 and stayed there until 17 May.[125]

Trench Life

Text: ms. (Buffalo).

Posthumously published: *PAW*, p.53.

[125] *RPG 1*, pp.122-3.

Through the Periscope

Cf. *GTAT*, pp.142/91:

> At stand-to rum and tea were served out. I had a look at the German trenches through a periscope – a streak of sandbags four hundred yards away. Some of these were made of coloured stuff, whether for camouflage or from a shortage of plain canvas I do not know. There was no sign of the enemy, except for a wisp or two of wood-smoke where they, too, were boiling up a hot drink. Between us and them was a flat meadow with cornflowers, marguerites and poppies growing in the long grass, a few shell holes, the bushes I had seen the night before, the wreck of an aeroplane, our barbed wire and theirs. A thousand yards away was a big ruined house, behind that a red-brick village (Auchy), poplars and haystacks, a tall chimney, another village (Haisnes). Half-right was a pithead and smaller slag-heaps. La Bassée lay half-left; the sun caught the weathervane of the church and made it twinkle.

See also *GTAT57*, pp.123-4:

> I now had a trench periscope, a little rod-shaped metal one, sent me from home. When I poked it up above the parapet, it offered only an inch-square target to the German snipers; yet a sniper at Cuinchy, in May [1915], drilled it through, exactly central, at four hundred yards range. I sent it back as a souvenir; but my mother, practical as usual, returned it to the makers and made them change it for a new one.

Text: ms. (Berg), included in a letter to Edward Marsh, October 1915, *SL 1*, pp.34-6, quoted in the note on 'The Fusilier', below.

A manuscript at Buffalo of an apparently earlier version is dated 'June '15'.

Emendations:

st.1 l.1	shallow-buried *ms.(Buffalo)*] shallow buried *ms.(Berg)*
l.2	stands *ms.(Buffalo)*] stand *ms.(Berg)*
l.4	fear, *ms.(Buffalo)*] fear *ms.(Berg)*
	faith, *Ed.*] faith *ms.(Berg)*
	hate, *Ed.*] hate *ms.(Berg)*
st.3 l.3	trees, *ms.(Buffalo)*] trees *ms.(Berg)*
l.4	La Bassée *ms.(Buffalo)*] *accent omitted ms.(Berg)*
	sunshine. *Ed.*] sunshine *ms.(Berg)*
st.4 l.1	brain, *Ed.*] brain *ms.(Berg)*
st.5 l.2	Since *ms.(Buffalo)*] That *ms.(Berg)*

Posthumously published: *PAW*, p.50.[126]

Discussing the proposed contents of *OB* with Marsh, Graves wrote: 'I quite agree "Through the Periscope" should go'.[127]

[126] In *PAW* 'he' has been added in st.7 l.1.

[127] Graves to Marsh, 'St David's Day' [1 March] 1916 (Berg); quoted in *PAW*, p.89.

Machine Gun Fire: Cambrin

The manuscript has '(Sept 25 1915)' after the title – the first day of the Battle of Loos. For Graves's prose account of the episode in the poem, see *GTAT*, pp.201-3/137-8.

Text: ms. (Buffalo).

Emendation:

l.6 it's *Ed.*] its *ms.(Buffalo)*

The Fusilier

Graves sent this poem in a letter to Marsh dated 9 February 1916, describing his life as an instructor at the central training camp at Le Havre:[128]

> I have to live up to my part here as I have learned to worship my Regiment: in sheer self-defence I had to find something to idealize in the Service & the amazing sequence of R.W.Fus suicides in defence of their 'never-lost-a-trench' boast is really quite irresistible. Result: I am getting horribly Praetorian & drill-bookish & find it impossible to write you a decent letter.
>
> Tonight however my dormitory-fellow has returned off leave with a half dozen of very ancient port, & my hard military frown is softened a little by Bacchus. We are now drinking the glorious year that Erewhon appeared & beneath Philpott's bed lurks another bottle, of 1834, fragrant with still more romantic possibilities.
>
> Havre is a dull place, full of horrible painted women[,] cheap cinemas, Belgians, A.S.C, slatternly French tradespeople & various kinds of embusqués. I don't go there much. After my long-hoped leave I want to go straight away back to my battalion. [. . .]
>
> I haven't written a line of verse here – oh, yes I have one poem but its rather the private kind of poetry so I'll send it to you only, & won't risk sending it home – I'm always forgetting that my people take things I write frightfully seriously & last month I had an absolute *snorter* from Father about a set of verses which were really very good but expressed a point of view he regarded as immoral[.][129] I'll show them you when I get my leave (oh vain hopes deferred!) because I want sympathy. There is nothing about this one which he could consider so, but I'm very sensitive: here goes:– ['The Fusilier' follows].

---

[128] Graves to Marsh, 9 Feb. 1916 (Berg); the first paragraph is quoted in *SL 1*, pp.38-9.

[129] 'To Francis', in the typescript notebook at Buffalo (dated 'January 1916'). The first of its six stanzas:

> It's not for the lewdness of the tale you told
>   That I'm so angry, dear,
> For who could be so foolish or so bold
>   As to hope virgins here?

Graves had already told Marsh about 'Peter' in a previous letter:

> But my chief solace which makes up for everything really, is a fairly regular correspondence with Peter – or so the gods call him, as Homer would say, tho' men call him George Johnstone[130] – my best friend, a poet long before I'll ever be, a radiant & unusual creature whose age hovers between seven & seventy, & tho' now in the first half-dozen of VIth Form at Ch'ouse he's still whole-some minded & clean-living. Thank God he's too young to come out & get killed before another year or so. When I go West I want you to write to him & look him out & be as good a friend to him as you have been to me. He'll repay it.[131]

For Graves's account of his relationship with Johnstone, see *GTAT* (where he is called 'Dick'), pp.40-1/17, 76-7/42, 85-7/49-50, 162-4/107-8, 220/151, 368/262; and *SL 1*, pp.35-6, 46, 50-1, 57, 63, 77-8, 89, 100, 150.

Text: ms. (Berg). Punctuation has not been added to the text, to preserve its character.

O

Text: ms. (Berg).

Emendations:

l.5 It's *Ed.*] Its *ms.(Berg)*

l.6 alphabet. *Ed.*] alphabet *ms.(Berg)*

A letter containing the poem was written to Marsh on 4 April 1916 at the Millbank private hospital in London, while Graves was on leave from the Somme for a nose operation; he also sent 'The Lady Visitor in the Pauper Ward' and 'Not Dead' (*GD*).

A later poem with this title was published in *MDWI*, and reprinted in *CP65* and *CP75*.

To My Unborn Son

Objections to this poem twice prevented it from being published in one of Graves's books. Sassoon removed it from the proofs of *GD* after Graves had returned to France in January 1917:

> Robbie [Ross] & I have (with Eddie Marsh's sanction) taken the responsibility of inserting 'Careers' – (& 'The Work-House' ['The Lady Visitor in the Pauper Ward']) in place of 'My Unborn Son' – which Robbie was *very much* against. He says it spoils the book. I myself had serious doubts of it – as it practically describes a wet dream. (Pardon my frank way of expressing myself).[132]

---

[130] George Harcourt Johnstone (1899-1946), later third Baron Derwent.

[131] Graves to Marsh, Oct. 1915; *SL 1*, p.35.

[132] Sassoon to Graves, 27 Feb. [1917]; Carbondale.

Later that year it was rejected by William Heinemann, who was publishing *FF* (with the ten poems from *GD* reprinted in it):

> Only one poem fails to please H. & after consultation with Gosse this has been removed[:] 'The Unborn Son' supposedly too erotic. A new poem called 'the caterpillar' goes in instead [. . .].[133]

Text: revised ts. (Buffalo); though undated, it is placed in the notebook (see the note on 'The First Poem', above) within a group of poems dated 1916.

Posthumously published: *Observer*, 8 Nov. 1992, p.60.

A manuscript fair copy (Imperial War Museum) has 'lonely' for 'pretty' in st.4 l.4, no sub-title, and ll.2 and 4 of each stanza indented; there are also differences in punctuation.[134]

Return

Text: ts. (Buffalo); dated 'July 1916'.

Emendation:

st.1 l.4 Blighty.' *Ed.*] Blitey.' *ts.(Buffalo).*

Graves included an earlier version (which he referred to as 'Eight lines of doggerel') in a letter to Marsh.[135]

The Savage Story of Cardonette

See *GTAT*, pp.237/164:

> The only first-hand account I heard of large-scale atrocities was from an old woman at Cardonette on the Somme, with whom I was billeted in July 1916. It was at Cardonette that a battalion of French Turcos overtook the rear guard of a German division retreating from the Marne in September 1914. The Turcos surprised the dead-weary Germans while they were still marching in column. The old woman went, with gestures, through a pantomime of slaughter, ending: 'Et enfin, ces animaux leur ont arraché les oreilles et les ont mis à la poche.'[136]

The poem was one of four sent with a letter to Marsh dated 14 August 1916 (Berg) (the manuscript of the poem, a fair copy, also has the date 'Aug 14 '16') from Queen Alexandra's Hospital, Highgate, London, where

[133] Graves to Marsh, 25 Aug. 1917; Berg.

[134] The text in the *Observer* is apparently that of the manuscript fair copy, previously in Sassoon's library (though there are four differences in punctuation); see Martin Taylor, '"Two Fusiliers": The First World War Friendship of Robert Graves and Siegfried Sassoon', *Imperial War Museum Review*, 7 (Nov. 1992), 4-14 (the manuscript is reproduced on p.10).

[135] Graves to Marsh, n.d. [July 1916], *SL 1*, pp.53-4. (There is an error in transcription: in l.6, 'long,' should be suppressed.)

[136] Quoted in *PAW*, p.52, with the note: 'A Turco was one of a body of native Algerian light infantry in the French Army.'

Graves was being treated for wounds he received in the Battle of the Somme; the other poems included 'To S.S. who mourned me dead', an earlier version of 'Escape' (*GD*) (see the note on 'Died of Wounds', below).

Text: ms. (Berg).

Emendation:

st.1 l.4 morning. *Ed.*] morning *ms.(Berg)*

Posthumously published: *PAW*, p.52.[137]

Died of Wounds

While Graves was convalescing at the family's country house, Erinfa, near Harlech, in North Wales, he sent this poem in a letter to Marsh dated 18 October 1916 (Berg):

> I wrote the following silly thing last night in a moment of abstraction (I told you I died of wounds on my 21st birthday? Well! I call it "Died of Wounds" & have made it into the shape of a funeral urn, as George Herbert might have done.[)]

For Graves's reported death in the Battle of the Somme in July 1916, see the note on 'Escape' (*GD*), *Complete Poems*, Volume I, pp.342-3.

Text: ms. (Berg).

Posthumously published: *PAW*, p.51.[138]

Six Poems from 'The Patchwork Flag' (1918)

During the summer of 1918 Graves prepared a new book of poems, to be called 'The Patchwork Flag'. After criticisms by Siegfried Sassoon and Robert Ross, however, he decided not to publish it, though thirty-two of the forty-three poems did eventually appear in print, twenty-four of them in *CS* in 1920. A carbon typescript revised by Graves in pencil and red ink, with a sheet of comments by Sassoon dated 'Aug. 21', is in the Berg Collection in the New York Public Library. See the note on *CS, Complete Poems*, Volume I, pp.350-2, and Dominic Hibberd, '"The Patchwork Flag" (1918): An Unrecorded Book by Robert Graves', *Review of English Studies*, new series, XLI, 164 (1990), 521-32.

The following six poems are in the same order as in the typescript.

Foreword

See Graves to Sassoon, 9 July 1918:

> I've almost got the new book together & I forbid you to get the posthumous V.C. till it's published. It wont be as striking as yours[139] but

---

[137] *PAW* has an error in st.2 l.3, 'stop' instead of 'loot', and 'Bosche' is spelt 'Boche' (for the former spelling, see the note on 'It's a Queer Time' (*OB*), *Complete Poems*, Volume I, p.340.

[138] *PAW* omits 'day' in l.13.

[139] Sassoon's *Counter-Attack and Other Poems* was published on 27 June 1918.

it will be damned good in spite of occasional corpses that blunder up among the nursery toys. It shall be called 'The Patchwork quilt' I think with an explanation perhaps of this kind [an earlier version of 'Foreword', without a title, follows].[140]

See also the note on 'The Treasure Box' (*TB*), *Complete Poems*, Volume I, pp.349-50.

Text: 'The Patchwork Flag' ts. (Berg).

Letter to S.S. from Bryn-y-pin

Graves and his wife spent six months from March to September 1918 at Bryn-y-pin, a farmhouse above the Royal Welch Fusiliers' camp at Kinmel Park, near Rhyl on the North Welsh coast (*RPG 1*, pp.194-9; see note on 'Night March', below). The poem was his response to the 'anger' and 'jealousy' in a letter from Sassoon at the end of June 1918, which charged him with not 'writing deeply'.[141] Noting that it was two years to the day since he had written his 'Letter to S.S. from Mametz Wood' (*FF*), Graves sent the first ten lines (an earlier version) in a letter dated 16 July; by then, however, Sassoon had been invalided out, after being shot in the head on 13 July, and so the poem would 'have to be rewritten'.[142]

Sassoon found the poem 'Full of nice things', but objected: 'The only thing is that I *wasn't* "lone & drear". I was filled with a deeper passion than ever before; & *much better* at the job of soldiering. Like all war feelings, it was an abnormal effort. But I never thought much about the old 1st Battn. days – the men I'd got were too good for that. I would like you to wash out the impression of a disconsolate survivor, because it isn't true at all.'[143]

Text: 'The Patchwork Flag' ts. (Berg).

Posthumously published: Hibberd, '"The Patchwork Flag" (1918)', 528-9; *PAW* (American edition), pp.81-2.

Night March

After hearing Graves read 'Night March' in December 1917, Sassoon described it as 'a wonderful thing – his most sustained effort'.[144]

---

[140] See *SL 1*, p.95; this version, which is also printed in *PAW*, p.53, has as its final line 'Blame my dazed head, blame bloody war'.

[141] *SL 1*, pp.94-5.

[142] *SL 1*, p.97; the version in 'The Patchwork Flag' makes, nonetheless, no mention of this.

[143] Ms. with ts. (Berg). In a carbon copy of one page of the typescript at Buffalo, 'drear' in l.9 has been lightly cancelled in pencil; but so too has 'dread' in l.36, while in place of 'frightened' in l.33 'fearful' has been faintly pencilled in the margin, then cancelled and 'anxious' substituted. The only substantive revision in the Berg typescript is 'foul' in l.25 in place of 'sad'; in l.24, a full stop after 'sick', retained in Hibberd and *PAW*, has been circled in pencil, i.e. cancelled.

[144] Sassoon to Marsh, 22 Dec. 1917, quoted in Hibberd, '"The Patchwork Flag" (1918)', 524.

Text: 'The Patchwork Flag' ts. (Berg).

Emendation:

st.22 l.2 withholding *Ed.*] witholding *ts.(Berg)*

Posthumously published: Hibberd, '"The Patchwork Flag" (1918)', 529-32; *PAW* (American edition), pp.83-5.

There are incomplete manuscript drafts in a notebook at Buffalo inscribed 'Oct 1917 | Kinmel Park'.[145]

Poetic Injustice

Text: 'The Patchwork Flag' ts. (Berg).

Posthumously published: *PAW* (American edition), p.86.

The Survivor Comes Home

On a manuscript (pencil) of the poem at Buffalo, Graves has written (in ink) up the left-hand margin: 'This was when I had the horrors. It reads silly now.'

Text: 'The Patchwork Flag' ts. (Berg).

Emendations:

st.2 l.2 weasel, *ms.(Buffalo)*] weazel, *'Patchwork Flag' ts.* (The ms. has 'owl' in place of 'bird')

st.3 l.2 waste, *ms.(Buffalo)*] noise, *'Patchwork Flag' ts.*

l.5 Death *ms.(Buffalo)*] death *'Patchwork Flag' ts.*

st.6 l.1 Death: *ms.(Buffalo)*] Death *'Patchwork Flag' ts.*

l.2 scorned you, *ms.(Buffalo)*] scorned you *'Patchwork Flag' ts.*

l.3 breath . . . *ms.(Buffalo)*] breath *'Patchwork Flag' ts.*

Posthumously published: Hibberd, '"The Patchwork Flag" (1918)', 532; *PAW* (American edition), p.87.

'Too long to get harrowing effect' was Sassoon's comment on the poem.[146] There is a shorter version at Buffalo, a typescript comprising sts.1, 4, 3 and 6, in that order, with these differences in wording:

st.3 l.2 shrieking *'Patchwork Flag' ts.*] roaring *ts.(Buffalo)*
noise,] waste

st.4 l.1 alive and] alive, are

l.2 sweet] Brave

l.3 journeyed] travelled

l.4 me now] me, cold

st.6 l.1 Death! O great king Death!

---

[145] It contains notes on trench warfare together with drafts of poems and cuttings of reviews; Graves was training young officers at Kinmel Park from the beginning of October 1917 (*RPG 1*, p.183); see the note on 'Letter to S.S. from Bryn-y-pin', above.

[146] Ms. with ts. (Berg).

The Pudding

Text: 'The Patchwork Flag' ts. (Berg).

Emendations:

l.1 'Eat *Ed.*] Eat *'Patchwork Flag' ts.*

l.3 Alexander.' *Ed.*] Alexander,' *'Patchwork Flag' ts.*

This is the fifth of six 'Rhymes' in 'The Patchwork Flag'; see the note on *CS, Complete Poems,* Volume I.

Graves sent 'The Pudding' in a letter to Sassoon in July 1918, with the comment, 'Haven't had time to write anything lately except a few children's rhymes for Nancy to illustrate, which are not particularly anything great'.[147] The other rhymes were 'The Dream' ('What Did I Dream?' (*TB*)) and 'The King's Story Teller' ('Jock o' Binnorie' (*PF*)), also in 'The Patchwork Flag'.

Mother's Song in Winter

For l.3, cf. 'Song for New Year's Eve' (*5PH*), st.3 l.2, *Complete Poems,* Volume II.

Text: ms. (Buffalo).

Emendation:

l.9 sings, *Ed.*] sings *ms.(Buffalo)*

The manuscript is inscribed 'For Collins', like the accompanying manuscripts of 'The Penny Fiddle' and 'The Story Teller' ('Jock o' Binnorie') (*PF*), first published in *Collins' Children's Annual* (London: Collins, 1926) (see notes).

To Jean and John

In l.4, the word 'wingle' was coined by the younger of Graves's two brothers, John; cf. 'Mr Philosopher'(*FF*), st.7 l.3, and 'Finland' (*FF*), st.1 l.3.

Text: ms. (Buffalo).

Emendation:

l.10 bother. *Ed.*] bother *ms.(Buffalo)*

The manuscript of this rhyme, a fair copy, is in 'New Poems', a collection of poems superseded by *CS* (1920). See the note on ['The Untidy Man'] ('Uncollected Poems').

---

147 Graves to Sassoon, n.d. [early July 1918]; Berg. In this version ll.1 and 3 are designated 'Nurse', the other lines 'A'. Graves had been thinking of the children he and Nancy, who was pregnant, were going to have, and adds that 'if ever I make any name for myself for poetry & stories, its the children's stunt that I'm going to succeed in, I'm sure'.

1920s–1930s

From an Upper Window

Text: ms. book 'Suavia, Gravioia' (1925) (William S. Reese collection). Emendation:

st.4 l.5 climb. *Ed.*] climb *ms.'Suavia, Gravioia'*

To express his gratitude to Sassoon for once again helping him financially – with a gift of £150 – Graves sent him a bound manuscript book of eighteen poems, entitled 'Suavia, Gravioia', and inscribed 'Siegfried with love from | Robert & Nancy | Christmas 1925'.[148] In an accompanying letter he thanks him for the money – 'It has made life a different thing' – and adds, 'This book is the best I can do to show my devotion'.

The contents of the manuscript book (which has a final page for 'Notes') are as follows (unpublished poems are indicated with an asterix):

> A History of Deification* (sonnet); From an Upper Window*; A Dedication of Three Hats (*P14-26*); The Country Dance (*P14-26*); Degrees of Vision* (forty lines in rhyming couplets); The Rose and the Lily (*P14-26*); The Hill of Rhododendrons* (sixteen five-line stanzas); The Hobby Horse (see the note on 'The College Debate' (*WH*), *Complete Poems*, Volume I, pp.403-4); An Occasion (*P14-26*); Four Children ('Uncollected Poems'); The Corner Knot (*P14-26*); A Letter to a Friend (*P14-26*); Pygmalion to Galatea (*P14-26*); Ancestors (*P14-26*); The Toads ('Uncollected Poems'); Virgil the Sorcerer (*P14-26*); The Bargain ('Uncollected Poems'); A Study in Norman Influences (The Oxford English School) ('Uncollected Poems').

There is an earlier version of st.1 of 'From an Upper Window' in the notebook 'Tasters, Wasters, Odd ends.' at Buffalo; extracts from the notebook were published in January 1921 (see *Complete Poems*, Volume I, p.374, footnote 42).

Drink and Fever

Text: revised ts. (Buffalo).

'Drink and Fever' is one of three unpublished poems in a typescript contents list headed 'Poems 1928' (Buffalo); the others are 'Story Told to a Goat' ('Vestry') and 'The End' (see the following two notes). The remaining eighteen poems appeared in *P29* and (one only) *10PM*.

Vestry

'Vestry' began as a four-line version of st.4 entitled 'Additional verse to a ballad in *Ulysses*' (with 'I took my disciples and gave them advice' as its

---

[148] The title is apparently from a family motto, 'Suaves dum Graves' ('Pleasant while serious'); see *But It Still Goes On* (London: Cape, 1930), p.13.

first line, and 'pennies' in place of 'rubies' (l.3)); see 'The Ballad of Joking Jesus' recited by Buck Mulligan in James Joyce's *Ulysses*:

I'm the queerest young fellow that ever you heard.
My mother's a jew, my father's a bird.
With Joseph the joiner I cannot agree,
So here's to disciples and Calvary.

If anyone thinks that I amn't divine
He'll get no free drinks when I'm making the wine
But have to drink water and wish it were plain
That I make when the wine becomes water again.

Goodbye, now, goodbye. Write down all I said
And tell Tom, Dick and Harry I rose from the dead.
What's bred in the bone cannot fail me to fly
And Olivet's breezy . . . Goodbye, now, goodbye. [149]

Among the other titles in the drafts are 'Apology', 'To a Churchwarden' and 'Story Told to a Goat'.

Text: revised ts. (Buffalo).

Emendation:

st.3 l.8 quarter-day *ms.(Buffalo)*] quarter day *ts.(Buffalo)*

See the previous note.

The End

For 'Pepper's Ghost' (l.19), cf. James Joyce, *Ulysses*: 'Where was that ad some Birmingham firm the luminous crucifix? Our Saviour. Wake up in the dead of night and see him on the wall, hanging. Pepper's ghost idea.'[150]

Text: revised ts. (Buffalo).

Emendation:

sect.1 l.23 halitosis. *Ed.*] halytosis. *ts., mss (Buffalo).*

See the note on 'Drink and Fever', above.

The Sand Glass

Text: ms. (Buffalo).

The manuscript is a fair copy which was among material at Buffalo – sheets of manuscript and cut-and-paste typescript – from Graves's revision of his story 'The Shout' for publication in 1929.

---

[149] James Joyce, *Ulysses* (Paris: Shakespeare and Company, 1926), pp.18-19 (edition in Graves's library).

[150] *Ulysses* (see previous footnote), p.144. See Weldon Thornton, *Allusions in Ulysses: An Annotated List* (Chapel Hill: University of North Carolina Press, 1968), p.131: 'Pepper's ghost seems to have been a character of a dramatic company that specialized in presenting plays involving a spectral effect, probably through the use of some phosphorescent substance on their costumes.'

This What-I-Mean

For Laura Riding's membership of the Fugitive group of American poets, and her attempted suicide on 27 April 1929 by throwing herself from a window after drinking Lysol, a disinfectant (sect.4), see *RPG 2*, pp.6-9 and 71-116 (especially p.84), and *GTAT29*, p.445.

Text: ms. (Buffalo).

The Fingerhold

'The Fingerhold' is one of a group of seven discarded poems from 'Man Ending', a poem sequence superseded by *P30-33*. The sequence has an introductory prose 'argument' (ms. Buffalo) consisting of brief linked commentaries on each of the twenty-seven poems; 'The Fingerhold' is the eighteenth, followed by 'The Foolish Senses' (*TWE*).

Text: ms. (Buffalo).

Emendations:

'Fingerhold' is hyphenated in the title above the poem but not in st.2 l.3, nor in the prose 'argument'; the hyphen has been omitted in the present edition.

st.2 l.9 uphold. *Ed.*] uphold *ms.(Buffalo)*

Then What?

Text: ms. (Buffalo); a fair copy.

Emendations:

l.9 gate, *ms. drafts (Buffalo)*] gate *ms. fair copy (Buffalo)*

l.13 event, *ms. drafts (Buffalo)*] event *ms. fair copy (Buffalo)*

Historical Particulars

Text: ms., ts. (Buffalo).

Graves worked on this poem intermittently over a period of fourteen months. In his diary he records that he started a poem 'about place in history' on 21 March 1935, and wrote four more drafts in the next two days, changing the title from 'And Should I Fail?' to 'What Then?'; Laura Riding went over it with him on 25 March and 'made suggestions'. He resumed composition on 22-3 June, producing a version on 25 June to which he gave the ultimate title; further drafts followed on 11 October. Finally he returned to the poem on 19 May 1936, recording the following day: 'Finished *Historical Particulars*'.

The title is in a manuscript list of poems written in 1935-36 (Buffalo), almost all of which were printed in *CP38*.

Address to Self

Text: ms. (Buffalo).

Graves's diary records the composition of this poem on 22-3 June 1935 (see the previous note). On 11 August Riding went over his recent poems with him: 'It was agreed to scrap *Address to Myself* & I to rewrite two more.'

Prosperity of Poets

The origin of this poem is revealed in Graves's diary. On the morning of 13 December 1935 he 'wrote set poem on words listed (originals noted for title of poem book)'. The typed list is on the facing page: 'sample, arbiter, quorum, escort, consort, instances, numbers, array, several, plural, certain poems, mutual, agenda'. 'Laura read & passed my set poem, now called *Prosperity of Poets*', the entry for 18 December concludes. 'Never wrote a poem so easily.'

Riding's set poem written with the same words (Diary, 16-17 Dec.) was 'Friendship on Visit', nine seven-line stanzas about her relationship with James Reeves,[151] who had just spent a month in Deyá; see Riding's *Collected Poems* (London: Cassell, 1938; reprinted Manchester: Carcanet, 1980), pp.305-7 and 271-2. There was also to have been a poem by Reeves – 'Did you write your Task in the end?' Graves asked him in January[152] – but it has not been traced.

Text: ts. (Buffalo).

1940s–1950s

Diotima Dead

Written in eight drafts over eleven worksheets, 'Diotima Dead' apparently dates from the first half of 1940. The initial draft is on the back of a sheet of carbon typescript of *Sergeant Lamb of the Ninth*, Chapter 8.[153] Graves was working on this historical novel in January-February 1940 when he received two hostile letters from Laura Riding, dissociating herself from the 'Covenant of Literal Morality' she had established with her circle, and, in the second, written on 17 February,[154] repudiating her fourteen-year association with Graves; see *SL 1*, pp.290-1, and *RPG 3*, pp.7-9. See also Graves's letter of 19 February 1940 to Basil Liddell Hart:

> What can I say about Laura? She reached (for me) a point of shall we say poetic (i.e. hyper-moral) excellence that nobody has ever attained before; and then – what shall I say? Her oldest friends consider it an inexplicable abandonment of the principles that she once guarded with the fiercest intensity.[155]

The poem starts in autobiographical mode, using first- and second-person pronouns, with the final line, 'And two lives ended.'; Diotima and Socrates emerge in the second draft.

Cf. Laura Riding's 'Many Gentlemen', *Collected Poems* (London: Cassell,

---

151 See *Complete Poems*, Volume II, p.317, footnote 40.
152 Graves to James Reeves, 24 Jan. 1936; Texas.
153 *Sergeant Lamb of the Ninth* (London: Methuen, 1940).
154 *RPG 3*, p.8.
155 *SL 2*, p.292.

1938; and Manchester: Carcanet, 1980), pp.75/81, and *WG61*, pp.11-12/7-8.

Text: revised ts. (Buffalo).

Graves removed 'Diotima Dead' from *WIH* (1942) in October 1941 when his co-author Alan Hodge wrote that the printers wanted three poems to be cut.[156]

The Hearth

Text: revised ts. (Buffalo).

Graves at first intended to put 'The Hearth' in *WIH* ; see the following note.

A later poem with this title was published in *MDWI*, and reprinted in *CP65*, *PAL* and *CP75*.

In the Lion House

Text: ms. (Texas).

Emendation:

st.3 l.4 half-hearted *ms.(Buffalo)*] half hearted *ms.(Texas)*

Graves sent 'In the Lion House' (with the comment 'not a good title') in a letter to James Reeves, explaining that he was substituting it for 'The Hearth' in *WIH*;[157] he subsequently wrote that on reading *WIH* as a book he found the poem 'out of key', and removed it.[158]

An Appeal

Cf. 'The Simpleton' (*MP61*).

Text: ts. (Buffalo).

A Ghost from Arakan

'I have never really got over David's death', Graves told a friend in 1961.[159] The poet's eldest son by his first marriage, David Graves (born on 7 March 1920)[160] was a lieutenant with the Royal Welch Fusiliers in the Second World War; he died heroically in combat against the Japanese on the Arakan coast, Burma, on 18 March 1943. See *RPG 3*, pp.64-9, 100, 109-11, and 'Kill Them! Kill Them!', in *CSS*, pp.167-8.[161]

---

[156] Alan Hodge to Graves, 3 and 12 Oct. 1941; Canelluñ. For *WIH*, which Graves and Hodge shared with Norman Cameron, see *Complete Poems*, Volume II, p.322. Hodge's handwriting appears on a typescript of the fifth draft of the poem, querying two words, one of which Graves changed.

[157] Graves to Reeves, n.d. [late Feb.-early March 1941]; Texas. A group of Reeves's poems was to have been included in *WIH*.

[158] Graves to Reeves, 22 March 1941; Texas.

[159] Graves to Tom Matthews, 5 Aug. 1961; *SL 2*, p.206.

[160] In the preceding drafts he is 'not yet twenty-four' (st.2 l.4).

[161] First published in 1956 in *¡Catacrok!: Mostly Stories, Mostly Funny* (London: Cassell), pp.148-50; in the 'Foreword' Graves calls the story the 'deuce of clubs in this pack of jokers', adding that it 'really happened'.

Text: revised ts. (Buffalo).

The poem was first recorded in Graves's diary on 12 October 1956, under the title 'The Tear', and 'finished' on 15 October, though 'another version' was written on 2 January 1957.

1960s–1970s

Robin and Marian

Text: ms. (Carbondale).

The drafts of this poem are written on the backs of eight sheets of typescript of 'The Anti-Poet', the second of Graves's lectures as Professor of Poetry at Oxford,[162] which he was writing in the summer of 1961.[163]

Never Yet

Text: ts. (Carbondale).

Graves's diary records this poem on 16 June and 19 July 1962.

Tanka

Text: ts. (Canelluñ); l.2 'Tassel' is misspelt 'Tassle'.

Written in April 1963,[164] 'Tanka' was to have been published the following year in *MDWI*, at the beginning of section XVII; however, Graves asked his publishers to remove it from the manuscript and substitute a revised version of 'The Green Castle', inserting it in section XVI.[165]

House on Fire

Text: ms. (Carbondale); a fair copy.

In a draft contents list of sixty-one poems from the mid-1960s, 'House on Fire', the fifty-second title, is placed above 'The Lilac Frock' (fifty-sixth).[166]

The Lilac Frock

In sect.1, ll.3-6 are based on a 'dream of violence' with 'curiously accurate detail' which a friend in Deyá had 'the same night as I dreamed of screaming', 10 September 1964; see *RPG 3*, pp.396-7.[167]

For sect.2 ll.2-4, cf. 'Gooseflesh Abbey' (*P65-68*), ll.2-4.

---

[162] *OAP*, pp.29-53, and *CWP*, pp.320-35.

[163] See Graves to Martin Seymour-Smith, 22 June 1961, *SL 2*, p.204, and Graves to Selwyn Jepson, 29 Aug. 1961, *SL 2*, p.207.

[164] Graves's diary records a draft on 14 April 1963.

[165] Bryen Gentry, of Cassells, to Graves, 17 Jan. 1964, returning 'Tanka' and the earlier version of 'The Green Castle'; Canelluñ.

[166] Ms. (Berg).

[167] Graves to Ralph Jacobs, 13 and 30 Sept. 1964; Canelluñ. (In *RGP 3* the friend's dream is misattributed to Graves.)

Text: ms. (Carbondale); a fair copy.

Emendation:

sect.1 l.4 'Escape!' *ms. drafts (Carbondale)*] 'Escape' *ms. fair copy (Carbondale).*

See the note on 'House on Fire', above.

Departure

Text: revised ts. (Carbondale).

On 10 February 1965 Graves, now in his seventieth year, left for New York and then went with his 'muse' Aemilia Laraçuen (Cindy Lee) to Puerto Vallarto, Mexico; he returned to Deyá, alone, after two months. See *RPG 3*, pp.406-8.

North Side

Text: ms. (Texas); a fair copy, dated 'June 26 1965'.

A

On 19 November 1966 Graves, who was about to leave on another American lecture tour (his ninth since 1957), wrote from Madrid to his wife: 'Supper at Ava's. She gave me a blonde, kneeling angel doll with one wing: [the poem follows].'[168]

Ava Gardner's enduring friendship with Graves began in November 1955; for his account of her 1956 visit to Mallorca, see 'A Toast to Ava Gardner', *CSS*, pp.207-17.

Text: ms. (Victoria).

Emendation:

l.1 Gardner *ms. (Canelluñ)*] Gardener *ms. (Victoria).*

Song: John Truelove

Text: ms. (Victoria).

Emendation:

Title *Song: ms.(JS)*] *Song ms.(Victoria)*

The manuscript (JS) of an almost identical version is dated 'Dec 31 1967'.

Requirements for a Poem

Text: *Winged by Their Own Need: Poems by the Winners and the Jurors of the Robert Graves Prize for Best Hungarian Poem of the Year 1970-1986*, edited by Miklós Vajda (Deyá, Mallorca: New Seizin Press, 1988), p.14. The manuscript of the poem, reproduced in facsimile on the cover, is signed 'Robert Graves | Budapest | May 8 | – 1968 –'.

In his introduction, Vajda describes how 'Requirements for a Poem' was written extempore as the 'charter' of the Robert Graves Prize, which Graves founded with royalties he had accumulated in Hungarian currency.

See also the note on 'Women and Masks' (*P70-72*).

---

[168] Graves to Beryl Graves, 19 Nov. 1966; Canelluñ.

The Atom

Text: *Nagyvilág*, 27, no.8 (Aug. 1982), 1110.

Graves evidently left a manuscript of the poem on one of his four visits to Hungary between 1968 and 1973. (Permission for publication was granted in 1982 by Graves's wife, as was the usual procedure in his last years, hence the inclusion of the poem in this section rather than among the 'Uncollected Poems', publication of which was approved by Graves himself.)

The manuscript is reproduced with a transcription and a Hungarian translation by Tandori Dezső (an error in the transcription, 'heat' for 'host' in l.2, is repeated in the translation).

The Cupid

Text: ms. (Canelluñ); a fair copy.

In the penultimate line, a comma after 'God' in the revised manuscript from which the fair copy was made (and in preceding drafts) has been restored.

'The Cupid' is the sixteenth of twenty-one titles in a contents list for 'New Poems 1970', a collection superseded by *GSV* (carbon ts., Canelluñ).

Olives of March

See *GM*, 16.*c*,*4*, 106.*h*,*3*.

Cf. 'The Oleaster' (*MDWI*).

Text: ms. (Canelluñ).

The Undying Worm

See Isaiah 66. 24.

Text: ms. (Canelluñ).

An earlier version is dated 'Ap 22 1970' (ms.(JS)).

Song: Though Time Conceals Much

Text: ms. (Canelluñ).

The second and third of eleven drafts (Canelluñ) are on the back of a letter to Graves dated 30 December 1970; another manuscript (JS) of the eighth draft is dated 'Jan 12 1971'.

Always and For Ever

Text: ms. (JS).

Dated 'Sept 4th. 1972', 'Always and For Ever' was sent on the back of a letter to Juli Simon; in the top left-hand corner Graves has added 'Poem written with a temperature' (JS).

Across the Gulf (1992)

The colophon to *Across the Gulf* states:

> These poems, written by Robert Graves when he was in his seventies, were selected from his unpublished work by Beryl Graves. The text was

prepared for publication by Beryl Graves, Lucia Graves and Dunstan Ward; it was hand-set and printed by Tomás Graves and bound by Carmen García-Gutierrez, at The New Seizin Press, Deià, Mallorca.

The fourteen poems in the book are arranged in the order below.

The Snapped Rope

Text: revised ts. (Canelluñ).

The Goldsmiths

Text: ms. (Canelluñ).
A draft of the poem is dated 'March 21st 1969' (Berg).

Adam in Hell

For sect.3 ll.3-5, see Genesis 3. 15.
Text: revised typescript (Canelluñ).
An earlier version is dated 'Dec. 25 1969' (ms.(JS)).

The Cards Are Wild

Text: ms. (Canelluñ).
Earlier versions are dated 17 and 18 April 1970 (ms.(Tulsa), ms.(JS)).

Unless

Text: ms. (JS); a fair copy.

The Poised Pen

Text: revised ts. (JS).
The typescript is dated 'Sept 14 1972'.

[Fragment]

Text: ms. (Canelluñ), ms. (JS).

After these lines from an untitled manuscript draft (Canelluñ) were published in *ATG*, they were identified as the first stanza of 'Birthday Letter', a manuscript poem dated 'Feb 1 1974' on the back of a letter from Graves (JS). They are so different from the second, six-line stanza as to constitute, in effect, a separate poem, and are printed in the present edition as in *ATG*, with one change: the 'Birthday Letter' version omits a comma after l.2 'broad'.

St.2 of 'Birthday Letter' is as follows:

Her birthday letter reached me yesterday
Criss-crossed with kisses, far away,
And the home stream hisses
From a distant continent where she had gone
To tan her cheeks under a vulture sun.
How should I answer save with silent kisses?

[How Is It a Man Dies?]

Text: ms., untitled (Canelluñ).

A third stanza has been cancelled with two diagonal lines.

Green Flash

For l.7, see *HM*, 13.*3*.

Text: *P65-68* proof (Canelluñ).

This poem appears in the proof of *P65-68* on p.94; in his copy (Canelluñ), Graves has cancelled it in ink with a diagonal line and pasted in a typescript of 'The Yet Unsayable', which replaced it.

An earlier version entitled 'The Green Flash' was printed in *ATG*; the manuscript, a fair copy, is dated 'June 18 1967' (Texas).

Peisinoë

For the Siren Peisinoë ('persuading the mind'), see *GM*, 154.*d*,*3*, 170.*q*,*r*,*s*.

Text: ms. (Canelluñ).

Across the Gulf

See Luke 16. 19-26.

Text: ms. (Canelluñ).

To His Temperate Mistress

Text: ms. (Canelluñ).

Foot-Holder-Royal

For the 'office of royal foot-holder', see *WG61*, pp.303/295.

Text: ms. (Canelluñ).

The hyphen in l.1 'foot-holder', omitted in the manuscript, has been inserted to make it consistent with the title.

An earlier version is dated '7-14 March 1970' (ms.(JS)).

The Pressure Gauge

Text: ms. (Canelluñ).

In st.2 l.4 a closing quotation mark, omitted in the manuscript, has been inserted.

The first draft (Canelluñ) is on the back of a letter to Graves dated 3 February 1969. Graves sent Juli Simon an earlier version in a letter dated 18 February 1969 (JS), adding: 'I'll sing it to you with the tune when we meet'.

INDEX OF TITLES

Robert Graves